Borland C++
Power Programming

Clayton Walnum

PROGRAMMING
SERIES

que

Library of Congress Catalog No.: 93-83382

ISBN: 1-56529-172-7

96 95 94 93   8 7 6 5 4 3 2 1

Interpretation of the printing code: the rightmost double-digit number is the year of the book's printing; the rightmost single-digit number, the number of the book's printing. For example, a printing code of 93-1 shows that the first printing of the book occurred in 1993.

Trademarks

Publisher: Lloyd J. Short

Associate Publisher: Rick Ranucci

Operations Manager: Sheila Cunningham

Acquisitions Editor: Joseph B. Wikert

Dedication

To my wife, Lynn, for her love and understanding.

Credits

Title Manager
Joseph B. Wikert

Product Director
Jay Munro

Production Editor
Kezia Endsley

Copy Editors
Susan Pink
Judy Brunetti
Lori Cates

Technical Editor
Jeffrey D. Clark

Editorial Assistants
Elizabeth D. Brown
Stacey Beheler

Production Manager
Corinne Walls

**Proofreading/Indexing
Coordinator**
Joelynn Gifford

Production Analyst
Mary Beth Wakefield

Book Designer
Scott Cook

Cover Designer
Jay Corpus

Graphic Image Specialists
Jerry Ellis
Dennis Sheehan
Susan VandeWalle

Production Team
Katy Bodenmiller
Julie Brown
Laurie Casey
Brook Farling
Dennis Clay Hager
Heather Kaufman
Bob LaRoche
Jay Lesandrini
Caroline Roop
Linda Seifert
Susan Shepard
Sandra Shay
Phil Worthington

Indexer
Johnna VanHoose

Composed in ITC Century Light and MCPdigital by
Prentice Hall Computer Publishing.

About The Author

Clayton Walnum has been writing about computers for a decade and has published over 300 articles in major computer publications. He is also the author of 10 books, which cover such diverse topics as programming, computer gaming, and application programs. He lives in Connecticut with his wife and their three children, Christopher, Justin, and Stephen.

Acknowledgments

I would like to thank the following people for their contribution to this book: Joe Wikert for giving me the project; Jay Munro for his encouragement and invaluable guidance; Kezia Endsley, Susan Pink, Judy Brunetti, and Lori Cates for making the words right; and Jeff Clark for checking the facts. Thanks to Bryan Schappel and Computer Components Inc. of Middleton, Wisconsin for bailing me out when the equipment went bad. Finally, a special thank you is due to some special people—my wife, Lynn, and my three great kids, Christopher, Justin, and Stephen—who make many sacrifices so Dad can do his writing thing.

Overview

Table of Contents

5 Playing with Life   143

6 An Introduction to Recursion   191

7 Using Recursion to Parse Formulas 229

8 Writing Interrupt Handlers and TSR Programs 259

II Windows Topics

9 Creating Status Bars and Toolbars 291

13 Writing Dynamic Link Libraries 481

14 Using Multimedia Sound with Windows 501

15 Writing Screen Savers for Windows 3.1 527

III References

A DOS Window Library Quick Reference 557

Introduction

I t wasn't too long ago that a hobbyist programmer got by with a monochrome monitor, two floppy drives, 16K of RAM, and a decent understanding of BASIC. Back then, a big program may have comprised 500 lines and taken a few days to write. Even professional programmers—the folks who produced commercial-quality software—had it much easier. Most commercial programs took a single author six months to a year to write.

The New Age

N ow, programmers (even hobbyist programmers) have to know their machines inside and out and be familiar with two or three operating systems if they are to survive in a world in which a typical commercial-quality program may take up an astounding 50,000 (or more) lines of code. And it's not only the programs that have expanded—Borland C++ 3.1 requires over 40 megabytes of disk space for a full installation. The scary part is that you need most of that 40 megabytes to create programs for today's complex operating systems and state-of-the-art computers.

Learning a complex language like C++ is a tough enough job without finding yourself lost in an ocean of questions every time you sit down to write a program. With the power of a language like C++ comes a seemingly infinite number of ways to complete even the simplest task. This complexity is multiplied by the huge libraries of functions that make up a graphical user interface like Microsoft Windows 3.1, which boasts nearly 1,000 functions in its *Application Programming Interface* (API).

This book, *Borland C++ Power Programming,* was written to provide you with some of the answers you need to write the type of programs you've only dreamed of before. With the techniques presented here, you are able to write your own Windows-like programs without ever leaving DOS.

In addition, you learn to handle such tricky tasks as designing classes, parsing formulas, installing interrupt handlers, and much more. In the Windows section of the book, you learn to create professional-looking applications with status bars, toolboxes, custom controls, and snazzy sound effects. You even learn to program screen savers, those delightful graphical interludes that have become so popular.

Who This Book Is For

T his book is *not* an introductory text for programmers interested in learning Borland C++ programming. To understand the lessons included here, you must have a working knowledge of C++ and be comfortable with Borland's C++ development system. Obviously, you should have experience programming in MS-DOS, but it also helps to have a basic understanding of programming in Microsoft Windows, particularly using Borland's ObjectWindows library. This is not to say that you have to be a Windows guru, only that some Windows programming experience is helpful.

In short, if you are at least an intermediate-level C++ programmer, you should have the skills and knowledge necessary to get the most from this book.

Hardware and Software Requirements

T o compile and run the programs on this book's disk, and to get the most out of the upcoming lessons, you must have the following:

- An IBM-compatible 80286 with at least two megabytes of RAM (a 80386 or better with four or more megabytes is recommended)

- MS-DOS 3.31 or greater (MS-DOS 5.0 recommended)

- VGA graphics

- A hard drive

- Microsoft Windows 3.1

- Borland C++ 3.1

As always, the faster your processor, the better. Fast processors mean fast compiles and zippy programs. This is especially true for Windows programs, because Windows pushes your hardware to the limits.

 Note: If your system doesn't meet the requirements listed, you may still be able to use this book. However, you are limited to those programs and chapters that your system can handle. For example, if your system is not capable of VGA graphics, you are unable to run programs that display graphics in VGA mode. Other programs, however, may run fine in any graphics mode. Similarly, if you don't have Microsoft Windows, you are unable to compile and run the programs from the Windows section of this book. The programs in the DOS section, however, do not require Microsoft Windows.

An Overview of the Book

This book contains a wealth of programming tips and techniques that help you produce more efficient and powerful C++ programs. The following is a brief outline of the three sections of this book.

These chapters compose Part I, "DOS Topics":

- *Chapter 1* offers an overview of the C++ programming style with a concentration on object-oriented program design. Discussed in this chapter are some of C++'s more difficult topics, including class design, polymorphism, function and operator overloading, and virtual functions.

- *Chapter 2* extends the discussion in Chapter 1 by applying object-oriented programming techniques to the creation of a string-handling class. This string class gives your C++ programs the power to handle strings like Borland's Turbo Pascal does.

- *Chapter 3* begins a discussion of event-driven programming in DOS. It discusses event handlers and dispatchers, and presents a basic class for handling a mouse in your programs. Both keyboard and mouse events are covered.

- *Chapter 4* adds graphical windows and controls to the event-driven programming concepts discussed in Chapter 3. A basic library of windows, dialog boxes, and button controls is developed using object-oriented programming techniques.

- *Chapter 5* takes the window library developed in Chapter 4 and shows how to use it in a full-feature program. The simulation program, based on Conway's famous *Life*, also shows how to use linked lists effectively, incorporating a list class developed especially for the program.

- *Chapter 6* offers an in-depth discussion of recursion and how it can be used to simplify complex algorithms. A commercial-quality game, *Trap Hunt*, is developed, using the recursive techniques presented in the chapter and providing further use for Chapter 4's window library.

- *Chapter 7* continues the recursion topic by exploring a method for parsing mathematical formulas such as those used in spreadsheet programs. Topics include grammar syntax, Backus-Naur Form, and recursive-descent parsing.

- *Chapter 8* discusses the basics of programming interrupt handlers and TSR programs. Installing interrupt handlers, hooking and chaining interrupts, and calling DOS from a TSR are some topics covered during the development of an on-screen clock TSR.

The remaining chapters compose Part II, "Windows Topics":

- *Chapter 9,* the first on Windows programming, shows how to create status bars and toolbars in your ObjectWindows programs. Several demonstration programs are included, and a brief explanation of the *Multiple Document Interface* (MDI) is featured.

- *Chapter 10* explores the topic of custom controls by showing how to handle owner-draw buttons, how to add bitmaps to menus, and how to create custom toolboxes that can be moved around the screen, yet remain accessible at all times.

- *Chapter 11* tackles the tricky task of printer output in Windows. Besides the basics of sending data to a printer, font creation and image scaling are covered. The techniques discussed are demonstrated with a program that prints audio-cassette labels.

- *Chapter 12* introduces the Windows Clipboard. Here, you learn to transfer text and bitmaps to and from the Clipboard. You also learn important rules for handling the Clipboard, rules that ensure that all applications have access to the Clipboard when necessary.

- *Chapter 13* covers the mysterious topic of programming Dynamic Link Libraries (DLLs). Discussions include the differences between a DLL and an executable program and how to set up Borland C++ to compile DLLs. A sample DLL that draws shapes in a window is included.

- *Chapter 14* features two sample programs that show how to use multimedia sound in your applications. Two ways of playing waveform files are described, including methods for stopping, pausing, and resuming a sound.

- *Chapter 15* closes Part II of the book with a tutorial on writing Windows 3.1 screen savers. Here, you learn how screen savers blank the screen, how to draw graphics as other applications run in the background, and how to close a screen saver when the user presses a key or moves the mouse.

These appendixes compose Part III, "References":

- *Appendix A* contains a complete reference to the window library developed in Chapter 4.

- *Appendix B,* for advanced programmers, contains additional information about writing TSR programs.

Compiling the Programs in This Book

T he programs in this book were written with *Borland C++ 3.1*. It is best if your copy of Borland C++ was installed using all the default settings and directories. If you have changed any of the default settings or directories, and are not sure how to fix errors that might result from these changes, you should reinstall Borland C++. You can also use Turbo C++ to compile the programs in Part I of this book, and Turbo C++ for Windows to compile the programs in Part II.

The programs that follow are organized on the disk by chapter. Each chapter's programs are found in their own directory on-disk. The programs in Chapter 1 are in the CHAP1 directory, the programs in Chapter 2 are in the CHAP2 directory, and so on.

To compile the programs for a specific chapter, copy all the files from the chapter's directory to your main Borland C++ directory. Then start Borland C++ and load the project file for the program you want to compile. Selecting the Run entry of the Run menu compiles and runs the program. To only compile the program, select the Build All entry of the Compile menu.

Many programs in this book require that you set certain options of the compiler. In particular, when compiling programs that require Borland's graphics library, you must enable that library by selecting the Graphics library in the Libraries dialog box. Display this dialog box by selecting the Options/Linker/Libraries menu item.

Windows programs must be compiled with WIN31 defined. This is accomplished by selecting the Options/Compiler/Code generation menu item, which displays the Code Generation Options dialog box. Be sure that you type WIN31 in the Defines text field.

Conventions Used in This Book

T o get the most out of this book, you should know how it is designed. New terms and emphasized words are presented in *italicized text* and are defined on first reference. Pay close attention to italicized text. Functions, commands, parameters, and the like are set in `monospace` text; for example, the `main()` function.

Full C++ programs appear as listings with listing heads, whereas code fragments appear alone within the text. All full listings are also included on the disk. Tables and figures (all numbered) also help organize material within the chapters.

Other visual pointers found in this book include:

 Caution: Caution boxes that warn you of problem areas, including possible cases in which you might introduce bugs into your program or crash your system.

and

 Note: Note boxes that provide you with extraneous information. Many times, this information helps speed your learning process and provides you with shortcuts in C++. Other times, it simply reminds you of information important enough to be mentioned twice.

All these conventions are used simply to help arrange the material in a logical manner, thus helping you quickly find the information you need.

A Word to the Wise

As every developer knows, a good program is virtually crash proof. Error-checking must be done for every action that might fail, and appropriate error messages must be provided to the user. Unfortunately, good error-checking requires a lot of extra program code. For the programmer working on her or his next magnum opus, this is all just part of the game. But for an author writing a programming book, this extra code has different implications.

A programming book should present its topics in as clear a manner as possible. This means featuring programs with source code that is not obscured by details that don't apply directly to the topic at hand. For this reason, the programs in this book do not always employ proper error-checking. User input might sometimes go unverified, memory-allocation routines might sometimes assume that memory is available, and (horror of horrors) pointers might be assumed to be valid—all for the clarity and conciseness of the code.

In short, if you use any of the code in this book in your own programs, it's up to you to add the error-checking procedures. Never assume anything in your programs. Add error-checking whenever you can't be 100 percent sure that your program will function correctly. This ensures that the program doesn't come crashing down on your user.

Now, let's get programming!

DOS Topics

I

1

C++ Style Considerations

Mastering a new programming language, particularly one that requires a new way of thinking, can be a frustrating and difficult task. C++ is no exception. Because C++ adds many powerful features to the C language—not the least of which is object-oriented programming—many programmers, once they learn the language's syntax, are often unsure of how to apply what they've learned to problems at hand. Knowing how to hammer is not the same as knowing how to build a house.

Before you get into the main topics in this book, review the basics of object-oriented programming and C++ programming style, with an eye toward using new features of the language in an appropriate and sensible way. An excellent book you might want to check into is *Tom Swan's C++ Primer,* published by Sams Publishing. In this 750-page tome, Tom starts with the very basics of C++ programming and leads his readers through to the more advanced topics, including class design and operator overloading.

A Programming History

Programming languages, like spoken languages, evolve over time. They are constantly refined and focused to meet the ever-changing needs of their users. The C++ language that you use today—possibly the most powerful high-level language in existence—is an amalgamation of all the techniques developed over the years. Therefore, start exploring C++ by briefly looking at the history of programming languages.

From Switches to Objects

Way back in the dark ages of computing, technicians programmed computers by flipping banks of switches; each switch represented a single bit of information. In those days, even simple programs required agonizing patience and precision to create. As the need for more sophisticated programs grew, however, so did the need for better ways to write these programs. Assembly language and—shortly thereafter—high-level languages like FORTRAN were invented to speed and simplify the programming task.

With the advent of high-level languages, programming became accessible to more people; writing code was no longer the domain of highly trained scientists. As a result, computing was used in increasingly complex roles. It was soon clear, however, that a more efficient way of programming was needed, one that would eliminate the obscure "spaghetti" code produced by these early languages.

Programmers needed a new way of using high-level languages, one that enabled them to partition their programs into logical sections that represented the general tasks to be completed. Thus, the structured-programming paradigm was born. Structured programming encourages a *top-down* approach to programming, in which the programmer focuses on the general functions a program must accomplish, rather than the details of how those functions are implemented. When programmers think and program in top-down fashion, it is easier for them to handle large projects without the tangled code that results from GOTO-ridden programs. Moreover, programmers can write *black-box routines,* general functions that can be reused in many programs.

Today, the need for efficient programming is more important than ever. Computer programs have grown dramatically, comprising hundreds of thousands of code lines. With these huge programs, reusability is even more critical.

Again, a better way of programming is needed; that better way is object-oriented programming.

An Obvious, Yet Brilliant, Solution

Our world is made up of many objects, most of which manipulate other objects or data. For example, a car is an object that manipulates its speed and direction to transport people to a different location. This car object encapsulates all the functions and data it needs to get its job done. It has a switch to turn it on, a wheel to control its direction, and brakes to slow it down. These functions directly manipulate the car's data, including direction, position, and speed.

When you travel in a car, however, you don't have to know the details of how these operations work. To stop a car, for example, you simply step on the brake pedal. You don't have to know how the pedal stops the car. You simply know that it works.

All these functions and data work together to define the object called a car. You're not likely to confuse a car with a dishwasher, a tree, or a playground. A car is a complete unit—an object with unique properties.

You can also think of computer programs as objects. Instead of thinking of a piece of code that, for example, draws a rectangle on-screen, and another piece of code that fills the rectangle with text, and still another piece of code that enables you to move the rectangle around the screen, you can think of a single object: a window. This window object contains all the code it needs to operate. Moreover, it also contains all the data it needs. This is the philosophy behind object-oriented programming.

A Review of Object-Oriented Programming

Object-oriented programming enables you to think of program elements as objects. In the case of a window object, you don't need to know the details of how it works. Nor do you need to know about the window's private data. You need to know only how to call the various functions that make the window operate. Think about the car object discussed in the previous section. To drive a car, you don't have to know the details of how a car works. You need to know only how to drive it. What's going on under the hood is none of your business. (And, if you try to make it your business, plan to face an amused mechanic who will have to straighten out your mess!)

If this were all there was to object-oriented programming, you wouldn't have gained much over structured programming techniques. After all, with structured programming, you could create black-box routines, which you could then use without knowing how they worked. Obviously, there must be much more to object-oriented programming than just hiding the details of a process.

Encapsulation

One major difference between conventional procedural programming and object-oriented programming is a handy thing called *encapsulation.* Encapsulation enables you to hide both the data and the functions that act on that data inside the object. Once you do this, you can control access to the data, forcing programs to retrieve or modify data only through the object's interface. In strict object-oriented design, an object's data is always private to the object. Other parts of a program should never have direct access to that data.

How is this data-hiding different from a structured-programming approach? After all, you could always hide data inside functions, just by making that data local to the function. A problem arises, however, when you want to make the data of one function available to other functions. The way to do this in a structured program is to make the data global to the program, which gives *any* function access to it. It seems that you could use another level of scope—one that would make your data global to the functions that need it—but still prevent other functions from gaining access. Encapsulation does just that.

The best way to understand object-oriented programming is to compare a structured program to an object-oriented program. Now you can extend the car-object metaphor by writing a program that simulates a car trip. The first version of the program, shown in Listing 1.1, uses a typical structured design.

Listing 1.1. CAR1.CPP—a program that simulates a car trip.

```
#include <iostream.h>
#include <stdlib.h>
#include <conio.h>
#include <time.h>

#define HOME 10

void StartCar(void)
{
```

```cpp
  cout << "Car started.\n";
  getch();
}

int SteerCar(int destination, int &position)
{
  cout << "Driving...\n";
  getch();
  if (++position == destination) return 1;
  return 0;
}

void BrakeCar(void)
{
  cout << "Braking.\n";
  getch();
}

void ReverseCar(int &forward, int &position)
{
  if (forward)
  {
    cout << "Backing up.\n";
    getch();
    --position;
    forward = 0;
  }
  else forward = 1;
}

void TurnOffCar(void)
{
  cout << "Turning off car.\n";
  getch();
}

int FindObstacle(void)
{
  int r = random(4);
  if (r) return 0;
  return 1;
}
```

continues

Listing 1.1. Continued

```
int position = 0, destination = HOME;
int at_destination = 0;
int obstacle, forward = 1;

void main()
{
  randomize();
  StartCar();
  while (!at_destination)
  {
    at_destination = SteerCar(destination, position);
    obstacle = FindObstacle();
    if (obstacle && !at_destination)
    {
      cout << "Look out! There's something in the road!\n";
      getch();
      BrakeCar();
      ReverseCar(forward, position);
      ReverseCar(forward, position);
    }
  }
  cout << "Ah, home at last.\n";
  TurnOffCar();
}
```

Now examine this program, starting with `main()`. The call to `Randomize()`
initializes the random-number generator, which is used to simulate obstacles
in the road. Then the function `StartCar()` simply prints the message `Car`
`started`, informing the user that the trip is about to begin.

The program simulates the trip with a `while` loop that iterates until
`at_destination` becomes true (1). In the loop, the car moves forward by calling
the function `SteerCar()`. This function prints the message `Driving...` and
moves the car one unit closer to the destination. When the integer `position` is
equal to the destination, this function returns a 1, indicating that the trip is
over. Otherwise, it returns 0.

Of course, the car's driver must always watch for obstacles. The function
`FindObstacle()` acts as your eyes by looking for obstacles and reporting what
it finds. In this function, each time the random-number generator comes up

with a 0, `FindObstacle()` informs you that something is blocking the route, by returning 1 rather than 0.

If the car reaches an obstacle, the function `BrakeCar()` puts on the brakes and the function `ReverseCar()` backs up the car. Both functions print an appropriate message; however, `ReverseCar()` also sets the car's position back one unit—unless it was already moving backward, in which case it just reverses the direction again, setting the car back in the forward direction. (The variable `forward` keeps track of the car's current direction.) The second call to `ReverseCar()` gets the car moving forward again. Finally, when the car reaches its destination, the function `TurnOffCar()` ends the program. Here is the output from a typical run of the program:

```
Car started.
Driving...
Driving...
Driving...
Driving...
Look out! There's something in the road!
Braking.
Backing up.
Driving...
Driving...
Driving...
Driving...
Driving...
Look out! There's something in the road!
Braking.
Backing up.
Driving...
Driving...
Driving...
Ah, home at last.
Turning off car.
```

Note that when the program is running, you must press a key after each message is printed to the screen.

Listing 1.2 is the object-oriented version of the program. This version includes the same functions and data. However, now everything unique to a car is encapsulated as part of the `Car` object.

Listing 1.2. CAR2.CPP—the object-oriented version of the car-driving program.

```cpp
#include <iostream.h>
#include <stdlib.h>
#include <conio.h>
#include <time.h>

#define HOME 10

class Car
{
  int test, position, forward;

public:
  Car(int destination);
  void StartCar(void) { cout<<"Car started.\n"; getch(); }
  int SteerCar(void);
  void BrakeCar(void) { cout<<"Braking.\n"; getch(); }
  void ReverseCar(void);
  void TurnOffCar(void) { cout<<"Turning off car.\n"; getch(); }
};

Car::Car(int destination)
{
  randomize();
  test = destination;
  forward = 1;
  position = 0;
}

int Car::SteerCar(void)
{
  cout << "Driving...\n";
  getch();
  if (++position == test) return 1;
  return 0;
}

void Car::ReverseCar(void)
{
  if (forward)
  {
    cout << "Backing up.\n";
```

```
      getch();
      --position;
      forward = 0;
    }
    else forward = 1;
}

int FindObstacle(void)
{
    int r = random(4);
    if (r) return 0;
    return 1;
}

int obstacle, at_destination = 0;
Car car(HOME);

void main()
{
    randomize();
    car.StartCar();
    while (!at_destination)
    {
        at_destination = car.SteerCar();
        obstacle = FindObstacle();
        if (obstacle && !at_destination)
        {
            cout << "Look out! There's something in the road!\n";
            getch();
            car.BrakeCar();
            car.ReverseCar();
            car.ReverseCar();
        }
    }
    cout << "Ah, home at last.\n";
    car.TurnOffCar();
}
```

Because the program encapsulates much of the data into the class Car, rather than using global variables as in the first version, fewer variables are passed to functions that make up the car. This points out a subtle stylistic difference between structured programming and object-oriented programming. The first version of the program passed variables into functions—even though those variables were global—so the programmer had a clear idea of what data the function used. This is a form of self-documentation; the style of the code says something about what the code does.

In an object, the encapsulated data members are global to the object's function members, yet they are local to the object. They are not global variables. Because objects represent smaller portions of an entire program, there's no need to pass data members into member functions to help document a function's purpose. Objects are usually concise enough that this type of self-documentation is unnecessary. In Listing 1.2, no variables are passed into functions (except into the class' constructor).

Another advantage of the object-oriented approach taken in Listing 1.2 is that the car object is clearly defined. All the data and functions required for a car (at least, all that's needed for this simple computer car) are encapsulated into the class. That means there is less clutter in the main program. It also means that the code is more logically organized. In Listing 1.1, you have no clear idea of what makes up a car. The functions and data needed for the entire program are defined on the same level. For example, whereas starting a car is clearly a function of a car, finding an obstacle is not. (If you don't agree, go out to your car, climb in, and press the find-obstacle button.) Yet the scope of both the `StartCar()` and `FindObstacle()` functions are the same. This is also true of the data. Whereas the car's destination, position, and direction are all information that help define a car, obstacles are not. You don't need an obstacle to drive a car; you do need a destination, a position, and a direction.

In Listing 1.2, every element that makes up a car is part of the class. To drive the car, the program doesn't have to deal with the car's data members. The class takes care of them. The only data the program needs from `Car` is whether the car has arrived at its destination. The only function left in the main program is `FindObstacle()`, the one function in the program that has nothing to do with being a car. Finding obstacles is not a car's job. In all these ways, encapsulation makes the programming task more logical and organized.

Classes as Data Types

Classes are really nothing more than user-defined data types. As with any data type, you can have as many instances of the data type as you need. For example, you can have more than one car in the car program, each with its own destination. This is because a class is really nothing more than a custom data type. Once you have created a data type, you can create as many instances of that data as you need.

For example, one standard data type is an integer. It's absurd to think that a program can have only one integer. You can declare many integers, just about all you want. The same is true of classes. Once you define a new class, you can create many instances of the class. Each instance (called an object) normally has full access to the class' member functions and gets its own copy of the data members. In the car simulation, you can create two cars, each with its own destination, as in the following:

```
Car car1(10), car2(20);
```

Although these cars derive from the same class, they are completely separate objects. The object `car2` has to go twice as far as `car1` to reach its destination.

Header Files and Implementation Files

In Listing 1.2, all the program code is in a single file. This makes it easy to compare the first version with the second. When using object-oriented programming techniques, however, it's standard practice to place each class into two files of its own. The first, the header file, contains the class' definition. Usually, the header file contains all the information you need to use the class. The header file traditionally has an *.H* extension. The actual implementation of a class' functions goes into the implementation file, which usually has the extension *.CPP*. From this point on in the book, most classes are organized in this way.

The header and implementation files for the `Car` class are shown in Listings 1.3 and 1.4, respectively. Note that the class definition has been slightly modified by adding the keyword `protected` to the data member section. This is done so derived classes can inherit these data members. (You read about inheritance in the next section.)

Listing 1.3. CAR.H—the header file for the *Car* class.

```
#ifndef _CAR_H
#define _CAR_H

#include <iostream.h>
```

continues

Listing 1.3. Continued

```
#include <stdlib.h>
#include <conio.h>
#include <time.h>

class Car
{
protected:
  int test, position, forward;

public:
  Car(int destination);
  void StartCar(void)
    { cout<<"Car started.\n"; getch(); }
  int SteerCar(void);
  void BrakeCar(void)
    { cout<<"Braking.\n"; getch(); }
  void ReverseCar(void);
  void TurnOffCar(void)
    { cout<<"Turning off car.\n"; getch(); }
};


#endif
```

Listing 1.4. CAR.CPP—the implementation file for the *Car* class.

```
#include "car.h"

Car::Car(int destination)
{
  randomize();
  test = destination;
  forward = 1;
  position = 0;
}

int Car::SteerCar(void)
{
  cout << "Driving...\n";
  getch();
```

```
  if (++position == test) return 1;
  return 0;
}

void Car::ReverseCar(void)
{
  if (forward)
  {
    cout << "Backing up.\n";
    getch();
    --position;
    forward = 0;
  }
  else forward = 1;
}
```

Inheritance

Inheritance enables you to create a class that is similar to a previously defined class, but one that still has some of its own properties. Consider the car simulation. Suppose you want to create a car that has a high-speed passing gear. In a traditional program, that would require much code modification. As you modified the code, you would probably introduce bugs into a tested program. To avoid these hassles, use the object-oriented approach: create a new class by inheritance. This new class inherits all the data and function members from the ancestor class. (You can control the level of inheritance with the `public`, `private`, and `protected` keywords.)

Listings 1.5 and 1.6 show the header and implementation files for a new class of car, `PassingCar`. This car inherits the member functions and data from its ancestor class, `Car`, and adds two member functions of its own. The constructor, `PassingCar()`, does nothing but pass parameters to the ancestor class' constructor. The member function `pass()`, however, is unique to `PassingCar`. This is the function that gives the new car its passing gear. (Ignore the keyword `virtual` for a moment. You learn about virtual functions in the next section.)

If you look at Listing 1.6, you see that `Pass()` is similar to `Car`'s `SteerCar()` function, the difference being that `Pass()` increments the car's position by two units rather than one, which simulates a faster speed. Remember that although `PassingCar` has a new passing gear (implemented in the `Pass()` function), it still has access to `SteerCar()`.

Listing 1.5. PASSCAR.H—the header file for *PassingCar*.

```
#ifndef _PASSCAR_H
#define _PASSCAR_H

#include "car.h"

class PassingCar: public Car
{
public:
  PassingCar::PassingCar(int destination): Car(destination) {}
  virtual int Pass(void);
};

#endif
```

Listing 1.6. PASSCAR.CPP—the implementation file for *PassingCar*.

```
#include "passcar.h"

int PassingCar::Pass(void)
{
  cout << "Passing...\n";
  getch();
  position += 2;
  if (position >= test) return 1;
  return 0;
}
```

Listing 1.7, a new version of the simulation's main program, gives `PassingCar` a test drive. When you run the program, `PassingCar` reaches its destination a little faster because after it backs up, it makes up time by going into passing gear. By using inheritance, this program creates a new kind of car, with only a few lines of code. And the original class remains unchanged (except for the addition of the `protected` keyword). Impressed?

Listing 1.7. CAR3.CPP—a new version of the car-driving program that gives *PassingCar* a test drive.

```
#include "passcar.h"
#define HOME 10

int FindObstacle(void)
{
  int r = random(4);
  if (r) return 0;
  return 1;
}

int obstacle, at_destination = 0;
PassingCar car2(HOME);

void main()
{
  randomize();
  car2.StartCar();
  while (!at_destination)
  {
    at_destination = car2.SteerCar();
    obstacle = FindObstacle();
    if (obstacle && !at_destination)
    {
      cout << "Look out! There's something in the road!\n";
      getch();
      car2.BrakeCar();
      car2.ReverseCar();
      car2.ReverseCar();
      at_destination = car2.Pass();
    }
  }
  cout << "Ah, home at last.\n";
  car2.TurnOffCar();
}
```

25

Polymorphism

The last major feature of object-oriented programming is *polymorphism*. By using polymorphism, you can create new objects that perform the same functions found in the ancestor object, but which perform one or more of these functions in a different way. For example, when the previous program used inheritance, it created a new car with a passing gear. This isn't polymorphism because the original car didn't have a passing gear. Adding the passing gear didn't change the way an inherited function worked; it simply added a new function. Suppose, however, you want an even faster passing gear, without having to change the existing classes? You can do that easily with polymorphism.

Listings 1.8 and 1.9 show the header and implementation files for a new class, called FastCar. A FastCar is exactly like a PassingCar, except it uses its passing gear a little differently: A FastCar moves three units forward (rather than two) when passing. To do this, the program takes an already existing member function and changes how it works relative to the derived class. This is polymorphism. Remember that when you create a polymorphic function, you must preface its definition with the keyword virtual.

Listing 1.8. FASTCAR.H—the header file for *FastCar*.

```
#ifndef _FASTCAR_H
#define _FASTCAR_H

#include "passcar.h"

class FastCar: public PassingCar
{
public:
  FastCar(int destination):
    PassingCar(destination) {}
  virtual int Pass(void);
};

#endif
```

Listing 1.9. FASTCAR.CPP—the implementation file for *FastCar*.

```
#include "fastcar.h"

int FastCar::Pass(void)
{
  cout << "High-speed pass!\n";
  getch();
  position += 3;
  if (position >= test) return 1;
  return 0;
}
```

Look at Listing 1.10, the new main program for the car simulation. To take advantage of polymorphism, the program allocates the new `FastCar` dynamically—that is, it creates a pointer to the base class and then uses the `new` keyword to create the object. Remember that you can use a pointer to a base class to access any derived classes. Note also that the base class for `FastCar` is not `Car`, but rather `PassingCar`, because this is the first class that declares the virtual function `Pass`. If you tried to use `Car` as a base class, the compiler would complain, informing you that `Pass` is not a member of `Car`. One way around this is to give `Car` a virtual `Pass` function, too. This would make all car classes uniform with respect to a base class. (And that would probably be the best program design.)

Listing 1.10. CAR4.CPP—the new main program for the car simulation.

```
#include "fastcar.h"
#define HOME 10

int FindObstacle(void)
{
  int r = random(4);
  if (r) return 0;
  return 1;
}

int obstacle, at_destination = 0;
PassingCar *car3;
```

continues

Listing 1.10. Continued

```
void main()
{
  randomize();
  car3 = new FastCar(10);
  car3->StartCar();
  while (!at_destination)
  {
    at_destination = car3->SteerCar();
    obstacle = FindObstacle();
    if (obstacle && !at_destination)
    {
      cout << "Look out! There's something in the road!\n";
      getch();
      car3->BrakeCar();
      car3->ReverseCar();
      car3->ReverseCar();
      at_destination = car3->Pass();
    }
  }
  cout << "Ah, home at last.\n";
  car3->TurnOffCar();
}
```

You must use pointers with polymorphism because the point of polymorphism is to enable you to access different types of objects through a common pointer to a base class. You might want to do this, for example, to iterate through an array of objects. To see polymorphism work, change the line

```
car3 = new FastCar(10)
```

to

```
car3 = new PassingCar(10).
```

When you run the new version, you will be back using the slower passing gear, even though both cars use a pointer to the class `PassingCar`.

Now that you've reviewed the basics of object-oriented programming and have discovered some ways it makes programming easier, it's time to learn some usage and style considerations that are unique to the object-oriented paradigm and C++.

Classes: From General to Specific

S tarting with object-oriented programming can be a daunting experience; it's unlike other programming methods and requires adherence to a new set of principles. The process of designing a class is rarely as easy as it was with the car simulation, because classes are often based on abstractions rather than physical objects like automobiles. This makes it difficult to know which parts of a program belong in the object and which don't. Moreover, a complex program has many classes, many of which are derived from classes that may have been derived from still other classes. And each class may have many data and function members. Obviously, designing classes requires some thought and the careful application of the object-oriented philosophy.

The first step in designing a class is to determine the most general form of an object in that class. For example, suppose you're writing a graphics program and you need a class to organize the types of shapes it can draw. (In this new class, you draw only points and rectangles, to keep things simple.) Determining the most general class means determining what the objects in the class have in common. Two things that come to mind are color and position. These attributes become data members in the base class. Now, what functions must a shape perform? Each shape object needs a constructor and a way to draw itself on-screen. Because drawing a point is different from drawing a square, you have to put polymorphism to work and use a virtual function for the drawing task.

Listing 1.11 is the header file for a `Shape` class. This class needs no implementation file because the class is fully implemented in the header file. The constructor is implemented in-line, and the pure virtual function `DrawShape()` requires no implementation because it is only a placeholder for derived classes.

Listing 1.11. SHAPE.H—the header file for the *Shape* class.

```
#ifndef _SHAPE_H
#define _SHAPE_H

class Shape
{
protected:
  int color, sx, sy;

public:
```

continues

Listing 1.11. Continued

```
  Shape(int x, int y, int c)
    { sx=x; sy=y; color=c; }
  virtual void DrawShape(void) = 0;
};


#endif
```

As you can see from Listing 1.11, Shape does nothing but initialize the data members color, sx, and sy, which are the color and x,y coordinates of the object. To do anything meaningful with the class, you must derive a new class for each shape you want to draw. Start with the point. Listings 1.12 and 1.13 are the header and implementation files for this new class.

Listing 1.12. POINT.H—the header file for the *Point* class.

```
#ifndef _POINT_H
#define _POINT_H

#include <graphics.h>
#include "shape.h"

class Point: public Shape
{
public:
  Point(int x, int y, int c): Shape(x, y, c) {};
  virtual void DrawShape(void);
};

#endif
```

Listing 1.13. POINT.CPP—the implementation file for the *Point* class.

```
#include "point.h"

void Point::DrawShape(void)
{
  putpixel(sx, sy, color);
}
```

The constructor for this class does nothing but pass parameters to the base class' constructor; thus it is implemented in-line. The `DrawShape()` function, however, must draw the shape—in this case, a dot on-screen at the coordinates and in the color found in the `sx`, `sy`, and `color` data members. This function, too, is short and could have been implemented in-line. However, to keep the program construction parallel with the next example, there is a separate implementation file for the `Point` class.

Listing 1.14 is the test program for the shape classes. Because polymorphism is used to create shape classes, and because each class is derived from the `Shape` base class, the program can test a new shape class simply by changing the type of object created by the `new` statement. Run the program now. A dot should appear in the middle of your screen.

Listing 1.14. TSTSHAPE.CPP—the test program for the *Shape* classes.

```
#include <graphics.h>
#include <iostream.h>
#include <conio.h>
#include "point.h"
#include "rectngle.h"
#include "barrec.h"


void main()
{
  int gdriver = VGA, gmode = VGAHI, errorcode;
  Shape *r;

  initgraph(&gdriver, &gmode, "");
  if ( (errorcode = graphresult()) != grOk)
    cout << "Graphics not initialized: " << errorcode << '\n';
  else {
    int maxx = getmaxx();
    int maxy = getmaxy();
    r = new BarRec(maxx/2, maxy/2, 100, 100, WHITE);
    r->DrawShape();
    getch();
  }
  delete r;
  closegraph();
}
```

To make things interesting, add a second shape, Rectngle, to the classes. Rectngle is also derived from Shape. Listings 1.15 and 1.16 show the files for this new class.

Listing 1.15. RECTNGLE.H—the header file for the *Rectngle* class.

```
#ifndef _RECTNGLE_H
#define _RECTNGLE_H

#include <graphics.h>
#include "shape.h"

class Rectngle: public Shape
{
protected:
  int x2, y2;

public:
  Rectngle(int x1, int y1, int w, int h, int c);
  virtual void DrawShape(void);
};

#endif
```

Listing 1.16. RECTNGLE.CPP—the implementation file for the *Rectngle* class.

```
#include "rectngle.h"

Rectngle::Rectngle(int x1, int y1, int w, int h, int c):
        Shape(x1, y1, c)
{
  x2 = sx + w;
  y2 =  sy + h;
}

void Rectngle::DrawShape(void)
{
  setcolor(color);
  rectangle(sx, sy, x2, y2);
}
```

To test this new class in the main program, change the line

```
r = new Point(maxx/2, maxy/2, WHITE);
```

to

```
r = new Rectngle(maxx/2, maxy/2, 100, 100, WHITE);
```

Thanks to polymorphism, this is the only change you need in the main program to draw a rectangle.

The class `Rectngle` is more complicated than the `Point` class. To draw a rectangle the program needs—besides the rectangle's x,y coordinates—the rectangle's width and height. This means that `Rectngle`'s constructor does more than send parameters to the base class. It also initializes two extra data members, `x2` and `y2`. `Rectngle`'s `DrawShape()` function, too, is more complicated than `Point`'s, because drawing a rectangle takes more work than drawing a dot.

So far, you've gone from an abstract shape, which did nothing but initialize a couple of data members, to drawing two simple shapes on-screen. You can now move down another level, from the general shape of a rectangle to a more specific type: a rectangle with a colored bar at the top. This type of rectangle might, for example, be the starting point for a labeled window. Listings 1.17 and 1.18 are the source code for the `BarRec` object.

Listing 1.17. BARREC.H—the header file for the *BarRec* object.

```
#ifndef _BARREC_H
#define _BARREC_H

#include <graphics.h>
#include "rectngle.h"

class BarRec: public Rectngle
{
public:
  BarRec(int x1, int y1, int w, int h, int c):
        Rectngle(x1, y1, w, h, c) {}
  virtual void DrawShape(void);
};

#endif
```

Listing 1.18. BARREC.CPP—the implementation file for the *BarRec* object.

```
#include "barrec.h"

void BarRec::DrawShape(void)
{
  setcolor(color);
  rectangle(sx, sy, x2, y2);
  setfillstyle(SOLID_FILL, RED);
  bar(sx+2, sy+2, x2+-2, sy+15);
}
```

To test this new shape, change the `new` statement in the main program to

```
r = new BarRec(maxx/2, maxy/2, 100, 100, WHITE);
```

Now, when you run the program, the new type of rectangle object appears on-screen.

You could easily continue creating new types of rectangles. For example, if you want a rectangle with both a bar at the top and a double-line border, you can derive a new type from `BarRec`, overriding its virtual `DrawShape()` with one of its own. (This new function would probably need to call its ancestor's `DrawShape()` function to draw the bar at the top and then do the extra drawing required for the double border.)

 Note: By using the general-to-specific method of creating classes, you end up with extremely flexible code. You have many classes from which to choose when it comes time to derive a new one. Moreover, classes are less complex than they would be if you tried to cram a lot of extra functionality into them. Remember that the more general you make your classes, the more flexible they are.

Single-Instance Classes

O bject-oriented programming means power. When programmers first experience this power, they find it irresistible. Suddenly, they're using objects for everything in their programs, without thinking about whether each use is appropriate. Remember that C++ is both an object-oriented language and a procedural language. In other words, C++ programmers get the best of both worlds and can develop a strategy for a particular programming problem that best suits the current task. That strategy may or may not include an object-oriented approach.

Classes are most powerful when used as the basis for many instances. For example, in the next chapter you delve more deeply into object-oriented programming techniques by putting together a string class to help overcome C++'s limited string-handling capabilities. After developing the class, you're likely to have many instances of strings in your programs, each inheriting all the functionality of its class.

Nothing comes free, however. There is always a price. For example, to call an object's member functions, you must use a more complicated syntax than you need for ordinary function calls; you must supply the object and function name. Moreover, creating classes is a lot of work. Why go through all the extra effort if the advantages don't balance the disadvantages?

Although classes are most appropriate when used to define a set of objects, there are times when creating a single-instance class is a reasonable strategy. For example, later in the book, you study a class for controlling a mouse. Although you'll never have more than one mouse operating simultaneously, writing mouse functions into a single-instance class enables you to conveniently package and organize routines that you'll need often.

Generally, a single-instance class is appropriate for wrapping up a big idea, like a screen display, a mouse driver, or a graphics library. It may not, however, be appropriate for smaller uses that suffer from the overhead inherent in using classes.

 Note: Just because you are programming in C++ doesn't mean you can't use simpler data structures like structures and arrays. When you need to create a new data type, don't automatically assume that the object-oriented approach is best. Often, it's not.

Responsible Overloading

One of the things that differentiates C from C++ is function and operator *overloading*. Overloading is the capability to create several versions of a function or operator, each version of which has an identical name but requires different arguments. For example, in C++, you can have two functions named `Sum()`, one that adds integers and another that adds floating-point numbers. When you call `Sum()` in a program, the compiler can determine which function you mean by checking the function's parameters.

The capability of C++ to overload functions and operators offers immense flexibility. You no longer have to come up with different names for functions that, although they take different parameters, perform virtually identical operations. You can simply write several versions of the function, using the same name, each version with its own set of arguments. As you've already learned, however, powerful techniques are often misused. In this section, you examine function and operator overloading etiquette.

Overloading Versus Default Arguments

There's no question that function overloading is a great feature of C++ programming. However, when overused, it can make code more difficult to understand. If nothing else, having several versions of a function considerably increases program maintenance. The solution? Default arguments also enable you to call functions with different parameters, but without resorting to overloading. For example, consider the following overloaded function:

```
int Example(int x);
int Example(int x, int y);
```

Because of overloading, you can call the function `Example()` with one or two integer arguments:

```
Example(1);
Example(1,2);
```

This adds much to the function's flexibility. However, do you really need two copies of the function to get this flexibility? Not really. By using default arguments, you can create one version of `Example()` that accepts either one or two integer arguments:

```
int Example(int x, int y = 0);
```

This new function retains the flexibility of the overloaded function, but without the extra baggage. Of course, you can't always replace overloaded functions with default arguments. For example, if the parameter types of overloaded functions are different, the default argument technique won't work. The following overloaded function cannot be written using default arguments:

```
int Example(int x);
float Example(float x);
```

You can't have a default type, only a default value. When you get the urge to overload a function, first consider whether it would be more expedient to use default arguments.

Using Operator Overloading Logically

You've seen how function overloading can be both bounty and bane. Operator overloading, too, requires thought before you use it. Although the use of default arguments doesn't apply here, there are still important considerations. The most important is using overloaded operators logically—in other words, using them as they were originally designed to be used.

Using operator overloading, you can make any of C++'s operators perform whatever task you want. For example, the + operator sums two values. Without operator overloading, this operator can be used only on C++'s built-in data types—in other words, types like int, float, and long. Suppose, however, you want to add two arrays and assign the result to a third array? You can then overload the + and = operators in an array class so they can take arrays as arguments. Assuming you've done this, what do you suppose the following line would do (where a, b, and c are objects of your array class)?

```
c = a + b;
```

You'd expect that the equals sign acts as an assignment operator, because that is normally its purpose. Similarly, you'd expect that the + operator summed the elements of each array. (You can find the code that performs this overloading in Listing 1.19.) What you wouldn't expect is for the sum operator to take, for example, two two-element arrays and combine them into a four-element array. This type of operation would not be consistent with the operator's conventional usage.

Listing 1.19. OVERLOAD.CPP—code that uses the + operator to sum the elements of two arrays.

```cpp
#include <iostream.h>
#include <conio.h>

class Array
{
  int a[2];

public:
  Array(int x=0, int y=0);
  void Print(void);
  Array operator=(Array b);
  Array operator+(Array b);
};

Array::Array(int x, int y)
{
  a[0] = x;
  a[1] = y;
}

void Array::Print(void)
{
  cout << a[0] << ' ' << a[1] << '\n';
}

Array Array::operator=(Array b)
{
  a[0] = b.a[0];
  a[1] = b.a[1];
  return *this;
}

Array Array::operator+(Array b)
{
  Array c;

  c.a[0] = a[0] + b.a[0];
  c.a[1] = a[1] + b.a[1];
  return c;
}
```

```
void main()
{
  Array a(10, 15);
  Array b(20, 30);
  Array c;

  a.Print();
  b.Print();
  c.Print();
  c = a + b;
  c.Print();
  getch();
}
```

Operators should perform as expected. This means more than just using them for the expected operation. It also means performing that operation in a way that is consistent with the language's implementation. For example, look at the code for the + operator in the array class (Listing 1.19). Notice that the source arrays are unchanged by the operation. Instead, a third array is used to hold the results of the addition. This third array is returned from the function. This is how you expect the addition operator to work in C++. Contrast this with the way an addition instruction works in assembly language, by storing the result of the operation into one of the two operands. In most assembly languages, one of the operands is changed by the operation. In C++, it is not.

 Note: Overloading functions and operators is a powerful technique. Like all powerful features of a language, however, it must be used with thought and style. Don't use overloading when a simpler method will do, and ensure that overloaded operators perform in the expected way.

When to Use Virtual Functions

Using virtual functions, you can create classes that, like the simple graphics demonstration in a previous section, perform the same general functions, but perform those functions differently for each derived class. Like overloading, however, virtual functions are often misused.

Before using a virtual function, consider how the classes in the hierarchy differ. Do they need to perform different actions? Or do the classes require only different values? For example, in the shapes demonstration, the program used virtual functions so each class could draw its shape properly. Every shape object must know how to draw itself; however, every object needs to do it differently. Drawing a shape is an action. It's inappropriate, however, to use a virtual function to assign a color to an object. Although each shape object has its own color attribute, the color attribute is a *value* rather than an *action,* and so it is best represented by a data member in the base class. Using polymorphism to set an object's color is like trying to kill a mosquito with a machine gun.

 Note: Make sure that when you use virtual functions you are creating classes that differ in action rather than value.

Conclusion

C++ programming—and object-oriented programming in particular—requires thought and practice to master. By following the guidelines presented in this chapter, you can design C++ programs that are easier to understand and maintain than programs written using traditional methods.

In the next chapter, you put this new knowledge to work by creating a string class for your C++ programs.

2

Developing a String Class

In the preceding chapter, you reviewed object-oriented program design and some C++ style considerations. In this chapter, you will apply much of what you learned to create a string class for your C++ programs.

Handling strings in C has always been tougher than pulling meat from a lion's mouth, especially when compared with the excellent string-handling capabilities of many other high-level languages. Unfortunately, in C, you can't create classes and overload operators, so good string handling can't be incorporated into the language, even by user-written routines. For example, in C, strings cannot be assigned by the simple expression A = B.

Thankfully, you're a C++ programmer. By using C++'s overloading capabilities, both for functions and operators, as well as taking advantage of its object-oriented programming features, you can create a string class that provides all the string-manipulation features of languages like Pascal. In fact, the string class presented in this chapter uses Borland's excellent Turbo Pascal as a model.

How do you design a string class? I'm glad you asked!

Designing a String Class

To design your own string class, ask yourself a couple of questions. First, how should you represent the string? There are two approaches you can take: a standard character array or dynamically allocated memory. Both approaches have strong and weak points. For example, the character-array approach is the simplest, enabling you to use C++'s array-handling capabilities without having to worry about the details of memory allocation.

On the other hand, using a character array is the least flexible of the choices, because you must choose a maximum string size and stick with it. Moreover, your character array will take up the same amount of memory regardless of the actual length of the string. Suppose you choose an 81-element character array, which has enough space for 80 characters, plus a null. Then, each string you create will take up 81 bytes of memory, although the string data may be only a few bytes. Figure 2.1 illustrates this problem.

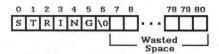

Figure 2.1. The standard character-array approach sometimes results in wasted memory space.

By dynamically allocating space for a string and by grabbing only the memory you actually need to contain the string, you can use memory more efficiently. This method, however, requires a lot of program overhead. You must write code to handle memory allocation and deallocation, check for allocation errors and null strings, keep track of a string's size, and take care of other messy details. In fact, the extra code required for a dynamically allocated string class would probably use as much memory as you'd waste with the character-array approach (depending on the number of strings a program uses, of course). To keep things simple and clean, then, the class presented in this chapter uses the character-array method, with an 81-element array.

Now that you've chosen a type of storage, consider how your programs will use strings. To be as flexible as possible, your programs must be able to handle two types of strings: standard character arrays and String objects (instances of the String class). For example, you must allow string assignments such as str1 = str2 (in which str1 and str2 are String objects) and str1 = "STRING" (in which str1 is a String object and "STRING" is a standard C character array). This means you're going to have to overload functions to accept either type of parameter.

You now have a general strategy for string storage and string usage. Next, you need to decide what functions will give you the string-handling power you want.

The Components of a String Class

The basic functions required in a string class vary with the needs of each programmer; everyone programs differently. Moreover, each program has its own requirements. The string class in this chapter contains the most often-used functions. When the string class is complete and you've used it in your own programs, you may find you need additional functions. No problem! Add them by modifying the original class. When you understand how the basic class was created, you should have no difficulty modifying it to meet specific needs.

What are the basic functions a string class requires? You can answer this question easily, by examining a popular high-level language with good string handling, such as Borland's Turbo Pascal. Examining Turbo Pascal yields a list of important string-handling functions. These functions are

- String construction and destruction
- String assignment
- String concatenation
- String comparison
- String searches
- String insertion
- String deletion
- String extraction
- String retrieval

Each function in the string class is covered in its own section.

Before you get started, however, look at Listing 2.1, the header file for the string class. Compare it with Table 2.1, which lists each function and its usage.

Obviously, if you understand how to use the class, you'll better understand the programming involved. You might also want to look over Listing 2.3 to get a general idea of how the string functions are used in a program.

Listing 2.1. STRNG.H—the header file for the string class.

```
#ifndef _STRNG_H
#define _STRNG_H

#include <string.h>
#include <conio.h>
#include <iostream.h>

class String
{
  char s[81];

public:
  String(char *ch);
  String(String &str) { strcpy(s, str.s); }
  void Show(void) { cout << s << '\n'; }
  void GetStr(char *ch, int size);
  String GetSubStr(int index, int count);
  void Delete(int index, int count);
  void Insert(String str, int index);
  void Insert(char *ch, int index);
  int Length() { return strlen(s); }
  int Pos(String str);
  int Pos(char *ch);
  String operator=(String str);
  String operator=(char *ch);
  String operator+(String str);
  String operator+(char *ch);
  int operator==(String str);
  int operator==(char *ch);
  int operator!=(String str);
  int operator!=(char *ch);
  int operator<(String str);
  int operator<(char *ch);
  int operator>(String str);
  int operator>(char *ch);
  int operator>=(String str);
  int operator>=(char *ch);
```

44

```
  int operator<=(String str);
  int operator<=(char *ch);
};

#endif
```

Table 2.1. String class description.

String Function	Use
`String(char *ch)` `String(String &str)`	These are the class' constructors. The constructor accepts as a parameter either a character array or a `String` object.
`void Show(void)`	This function is mostly for testing purposes. It displays a `String` on-screen using standard stream output.
`void GetStr` `(char *ch, int size)`	This function retrieves a `String` and places it into a character array. The parameter `ch` is a pointer to the destination character array, and `size` is the length of the destination array.
`String GetSubStr` `(int index, int count)`	This function returns a `String` made up of `count` characters. The characters are extracted from the `String` starting with the character at position `index`.
`void Delete` `(int index, int count)`	This function deletes `count` characters from the `String` object, starting with the character at position `index`.
`void Insert` `(String str, int index)`	This function inserts `str` into a `String`, at position `index`.
`void Insert` `(char *ch, int index)`	This function inserts a character array pointed to by `ch` into a `String`, starting at `String` character position `index`.
`int Length()`	This function returns the length of a `String`.

continues

45

Table 2.1. String class description (*continued*).

String Function	Use
`int Pos(String str)`	This function returns the character position of the first occurrence of `str` within a `String`.
`int Pos(char *ch)`	This function returns the character position of the first occurrence of `ch` (a character array) within a `String`.
`String operator=` `(String str)`	This function assigns `str` to a `String`.
`String operator=` `(char *ch)`	This function assigns `ch` (a character array) to a `String`.
`String operator+` `(String str)`	This function concatenates a `String` and `str`.
`String operator+` `(char *ch)`	This function concatenates a `String` and `ch` (a character array).
`int operator==` `(String str)`	This function compares a `String` with `str`, returning 1 if they are equal or 0 if they are not equal.
`int operator==` `(char *ch)`	This function compares a `String` to `ch` (a character array), returning 1 if they are equal or 0 if they are not equal.
`int operator<` `(String str)`	This function returns 1 if `String` is less than `str`, else returns 0.
`int operator<` `(char *ch)`	This function returns 1 if `String` is less than `ch`, else returns 0.
`int operator>` `(String str)`	This function returns 1 if `String` is greater than `str`, else returns 0.
`int operator>` `(char *ch)`	This function returns 1 if `String` is greater than `ch`, else returns 0.
`int operator<=` `(String str)`	This function returns 1 if `String` is less than or equal to `str`, else returns 0.

String Function	Use
int operator<= (char *ch)	This function returns 1 if String is less than or equal to ch, else returns 0.
int operator>= (String str)	This function returns 1 if String is greater than or equal to str, else returns 0.
int operator>= (char *ch)	This function returns 1 if String is greater than or equal to ch, else returns 0.

String Construction and Destruction

Thanks to object-oriented programming, String initialization can be handled by the class' constructor. This means you can create and initialize a new String with a single declaration—for example, String str("TEST STRING")—or, to create an empty string, String str("").

By using conventional character arrays, rather than dynamically allocated memory, the class needs no string destructor. The class creates nothing that can't be handled automatically by C++. If, however, the string class used dynamically allocated memory, its destructor would have been responsible for releasing memory allocated to a String.

Finally, as mentioned previously, the string class must deal with both String objects and standard C character arrays. Therefore, it has to overload the constructor. One version constructs a String from an existing String and another constructs a String from a character array. The former is implemented in-line:

```
String(String &str) { strcpy(s, str.s); }
```

The constructor doesn't have to worry about the length of str.s. It's already a String object; thus, it is guaranteed to be 80 characters or less. To construct the new String, the function simply copies one string into the other.

The following is the source code for the character-array version of the constructor:

```
String::String(char *ch)
{
  if (strlen(ch) > 80) ch[80] = 0;
  strcpy(s, ch);
}
```

Here, the function first checks the length of `ch`. If it's larger than 80 characters, it places a null in `ch[80]`, which truncates the array to the correct size. The function then uses the C function `strcpy()` to copy the source array, `ch`, into the destination array, `s`.

String Assignments

To handle string assignments conveniently, the string class overloads C++'s assignment operator (=). In fact, it overloads it twice: once for character arrays and once for `String` objects. An assignment operator would be crippled if it couldn't accept string constants, which are represented in C++ by character arrays. The following is the source code for the `String` version:

```
String String::operator=(String str)
{
  strcpy(s, str.s);
  return *this;
}
```

As with the string constructor, the source `String` is already in the acceptable format, so the function can just copy it directly into the destination `String`. Note the use of the pointer `this`, which is a pointer to the object that called the function. Every call to a class' function gets `this` as a hidden parameter. So, the previous function returns a pointer to the object. This makes it possible to use the new assignment operator in such expressions as `str1 = str2 = "TEST STRING"`. Also, this is the way programmers expect the C++ assignment operator to work. You should avoid giving programmers nasty surprises. Surprises make them cranky.

The following is the character-array version of the function:

```
String String::operator=(char *ch)
{
  if (strlen(ch) > 80) ch[80] = 0;
  strcpy(s, ch);
  return *this;
}
```

This version works much like the first, except the function can no longer assume that the source character array is 80 characters or less. As with the character-array version of the constructor, therefore, the function checks the length of `ch` and truncates it if necessary. Then, it uses `strcpy()` to copy the array into `s`.

String Concatenation

There probably aren't too many string-intensive programs that couldn't benefit from a string-concatenation function. For example, a program may need to combine a person's first and last names, build a complete pathname out of directory and filename strings, or assemble phrases into sentences.

Concatenating strings is trickier than making simple string assignments. First, you must be sure that the final String is no longer than the allowable 80 characters. Also, as discussed in the previous chapter, you must use the + operator in the expected way. Specifically, you must not change either of the source strings, but rather return a third string that is the concatenation of the source strings. Also, you need two versions of the function, one for Strings and one for character arrays. The following is the String version:

```
String String::operator+(String str)
{
  char ch[161];
  String str1("");

  strcpy(ch, s);
  strcpy(&ch[strlen(s)], str.s);
  ch[80] = 0;
  strcpy(str1.s, ch);
  return str1;
}
```

Although the function concatenates two strings, you may wonder why only one string is listed in the function's parameters. This is because the other source string is the String object that called the function.

Which object calls the operator function? With operators, the object on the left is always the one that makes the function call. For example, in the statement str2 = str1 + "TEST STRING", the object str1 calls the concatenation function. You don't have to pass str1 as a parameter, because you already have access to it within the class.

The previous function uses a 161-element character array as temporary storage for the Strings being concatenated. By using this double-sized character array, the function can concatenate the two Strings (which are 80 characters or less) without worrying about overrunning the destination array. To return a String in the proper format, the function simply places a null in ch[80], which truncates ch if it's larger than 80 characters. After concatenating the String, the function copies the resulting character string into a new String object, str1, which is the String returned.

The character-array version of the concatenation function is much simpler:

```
String String::operator+(char *ch)
{
   String str(ch);
   return *this + str;
}
```

Rather than duplicate a lot of code, it's much easier to convert the character array to a string object and then use the String version of the concatenation function to do the dirty work. Notice that the function uses a dereferenced this pointer to access the String object that called the function.

String Comparison

Comparing strings is a particularly handy function. Often, for example, in an interactive program, you have to check a user's input against some expected response. C++ already provides string-comparison functions, but those functions can be improved by hiding their somewhat clumsy implementation inside the string class. By overloading C++'s == operator, you can compare strings in a more natural way. The following is the implementation for both versions of this function:

```
int String::operator==(String str)
{
   if (strcmp(s, str.s) == 0) return 1;
   return 0;
}

int String::operator==(char *ch)
{
   if (strcmp(s, ch) == 0) return 1;
   return 0;
}
```

These functions differ only in the type of parameter they accept. Both use the C++ function strcmp() to compare two character arrays. Unlike the strcmp() function, however, which returns a false (0) value when the strings match, the string class' comparison function returns true (1) for a match, and false (0) otherwise. This is the way you would expect the == comparison operator to work.

The string class also includes overloaded functions for all other types of comparisons, as shown in Table 2.1. Note that the comparison functions provided here are case-sensitive. You might want to develop comparison operators that are not case-sensitive.

String Searches

Sometimes, you may want to locate a series of characters within a string. Again, as with string comparisons, C++'s string library already provides a function for locating substrings. The `strncmp()` function works like `strcmp()`, except it limits its comparison to the number of characters specified in the last parameter. You can easily use `strncmp()` to locate a substring and return its position. The string class' `Pos()` function uses `strncmp()` for just this task:

```
int String::Pos(String str)
{
  int found = 0;

  if ((str == "") || (str.Length() > Length())) return 0;
  int i = 0;
  while ((!found) && (i<Length()))
  {
    if (strncmp(&s[i], str.s, str.Length()) == 0)
      found = 1;
    else ++i;
  }
  if (found) return i+1;
  return 0;
}
```

Here, the function first checks whether the passed `String` is null or is longer than the `String` that called the function. In either case, there can't possibly be a match; therefore, the function returns a 0. If the function gets past this first check, it enters a `while` loop that uses the index `i` to cycle through each character of the `String` object. In the call to `strncmp()`, the index is used to calculate the address of the character with which to start the comparison (`&s[i]`) with the search `String`. If `strncmp()` finds a match, the flag `found` is set, which causes the loop to end. Then the value `i+1`, the position of the character that begins the substring, is returned from the function.

The character-array version of `Pos()`, like the character-array version of the concatenation function, simply converts the character array to a `String` object, and then calls the String version of Pos(). This trick makes adding a character-array version of most functions easier than toasting marshmallows in a forest fire.

```
int String::Pos(char *ch)
{
  String str(ch);
  return Pos(str);
}
```

String Insertion

Another handy string operation—one that's similar to string concatenation—is *string insertion* (placing one string into another). The String class accomplishes this task with the function Insert(). The String version follows:

```
void String::Insert(String str, int index)
{
  char ch[161];

  if ((index <= Length()) && (index > 0))
  {
    strncpy(ch, s, index-1);
    strcpy(&ch[index-1], str.s);
    strcpy(&ch[strlen(ch)], &s[index-1]);
    ch[80] = 0;
    strcpy(s, ch);
  }
}
```

This function first checks for a valid index. If the index is okay, it uses strncpy() to copy all the characters, up to the index, into a temporary character array. Then it adds the string you want to insert to the array. Finally, it copies the remaining characters in the original String into the temporary array, placing a null in ch[80] to ensure that the returned string is 80 characters or less, as required by the String class. Note that this function returns no value; it operates directly on the String object that calls the function.

The character-array version of Insert(), again, does nothing more than convert the array to a String object and then call the String version of the function. Following is that version of the function:

```
void String::Insert(char *ch, int index)
{
   String s1(ch);
   Insert(s1, index);
}
```

String Deletion

The opposite of insertion is, of course, deletion. A *string-deletion* function enables you to remove a substring from a String object. In the String class, the function Delete() does the job:

```
void String::Delete(int index, int count)
{
   String s1("");

   if ((index <= strlen(s)) && (index > 0) && (count > 0))
   {
     strncpy(s1.s, s, index-1);
     if ((index+count-1) <= strlen(s))
       strcpy(&s1.s[index-1], &s[index+count-1]);
     else s1.s[index-1] = 0;
     *this = s1;
   }
}
```

This function works similarly to the insertion function. It first checks that the index is valid. It also checks that count is greater than 0. If the index or the count is invalid, the function does nothing. If the index is valid (greater than zero and less than or equal to the length of the string) and count is greater than zero, index-1 characters are copied from the beginning of the source String (the one that called the function) into a temporary String. Then the function checks whether the source String, starting at index, contains at least count characters. If it does, the characters starting at index+count-1 are added to the temporary String. Otherwise, if count is larger than the number of remaining characters in the source String, the function just adds a null to the temporary String, which effectively deletes all remaining characters in the String. Note that in the last line, *this = s1, the assignment operator is the one defined for the String class, not the usual C++ assignment operator.

String Extraction

A *string-extraction* function is much like a string-deletion function, except the extraction function returns a new string containing the requested characters, without deleting the characters from the original string. In the `String` class, the function `GetSubStr()` takes on this chore. Because the function takes only integer parameters, only one version is needed:

```
String String::GetSubStr(int index, int count)
{
  String s1("");

  if ((index <= strlen(s)) && (index > 0) && (count > 0))
  {
    int c = Length() - index + 1;
    if (count > c) count = c;
    strncpy(s1.s, &s[index-1], count);
    s1.s[count] = 0;
  }
  return s1;
}
```

As always, the function first checks for a valid index and count. If the index is valid (less than or equal to the length of the string and greater than zero) or the count less than 1, it returns a null `String` from the function. If the index and count are valid, the number of characters in the `String` starting at `index` are calculated, and `count` is adjusted if necessary. (You don't want to try to copy more characters than exist in the `String`.) Finally, `strncpy()` copies the requested characters into the new `String` object and that `String` is returned from the function.

String Retrieval

The last function in the `String` class enables you to convert the contents of a `String` back to a character array. You might need to do this, for example, to manipulate the string in a manner that is not supported by the `String` class. The `GetStr()` function handles the following conversion task:

```
void String::GetStr(char *ch, int size)
{
  strncpy(ch, s, size-1);
  ch[size-1] = 0;
}
```

Here, the function simply copies the String object's character array into the array pointed to by ch. Note that it's imperative that the size parameter, which informs the function of the size of ch, be correct. To be sure of this, you should always use sizeof() as the second parameter in a call to this function, as in the following:

```
str.GetStr(ch, sizeof(ch));
```

Why can't you use the sizeof() function inside GetStr() and avoid having to pass it as a parameter? Because GetStr() only knows that ch is a pointer to char; the size of a pointer is four bytes. Dereferencing the pointer won't work either, because then you'd be asking for the size of the data to which ch pointed. What does ch point to? Characters, of course, which are actually integers, so their size is two bytes. GetStr() has no way of knowing that ch actually points to an array of characters.

Conclusion

That's it! You now have a versatile string class that relieves you from having to manipulate character arrays the old-fashioned C way. Listing 2.2 is the complete source code for the String class' implementation. Listing 2.3 is a program that tests the new class and shows how each function is called.

Listing 2.2. STRNG.CPP—the complete source code for the *String* class' implementation.

```
#include "strng.h"

String::String(char *ch)
{
  if (strlen(ch) > 80) ch[80] = 0;
  strcpy(s, ch);
}

void String::GetStr(char *ch, int size)
{
  strncpy(ch, s, size-1);
  ch[size-1] = 0;
}
```

continues

Listing 2.2. Continued

```
String String::GetSubStr(int index, int count)
{
  String s1("");

  if ((index <= strlen(s)) && (index > 0) && (count > 0))
  {
    int c = Length() - index + 1;
    if (count > c) count = c;
    strncpy(s1.s, &s[index-1], count);
    s1.s[count] = 0;
  }
  return s1;
}


void String::Delete(int index, int count)
{
  String s1("");

  if ((index <= strlen(s)) && (index > 0) && (count > 0))
  {
    strncpy(s1.s, s, index-1);
    if ((index+count-1) <= strlen(s))
      strcpy(&s1.s[index-1], &s[index+count-1]);
    else s1.s[index-1] = 0;
    *this = s1;
  }
}


void String::Insert(String str, int index)
{
  char ch[161];

  if ((index <= Length()) && (index > 0))
  {
    strncpy(ch, s, index-1);
    strcpy(&ch[index-1], str.s);
    strcpy(&ch[strlen(ch)], &s[index-1]);
    ch[80] = 0;
    strcpy(s, ch);
  }
}
```

```
void String::Insert(char *ch, int index)
{
  String s1(ch);
  Insert(s1, index);
}

int String::Pos(String str)
{
  int found = 0;

  if ((str == "") || (str.Length() > Length())) return 0;
  int i = 0;
  while ((!found) && (i<Length()))
  {
    if (strncmp(&s[i], str.s, str.Length()) == 0)
      found = 1;
    else ++i;
  }
  if (found) return i+1;
  return 0;
}

int String::Pos(char *ch)
{
  String str(ch);
  return Pos(str);
}

String String::operator=(String str)
{
  strcpy(s, str.s);
  return *this;
}

String String::operator=(char *ch)
{
  if (strlen(ch) > 80) ch[80] = 0;
  strcpy(s, ch);
  return *this;
}
```

continues

Listing 2.2. Continued

```
String String::operator+(String str)
{
  char ch[161];
  String str1("");

  strcpy(ch, s);
  strcpy(&ch[strlen(s)], str.s);
  ch[80] = 0;
  strcpy(str1.s, ch);
  return str1;
}

String String::operator+(char *ch)
{
  String str(ch);
  return *this + str;
}

int String::operator==(String str)
{
  if (strcmp(s, str.s) == 0) return 1;
  return 0;
}

int String::operator==(char *ch)
{
  if (strcmp(s, ch) == 0) return 1;
  return 0;
}

int String::operator!=(String str)
{
  if (strcmp(s, str.s) != 0) return 1;
  return 0;
}

int String::operator!=(char *ch)
{
  if (strcmp(s, ch) != 0) return 1;
  return 0;
}
```

```
int String::operator<(String str)
{
  if (strcmp(s, str.s) < 0) return 1;
  return 0;
}

int String::operator<(char *ch)
{
  if (strcmp(s, ch) < 0) return 1;
  return 0;
}

int String::operator>(String str)
{
  if (strcmp(s, str.s) > 0) return 1;
  return 0;
}

int String::operator>(char *ch)
{
  if (strcmp(s, ch) > 0) return 1;
  return 0;
}

int String::operator>=(String str)
{
  if (strcmp(s, str.s) >= 0) return 1;
  return 0;
}

int String::operator>=(char *ch)
{
  if (strcmp(s, ch) >= 0) return 1;
  return 0;
}

int String::operator<=(String str)
{
  if (strcmp(s, str.s) <= 0) return 1;
  return 0;
}
```

continues

Listing 2.2. Continued

```
int String::operator<=(char *ch)
{
  if (strcmp(s, ch) <= 0) return 1;
  return 0;
}
```

Listing 2.3. TSTSTRNG.CPP—a program that tests the new class and shows how each function is called.

```
#include "strng.h"
#include "iostream.h"
#include "conio.h"

void main ()
{
  String s1("THE HAT");
  String s2(s1);
  String s3("");
  char ch[81];

  cout<<'\n';
  s1.Show();
  s2.Show();
  s2.Insert("CAT ", 5);
  s2.Show();
  s3 = "IN THE THE";
  s3.Show();
  s2.Insert(s3, 9);
  s2.Show();
  s2.Delete(16, 3);
  s2.Show();
  s3 = s2;
  s3.Show();
  cout << "s3 is " << s3.Length() << " characters long.\n";
  cout << "'CAT' is at position " << s3.Pos("CAT") << ".\n";
  s2 = "HAT";
  cout << "'HAT' is at position " << s3.Pos(s2) << ".\n";
  s3 = s2 + " TRICKS";
  s3.Show();
```

```
  s3 = s3 + " " + s3;
  s3.Show();
  s1 = s3.GetSubStr(5, 6);
  s1.Show();
  s3 = s2;
  if ((s2 == "HAT") && (s2 == s3))
    cout << "The strings are equal.\n";
  s2.GetStr(ch, sizeof(ch));
  cout << ch << '\n';
  getch();
}
```

The output from the test program should look like this:

```
THE HAT
THE HAT
THE CAT HAT
IN THE THE
THE CAT IN THE THEHAT
THE CAT IN THE HAT
THE CAT IN THE HAT
s3 is 18 characters long.
'CAT' is at position 5.
'HAT' is at position 16.
HAT TRICKS
HAT TRICKS HAT TRICKS
TRICKS
The strings are equal.
HAT
```

Now, not only do you have a handy programming tool, but you have also reinforced some of what you learned in Chapter 1—specifically, what you learned about the proper use of function and operator overloading.

This class overloads functions that vary in parameter type, not parameter count. Also, it overloads operators in a way consistent with their intended use—except in one instance.

Note: Do you see a problem with the concatenation function? The concatenation function allows an expression like

```
str3 = str1 + str2
```

or

```
str3 = str1 + "TEST"
```

It doesn't, however, allow an expression like

```
str3 = "TEST" + str1
```

Why? Because, if you recall, it's the object on the left of the operator that calls the overloaded operator function. Because `"TEST"` is a character array and not a `String` object, the previous expression is invalid. It doesn't even compile. To perform the operation in question, `"TEST"` must first be converted to a `String` object.

In Chapter 3, "Event-Driven Programming in DOS," you get more practice developing classes. You also see how to write event-driven DOS programs.

3

Event-Driven Programming in DOS

I n these days of *graphical user interfaces* (GUIs), any program worth its weight in microchips features sophisticated screen elements like windows, buttons, and dialog boxes. The immense popularity of Microsoft Windows is testament that GUIs have not only moved in, but have brought enough luggage to stay. Undoubtedly, designing a program interface is much more difficult than it used to be. If you want your software to get rave reviews, however, you have no choice but to knuckle under and give the people what they want.

In the next couple of chapters, you learn to create event-driven programs featuring interactive screen objects such as windows, dialog boxes, and button controls. Before you can start thinking about these objects, however, you must learn the basics of event-driven program design, which you do in this chapter. You also develop a basic mouse class that instantly adds mouse support to your programs.

Note: If you have a strong urge to bolt for the nearest exit, please stick around. You may find that the job at hand is easier than you expect—and maybe even a little fun.

What Is an Event-Driven Program?

With an application written using conventional procedural programming techniques, the user has limited control over the program's features. For example, suppose an application requires keyboard input from a user. In a typical program, the application waits until the user enters the required string (or an escape code of some type from the keyboard). Until the user enters the requested information, he cannot go on to something else. What if the user wants to use her mouse to select a different option? It doesn't matter. The program is expecting character input and nothing short of a reboot is going to interrupt it.

In an event-driven program, input comes from any device at any time. For example, when the user requests a string, she would probably use a dialog box. While the dialog box is active, the program isn't locked onto the keyboard; it's still ready to accept input from any device. After all, the program has no way of knowing in advance whether the user is going to type characters or click a button.

When the user chooses an action, the program receives a message, which it then interprets and routes to the appropriate functions. This interpretation and routing is performed by the program's *event loop,* a short section of code that loops continuously, receiving events from the user and dispatching those events to the parts of the program designed to handle them. This loop iterates endlessly, doing nothing until the user interacts with the program in some way, usually by pressing a key on the keyboard or selecting a control with the mouse.

To create event-driven programs, you must do the following:

- Decide which devices to support.
- Define message types for each device.
- Write a handler for each device.

- Write an event loop to gather messages.

- Write an event dispatcher to send messages to their appropriate functions.

These steps are discussed in the sections that follow.

Developing an Event Handler

Because a program's event handler defines the program's interactive nature, you must carefully consider what types of events your programs have to handle in order to provide a flexible and easy-to-use interface. In a full-scale GUI, this is no small matter. Programs written for Microsoft Windows, for example, must deal with hundreds of different types of events.

The next two chapters discuss the techniques you need to build event-handling into your DOS programs. Instead of obscuring the principles by trying to create the ultimate event-driven program interface, the discussion keeps things simple. Then, you can expand on what you've learned and enhance the basic routines presented here to better suit your specific programming needs.

With this in mind, think about the events you need to handle to provide a solid program interface. First, which input devices will your programs support? There are many types, including keyboards, graphics tablets, joysticks, mice, light pens, trackballs, and more. For the sake of clarity and simplicity, however, this chapter considers only the two most useful: the keyboard and the mouse. Using these two input devices, you can write just about any type of program, including applications, utilities, and even games.

Now you need to consider how those devices generate input. You can then gather that input, translate it into an appropriate event message, and dispatch that message to the proper part of your program. Gathering input events requires a programming technique called *polling*.

Polling for Events

If you have no experience with event-driven programming, you probably think all this stuff about event loops, message translating, and message dispatching sounds complex. Actually, however, it's not difficult to implement, and the code involved is surprisingly short. In the event handler, you need only two functions. These functions are `GetEvent()` and `DispatchEvent()`. The following is a typical event loop:

```
int repeat = 1;
while (repeat)
{
  GetEvent(evntmsg);
  DispatchEvent(evntmsg);
}
```

The function `GetEvent()` is a general function that you can use in any event-driven program. It simply polls the devices until it gets input. It then uses the input to formulate an event message, which it passes to the second function, `DispatchMessage()`. The basic event handler presented in this chapter handles only two types of events: mouse-button events and keyboard events. The `GetEvent()` function loops until the user types a key or presses a mouse button. Here's the code for `GetEvent()`:

```
void GetEvent(EvntMsg &evntmsg)
{
  while ((!mouse.Event()) && (!(evntmsg.key = KeyEvent()))) {}
  evntmsg.button = mouse.GetButton();
  if (evntmsg.button)
  {
    evntmsg.type = MBUTTON;
    mouse.GetXY(evntmsg.mx, evntmsg.my);
  }
  else
  {
    evntmsg.type = KEYBD;
    evntmsg.mx = -1;
    evntmsg.my = -1;
  }
}
```

Although the details of how to retrieve input from the devices haven't been discussed, you should be able to make some general sense out of this function. In the first line, the `while` loop iterates until it senses either a mouse-button or keyboard event. If it senses a mouse-button event, it constructs a mouse-button message, which includes the message type, the number of the button pressed, and the coordinates of the mouse when the button was pressed. If the function gets a keyboard event, it constructs a keyboard message, which contains the key that was pressed and the message type. The structure that contains these messages (which is defined in the next chapter) looks like this:

```
typedef struct EvntMsg
{
  int type,       // Event type.
      mx, my,     // Mouse coords.
      button;     // Mouse button pressed.
  unsigned key; // Key pressed.
};
```

The function DispatchEvent(), unlike GetEvent(), is closely tied to a specific program. It is here that a general keyboard or mouse event is directed to a specific function. Because every program has different functions, DispatchEvent() is different in every program. Here's what DispatchEvent() looks like in a program from Chapter 4:

```
void DispatchEvent(EvntMsg evntmsg)
{
  if ( startbut.Clicked(evntmsg) )
    Life();
  else if ( clearbut.Clicked(evntmsg) )
    ClearWorld();
  else if ( generatebut.Clicked(evntmsg) )
    GetGens();
  else if ( speedbut.Clicked(evntmsg) )
    GetSpeed();
  else if ( quitbut.Clicked(evntmsg) )
    repeat = 0;
  else PlaceCell(evntmsg);
}
```

Again, although the details have not been discussed, you can see that this function checks which button control the user clicked and then calls the appropriate function.

Chapter 4 returns to GetEvent() and DispatchEvent(). For now, you need to know how to receive keyboard and mouse events. Gathering keyboard events is easy: You only have to poll for a keystroke, and, if one is received, translate that keystroke into the appropriate message. Handling a mouse, however, is more complex: You must access the operating system at an assembly-language level. This is because C++ provides no direct mouse support. Instead, you must control the mouse with calls to a mouse handler.

Keyboard Events

Consider the keyboard first. In a *nonevent-driven program,* handling the keyboard is easy. For example, it's not uncommon to prompt for a string and then wait for the user to enter it. Until the user enters the string, the program is idle. Because no further processing is possible anyway, you can use a function like `getch()`, which waits for a keystroke, to gather input.

An *event-driven program,* however, must never wait for a specific type of input. This is, in fact, what distinguishes an event-driven program from a nonevent-driven program. An event-driven program must always be ready to accept any type of event from the user. This means that you can't gather keystrokes with a function like `getch()`.

Suppose your program has displayed a dialog box in response to a user's menu selection. This dialog, which prompts for a line of text, contains an editable text line, along with OK and Cancel buttons. When your program starts the dialog, it has no idea what the user will do with it. The user may enter the string you've requested and click the OK button. He may enter the string, change his mind, and click the Cancel button. Or the user may press the Cancel button without attempting to enter a string. Obviously, you can't wait for any particular type of event. Instead, you must poll the devices your program supports.

To get keyboard input under these conditions, you need a function that only inquires whether a key has been pressed, without waiting for a key. If this function informs you that a key was pressed, you can then read the keystroke and decide what to do with it. If there is no keystroke available, you are free to check other devices (in this case, the mouse) for input. The event-driven programs in this book handle keyboard input with the function `KeyEvent()`:

```
int KeyEvent(void)
{
  // Check for key press.
  int key = bioskey(1);

  // Get key if one is available.
  if (key) key = bioskey(0);

  return key;
}
```

As you can see from this function, Borland C++ provides exactly the keyboard function you need to inquire about the keyboard's state, without stalling your program. The function `bioskey()` directly calls the BIOS via interrupt 0x16 to return information about the keyboard's status. This function accepts one of three values as a parameter. The value of the parameter determines the type of information the function will return. If this parameter is 1, `bioskey()` checks whether a key is available. If this parameter is 0, `bioskey()` returns the last keystroke. If this parameter is 2, `bioskey` returns the status of certain special keys, including the Shift, Alt, and Ctrl keys. (You can read more about this function in the *Borland C++ Library Reference.*)

`KeyEvent()` first calls `bioskey(1)` to determine whether a key has been pressed. If a key has, the function retrieves its value with another call to `bioskey()`, this time with the parameter 0. In either case, the value of `key` is returned from the function. This value will be 0 if no key was retrieved, or the value of the key if a key was available. This function doesn't wait for input. It does its job and returns control to the event loop.

Listing 3.1 demonstrates `KeyEvent()`. Try the program now. When you're through, press Ctrl-C to exit the program.

Listing 3.1. KEY1.CPP—a demonstration of *KeyEvent()*.

```
// KEY1.CPP: Test Program for KeyEvent().

#include <iostream.h>
#include <bios.h>

#define CTRL_C 0x2e03

//Function prototype.
int KeyEvent(void);

void main()
{
  int k = 0;
  while ((k=KeyEvent()) != CTRL_C)
    if (k) cout << "Key value: " << k << '\n';
}

int KeyEvent(void)
{
```

continues

Listing 3.1. Continued

```
// Check for key press.
int key = bioskey(1);

// Get key if one is available.
if (key) key = bioskey(0);
return key;
}
```

When you run KEY1.CPP, you'll discover that values returned from `bioskey(0)` are quite cryptic. This is because `bioskey(0)`, a call to the BIOS function 0x00 (`Int 0x16`), returns both the key's scan code and the key's ASCII code (if appropriate) combined into a single integer. The scan code is in the upper byte and the ASCII code is in the lower byte, as shown in Figure 3.1. (A *scan code* is a special code assigned to every key on the keyboard, even keys that have no ASCII representation.)

To get the ASCII code of the key pressed, you must mask out the upper byte of the value returned from `bioskey(0)`. Listing 3.2 is a refinement of KEY1.CPP that uses a key's ASCII code to print the actual key pressed.

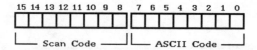

Figure 3.1. The *bioskey(0)* function returns both the key's scan code and the key's ASCII code as a single integer.

Listing 3.2. KEY2.CPP—a refinement of Listing 3.1.

```
// KEY2.CPP: Test Program for KeyEvent().

#include <iostream.h>
#include <bios.h>

#define CTRL_C 0x2e03

//Function prototype.
int KeyEvent(void);

void main()
```

```
{
  int k = 0;
  while ((k=KeyEvent()) != CTRL_C)
  {
    if (k)
    {
      cout << "Key value: " << k << ". ";

      // Mask out the key's scan code.
      k &= 0x00ff;

      if (!k) cout << "Not an ASCII character.\n";
      else cout << "The character is: " << (char) k << '\n';
    }
  }
}

int KeyEvent(void)
{
  // Check for key press.
  unsigned key = bioskey(1);

  // Get key if one is available.
  if (key) key = bioskey(0);

  return key;
}
```

Using `KeyEvent()`, you can now retrieve keyboard events on the fly. In fact, `KeyEvent()` is all the event handler you need for an event-driven program—albeit one that supports only the keyboard. After all, a user can select interactive objects like buttons from the keyboard, right? However, because most modern programs support mice, you can't get off this easily. At the least, you need minimal mouse support in your programs.

Mouse Events

When PCs were first introduced, there were no mice. Virtually all program input was entered through the keyboard. Today, however, a program's interface must be as interactive as possible, and this means providing mouse support. Although you may grumble and groan about the extra work, in all fairness to the user you must accept the responsibility.

71

Because a mouse is not a standard PC device, mouse support is not built into the operating system. To add mouse support to a system, the user must first load a mouse driver. This is typically done in the user's CONFIG.SYS or AUTOEXEC.BAT files. Once the driver is loaded, a program can access the mouse through interrupt 0x33.

Although there are many mouse manufacturers, there is one standard driver. This standard mouse driver, developed by Microsoft Corporation, supplies more than 30 functions for controlling a mouse, including not only the capability to respond to mouse-button presses, but also to get the mouse's location, adjust the mouse's sensitivity, change the mouse pointer's shape, detect mouse motion, and much more. Most mouse manufacturers have adopted this standard and incorporated it into their own mouse drivers.

To access a mouse driver, you must call functions at an assembly-language level. This task isn't as scary as it sounds. Read on to assemble a basic mouse class. Once you understand how to call mouse functions, you can extend the class to provide additional mouse functions.

In a basic mouse class, you need to support the mouse driver's most-used functions. These functions enable you to initialize the mouse, check that a mouse exists, set the limits of its screen coordinates, hide and show the mouse pointer, and read the mouse's buttons and current location.

The header file for this chapter's mouse class is shown in Listing 3.3, MOUS.H. A description of each function is included in Table 3.1.

 Note: This chapter's mouse class is developed for use only with a graphics screen, not a text screen. If you want to develop text-based programs with mouse support, you might as well use Borland's Turbo Vision, which comes with Borland C++.

Listing 3.3. MOUS.H—the header file for the *Mouse* class.

```
// MOUS.H: Mouse class header file.

#ifndef MOUSE_H
#define MOUSE_H


// Mouse button values.
```

```
#define LEFT 1
#define RIGHT 2
#define CENTER 3

class Mouse {

    int mx, my,    // Mouse coordinates.
     got_mouse,    // Mouse init flag.
     num_buttons,  // # buttons on mouse.
     button,       // Button status.
     ax,bx,cx,dx;  // Register saves.

  public:
    Mouse(void);
    ~Mouse(void) { MouseIntr(0x00); }
    int GotMouse(void) { return got_mouse; }
    void SetLimits(int min_Xlimit, int max_Xlimit,
             int min_Ylimit, int max_Ylimit);
    void ShowMouse(void) { MouseIntr(0x01); }
    void HideMouse(void) { MouseIntr(0x02); }
    int Event(void);
    int GetButton(void) { return button; }
    void GetXY(int &x, int &y) { x=mx; y=my; }
    void ButtonUp(void);
  private:
    void MouseIntr(int func);
};

extern Mouse mouse;

#endif
```

Table 3.1. Functions in the *Mouse* class.

Mouse Class	Description
Mouse(void)	This is the class' constructor. It calls mouse function 0x00 to initialize the mouse driver.

continues

73

Table 3.1. Functions in the *Mouse* class (*continued*).

Mouse Class	Description
~Mouse(void)	This is the class' destructor. It calls mouse function 0x00 a second time to reset the mouse driver to its default state.
int GotMouse(void)	Returns a –1 if a mouse is present and a 0 if a mouse is not present.
void SetLimits(int min_Xlimit, int max_Ylimit, int max_Xlimit, int min_Ylimit)	Sets the horizontal and vertical screen coordinate limits for the the mouse. Usually, these limits are set to the full screen.
void ShowMouse(void)	Displays the mouse pointer on-screen.
void HideMouse(void)	Removes the mouse pointer from the screen.
int Event(void)	Updates the mouse's button and position variables. This function should always be called immediately before retrieving the values of the button, mx, and my mouse variables.
int GetButton(void)	Gets the value of button returned from the last call to Event().
void GetXY(int &x, int &y)	Gets the coordinates of the mouse returned from the last call to Event().
void ButtonUp(void)	Waits for all mouse buttons to be released.

The Mouse class is a single-instance class (in other words, you'll never have more than one mouse in a program) that provides all the basic mouse functions. To include a mouse in a program, you need only include the mouse class. A mouse object is already declared as part of the class. Now you can examine the Mouse class a function at a time.

Initializing a Mouse

As with most classes, `Mouse` contains a constructor that initializes a `Mouse` object:

```
Mouse::Mouse(void)
{
  got_mouse = 0;
  if (getvect(0x33))
  {
    _AX = 0x00;
    geninterrupt(0x33);
    got_mouse = _AX;
    num_buttons = _BX;
  }
}
```

Here, after checking that the mouse driver is installed (by calling `getvect()`), this function makes the first call to the mouse driver with the 0x33 interrupt. To call an interrupt, you must first place appropriate values into the CPU's registers. Then, generate the interrupt by calling Borland C++'s `geninterrupt()` function. When the interrupt takes over, the values you placed in the registers inform the mouse driver what function you've requested and the parameters you want to send to that function. Borland C++ provides easy access to registers, through the pseudovariables `_AX`, `_BX`, `_CX`, and `_DX`. (There are other registers, but these are all you have to be concerned with for now.)

To initialize a mouse, you must call interrupt 0x33 with a 0 in `AX`. The mouse function 0x00 initializes the mouse driver and sets the mouse to its default state, returning a –1 in `AX` if a mouse is available, and a 0 if a mouse is not available. It also returns, in `BX`, the number of buttons on the mouse. In the previous constructor, the function saves these return values in the data members `got_mouse` and `num_buttons`.

Setting Mouse Screen Limits

After initializing your mouse, you need to set its screen limits. Normally, this task is handled by the mouse initialization; however, for some reason, when you use a mouse with high-resolution graphics screens, you need to remind the driver of the screen's resolution. If you fail to do this, the mouse will be unable to traverse the full screen.

75

To set a mouse's screen coordinate limits, call function 0x07 for the horizontal limits and 0x08 for the vertical limits. In the `Mouse` class, the function `SetLimits()` handles this task:

```
void Mouse::SetLimits(int min_Xlimit, int max_Xlimit,
                 int min_Ylimit, int max_Ylimit)
{
  if (!got_mouse) return;
  _AX = 0x07;
  _CX = min_Xlimit;
  _DX = max_Xlimit;
  geninterrupt(0x33);
  _AX = 0x08;
  _CX = min_Ylimit;
  _DX = max_Ylimit;
  geninterrupt(0x33);
}
```

Here, the function first checks that the mouse is present. There's no need to set the screen limits of a nonexistent mouse. If there's no mouse, the function returns immediately. If the mouse is present, `SetLimits()` loads the registers with the function number 0x07 and the horizontal screen limits, after which it generates an interrupt 0x33. It sets the vertical screen limits the same way, with the exception of using function 0x08 and the vertical coordinates.

 Caution: In spite of the fact that the function checks for a mouse, you should always check whether the mouse exists before you call other mouse functions. This is especially important if your program cannot run properly without a mouse.

There are many other uses for the `SetLimits()` function. For example, there may be times when you want to limit mouse movement to a particular rectangle on-screen. You could, if you wanted, force the mouse to stay within the boundaries of a particular window.

Showing and Hiding a Mouse Pointer

Showing and hiding the mouse pointer is critical. Without this capability, screen displays would soon become corrupted. Why? First, when you write to the screen, you may erase the mouse pointer. (The mouse pointer isn't magical; it's simply a graphic drawn on-screen.) This, by itself, is no big deal.

After all, the pointer is redrawn the next time you move the mouse. However, if you don't disable the mouse before drawing to the screen, something else is restored along with the mouse pointer: the data that was behind the pointer when it was last drawn. This saved data writes over your new screen, erasing what you just drew in the mouse's location.

In short, whenever you want to draw on-screen, you must first turn off (or hide) the mouse pointer. When you're finished drawing, turn the mouse pointer back on. If you fail to follow this rule (and sooner or later, we all do), the user of your program may not notice it at first, because the faulty screen update occurs only when the mouse pointer happens to be where your program is drawing. However, the first time the mouse is in the way of your drawing, you've got a faulty screen.

The Mouse class can show or hide the mouse pointer through calls to its HideMouse() and ShowMouse() member functions, both of which are written in-line in the MOUS.H header file:

```
void ShowMouse(void) { MouseIntr(0x01); }
void HideMouse(void) { MouseIntr(0x02); }
```

These functions call the private member function MouseIntr(). Because many mouse functions require only the function number in AX before calling the interrupt, MouseIntr() saves a lot of duplicated code. You simply supply the value to be placed in AX, and the function takes care of the rest. The MouseIntr() function looks like this:

```
void Mouse::MouseIntr(int func)
{
  if (!got_mouse) return;
  _AX = func;
  geninterrupt(0x33);
  ax = _AX;
  bx = _BX;
  cx = _CX;
  dx = _DX;
}
```

This function simply loads the value func into the AX register and then generates an interrupt 0x33. It saves the values returned in the AX, BX, CX, and DX registers right after the interrupt returns, because the registers may change when the function exits. Note that this function is private to the Mouse class—in other words, it can be called only by a class member function. It cannot be called directly from your programs.

77

Note: A final note about hiding and showing a mouse: The mouse functions, 0x01 and 0x02, count the number of times the pointer has been hidden and shown. If you don't want your mouse pointer to disappear, every *hide* function must be matched with a *show* function. In other words, if you call the `HideMouse()` function three times in a row (usually due to nested function calls), you must also call `ShowMouse()` three times to restore the mouse pointer.

Retrieving Mouse Events

Now that the mouse is functioning, you have to know when it is used. If the user clicks an on-screen button, for example, you must determine which on-screen button was clicked so you can perform the requested operation. Gathering this information is a snap. First, when the user clicks a mouse button, `GetEvent()` sends a mouse-button event. Use the data stored in this event to determine the mouse's coordinates at the time of the click. If these coordinates match those of your on-screen button, you know the button was selected.

In the `Mouse` class, the function that checks for mouse-button presses is `Event()`, which calls mouse function 0x03, returning the mouse-button status and the current location of the pointer:

```
int Mouse::Event(void)
{
  if (!got_mouse) return 0;
  MouseIntr(0x03);
  button = bx;
  mx = cx;
  my = dx;
  if (button) return 1;
  else return 0;
}
```

Here, the function first checks that the mouse is present. Then it calls mouse function 0x03 with `MouseIntr()`. After the call, the button status and the mouse coordinates are saved in the data members `button`, `mx`, and `my`, respectively, from which your program can retrieve them when necessary.

When you use a mouse in your programs, remember that button, mx, and my are updated only when you call Event(). Therefore, you must process the information retrieved by this function immediately. Otherwise, the mouse-status data may be obsolete. In short, you should always call Event() before testing the button, mx, and my variables.

As you know, the object-oriented approach dictates that Mouse's data members be private—it never allows a program to access the members directly. By following this rule, you can change the class without affecting programs that use it. For example, suppose you want to store the mouse variables button, mx, and my in a structure. By keeping the data members private, you can make this change easily. You need not change anything more (other than the data) than the functions in the class that return the variable's values. In other words, although the class' interface must remain consistent, the way you implement that interface can change any way you want. This is one way object-oriented programming makes programs more maintainable.

Because the mouse variables are private, you need functions to retrieve those values. In the Mouse class, you do this with the in-line functions GotMouse(), GetButton(), and GetXY():

```
int GotMouse(void) { return got_mouse; }
int GetButton(void) { return button; }
void GetXY(int &x, int &y) { x=mx; y=my; }
```

There's little to say about these functions. GotMouse() checks the mouse-driver status returned from the class' constructor. GetButton() returns the button-press last retrieved by Event(). Finally, GetXY() returns the mouse coordinates last retrieved by Event(). Notice that, whereas GetButton() returns button directly from the function, GetXY() stores the mouse coordinates in variables you pass to the function.

Sticky Buttons

The last function in the Mouse class allows your program to wait until the user releases the mouse button. A program's event loop typically processes events very quickly. This means that if the user is a slow mouse clicker, several button clicks may be registered before she releases the button. To avoid this problem, you can call ButtonUp(), which loops until the user releases the mouse button:

```
void Mouse::ButtonUp(void)
{
  while (button) Event();
}
```

The Complete *Mouse* Class

Listing 3.4, MOUS.CPP, is the implementation source code for the complete Mouse class. (The listing is short because many functions are implemented in-line in the MOUS.H source listing.)

Listing 3.5 is a short program that demonstrates the Mouse class. When you run the program, click anywhere on-screen. The program prints the mouse's coordinates on-screen, at the location you click. To exit the program, click the right mouse button.

 Note: This program must be run on a VGA-compatible system and Borland's VGA graphics driver, EGAVGA.BGI, must be in the same directory as the program. Later, you learn how to link the graphics driver into your programs so you don't need the separate file.

Listing 3.4. MOUS.CPP—the implementation of the *Mouse* class.

```
// MOUS.CPP: Mouse class implementation.

#include <dos.h>
#include <conio.h>
#include "mous.h"

Mouse mouse;

// Initialize the mouse.
Mouse::Mouse(void)
{
  got_mouse = 0;
  if (getvect(0x33))
  {
    _AX = 0x00;
    geninterrupt(0x33);
```

```
      got_mouse = _AX;
      num_buttons = _BX;
   }
}


// Set the mouse's screen coord limits.
void Mouse::SetLimits(int min_Xlimit, int max_Xlimit,
                 int min_Ylimit, int max_Ylimit)
{
  if (!got_mouse) return;
  _AX = 0x07;
  _CX = min_Xlimit;
  _DX = max_Xlimit;
  geninterrupt(0x33);
  _AX = 0x08;
  _CX = min_Ylimit;
  _DX = max_Ylimit;
  geninterrupt(0x33);
}


// Check the status of the mouse's buttons
// and get the mouse's current position.
int Mouse::Event(void)
{
  if (!got_mouse) return 0;
  MouseIntr(0x03);
  button = bx;
  mx = cx;
  my = dx;
  if (button) return 1;
  else return 0;
}


// Wait for mouse button to be released.
void Mouse::ButtonUp(void)
{
  while (button) Event();
}


// Call a mouse function.
void Mouse::MouseIntr(int func)
{
  if (!got_mouse) return;
```

continues

81

Listing 3.4. Continued

```
_AX = func;
geninterrupt(0x33);
ax = _AX;
bx = _BX;
cx = _CX;
dx = _DX;
}
```

Listing 3.5. MDEMO.CPP—a demonstration of the *Mouse* class.

```
// MDEMO.CPP: Mouse test program.
// Before running, make sure the VGA graphics driver
// EGAVGA.BGI is in the same directory as the program.

#include <graphics.h>
#include <stdio.h>
#include <conio.h>
#include <iostream.h>
#include <stdlib.h>
#include "mous.h"

void main()
{
  int gdriver = VGA, gmode = VGAHI, errorcode;
  int mbutton, mouseX, mouseY;
  char s[10];

  // Initialize the graphics screen.
  initgraph(&gdriver, &gmode, "");
  if ( (errorcode = graphresult()) != grOk)
  {
    cout << "Graphics error: " << errorcode << '\n';
    getch();
    abort();
  }

  // Check that the mouse exists.
  if (!mouse.GotMouse())
  {
    cout<<"Got no Mouse!";
```

```
      getch();
    }
  else
  {
    // Allow mouse to use entire VGA screen.
    mouse.SetLimits(0,getmaxx(),0,getmaxy());

    // Display mouse pointer.
    mouse.ShowMouse();

    mbutton  = 0;
    while (mbutton != RIGHT)
    {
      // Update mouse data.
      mouse.Event();

      // Get mouse button status.
      mbutton = mouse.GetButton();

      if (mbutton == LEFT)
      {
    // Get new mouse coords.
    mouse.GetXY(mouseX, mouseY);

    sprintf(s, "%d,%d", mouseX, mouseY);

    // Hide pointer before drawing on-screen.
    mouse.HideMouse();

    outtextxy(mouseX, mouseY, s);

    // Restore mouse pointer.
    mouse.ShowMouse();

    // Wait for the mouse button to be released.
    mouse.ButtonUp();
      }
    }
  }
  closegraph();
}
```

You should now understand the basic mouse class. As you develop mouse-based programs, you may want to expand this basic class to include more sophisticated capabilities. To get you started, Table 3.2 lists some handy functions available in a Microsoft-compatible mouse driver. Look them over and try adding a few to the basic mouse class.

Table 3.2. Useful mouse functions.

Function 0x00	**Reset Mouse**
Entry:	AX = 0x00.
Exit:	AX = 0xFFFF if mouse is present or 0x00 if no mouse is present.
	BX = number of buttons on mouse.

Function 0x01	**Show Mouse Pointer**
Entry:	AX = 0x01.
Exit:	Returns nothing.

Function 0x02	**Hide Mouse Pointer**
Entry:	AX = 0x02.
Exit:	Returns nothing.

Function 0x03	**Get Mouse Status**
Entry:	AX = 0x03.
Exit:	BX = 0x00 if no button is pressed, 0x01 if left button is pressed, 0x02 if right button is pressed, and 0x04 if center button is pressed.
	CX = Horizontal coordinate.
	DX = Vertical coordinate.

Function 0x04	**Set Mouse Position**
Entry:	AX = 0x04.
	CX = New horizontal coordinate.
	DX = New vertical coordinate.
Exit:	Returns nothing.

Function 0x05	**Get Button Press Status**
Entry:	AX = 0x05.
	BX = 0x00 to check left button, 0x01 to check right button, and 0x02 to check center button.
Exit:	AX = 0x01 if left button is pressed, 0x02 if right button is pressed, and 0x04 if center button is pressed.
	BX = Number of button presses.
	CX = Horizontal coordinate of last button press.
	DX = Vertical coordinate of last button press.

Function 0x06	**Get Button Release Status**
Entry:	AX = 0x06.
	BX = 0x00 to check left button, 0x01 to check right button, and 0x02 to check center button.
Exit:	AX = 0x01 if left button is pressed, 0x02 if right button is pressed, and 0x04 if center button is pressed.
	BX = Number of button releases.
	CX = Horizontal coordinate of button release.
	DX = Vertical coordinate of button release.

continues

85

Table 3.2. Useful mouse functions (*continued*).

Function 0x07	Set Horizontal Limits
Entry:	AX = 0x07.
	CX = Minimum horizontal coordinate.
	DX = Maximum horizontal coordinate.
Exit:	Returns nothing.

Function 0x08	Set Vertical Limits
Entry:	AX = 0x08.
	CX = Minimum vertical coordinate.
	DX = Maximum vertical coordinate.
Exit:	Returns nothing.

Function 0x09	Set Graphical Shape
Entry:	AX = 0x09.
	BX = X coordinate of hot spot.
	CX = Y coordinate of hot spot.
	DS:DX = Address of bitmap image.
Exit:	Returns nothing.
	Note: The bitmap comprises 64 bytes, the first 32 bytes of which are the bit image for the pointer and the second 32 bytes of which are the bit image of the pointer mask.

Function 0x0B	Get Mouse Motion
Entry:	AX = 0x0B.
Exit:	CX = Number of mickeys moved horizontally.
	DX = Number of mickeys moved vertically.
	Note: Mickeys are equivalent to 1/200th of an inch. The values returned from this function are the number of mickeys moved since the last call to this function.

Function 0x10	Set Exclusion Rectangle
Entry:	AX = 0x10.
	CX = Left edge X coordinate.
	DX = Top edge Y coordinate.
	SI = Right edge X coordinate.
	DI = Bottom Y coordinate.
Exit:	Returns nothing.
	Note: An exclusion rectangle is an area of the screen in which the mouse pointer will not be shown.

Function 0x1A	Set Sensitivity
Entry:	AX = 0x1A.
	BX = Horizontal speed (number of mickeys per 8 pixels).
	CX = Vertical speed (number of mickeys per 8 pixels).
	DX = Double-speed threshold in mickeys per second.
Exit:	Returns nothing.
	Note: The double-speed threshold is the speed the mouse must travel before the pointer begins to move twice as fast.

Function 0x1B	Get Sensitivity
Entry:	AX = 0x1B.
Exit:	BX = Horizontal speed (number of mickeys per 8 pixels).
	CX = Vertical speed (number of mickeys per 8 pixels).
	DX = Double-speed threshold in mickeys per second.

The Event Handler

Now take a quick look at this chapter's complete event handler, which, now that you know how to handle keyboard and mouse input, is really quite simple. Listing 3.6 is the header file, which declares some constants and data types needed by programs that use the event handler.

Listing 3.6. EVENT.H—the header file for the event handler.

```
#ifndef _EVENT_H
#define _EVENT_H

#define MBUTTON 1
#define KEYBD   2

#define CR      13
#define ESC     27
#define BACKSP  8

typedef struct EvntMsg
{
  int type,       // Event type.
      mx, my,     // Mouse coords.
      button;     // Mouse button pressed.
  unsigned key;   // Key pressed.
};

#endif
```

The first two `#defines` define constants for the two types of messages (mouse button and keyboard) that the event handler supports. Next, constants for a few important keys are defined; you use these key constants in the next chapter. Finally, the header file defines the structure that carries event messages between your programs' functions. The event handler stores information in this structure, so your program can respond to the user's actions. Listing 3.7 is the implementation of the event handler.

Listing 3.7. EVENT.CPP—the implementation of the event handler.

```cpp
#include <bios.h>
#include "event.h"
#include "mous.h"

// Check for and retrieve key events.
int KeyEvent(void)
{
  // Check for key press.
  int key = bioskey(1);

  // Get key if one is available.
  if (key) key = bioskey(0);

  return key;
}

// Wait for an event. When one is received,
// construct an event message.
void GetEvent(EvntMsg &evntmsg)
{
  while ( ( !mouse.Event() ) &&
        ( !(evntmsg.key = KeyEvent()) ) ) {}
  evntmsg.button = mouse.GetButton();
  if (evntmsg.button)
  {
    evntmsg.type = MBUTTON;
    mouse.GetXY(evntmsg.mx, evntmsg.my);
  }
  else
  {
    evntmsg.type = KEYBD;
    evntmsg.mx = -1;
    evntmsg.my = -1;
  }
}
```

Earlier in this chapter, you saw the two functions that make up the event handler. At that time, however, the mouse class had not been discussed. Now, you can see exactly how the event handler works. Notice that it is the function GetEvent() that creates the event message, by storing appropriate values into the members of the evntmsg structure.

Conclusion

L earning about event-driven programming techniques is only half the battle. Now, you have to apply what you've learned and create an event-driven user interface that you can use in your programs. Chapter 4 presents a class of graphical windows and controls that provide this interface in an attractive and logical way.

4

Graphical Controls and Windows for DOS

Even the most casual computer user can't help but notice that most major software packages incorporate some type of windowing. Windows, after all, are handy entities that can display large amounts of data by overlapping information or by providing viewports into a small portion of a large data set. In addition, most windowing software enables the user to select commands in a logical and natural way, by activating on-screen controls. These controls make a computer program look and act more "physical," as if the program were just another piece of electronic equipment, such as a TV, stereo, or microwave oven.

The idea is to make computers less intimidating and easier to use. How do windows and interactive controls accomplish this? By replacing conceptual information with visual information. The human mind is visually oriented. You can interpret graphical information much faster than any other type of information. So, the more software looks like familiar objects, the less intimidating it becomes.

In this chapter, you design a set of graphical window classes. Using these classes, you can display program screens, button controls, and even dialog boxes. Because the windows you develop are graphical windows rather than text-based windows (like the windows you can create with Borland's Turbo Vision), you must decide on a graphics mode. Most computer systems can display VGA graphics, so you develop the windows for that graphics mode, using the high-resolution 640x480 mode in 16 colors.

Although the classes presented here are far from a full-fledged GUI, you'll be surprised at what you can do with even a limited window library. And, as always, after you understand how the basic window library works, you can extend the classes to include other graphical objects that more precisely fit your programming needs.

Designing the Basic Window

T o design the window library, you need a plan. What type of windows will you have? How will these windows be related? If you can decide on a minimum window, one that provides all the basic window characteristics, you can use this minimum window as a template for new types of windows. Object-oriented programming enables you to do this through *inheritance*, which enables you to build a new class on the foundation of a previous one.

To keep things simple, assume that your window library will feature the following:

- Blank windows that you can use as 3-D graphical screen elements or as backdrops for your programs.

- Dialog boxes of several types, from simple message boxes to data-entry boxes.

- Animated, 3-D button controls that can be used independently or as part of a dialog box. (Yes, buttons are windows.)

To come up with a minimum window, you must determine what the listed objects have in common. First, all are rectangles. So, the first step in creating any window is to draw some type of rectangle on-screen. To keep things interesting, all the windows will use 3-D rectangles that seem to stand out from the background. But whether you're drawing 3-D shapes or plain rectangles, you have to know the object's coordinates and size. Position and size, then, are two characteristics that all windows share.

Another characteristic all windows must have is the capability to restore the screen area they cover. Imagine a dialog box that, when closed, leaves a blank rectangle in the middle of your document! That's clearly unacceptable. Although every window you create may not have to restore the screen, it must at least have that capability. The basic window class will support this feature by having a buffer in which to hold screen data.

Finally, to make the basic window class more versatile, the basic window will be drawn with or without a border. A Boolean value controls this feature. If the value is true, the window is drawn with a border; otherwise, the window has no border.

Your Basic Window

Y ou've determined the data you need to handle a basic window. Now you must combine that data with the functions that will bring your window to life. In short, you must create a base class for your window hierarchy. As with most classes, every window always needs a constructor and sometimes needs a destructor. Every window needs also a way to draw itself and a way to interact with the user.

The basic window class, called Windw, is the base for every window in the window library. That is, you will derive new types of windows from this basic class, using inheritance to create more specialized windows. Figures 4.1 and 4.2 show unbordered and bordered windows, respectively, of the Windw class.

Figure 4.1. An unbordered window of the *Windw* class.

Figure 4.2. A bordered window of the *Windw* class.

The declaration for the base window class, `Windw`, follows:

```
class Windw
{
  int *buffer; // Pointer to screen buffer.

protected:
  int wx, wy, ww, wh; // Window coordinates.
  int border,         // Flag for border.
      buffered;       // Flag for buffer.
  EvntMsg evntmsg;    // Event message.

public:
  Windw(int x, int y, int w, int h, int bdr, int buf);
  virtual ~Windw(void);
  virtual void DrawWindow(void);
  virtual void RunWindow(void);

private:
  void WindwError(char *s);
};
```

The data members `wx`, `wy`, `ww`, and `wh` are the position and size of the window. The data member `border` is the Boolean value that determines whether a window has a 3-D border. Notice that all the data except `buffer` is declared as `protected` so the data can be inherited in derived classes. Notice also the extra data member named `evntmsg`, which you use to store event messages (see Chapter 3).

Constructing *Windw*

The first member function is the class' constructor:

```
Windw::Windw(int x, int y, int w,
             int h, int brd, int buf)
{
  wx = x; wy=y; ww=w; wh=h;
  border=brd;
  buffered = buf;
  buffer = NULL;
}
```

The parameters for calling the constructor are the x,y coordinates of the window, the width and height of the window, and two Boolean values, indicating whether the window will have a border and whether the window must buffer the screen area that it will cover.

In the constructor, the window's requested coordinates are copied into `wx`, `wy`, `ww`, and `wh`, and the `border` and `buffered` flags are set. Finally, the `buffer` pointer is set to NULL.

Destructing *Windw*

The next member function is the class' destructor:

```
Windw::~Windw(void)
{
  if (buffer != NULL)
  {
    mouse.HideMouse();
    putimage(wx, wy, buffer, COPY_PUT);
    free(buffer);
    mouse.ShowMouse();
  }
}
```

In this function, the value of `buffer` is checked. If it's NULL, there's no screen data to restore, so the function just exits. If `buffer` isn't NULL, the function hides the mouse and then copies the contents of the buffer back to the screen. This both erases the window and restores the screen. After redrawing the screen, the function frees the memory used by the buffer and turns back on the mouse.

Drawing *Windw*

Now that you know how the window is initialized and how it is erased, it would be nice to learn how to draw the window in the first place! That's the job of the virtual function `DrawWindow()`:

```
void Windw::DrawWindow (void)
{
  int size;

  mouse.HideMouse();
```

95

```
// Save window screen area, if requested.
if (buffered)
{
  if ((size = imagesize(wx, wy, wx+ww, wy+wh)) < 0)
    WindwError("Image too large to store.");
  else
  {
    if ((buffer = (int *)malloc(size)) == NULL)
   WindwError("Not enough memory.");
    else getimage(wx, wy, wx+ww, wy+wh, buffer);
  }
}

//Draw basic 3-D window.
setcolor(WHITE);
moveto(wx+ww, wy);
lineto(wx, wy);
lineto(wx, wy+wh);
moveto(wx+ww-1, wy+1);
lineto(wx+1, wy+1);
lineto(wx+1, wy+wh-1);
setcolor(DARKGRAY);
moveto(wx+1, wy+wh);
lineto(wx+ww, wy+wh);
lineto(wx+ww, wy);
moveto(wx+2, wy+wh-1);
lineto(wx+ww-1, wy+wh-1);
lineto(wx+ww-1, wy+1);
setfillstyle(SOLID_FILL, LIGHTGRAY);
bar(wx+2, wy+2, wx+ww-2, wy+wh-2);

//Draw border, if requested.
if (border) {
  setcolor(DARKGRAY);
  moveto(wx+ww-10, wy+10);
  lineto(wx+10, wy+10);
  lineto(wx+10, wy+wh-10);
  setcolor(WHITE);
  lineto(wx+ww-10, wy+wh-10);
  lineto(wx+ww-10, wy+10);
}
mouse.ShowMouse();
}
```

96

Here, as with all graphical operations, the function first turns off the mouse. Then it checks whether it must buffer the screen background. If `buffered` is false, it skips over this operation. Otherwise, it uses Borland's `imagesize()` function to determine how large the buffer must be.

If the image is too large to store (over 64K), `DrawWindow()` generates an error. (This means that large windows cannot be buffered, except by using multiple buffers to store segments of the screen. This operation is not included in the class, but you can add it.) If the image is not too large, the function obtains the memory needed with a call to `malloc()`, saving the buffer's address in the `buffer` pointer. It then copies the screen display data into the buffer, using Borland's `getimage()` function.

The function is now free to draw the window with calls to standard Borland graphics functions. The window's coordinates are used to calculate the coordinates for each of the window's graphics elements. For example, the first line is drawn from the upper-right corner of the window to the upper-left corner of the window. The X coordinate of this line is calculated by adding `wx` (the X position of the window's left edge) to `ww` (the window's width). The Y coordinate of this line is `wy` (the Y coordinate of the window's top edge). Notice that a border is drawn only if the `border` flag is true.

Running *Windw*

So far, you have functions to initialize a window, draw a window, and erase a window. Because your window class is interactive, you also need a way to receive commands from the user. The `RunWindow()` function, also a virtual function, takes care of this:

```
void Windw::RunWindow(void)
{
  GetEvent(evntmsg);
}
```

In the base class, `RunWindow()` doesn't accomplish much. It simply waits for an event of any type to occur. In derived window types, though, `RunWindow()` takes on greater responsibilities. In a dialog box, for example, `RunWindow()` gathers text input and responds to buttons. Note that the function `GetEvent()` is the event handler developed in Chapter 3.

When `RunWindow()` is called—usually by your main program, immediately after calling `DrawWindow()`—it takes over processing and returns only when the user exits the window. The base class could have implemented `RunWindow()` as an empty function. In that case, calling `RunWindow()` would immediately return control to the calling program. Because this might be deceptive, however, the simplest version of `RunWindow()` waits for a keypress or a mouse click before returning.

Keep in mind that not every window needs input, so not every window needs to call `RunWindow()`. For example, if you're using a window as a graphical screen frame, you shouldn't call `RunWindow()`. If you do, your program will halt until the user presses a key or clicks the mouse, at which time your frame window will vanish.

 Note: You should never call `RunWindow()` for a window that requires no interaction with the user. *Display windows* (windows used merely as screen dressing) require a call only to `DrawWindow()`.

Programming the Basic Window

The basic window class is now complete. Before examining the derived window classes, though, you should learn how to handle this basic class in your programs. Listing 4.1 is a program that shows how to display and run a window of the `Windw` class. Figure 4.3 shows the screen created by the program.

Listing 4.1. WNDW1.CPP—a program that displays and runs a *Windw* window.

```
#include <graphics.h>
#include <iostream.h>
#include <conio.h>
#include "windw.h"

void main(void)
{
  int gdriver = VGA, gmode = VGAHI, errorcode;

  initgraph(&gdriver, &gmode, "");
  if ( (errorcode = graphresult()) != grOk)
  {
    cout << "Graphics not initialized: " << errorcode << '\n';
    getch();
  }
```

```
  else
  {
    setbkcolor(BLUE);
    Windw wndw1(150, 100, 200, 200, FALSE, FALSE);
    wndw1.DrawWindow();
    Windw *wndw2 = new Windw(200, 150, 200, 200, TRUE, TRUE);
    wndw2->DrawWindow();
    wndw2->RunWindow();
    delete wndw2;
    getch();
    closegraph();
  }
}
```

Figure 4.3. The basic windows created by Listing 4.1 (WNDW1.CPP).

This program creates both an unbordered and bordered window, with the bordered window's coordinates overlapping the unbordered window. Because the bordered window overlaps important screen information, its screen buffering is turned on. To see how this works, run the program. Both windows appear on-screen. Press any key or click the mouse, and the top window vanishes, leaving the bottom window intact. That's the buffering in action. Press a key to exit the program.

Now you can examine the program in detail. First, the program initializes the screen for VGA graphics by loading Borland's EGAVGA.BGI graphics driver. (Note that this driver must be in the same directory as the program. In the next chapter, you'll learn to link the graphics driver directly into your programs.) After initializing the graphics driver, the program sets the screen's background color to blue. It then creates the first window with the statement:

```
Windw wndw1(150, 100, 200, 200, FALSE, FALSE);
```

99

This statement sets the window's x,y coordinates to 150,100, sets its width and height to 200, turns the window border off, and turns screen buffering off. The statement creates the window only in memory; the window is still not visible on-screen. So, the next line of the program calls the window's `DrawWindow()` function:

```
wndw1.DrawWindow();
```

This displays the window on-screen. If user interaction with this window was required, the program would call the window's `RunWindow()` function next. Instead, it creates a second window, with the statement:

```
Windw *wndw2 = new Windw(200, 150, 200, 200, TRUE, TRUE);
```

This statement creates a window at the coordinates 200,150. This window has a width and height of 200 pixels and a border, and buffers the screen area it covers.

Notice that this window is created dynamically on the heap. Why? First, you should see both methods of declaring a window. More importantly, however, without using dynamic allocation, this program cannot command the top window to erase itself. Remember: The windows are erased by their destructors, and destructors aren't called until an object is deleted or goes out of scope. Because the WNDW1.CPP program has only the `main()` function, none of the objects created in it can go out of scope until the program ends. This leaves no way to remove a statically allocated window from the display.

The solution is to create the window dynamically. Then, when you're ready to erase the window, you can call the window's destructor implicitly by deleting the window. Keep this in mind when you create your own windows. A statically allocated window's destructor is called only when the window goes out of scope. A dynamically allocated window's destructor is called indirectly by the `delete` instruction.

 Note: A statically allocated window's destructor is called only when the window goes out of scope. So, if you must display and erase a window in a single function, you must create the window with the new keyword, which allocates the window dynamically on the heap. To erase the window, you call `delete`.

After creating the second window, the program displays it by calling its `DrawWindow()` function:

```
wndw2->DrawWindow();
```

Notice that you must use the indirect component selector (->) to access members of the second window's class. You must use this syntax to access members of any dynamically allocated structures. You've probably used this operator frequently with pointers to structs.

After drawing the window, the program waits for user input by calling the window's RunWindow() function, which waits for a keypress or a mouse click:

```
wndw2->RunWindow();
```

When the window receives input, the program deletes the window by calling delete. When this dynamically allocated window is deleted, its destructor is called, which removes the window's image from the screen, leaving the first window intact. The program then waits for a keypress, after which the program closes the graphics driver and ends.

The Captioned Window

An empty window is fine to use as a background or as a screen element when creating a 3-D display. Other than adding interesting graphical effects to your programs, however, a basic, unadorned window is mostly useless. To do something more useful with your window class, you must create windows that display information and, in some cases, allow user input.

Now that you have a basic window class, you can create windows with new characteristics by deriving them from the basic class. When you do this, the new window class inherits all the characteristics of its ancestor class, leaving you free to add whatever you need, without worrying about introducing bugs into already tested code.

The next type of window you'll create is a captioned window. A *captioned window* is like a basic window, except it has a caption bar at the top, which enables you to label the window. Figure 4.4 shows a captioned window.

Figure 4.4. A captioned window has a caption bar at the top.

Here's the declaration for the new class:

```
class CapWindw: public Windw
{
protected:
  char label[61];

public:
  CapWindw(int x, int y, int w, int h,
          int bdr, int buf, char *s);
  virtual void DrawWindow(void);
  void SetCaption(char *s);
private:
  void DrawCapBar(void);
};
```

First, notice that CapWindw is derived publicly from Windw, which gives CapWindw access to all the public and protected data members and member functions of Windw. Without the public keyword in CapWindw's definition, this class would lose all of Windw's functionality. In fact, without the public keyword, the source code for the CapWindw class will not compile. The compiler will complain loudly, informing you that Windw's data members are not accessible.

The CapWindw class adds one data member, label, which is a character array that will hold the window's caption. Note that this array can hold only 60 characters plus the terminating null.

 Caution: CapWindw's member functions do not check the source string (the one you supply when you create a captioned window) for proper length. Therefore, you must be careful that your captions are no longer than 60 characters. If you aren't, the string-copying functions may overwrite other data, yielding unpredictable results. In a commercial program, this lack of error checking would be unacceptable. Keep this in mind when writing your own code.

Constructing *CapWindw*

Now, you can see how to construct a captioned window. This class' constructor requires the same parameters as the basic window, except it also needs a pointer to the caption string:

```
CapWindw::CapWindw(int x, int y, int w, int h,
            int brd, int buf, char *s) :
         Windw(x, y, w, h, brd, buf)
{
  strcpy(label, s);
}
```

This constructor lets the Windw class do the bulk of the initialization work by passing most of the parameters to that class' constructor. CapWindw() then takes the caption-string parameter and copies it into label. By using inheritance, this function creates a new window type, and only copied one string to do it! This is an example of the power of object-oriented programming.

Drawing *CapWindw*

Now that you've created a captioned window, you need to display it. You do that with its DrawWindow() function:

```
void CapWindw::DrawWindow(void)
{
  // Draw basic window.
  Windw::DrawWindow();

  // Draw caption bar.
  DrawCapBar();
}
```

This function takes advantage of its relationship with Windw by calling that class' version of DrawWindow() to draw the basic window. After calling that function, CapWindw::DrawWindow() must draw only the caption bar and the caption text. Again, OOP techniques have saved much work.

Notice that the caption-drawing code is placed into its own function, DrawCapBar(). This is because the class must call DrawCapBar() from more than one function. Here's the code for DrawCapBar():

```
void CapWindw::DrawCapBar(void)
{
  mouse.HideMouse();
  setcolor(WHITE);
  moveto(wx+20, wy+40);
  lineto(wx+20, wy+20);
  lineto(wx+ww-20, wy+20);
```

```
setcolor(BLACK);
lineto(wx+ww-20, wy+40);
lineto(wx+20, wy+40);
setfillstyle(SOLID_FILL, DARKGRAY);
bar(wx+21, wy+21, wx+ww-21, wy+39);
setcolor(WHITE);
int x = (wx+ww/2) - (strlen(label)*4);
outtextxy(x, wy+27, label);
mouse.ShowMouse();
}
```

First, the function uses Borland's graphics library to draw the 3-D bar at the top of the window. Then, it calculates the caption's x coordinate so the string is centered in the caption bar. Next, it draws the caption as graphics text, with the outtextxy() function.

In the class' declaration, DrawCapBar() is declared as private, which means only functions of the CapWindw class may access DrawCapBar(). New caption bars must be drawn through the public function SetCaption():

```
void CapWindw::SetCaption(char *s)
{
  strcpy(label, s);
  DrawCapBar();
}
```

This function, which takes as a parameter a pointer to the caption string, copies the new caption into label. It then draws the new caption bar by calling the private function DrawCapBar().

The Captioned Text Window

Many windows in your programs will be dialog boxes of one type or another, which means you need a way to display text in your windows. For example, before exiting a program, you may want to ask users whether they want to save the current file. As your window class stands now, you cannot create a window containing a text message, except to create a captioned window and then draw the text "by hand." Wouldn't it be nice to have a window class that can take care of this task?

The next derived class, CapTWindw (for *captioned text window*), is shown in Figure 4.5. It provides the basis for your dialog boxes:

```
class CapTWindw: public CapWindw
{
protected:
  char *line1, *line2;
  int button;

public:
  CapTWindw(char *s1, char *s2, char *s3);
  virtual void DrawWindow(void);
  int GetButton(void) { return button; }
};
```

Figure 4.5. A captioned window with a text display.

As you can see, this class is publicly derived from `CapWindw`. Thus, it inherits all the functionality of not only the `CapWindw` class but also the `Windw` class, because `CapWindw` is derived from that class.

This new class declares three new data members, `line1`, `line2`, and `button`. The first two are pointers to the lines of text that appear in the window when it is drawn. The integer `button` holds the value of the button that is clicked to exit the dialog. This data member isn't used in `CapTWindw` because windows of that class have no buttons. However, several classes that you derive from `CapTWindw` do have buttons. Rather than duplicate the `button` data member in each class, it has been moved back one step in the hierarchy, to the `CapTWindw` class.

Constructing *CapTWindw*

The `CapTWindw` constructor is very different from the constructors you've seen so far:

```
CapTWindw::CapTWindw(char *s1, char *s2, char *s3) :
     CapWindw(0, 0, 0, 150, FALSE, TRUE, s1)
{
```

105

```
// Calculate which string is the longest and
// use that width to calculate the window's width.
int w = strlen(s1) * 8 + 60;
if (strlen(s2) > strlen(s3))
  ww = strlen(s2) * 8 + 60;
else ww = strlen(s3) * 8 + 60;
if (w > ww) ww = w;

// Enforce a minimum width.
if (ww < 230) ww = 230;

// Calculate the window's x,y coordinates.
wx = 320 - ww/2;
wy = 164;

// Set the window's text.
line1 = s2;
line2 = s3;
}
```

To create a captioned text window, you need supply only three pointers to the strings used for the window's caption and body text. The other parameters needed by the base class constructor are supplied by CapTWindw's constructor. This is because a CapTWindw window, like all dialogs derived from it, always appears in the center of the screen, is always 150 pixels high, never has a border, and always buffers the screen background.

The CapTWindw constructor passes to the CapWindw constructor all zeroes for the window's wx, wy, and ww attributes because the CapTWindw constructor sizes its own windows. As mentioned, a CapTWindw window is always centered on-screen. In addition, the width of the window is determined by the width of the text the window must display.

The CapTWindw constructor first calls the CapWindw constructor, which in turn first calls the Windw constructor. It is Windw() that actually starts drawing the window. The window is created piece by piece, first drawing the basic window and then moving a step at a time back down through the hierarchy, from Windw() to CapWindw to CapTWindw(), drawing new window elements with each step. Each derived class adds to the previous classes, moving from a general form to a more specific implementation of the base object. The further down the hierarchy you go, the more specific the classes become.

After calling the base constructor, the CapTWindw constructor determines the longest of the three strings it must display, then uses that information to set the x,y coordinates and width of the window.

Drawing *CapTWindw*

A captioned text window, just like any of the windows, must have its own version of DrawWindow():

```
void CapTWindw::DrawWindow(void)
{
  // Draw the captioned window.
  CapWindw::DrawWindow();

  // Position and draw window body text.
  mouse.HideMouse();
  int x = (wx+ww/2) - (strlen(line1)*8)/2;
  setcolor(BLACK);
  if (strlen(line2)==0)
    outtextxy(x, wy+68, line1);
  else
  {
    outtextxy(x, wy+56, line1);
    x = (wx+ww/2) - (strlen(line2)*8)/2;
    outtextxy(x, wy+71, line2);
  }
  mouse.ShowMouse();
}
```

This version first calls the DrawWindow() function of its base class, CapWindw, which in turn calls Windw::DrawWindow(). When you draw the window (just as when you constructed the window), you move up through the hierarchy to the base class, then move down again a step at a time, drawing the appropriate window screen elements for each of the object's ancestor classes.

After those drawing operations are complete, the function draws the window's text. The text strings are centered horizontally in the box. The vertical spacing of the text is based on the number of lines to print. A single line of text (an option you can choose by sending the constructor an empty string for the third string parameter) is printed lower in the box than the first line of a two-line message.

Getting Button Presses

The last function in CapTWindw, GetButton(), is implemented in-line. GetButton(), like the data member it returns, is not used directly in this class. Rather, GetButton() is placed here to provide button support to all classes derived from CapTWindw.

107

The Button Window

S peaking of classes derived from `CapTWindw`, the first of these is the OK window, which is a message box containing an OK button. But before you can look at this class, you need to examine the `Button` class. After all, if you don't know how buttons work, how can you study classes that use them?

Here's the declaration for the `Button` class:

```
class Button: public Windw
{
  char label[20];
  unsigned hotkey;
  int altkey;

public:
  Button(int x, int y, char *s);
  void DrawWindow(void);
  int Clicked(EvntMsg evntmsg);
  void ClickButton(void);
};
```

A button is derived from the basic window class, `Windw`, because it has little in common with the other derived types created so far. In fact, a button is so radically different from even the basic window type that you may be surprised to discover it's a window.

The `Button` class adds three `private` data members to the data members inherited from `Windw`. The first is a character array that holds the button's label. The second is an integer that holds the value of the button's hot key, which is the key (rather than the mouse button) the user can press to select the button. For all buttons, hot keys are Ctrl-key combinations. For example, a Cancel button can be selected from the keyboard by pressing Ctrl-C.

The third data member, `altkey`, is similar to `hotkey`. This data member holds the value of an alternate hot key used specifically with OK buttons and Cancel buttons. This enables the user to press Enter to select an OK button and to press Esc to select the Cancel button. These are alternate keystrokes because both buttons also respond to their regular hot keys, Ctrl-O and Ctrl-C.

Constructing *Button*

Now look at `Button`'s member functions, starting with the constructor:

```
Button::Button(int x, int y, char *s) :
    Windw(x, y, 64, 32, FALSE, FALSE)
{
  strcpy(label, s);
  altkey = 0;
  hotkey = 0;
}
```

This constructor passes almost all initialization chores to its ancestor class, `Windw`, which sets most of the button's attributes. The only data left to initialize after the `Windw` constructor does its job are `Button`'s three `private` data members. This is accomplished by copying the string parameter into `label` and setting `hotkey` and `altkey` to 0.

The text in `label` appears on the button. This text has a special format that allows your button object to determine which character of the label is the button's hot key. When you enter the label text, you must place a caret (^) immediately before the hot-key character. When the button is drawn, the object searches for the caret in its label, sets the hot key to the appropriate Ctrl-key value, and underlines the hot-key character on the button.

Drawing *Button*

Study `Button`'s `DrawWindow()` function to see how the button-drawing works:

```
void Button::DrawWindow(void)
{
  int pos = -1;
  char tlabel[20];

  Windw::DrawWindow();
  mouse.HideMouse();

  // Find and remove the ^ character and
  // set the appropriate hot key.
  strcpy(tlabel, label);
  for (int i = 0; i<strlen(tlabel); ++i)
  {
```

```
      if (tlabel[i] == '^')
      {
        pos = i;
        hotkey = ctrlkeys[tlabel[i+1]-65];
        for (int j=i; j<strlen(tlabel); ++j)
       tlabel[j] = tlabel[j+1];
      }
    }


    if (strcmp(tlabel,"OK")==0) altkey = OKALT;
    else if (strcmp(tlabel, "CANCEL")==0) altkey = CANCELALT;

    // Center and draw text on button.
    int x = (wx+ww/2) - (strlen(tlabel)*4);
    setcolor(BLACK);
    outtextxy(x, wy+12, tlabel);

    // Underline the hot-key character.
    if (pos >= 0)
      line(x+pos*8, wy+20, x+pos*8+6, wy+20);

    mouse.ShowMouse();
}
```

This function has a lot of work to do. First, it makes a temporary copy of the button's label text. It then searches through the text, looking for the caret. When it finds the caret, it marks its position in the string with pos and sets the value of the hot key by using i to index an array of Ctrl-key values. This array, which contains a control value for every letter in the alphabet, is declared in the window library's implementation file, WINDW.CPP:

```
unsigned ctrlkeys[] =
   {0x1e01, 0x3002, 0x2e03, 0x2004, 0x1205, 0x2106,
    0x2207, 0x2308, 0x1709, 0x240a, 0x250b, 0x260c,
    0x320d, 0x310e, 0x180f, 0x1910, 0x1011, 0x1312,
    0x1f13, 0x1414, 0x1615, 0x2f16, 0x1117, 0x2d18,
    0x1519, 0x2c1a};
```

After assigning the hot key, the function removes the caret from the label string because you don't want the caret to show up on the button. It then checks the label text to see whether it is marked OK or CANCEL. If it finds a match, it sets the appropriate alternate hot key for the button. The values OKALT and CANCELALT are defined in the window library's header file, WINDW.H, and are the raw key codes for the Enter and Esc keys, respectively. Finally, the function centers and prints the button's text label and underlines the hot-key character.

Whew! That's a lot more work than drawing other classes of windows (except maybe the base class Windw). And the fun is far from over. A button is a sophisticated type of window. Besides being created and drawn, a button must know when the user has selected it.

Clicking *Button*

The Clicked() function handles the interaction when the user clicks the button or presses its hot key:

```
int Button::Clicked(EvntMsg evntmsg)
{
  int mx, my;
  int click = FALSE;

  // Check whether button was selected by the mouse.
  if  ((evntmsg.type == MBUTTON) &&
      (evntmsg.mx>wx) && (evntmsg.mx<wx+ww) &&
      (evntmsg.my>wy) && (evntmsg.my<wy+wh))
  {
    ClickButton();
    click = TRUE;
  }

  // Check whether button was selected from the keyboard.
  else if (evntmsg.type == KEYBD)
  {
    if ((evntmsg.key == hotkey) ¦¦ (evntmsg.key == altkey))
    {
      ClickButton();
      click = TRUE;
    }
  }
  return click;
}
```

This function returns a 0 if the button was not selected or a 1 if the button was selected. The value is returned to the button's owner, either a dialog box or your main program. To determine the return value, Clicked() compares the

111

values in the event message you pass to it with its own coordinates and hot keys. Because you must pass a current event message to this function, `GetEvent()` (found in the message handler) must be called before `Clicked()`. You can then call `Clicked()` for each button you need to check. If a button returns true, your program knows what action the user has requested.

The function `Clicked()` first checks for a mouse-button event. If it has one, it compares the mouse's coordinates at the time of the event with the button's coordinates. If they match, the user has selected the button with the mouse. So the function animates the button by calling the `ClickButton()` member function, then sets the function's return value to true.

If the function didn't get a mouse-button event, it checks for a keyboard event. If there was a keystroke, and the key pressed matches either the button's hot key or the alternate hot key, the function animates the button and sets the function's return value to true.

Note that both `if` statements could have been combined into one gigantic and complicated one, but that would have made the code almost impossible to read. Nothing will fry your brain faster than an `if` statement with a dozen conditions. Just figuring out where to put all the parentheses is enough to render your gray matter useless for the rest of the day.

The `Clicked()` function is straightforward. But before you move on, you'd probably like to know how the `ClickButton()` function works, because it makes your buttons act like buttons. Here it is

```
void Button::ClickButton(void)
{
  int *buff;

  mouse.HideMouse();

  // Shift the image on the button down and right
  // to simulate button movement.
  int size = imagesize(wx+2, wy+2, wx+ww-2, wy+wh-2);
  buff = (int *)malloc(size);
  if (buff)
  {
    getimage(wx+2, wy+2, wx+ww-2, wy+wh-2, buff);
    putimage(wx+3, wy+3, buff, COPY_PUT);
    free(buff);
  }
```

```
// Draw the button's borders so the
// button appears to be pressed.
setcolor(DARKGRAY);
moveto(wx+ww, wy);
lineto(wx, wy); lineto(wx, wy+wh);
moveto(wx+ww-1, wy+1);
lineto(wx+1, wy+1); lineto(wx+1, wy+wh-1);
setcolor(WHITE);
moveto(wx+1, wy+wh);
lineto(wx+ww, wy+wh); lineto(wx+ww, wy);
moveto(wx+2, wy+wh-1);
lineto(wx+ww-1, wy+wh-1);
lineto(wx+ww-1, wy+1);

// Make button beep.
sound ( 2000 );
delay ( 100 );
nosound();

// Redraw button in unselected form.
DrawWindow();

mouse.ShowMouse();
}
```

Here, the function first hides the mouse, so it stays out of the way of the screen-drawing operations. It then copies the image of the button's surface into a buffer and writes that image back to the screen, shifting it down and to the right one pixel. This gives the illusion of movement. To make the button look pressed, the function reverses its outline with a series of calls to moveto() and lineto(), after which it calls Borland's Sound(), delay(), and nosound() functions to make a beep. Finally, it restores the button's image by calling the button's DrawWindow() function.

 Note: If you add window types to the window library, you must be careful when calling DrawWindow(). Remember, for some window types, the DrawWindow() function creates a screen buffer. In other words, successive calls to this function for the same object may re-create the screen-image buffer, destroying the pointer to the previous buffer. Your screen may not be updated properly when the window is closed. The button objects have no screen buffers, so calling DrawWindow() does nothing more than draw the button.

Listing 4.2 is a program that demonstrates how to use a button object.

Listing 4.2. WNDW2.CPP—a demonstration of the button class.

```cpp
#include <graphics.h>
#include <iostream.h>
#include <conio.h>
#include "mous.h"
#include "windw.h"
#include "event.h"

void main(void)
{
  int gdriver = VGA, gmode = VGAHI, errorcode;
  EvntMsg evntmsg;

  initgraph(&gdriver, &gmode, "");
  if ( (errorcode = graphresult()) != grOk)
  {
    cout << "Graphics not initialized: " << errorcode << '\n';
    getch();
  }
  else
  {
    setfillstyle(SOLID_FILL, BLUE);
    bar(0, 0, getmaxx(), getmaxy());
    mouse.SetLimits(0,getmaxx(),0,getmaxy());
    mouse.ShowMouse();
    Button wndw1(200, 200, "^OK");
    Button wndw2(280, 200, "^CANCEL");
    wndw1.DrawWindow();
    wndw2.DrawWindow();

    // Loop until a button is chosen.
    int button = 0;
    while (!button)
    {
      GetEvent(evntmsg);

      // Check for button click.
      if (wndw1.Clicked(evntmsg))
        button = OK;
      else if (wndw2.Clicked(evntmsg))
        button = CANCEL;
    }
```

```
      mouse.HideMouse();
      if (button == OK)
        outtextxy(200, 300, "You clicked OK.");
      else
        outtextxy(200, 300, "You clicked CANCEL.");
      getch();
      closegraph();
  }
}
```

The program's display is shown in Figure 4.6. When you run the program, two button objects appear on-screen. To exit the program, simply select a button. Because the buttons are OK and Cancel buttons, you can select them in several ways. To select the OK button, click it with the mouse, press Enter, or press Ctrl-O. To select the Cancel button, click it with the mouse, press Esc, or press Ctrl-C.

Figure 4.6. The buttons created by WNDW2.CPP.

The OK Window

N ow that you know how buttons perform their magic, you can create window classes that use buttons. The first of these is an OK window, which displays messages to the user. After reading the message, the user can close the box by selecting the OK button with the mouse or the keyboard. Figure 4.7 shows an OK window. Its declaration is as follows:

```
class OKWindw: public CapTWindw
{
  Button *butn;

public:
  OKWindw(char *s1, char *s2, char *s3);
  virtual ~OKWindw(void);
  virtual void DrawWindow(void);
  virtual void RunWindow(void);
};
```

115

Figure 4.7. An OK window displays messages to the user.

The OK window is the first of several classes that will be derived from `CapTWindw`. Each class differs in the type of buttons it displays. The `OKWindw` declaration contains a new data member, `butn`, which is a pointer to a `Button` window. By declaring this pointer as a data member, any function in the `OKWindow` class can access it. The `DrawWindow()` and `RunWindow()` functions use this pointer.

Constructing *OKWindw*

The constructor for the `OKWindw` class is about as simple as it gets in a class hierarchy:

```
OKWindw::OKWindw(char *s1, char *s2, char *s3) :
      CapTWindw(s1, s2, s3)
{
  butn = NULL;
}
```

This constructor does little more than pass its parameters to the `CapTWindw` constructor, which does most of the required initialization. The only data member that an `OKWindw` object needs to initialize directly is its button pointer, `butn`, which the constructor sets to NULL.

Destructing *OKWindw*

`OKWindw` is the first class that has needed a destructor since the base class, `Windw`. The cleanup for the other classes could be handled by C++. However, an `OKWindw`, like other dialog classes to follow, creates a button window on the heap. This button must be deleted with the rest of the object when the destructor is called:

```
OKWindw::~OKWindw(void)
{
  if (butn != NULL) delete butn;
}
```

Drawing *OKWindw*

Drawing an OKWindw is much like drawing a CapTWindw:

```
void OKWindw::DrawWindow(void)
{
  CapTWindw::DrawWindow();
  butn = new Button(wx+ww/2-32, wy+wh-42, "^OK");
  butn->DrawWindow();
}
```

In fact, drawing an OKWindw is so much like drawing a CapTWindw that OKWindw::DrawWindow() first calls CapTWindw::DrawWindow() to do the bulk of the work. Then it simply draws the window's OK button by allocating a new button on the heap and calling the button's DrawWindow() function.

Running *OKWindw*

Because OKWindw is a dialog box (albeit a simple one), it must interact with the user. This means OKWindw must implement its own version of RunWindow():

```
void OKWindw::RunWindow(void)
{
  button = 0;

  // Loop until a button is chosen.
  while (!button)
  {
    GetEvent(evntmsg);

    // Check for mouse click on button.
    if (butn->Clicked(evntmsg))
      button = OK;

    // Check for a keyboard event.
    else if (evntmsg.type == KEYBD)
    {
```

117

```
        // Convert character code to ASCII,
        // and check for Esc key.
        char k = evntmsg.key & 0x00ff;
        if (k == ESC) button = CANCEL;
    }
  }
}
```

This function enables the user to close the dialog by selecting the OK button or pressing Enter (the alternate key for an OK button). First, the function sets the object's `button` data member to 0, which gets it into the `while` loop. In the loop, the `GetEvent()` function is called to poll for a mouse or keyboard event. When an event comes in, the function checks whether the user selected the OK button. If the user clicked the button, pressed the hot key, or the *alternate* hot key, `butn->Clicked()` returns true (as well as animates the button). In this case, the function sets `button` to OK (which indicates that the OK button was selected), and then returns.

If the button wasn't selected, the function checks for a keyboard event—specifically an Esc, which always cancels a dialog box. If Esc was pressed, the function sets `button` to Cancel, simulating a Cancel-button click, even though this window has no Cancel button. (The button values are defined in the WINDW.H header file.)

The Yes/No and Yes/No/Cancel Windows

M essage boxes require different types of responses, depending on the prompt they display. For example, when a user tries to quit your program, you may want to ask "Do you really want to quit?" This type of prompt requires only a yes or no answer. But suppose a user tries to close a file that hasn't been saved. You might display a message box asking "Do you want to save your file?" In this case, yes and no buttons are not adequate because both answers assume that the user wanted to close the file in the first place. (The user may have selected the close command accidentally.) Therefore, you also need a Cancel button, which terminates the command without taking an action.

Both of the Yes/No and Yes/No/Cancel types of message boxes are included in your window library. The first is called `YesNoWindw` and is defined as follows:

```
class YesNoWindw: public CapTWindw
{
protected:
  Button *butn1, *butn2;

public:
  YesNoWindw(char *s1, char *s2, char *s3);
  virtual ~YesNoWindw(void);
  virtual void DrawWindow(void);
  virtual void RunWindow(void);
};
```

Figure 4.8 shows a typical Yes/No window. Except for having two buttons instead of one, this type of window is almost identical to an OK window. For this reason, its member functions aren't discussed here. (If you'd like to compare them to the ones in OKWindw, see Listing 4.5 near the end of the chapter.)

Figure 4.8. A typical Yes/No window.

Your window library also features YesNoCanWindw, which displays Yes, No, and Cancel buttons in addition to the message box's prompt. Here's its declaration:

```
class YesNoCanWindw: public CapTWindw
{
  Button *butn1, *butn2, *butn3;

public:
  YesNoCanWindw(char *s1, char *s2, char *s3);
  virtual ~YesNoCanWindw(void);
  virtual void DrawWindow(void);
  virtual void RunWindow(void);
};
```

Again, except for the number of buttons, this window is almost identical to an OK window. Its member functions, too, are implemented in Listing 4.5. The window is shown in Figure 4.9.

119

Figure 4.9. A window of the *YesNoCanWindw* class.

The Input Window

Often your programs require the user to input short strings. You might need the user to supply a filename, for example. Your window library takes care of this requirement with a special dialog box, `InputWindw`:

```
class InputWindw: public CapTWindw
{
  char input[81];
  Button *butn1, *butn2;

public:
  InputWindw(char *s1, char *s2, char *s3);
  virtual ~InputWindw(void);
  void GetInput(char *s) { strcpy(s, input); }
  virtual void DrawWindow(void);
  virtual void RunWindow(void);
private:
  void HandleInput(char k);
};
```

Figure 4.10 shows a typical input window. In addition to button pointers, this type of window includes a data member in which it can store an array of characters—this is where input from the user is placed. As far as its data members go, this new character array is the only difference between `InputWindw` and the other dialogs in the window library.

Because constructing and destructing an input window is much like constructing and destructing the other dialog boxes, these functions are not examined here. Instead, take a quick look at `InputWindw`'s constructor and destructor in Listing 4.5 (at the end of this chapter).

Figure 4.10. An input window accepts short strings from the user.

Drawing *InputWindw*

On the screen, an input window is similar to any other dialog. The main difference is that an input window includes a data-entry field in which users can type their response to the dialog's prompt. As with any dialog, you draw an `InputWindw` by calling its `DrawWindow()` member function, shown in the following:

```
void InputWindw::DrawWindow(void)
{
  CapTWindw::DrawWindow();
  butn1 = new Button(wx+ww/2-70, wy+108, "^OK");
  butn1->DrawWindow();
  butn2 = new Button(wx+ww/2+6, wy+108, "^CANCEL");
  butn2->DrawWindow();
  mouse.HideMouse();
  setfillstyle(SOLID_FILL, BLACK);
  bar(wx+15, wy+85, wx+ww-15, wy+99);
  mouse.ShowMouse();
}
```

This function first calls the ancestor class' `DrawWindow()`, which draws the main window, the caption bar, and the dialog's text prompt. After that function returns, `InputWindw::DrawWindow()` creates and draws the input window's buttons and the text-entry field, which is simply a black bar.

Running *InputWindw*

When you run an input window, you must do more than check the dialog's buttons. You also must allow the user to enter text into the text-entry field.

This means you must capture and analyze every keyboard event that flows through your dialog. All this is handled in `InputWindw`'s `RunWindow()` member function:

```
void InputWindw::RunWindow(void)
{
  button = 0;
  while (!button)
  {
    GetEvent(evntmsg);
    if (butn1->Clicked(evntmsg))
      button = OK;
    else if (butn2->Clicked(evntmsg))
      button = CANCEL;
    else if (evntmsg.type == KEYBD)
    {
      char k = evntmsg.key & 0x00ff;
      HandleInput(k);
    }
  }
}
```

The button handling here is identical to the button handling in any other dialog box. The function grabs an event and then calls each button's `Clicked()` function to determine whether that button has been selected.

If `InputWindw::RunWindow()` gets a keyboard event (other than a keyboard event that selects a button), it must check the key's value and decide whether that key is intended for the text-entry field. First, the function translates the key into an ASCII code by masking the upper byte. It then sends the key to the `HandleInput()` private function:

```
void InputWindw::HandleInput(char k)
{
  int l = strlen(input);
  int w = (ww - 30)/8;
  settextjustify(LEFT_TEXT, TOP_TEXT);

  // Check that an appropriate key was pressed
  // and that the string can hold another character.
  if ((k>31) && (k<127) && (l<80))
  {
    // Add character to string.
```

```
  input[l+1] = 0;   input[l] = k;

  // Draw the portion of the string that will
  // fit into the text-entry field.
  setcolor(WHITE);
  if (l < w) outtextxy(wx+15, wy+88, input);
  else
  {
    int i = l - w + 1;
    setfillstyle(SOLID_FILL, BLACK);
    bar(wx+15, wy+85, wx+ww-15, wy+99);
    outtextxy(wx+15, wy+88, &input[i]);
  }
}

// Check for a Backspace character and that
// the string has a character to delete.
else if ((k==BACKSP) && (l>0))
{
  // Delete the last character.
  l -= 1;
  input[l] = 0;

  // Draw the portion of the string that
  // will fit in the text-entry field.
  setfillstyle(SOLID_FILL, BLACK);
  bar(wx+15, wy+85, wx+ww-15, wy+99);
  setcolor(WHITE);
  if (l < w+1) outtextxy(wx+15, wy+88, input);
  else
  {
    int i = l - w;
    outtextxy(wx+15, wy+88, &input[i]);
  }
}
}
```

The first if statement determines whether the key pressed is a text character. If it is, the function adds the character to the input string and draws the string in the text-entry field. However, because the text-entry field is only w characters wide (w is calculated by dividing the text field's width by a character's width) but allows strings as long as 80 characters, the function must provide text scrolling. This is accomplished by displaying only the characters of input that fit in the text-entry field, counting backward from the end of the string.

123

If the key received is a Backspace and the `input` string contains at least one character, the function removes the last character from the string. Again, it must then display the portion of the string that fits in the text-entry field.

To retrieve the string entered by the user, you must call the dialog's `GetInput()` function, which is implemented in-line, as shown in the class' declaration. When calling `GetInput()`, you must supply the address of a character array in which the function can store the input string. Size checking is not performed, so you must be sure that your character array can hold at least 81 characters, which provides enough space for 80 characters plus a NULL.

Listing 4.3 shows how to program an `InputWindw`. When you run the program, it draws an input window on-screen. You can then enter whatever you want into the window's text-entry field. If you exit the dialog by clicking the OK button, your input is displayed on-screen, after which you must press any key to exit the program. If you exit the dialog by selecting the Cancel key, your input is ignored.

Listing 4.3. WNDW3.CPP—this program shows how to program an input window.

```
#include <graphics.h>
#include <iostream.h>
#include <conio.h>
#include "mous.h"
#include "windw.h"

void main(void)
{
  int gdriver = VGA, gmode = VGAHI, errorcode;
  char s[81];

  initgraph(&gdriver, &gmode, "");
  if ( (errorcode = graphresult()) != grOk)
  {
    cout << "Graphics not initialized: " << errorcode << '\n';
    getch();
  }
  else
  {
    setfillstyle(SOLID_FILL, BLUE);
    bar(0, 0, getmaxx(), getmaxy());
```

```
      mouse.SetLimits(0,getmaxx(),0,getmaxy());
      mouse.ShowMouse();
      InputWindw *wndw1 = new InputWindw("INPUT WINDOW",
                  "Enter a text string:", "");
      wndw1->DrawWindow();
      wndw1->RunWindow();
      if (wndw1->GetButton() == OK)
      {
        wndw1->GetInput(s);
        mouse.HideMouse();
        outtextxy(0, 350, s);
        getch();
      }
      delete wndw1;
      closegraph();
  }
}
```

Conclusion

You now have a simple window library that you can use to create programs with an attractive and useful graphical interface. Because your library has many types of windows, each with its own set of functions, a quick reference for the library is provided in Appendix A. Also, Listing 4.4 shows the complete header file for your window classes, and Listing 4.5 shows the implementation file.

In the next chapter, you apply all you've learned to create an interesting simulation program. Along the way, you meet a handy data structure called a *linked list*.

Listing 4.4. WINDW.H—the header file for your window classes.

```
#ifndef _WINDW_H
#define _WINDW_H

#include <string.h>
#include "event.h"
```

continues

125

Listing 4.4. Continued

```
#define TRUE       1
#define FALSE      0
#define OK         1
#define YES        2
#define NO         3
#define CANCEL     4
#define OKALT      0x1c0d
#define CANCELALT 0x011b


// Function prototypes.
void GetEvent(EvntMsg &evntmsg);

class Windw
{
  int *buffer; // Pointer to screen buffer.

protected:
    int wx, wy, ww, wh; // Window coords.
    int border,          // Flag for border.
        buffered;        // Flag for buffer.
    EvntMsg evntmsg;     // Event message.

public:
    Windw(int x, int y, int w, int h, int bdr, int buf);
    virtual ~Windw(void);
    virtual void DrawWindow(void);
    virtual void RunWindow(void);

private:
    void WindwError(char *s);
};

class CapWindw: public Windw
{
protected:
    char label[61];

public:
    CapWindw(int x, int y, int w, int h, int bdr, int buf, char *s);
    virtual void DrawWindow(void);
    void SetCaption(char *s);
```

126

```
private:
  void DrawCapBar(void);
};

class CapTWindw: public CapWindw
{
protected:
  char *line1, *line2;
  int button;

public:
  CapTWindw(char *s1, char *s2, char *s3);
  virtual void DrawWindow(void);
  int GetButton(void) { return button; }
};

class Button: public Windw
{
  char label[20];
  unsigned hotkey;
  int altkey;

public:
  Button(int x, int y, char *s);
  void DrawWindow(void);
  int Clicked(EvntMsg evntmsg);
  void ClickButton(void);
};

class OKWindw: public CapTWindw
{
  Button *butn;

public:
  OKWindw(char *s1, char *s2, char *s3);
  virtual ~OKWindw(void);
  virtual void DrawWindow(void);
  virtual void RunWindow(void);
};

class YesNoWindw: public CapTWindw
{
```

continues

Listing 4.4. Continued

```
protected:
  Button *butn1, *butn2;

public:
  YesNoWindw(char *s1, char *s2, char *s3);
  virtual ~YesNoWindw(void);
  virtual void DrawWindow(void);
  virtual void RunWindow(void);
};

class YesNoCanWindw: public CapTWindw
{
  Button *butn1, *butn2, *butn3;

public:
  YesNoCanWindw(char *s1, char *s2, char *s3);
  virtual ~YesNoCanWindw(void);
  virtual void DrawWindow(void);
  virtual void RunWindow(void);
};

class InputWindw: public CapTWindw
{
  char input[81];
  Button *butn1, *butn2;

public:
  InputWindw(char *s1, char *s2, char *s3);
  virtual ~InputWindw(void);
  void GetInput(char *s) { strcpy(s, input); }
  virtual void DrawWindow(void);
  virtual void RunWindow(void);
private:
  void HandleInput(char k);
};

#endif
```

Listing 4.5. WINDW.CPP—the implementation file for window classes.

```cpp
#include <graphics.h>
#include <alloc.h>
#include <iostream.h>
#include <conio.h>
#include <stdlib.h>
#include <dos.h>
#include "mous.h"
#include "windw.h"

unsigned ctrlkeys[] =
  {0x1e01, 0x3002, 0x2e03, 0x2004, 0x1205, 0x2106,
   0x2207, 0x2308, 0x1709, 0x240a, 0x250b, 0x260c,
   0x320d, 0x310e, 0x180f, 0x1910, 0x1011, 0x1312,
   0x1f13, 0x1414, 0x1615, 0x2f16, 0x1117, 0x2d18,
   0x1519, 0x2c1a};


//////////////////////////////////////////////////////
// Implementation of the Windw class
//////////////////////////////////////////////////////
Windw::Windw(int x, int y, int w, int h, int brd, int buf)
{
  wx = x; wy=y; ww=w; wh=h;
  border=brd;
  buffered = buf;
  buffer = NULL;
}

Windw::~Windw(void)
{
  if (buffer != NULL)
  {
    mouse.HideMouse();
    putimage(wx, wy, buffer, COPY_PUT);
    free(buffer);
    mouse.ShowMouse();
  }
}

void Windw::DrawWindow (void)
{
```

continues

129

Listing 4.5. Continued

```
int size;

mouse.HideMouse();

// Save window screen area, if requested.
if (buffered)
{
  if ((size = imagesize(wx, wy, wx+ww, wy+wh)) < 0)
    WindwError("Image too large to store.");
  else
  {
    if ((buffer = (int *)malloc(size)) == NULL)
   WindwError("Not enough memory.");
    else getimage(wx, wy, wx+ww, wy+wh, buffer);
  }
}

//Draw basic 3-D window.
setcolor(WHITE);
moveto(wx+ww, wy);
lineto(wx, wy);
lineto(wx, wy+wh);
moveto(wx+ww-1, wy+1);
lineto(wx+1, wy+1);
lineto(wx+1, wy+wh-1);
setcolor(DARKGRAY);
moveto(wx+1, wy+wh);
lineto(wx+ww, wy+wh);
lineto(wx+ww, wy);
moveto(wx+2, wy+wh-1);
lineto(wx+ww-1, wy+wh-1);
lineto(wx+ww-1, wy+1);
setfillstyle(SOLID_FILL, LIGHTGRAY);
bar(wx+2, wy+2, wx+ww-2, wy+wh-2);

//Draw border, if requested.
if (border) {
  setcolor(DARKGRAY);
  moveto(wx+ww-10, wy+10);
  lineto(wx+10, wy+10);
  lineto(wx+10, wy+wh-10);
```

```
      setcolor(WHITE);
      lineto(wx+ww-10, wy+wh-10);
      lineto(wx+ww-10, wy+10);
  }
  mouse.ShowMouse();
}

void Windw::RunWindow(void)
{
  GetEvent(evntmsg);
}

void Windw::WindwError(char *s)
{
  cout << "ERROR: " << s << '\n';
  cout << "Press any key";
  getch();
  abort();
}


/////////////////////////////////////////////////////////
// Implementation of the CapWindw class
/////////////////////////////////////////////////////////
CapWindw::CapWindw(int x, int y, int w, int h,
              int brd, int buf, char *s) :
          Windw(x, y, w, h, brd, buf)
{
  strcpy(label, s);
}

void CapWindw::DrawWindow(void)
{
  // Draw basic window.
  Windw::DrawWindow();

  // Draw caption bar.
  DrawCapBar();
}

void CapWindw::SetCaption(char *s)
{
  strcpy(label, s);
```

continues

Listing 4.5. Continued

```
  DrawCapBar();
}

void CapWindw::DrawCapBar(void)
{
  mouse.HideMouse();
  setcolor(WHITE);
  moveto(wx+20, wy+40);
  lineto(wx+20, wy+20);
  lineto(wx+ww-20, wy+20);
  setcolor(BLACK);
  lineto(wx+ww-20, wy+40);
  lineto(wx+20, wy+40);
  setfillstyle(SOLID_FILL, DARKGRAY);
  bar(wx+21, wy+21, wx+ww-21, wy+39);
  setcolor(WHITE);
  int x = (wx+ww/2) - (strlen(label)*4);
  outtextxy(x, wy+27, label);
  mouse.ShowMouse();
}

CapTWindw::CapTWindw(char *s1, char *s2, char *s3) :
      CapWindw(0, 0, 0, 150, FALSE, TRUE, s1)
{
  // Calculate which string is the longest and
  // use that width to calculate the window's width.
  int w = strlen(s1) * 8 + 60;
  if (strlen(s2) > strlen(s3))
    ww = strlen(s2) * 8 + 60;
  else ww = strlen(s3) * 8 + 60;
  if (w > ww) ww = w;

  // Enforce a minimum width.
  if (ww < 230) ww = 230;

  // Calculate the window's x,y coordinates.
  wx = 320 - ww/2;
  wy = 164;

  // Set the window's text.
```

```
    line1 = s2;
    line2 = s3;
}


void CapTWindw::DrawWindow(void)
{
    // Draw the captioned window.
    CapWindw::DrawWindow();

    // Position and draw window body text.
    mouse.HideMouse();
    int x = (wx+ww/2) - (strlen(line1)*8)/2;
    setcolor(BLACK);
    if (strlen(line2)==0)
      outtextxy(x, wy+68, line1);
    else
    {
      outtextxy(x, wy+56, line1);
      x = (wx+ww/2) - (strlen(line2)*8)/2;
      outtextxy(x, wy+71, line2);
    }
    mouse.ShowMouse();
}


///////////////////////////////////////////////////////
// Implementation of the OKWindw class
///////////////////////////////////////////////////////
OKWindw::OKWindw(char *s1, char *s2, char *s3) :
      CapTWindw(s1, s2, s3)
{
    butn = NULL;
}


OKWindw::~OKWindw(void)
{
    if (butn != NULL) delete butn;
}


void OKWindw::DrawWindow(void)
{
    CapTWindw::DrawWindow();
```

continues

Listing 4.5. Continued

```
  butn = new Button(wx+ww/2-32, wy+wh-42, "^OK");
  butn->DrawWindow();
}

void OKWindw::RunWindow(void)
{
  button = 0;

  // Loop until a button is chosen.
  while (!button)
  {
    GetEvent(evntmsg);

    // Check for mouse click on button.
    if (butn->Clicked(evntmsg))
      button = OK;

    // Check for a keyboard event.
    else if (evntmsg.type == KEYBD)
    {
      // Convert character code to ASCII,
      // and check for Esc key.
      char k = evntmsg.key & 0x00ff;
      if (k == ESC) button = CANCEL;
    }
  }
}


///////////////////////////////////////////////////////
// Implementation of the YesNoWindw class
///////////////////////////////////////////////////////
YesNoWindw::YesNoWindw(char *s1, char *s2, char *s3) :
        CapTWindw(s1, s2, s3)
{
  butn1 = butn2 = NULL;
}

YesNoWindw::~YesNoWindw(void)
{
  if (butn1 != NULL) delete butn1;
```

```
    if (butn2 != NULL) delete butn2;
}

void YesNoWindw::DrawWindow(void)
{
  CapTWindw::DrawWindow();
  butn1 = new Button(wx+ww/2-70, wy+108, "^YES");
  butn1->DrawWindow();
  butn2 = new Button(wx+ww/2+6, wy+108, "^NO");
  butn2->DrawWindow();
}

void YesNoWindw::RunWindow(void)
{
  button = 0;
  while (!button)
  {
    GetEvent(evntmsg);
    if (butn1->Clicked(evntmsg))
      button = YES;
    else if (butn2->Clicked(evntmsg))
      button = NO;
    else if (evntmsg.type == KEYBD)
    {
      char k = evntmsg.key & 0x00ff;
      if (k == ESC) button = CANCEL;
    }
  }
}


//////////////////////////////////////////////////////////
// Implementation of the YesNoCanWindw class
//////////////////////////////////////////////////////////
YesNoCanWindw::YesNoCanWindw(char *s1, char *s2, char *s3) :
          CapTWindw(s1, s2, s3)
{
  butn1 = butn2 = butn3 = NULL;
}

YesNoCanWindw::~YesNoCanWindw(void)
{
  if (butn1 != NULL) delete butn1;
```

continues

135

Listing 4.5. Continued

```
  if (butn2 != NULL) delete butn2;
  if (butn3 != NULL) delete butn3;
}

void YesNoCanWindw::DrawWindow(void)
{
  CapTWindw::DrawWindow();
  butn1 = new Button(wx+ww/2-105, wy+wh-42, "^YES");
  butn1->DrawWindow();
  butn2 = new Button(wx+ww/2-32, wy+wh-42, "^NO");
  butn2->DrawWindow();
  butn3 = new Button(wx+ww/2+41, wy+wh-42, "^CANCEL");
  butn3->DrawWindow();
}

void YesNoCanWindw::RunWindow(void)
{
  button = 0;
  while (!button)
  {
    GetEvent(evntmsg);
    if (butn1->Clicked(evntmsg))
      button = YES;
    else if (butn2->Clicked(evntmsg))
      button = NO;
    else if (butn3->Clicked(evntmsg))
      button = CANCEL;
  }
}

//////////////////////////////////////////////////////
// Implementation of the InputWindw class
//////////////////////////////////////////////////////
InputWindw::InputWindw(char *s1, char *s2, char *s3) :
        CapTWindw(s1, s2, s3)
{
  input[0] = 0;
  butn1 = butn2 = NULL;
}

InputWindw::~InputWindw(void)
{
```

```
    if (butn1 != NULL) delete butn1;
    if (butn2 != NULL) delete butn2;
}

void InputWindw::DrawWindow(void)
{
  CapTWindw::DrawWindow();
  butn1 = new Button(wx+ww/2-70, wy+108, "^OK");
  butn1->DrawWindow();
  butn2 = new Button(wx+ww/2+6, wy+108, "^CANCEL");
  butn2->DrawWindow();
  mouse.HideMouse();
  setfillstyle(SOLID_FILL, BLACK);
  bar(wx+15, wy+85, wx+ww-15, wy+99);
  mouse.ShowMouse();
}

void InputWindw::RunWindow(void)
{
  button = 0;
  while (!button)
  {
    GetEvent(evntmsg);
    if (butn1->Clicked(evntmsg))
      button = OK;
    else if (butn2->Clicked(evntmsg))
      button = CANCEL;
    else if (evntmsg.type == KEYBD)
    {
      char k = evntmsg.key & 0x00ff;
      HandleInput(k);
    }
  }
}

void InputWindw::HandleInput(char k)
{
  int l = strlen(input);
  int w = (ww - 30)/8;
  settextjustify(LEFT_TEXT, TOP_TEXT);

  // Check that an appropriate key was pressed
  // and that the string can hold another character.
```

continues

Listing 4.5. Continued

```
if ((k>31) && (k<127) && (l<80))
{
  // Add character to string.
  input[l+1] = 0;  input[l] = k;

  // Draw the portion of the string that will
  // fit into the text-entry field.
  setcolor(WHITE);
  if (l < w) outtextxy(wx+15, wy+88, input);
  else
  {
    int i = l - w + 1;
    setfillstyle(SOLID_FILL, BLACK);
    bar(wx+15, wy+85, wx+ww-15, wy+99);
    outtextxy(wx+15, wy+88, &input[i]);
  }
}

// Check for a Backspace character and that
// the string has a character to delete.
else if ((k==BACKSP) && (l>0))
{
  // Delete the last character.
  l -= 1;
  input[l] = 0;

  // Draw the portion of the string that
  // will fit in the text-entry field.
  setfillstyle(SOLID_FILL, BLACK);
  bar(wx+15, wy+85, wx+ww-15, wy+99);
  setcolor(WHITE);
  if (l < w+1) outtextxy(wx+15, wy+88, input);
  else
  {
    int i = l - w;
    outtextxy(wx+15, wy+88, &input[i]);
  }
}
}
```

```
//////////////////////////////////////////////////////
// Implementation of the Button class
//////////////////////////////////////////////////////
Button::Button(int x, int y, char *s) :
     Windw(x, y, 64, 32, FALSE, FALSE)
{
  strcpy(label, s);
  altkey = 0;
  hotkey = 0;
}

void Button::DrawWindow(void)
{
  int pos = -1;
  char tlabel[20];

  Windw::DrawWindow();
  mouse.HideMouse();

  // Find and remove the ^ character and
  // set the appropriate hot key.
  strcpy(tlabel, label);
  for (int i = 0; i<strlen(tlabel); ++i)
  {
    if (tlabel[i] == '^')
    {
      pos = i;
      hotkey = ctrlkeys[tlabel[i+1]-65];
      for (int j=i; j<strlen(tlabel); ++j)
     tlabel[j] = tlabel[j+1];
    }
  }

  if (strcmp(tlabel,"OK")==0) altkey = OKALT;
  else if (strcmp(tlabel, "CANCEL")==0) altkey = CANCELALT;

  // Center and draw text on button.
  int x = (wx+ww/2) - (strlen(tlabel)*4);
  setcolor(BLACK);
  outtextxy(x, wy+12, tlabel);

  // Underline the hot-key character.
```

continues

139

Listing 4.5. Continued

```
  if (pos >= 0)
    line(x+pos*8, wy+20, x+pos*8+6, wy+20);

  mouse.ShowMouse();
}

int Button::Clicked(EvntMsg evntmsg)
{
  int mx, my;
  int click = FALSE;

  // Check whether button was selected by the mouse.
  if  ((evntmsg.type == MBUTTON) &&
       (evntmsg.mx>wx) && (evntmsg.mx<wx+ww) &&
       (evntmsg.my>wy) && (evntmsg.my<wy+wh))
  {
    ClickButton();
    click = TRUE;
  }

  // Check whether button was selected from the keyboard.

  else if (evntmsg.type == KEYBD)
  {
    if ((evntmsg.key == hotkey) ¦¦ (evntmsg.key == altkey))
    {
      ClickButton();
      click = TRUE;
    }
  }
  return click;
}

void Button::ClickButton(void)
{
  int *buff;

  mouse.HideMouse();

  // Shift the image on the button down and right
  // to simulate button movement.
```

```
int size = imagesize(wx+2, wy+2, wx+ww-2, wy+wh-2);
buff = (int *)malloc(size);
if (buff)
{
  getimage(wx+2, wy+2, wx+ww-2, wy+wh-2, buff);
  putimage(wx+3, wy+3, buff, COPY_PUT);
  free(buff);
}

// Draw the button's borders so the
// button appears to be pressed.
setcolor(DARKGRAY);
moveto(wx+ww, wy);
lineto(wx, wy); lineto(wx, wy+wh);
moveto(wx+ww-1, wy+1);
lineto(wx+1, wy+1); lineto(wx+1, wy+wh-1);
setcolor(WHITE);
moveto(wx+1, wy+wh);
lineto(wx+ww, wy+wh); lineto(wx+ww, wy);
moveto(wx+2, wy+wh-1);
lineto(wx+ww-1, wy+wh-1);
lineto(wx+ww-1, wy+1);

// Make button beep.
sound ( 2000 );
delay ( 100 );
nosound();

// Redraw button in unselected form.
DrawWindow();

  mouse.ShowMouse();
}
```

5

Playing with Life

I n Chapters 3 and 4, you developed powerful tools for writing interactive programs. Your event-handling system allows programs to accept continual keyboard and mouse input, by polling those devices in an event loop. This event-driven system gives users full control over your program; they can select program functions at almost any time, rather than in the manner dictated by the program. In addition, the window library provides attractive windows for organizing screens and displaying information, as well as interactive dialog boxes with animated controls. These interactive controls make function selection more natural, like changing a television channel or the volume of a stereo.

Now you will use these tools to create a commercial-quality simulation program, one that takes full advantage of the event-driven, windowing environment. This simulation uses windows of various types to build its main display. In addition, it uses button controls, not only in dialog boxes but also in a simple button-controlled menu bar that the user can access with the mouse or by pressing Ctrl-key combinations. And to add to the fun, you learn about a data structure that you may have not run into before: a *linked list*.

The Story of Life

A bout 30 years ago, a fine English fellow by the name of John Conway invented simple rules for a system that simulated the lives of special one-celled animals. Although the rules of the simulation were simple, the results were fascinating. Before long, every computer scientist worth his or her diploma had written a version of Life and had spent hours trying different combinations of cells to see what patterns might emerge.

Today, people are still fascinated by Conway's computer simulation. Many computer science books at least mention Life, and each year thousands of computer science students write versions of Life as part of their programming curriculum. The simplest implementations result in programs that accurately portray the simulation, but run too slowly to be practical. Other implementations blaze across the screen in vivid colors and kaleidoscopic patterns, hypnotizing any viewer that happens to glance in its direction.

In this chapter, you not only put your event-driven windows to work, but also examine a speedy algorithm for implementing the Life simulation.

 Caution: After you start dabbling with Life, you may find it hard to tear away. This author and his publisher cannot be held responsible for lost productivity!

The Rules of Life

T he Life simulation is played on a grid of any size. In the original rules, the grid is unbounded, but you can limit the grid to the screen. You might want to think of the screen display as a sort of petri dish holding a culture of microscopic cells. Cells are placed randomly on the grid and the simulation is started. The cells then run through their life cycles a given number of generations, living and dying according to the rules set forth by Mr. Conway.

The rules are simple and elegant, as follows:

- Any live cell with fewer than two neighbors dies of loneliness.

- Any live cell with more than three neighbors dies of crowding.

- Any dead cell with exactly three neighbors comes to life.

- Any live cell with two or three neighbors lives, unchanged, to the next generation.

Life Implementation

As you may imagine, a large grid could contain hundreds if not thousands of cells living and dying every generation. The computer must work furiously, calculating the number of neighbors for each cell in the grid, then creating or killing cells based on these counts. Keep in mind, too, that counting the neighbors for a single cell requires checking each adjacent cell—as many as eight.

Suppose you implemented the grid as a two-dimensional array of integers, like this:

```
int map[28][50];
```

Each element of the map can be one of two values: 0 if the cell is dead and 1 if the cell is alive. The logical way to process this grid is to check each element of the array, counting its neighbors and marking it as alive or dead.

In the example 28x50 array, 1400 cells must be processed every generation. Each cell processed must check the status of as many as eight adjacent cells to count its neighbors. That's about 11,000 operations for the entire grid. Worse yet, this processing must be performed for every generation of the simulation. A single run of the simulation may have as many as 10,000 generations!

All this calculating wouldn't be a problem if you planned to let the simulation run all night. However, to make the simulation interesting, you must update the screen as quickly as possible—ideally, several times a second. Obviously, this creates a problem in the speed department.

Speed is not the only problem. You also must consider the effects of prematurely creating or killing cells. It's not enough to scan though the grid, creating and killing cells as you go, because the cells you create or kill may affect cells you have not yet processed. Suppose cell X in a grid has only two neighbors. Now assume that a cell next to X dies as you process the grid. Although this cell died, cell X should still remain alive for this generation because it had two neighbors; it won't be lonely until the next generation. When you finally process cell X, however, the counting function recognizes cell X as having only one neighbor. As a result, cell X dies prematurely.

145

Confused? Look at Figure 5.1. Three cells are in the first-generation grid, which is on the left. In this generation, the top cell must die because it has only one neighbor. The middle cell must remain alive to the next generation, because it has two neighbors. The bottom cell must die because, like the top cell, it has only one neighbor. The empty cells to the left and right of the center cell must be brought to life because both have exactly three neighbors. After processing the grid, you should have the second-generation grid, which is on the right.

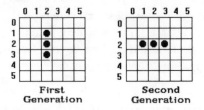

First
Generation

Second
Generation

Figure 5.1. Applying the rules of Life to three cells.

However, if you start at the top and process the grid by creating and killing cells as you go, you get incorrect results. First, you kill the top cell because it has only one neighbor. Then, when you get to empty cell 1,2, even though it should have come to life, you determine that it has only two neighbors and leave it alone. When you get to cell 2,2, you think it has only one neighbor and kill it, even though this cell should have survived to the next generation. After processing the entire grid, you don't have the correct second-generation result. Instead, you have an empty grid!

In short, in each generation, you must determine which cells live and die, without changing the grid. Then when you are finished, you must simultaneously create and kill the appropriate cells. This requires tricky algorithms, especially when you consider that all these calculations must be performed at a speed that allows fast screen updates. Sound like fun? Now give it a shot.

The Speed Problem

W hat can you do to speed things up? First, add another map array to keep a running count of each cell's neighbors. When the simulation starts, the program updates the neighbor count. From then on, rather than recalculating the entire grid in each generation, the program changes neighbor counts for only those cells adjacent to cells that have just been created or killed. This method cuts processing time significantly: In a given generation, the program must change the neighbor counts of only a small number of cells instead of the entire grid.

Then, although the original map grid records the status of each cell, you add two lists of cells, one for cells about to be created and one for cells about to die. These are the only cells that affect the map, so why check the entire grid every generation?

But what type of data structure enables you to build lists of items—lists that can grow or shrink dynamically? You've probably already guessed that the answer is a *linked list*.

Linked Lists

To create a linked list, you first must decide what information makes up the items, or *nodes*, that are to be stored in the list. In the simulation program, you must store enough data to identify a cell. All the information you need in order to identify a cell are its x and y coordinates in the grid, so a node could be

```
struct Node
{
  int x, y;
};
```

When a cell is born or dies, you can create a node for the cell like this:

```
Node *node = new Node;
node->x = x_ccord;
node->y = y_coord;
```

This code creates a new Node structure on the heap and sets its x and y members to the coordinates of a cell. But what good is it to have a bunch of these nodes sitting around in memory? You must link them into a list. To do this, you must add to your structure a pointer to a Node. You can then use this pointer to point to the next node in the list. The new Node structure, then, looks like this:

```
struct Node
{
  int x, y;
  Node *next;
};
```

147

In addition to the data structure for a node, you also need a pointer to the first node of the list (a *head pointer*) and a pointer to the end of the list (a *tail pointer*). Having a pointer to the head of the list is most important. Without it, you couldn't find the list in memory. A pointer to the tail is a convenience. You can use it to quickly add new nodes to the end of the list, without having to scan the list from the first node. The head and tail pointers look like this:

```
Node *list_h, *list_t;
```

Figure 5.2 illustrates how a linked list looks in memory. The `list_h` pointer points to the first node in the list. Each node has a pointer that leads to the next node in the list. The `next` pointer in the last node is left NULL, which indicates the end of the list. Finally, the `list_t` pointer points to the last node in the list.

Figure 5.2. A linked list in memory.

Listing 5.1 demonstrates this simple linked list.

Listing 5.1. LIST1.CPP—a simple linked-list demonstration.

```
#include <iostream.h>
#include <conio.h>

struct Node
{
  int x, y;
  Node *next;
};

Node *node = NULL,
     *list_h = NULL,
     *list_t = NULL;

void main(void)
{
  for (int i = 0; i < 10; ++i)
  {
    node = new Node;
    node->x = i;
```

```
      node->y = i * 10;
      if (!list_h) list_h = node;
      else list_t->next = node;
      list_t = node;
      list_t->next = NULL;
    }
    while (list_h)
    {
      node = list_h;
      list_h = list_h->next;
      cout << node->x << ',' << node->y << '\n';
      delete node;
    }
    getch();
}
```

Study Listing 5.1 carefully, so you're sure you understand how to create and manage a linked list. In this program, the Node structure is the type of item stored in the list. This structure contains two data elements, as well as a pointer to a Node. This pointer, next, is used to point to the next node in the list.

The program begins with a for loop, in which 10 nodes are created and linked. In the loop, the new command creates a new node on the heap, after which the node's data elements are set to the values of i and i*10. (These values hold no particular significance.) After creating the node, the program checks whether list_h is NULL. If it is, the program has a new list, so it sets list_h to point to node. Then list_t is set to point to the same node (if the list has only one item, the head and tail of the list are the same), and list_t's next pointer is set to NULL, indicating there are no other items in the list.

Getting back to the if statement, if list_h isn't NULL, there's already at least one node in the list. In this case, list_h shouldn't be changed. Rather, the new node must be added to the end of the list. This is where list_t comes in handy. Rather than having to scan through the entire list, looking for a NULL next, the program can use list_t to tack the new node to the end of the list. It does this by setting list_t's next pointer to point to the new node and then changing list_t to point to the new last node. Figures 5.3 through 5.6 illustrate this process.

After the program creates the linked list, a while loop scans the list, printing each node's contents before deleting the node. Notice how the temporary node pointer keeps track of the current node. By setting node to list_h, then setting

149

list_h to point to the next item in the list, you effectively "pop off" the first node. Without saving the pointer in node, you could not access this node. The program's output follows:

```
0,0
1,10
2,20
3,30
4,40
5,50
6,60
7,70
8,80
9,90
```

Step 1:
Create new node.

Figure 5.3. Creating a linked list—step one.

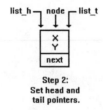

Step 2:
Set head and
tail pointers.

Figure 5.4. Creating a linked list—step two.

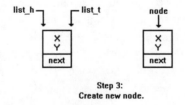

Step 3:
Create new node.

Figure 5.5. Creating a linked list—step three.

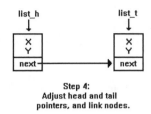

Step 4:
Adjust head and tail
pointers, and link nodes.

Figure 5.6. Creating a linked list—step four.

An Object-Oriented List

I f you've an idea that a linked list might be the perfect candidate for a class, you could be correct, depending on how you plan to use the list. Creating a linked-list class to handle only a single list in a small program such as Listing 5.1 is overkill. However, if you plan to use many different lists in a program— that is, the class won't be a single-instance class—it might be worthwhile to create a linked-list class.

For the sake of discussion, you can now convert Listing 5.1 into an object-oriented program. (For the moment, ignore that this results in a single-instance class.) Listing 5.2 is the header for the resultant List class.

Listing 5.2. LIST.H—the header file for the *List* class.

```
#ifndef _LIST_H
#define _LIST_H

class List
{
  struct Node
  {
    int x, y;
    Node *next;
  };

  Node *node, *list_h, *list_t;
```

continues

Listing 5.2. Continued

```
public:
  List(void);
  ~List(void);
  void MakeNewNode(int n1, int n2);
  void DisplayList(void);
};


#endif
```

As you can see, all the list-handling operations have been taken out of the main program and placed into the `List` class. The data that defines the list—the pointers and the node declaration—are placed inside the class also. The main program no longer has to know how a linked list works. It has only to draw on the capabilities of the class. Look at the class' constructor first:

```
List::List(void)
{
  list_h = list_t = NULL;
}
```

This function initializes a new list by setting its pointers to NULL. This creates an empty list. Of course, an empty list isn't particularly useful. Now, the class needs a way to add nodes to the list:

```
void List::MakeNewNode(int n1, int n2)
{
  node = new Node;
  node->x = n1;
  node->y = n2;
  if (!list_h) list_h = node;
  else list_t->next = node;
  list_t = node;
  list_t->next = NULL;
}
```

This function takes as parameters the values for the new node's x and y members. First, the new node is allocated on the heap, after which the x and y members are set to their appropriate values. Then, using the same code examined in Listing 5.1, the new node is added to the list.

To display the contents of the list, you call the class' `DisplayList()` function:

```
void List::DisplayList(void)
{
  node = list_h;
  while (node)
  {
    cout << node->x << ',' << node->y << '\n';
    node = node->next;
  }
}
```

This function simply scans the list (using the temporary `node` pointer, so it doesn't destroy `list_h`), printing the contents of x and y. Unlike the program in Listing 5.1, each node isn't deleted after it is printed. That job is left for the class' destructor:

```
List::~List(void)
{
  while (list_h)
  {
    node = list_h;
    list_h = list_h->next;
    delete node;
  }
}
```

As with any class, the `List` class' destructor is called when a `List` object goes out of scope or when a dynamically allocated `List` object is deleted. The destructor then deletes every node in the list, using the same method you saw in Listing 5.1 (but without printing the contents of the node before deleting it).

Listings 5.3 and 5.4 are the `List` class' implementation and the new main program, respectively.

Listing 5.3. LIST.CPP—the implementation of the *List* class.

```
#include <iostream.h>
#include "list.h"

List::List(void)
{
  list_h = list_t = NULL;
}
```

continues

153

Listing 5.3. Continued

```
List::~List(void)
{
  while (list_h)
  {
    node = list_h;
    list_h = list_h->next;
    delete node;
  }
}

void List::MakeNewNode(int n1, int n2)
{
  node = new Node;
  node->x = n1;
  node->y = n2;
  if (!list_h) list_h = node;
  else list_t->next = node;
  list_t = node;
  list_t->next = NULL;
}

void List::DisplayList(void)
{
  node = list_h;
  while (node)
  {
    cout << node->x << ',' << node->y << '\n';
    node = node->next;
  }
}
```

Listing 5.4. LIST2.CPP—a program for testing the *List* class.

```
#include <iostream.h>
#include <conio.h>
#include "list.h"

void main(void)
{
  List list;
```

```
    for (int i = 0; i < 10; ++i)
      list.MakeNewNode(i, i*10);
    list.DisplayList();
    getch();
}
```

The main program is much shorter and clearer. Although the effort of creating the class for such a small program is probably not worthwhile, imagine how much easier it would be to use a similar class in a large program that must handle multiple lists. By using a list class, you no longer must worry about initializing pointers or linking nodes. You don't even have to worry about releasing nodes from memory, because the class' destructor takes care of this task for you. Using the class, your main program is clean and to the point, uncluttered with the details of handling a linked list.

A Cell List

T he linked-list class in Listings 5.2 and 5.3 is far from complete. It's been used only to illustrate the process of creating a list class. In the Life program, the list class is more sophisticated, enabling you to do more than add, display, and delete nodes. Look at that class now. Listing 5.5 is the CList (Cell List) class header file, CLIST.H.

Listing 5.5. CLIST.H—the header file for the *CList* class.

```
#ifndef _CLIST_H
#define _CLIST_H

class CList
{
  struct Node
  {
    int x, y;
    Node *next;
  };

  Node *node, *list_h, *list_t;
```

continues

Listing 5.5. Continued

```
public:
  CList(void);
  ~CList(void);
  void MakeNewNode(int n1, int n2);
  void TransferList(CList &list2);
  void ClearList();
  int HasNodes();
  void GetNode(int &c, int &r);
  void DisplayList(void);
};

#endif
```

The CList class features several more functions than the List class. The class' constructor and destructor work similarly, however, so they aren't discussed. Likewise, the MakeNewNode() and DisplayList() functions are identical to the same functions in List. You can start by focusing on the TransferList() function:

```
void CList::TransferList(CList &list2)
{
  list2.ClearList();
  list2.list_h = list_h;
  list2.list_t = list_t;
  list_h = NULL;
  list_t = NULL;
}
```

This function enables you to transfer the contents of one list to another. No data is actually moved or copied. This task is accomplished simply by setting the destination-list pointers to the same values as the source-list pointers.

 Caution: The danger in setting the destination-list pointers to the same values as the source-list pointers is that after copying the pointers, you have two sets of pointers to the same data. When one of the lists is deleted, its destructor deletes all the nodes in the list. That leaves pointers to nodes that have been deleted, a dangerous situation. This problem is avoided in TransferList() by setting the source-list pointers to NULL after they are copied. This way, there is only one set of pointers to the nodes in the list.

You use `TransferList()` often in the Life program to shift the contents of lists. Another function you use often is `GetNode()`:

```
void CList::GetNode(int &c, int &r)
{
  if (list_h)
  {
    node = list_h;
    c = node->x;
    r = node->y;
    list_h = list_h->next;
    if (!list_h) list_t = NULL;
    delete node;
  }
}
```

This function retrieves the first cell node in a list, returns its contents in the variables c and r (column and row), then deletes the node from the list. Calling `GetNode()` for every node in a list results in an empty list.

Another handy function is `HasNodes()`, which returns a Boolean value indicating whether there are nodes in the list or the list is empty:

```
int CList::HasNodes()
{
  return ( list_h != NULL );
}
```

This function is particularly useful with a function such as `GetNodes()`. By using `HasNodes()` as the conditional for a `while` statement, you can scan an entire list, ending the looping when the list is empty, that is, when `HasNodes()` returns false.

The last new function in the `CList` class is `ClearList()`:

```
void CList::ClearList()
{
  while (list_h)
  {
    node = list_h;
    list_h = list_h->next;
    delete node;
  }
}
```

This function enables you to empty a list at any time. It simply reads through the list, deleting nodes as it goes. This function is called by CList's destructor, but you can use it also in your programs (and you use it in the Life program). The entire implementation for CList is shown is Listing 5.6.

Listing 5.6. CLIST.CPP—the implementation of the *CList* class.

```
#include <iostream.h>
#include "clist.h"

CList::CList(void)
{
  list_h = list_t = NULL;
}

CList::~CList(void)
{
  ClearList();
}

void CList::MakeNewNode(int n1, int n2)
{
  node = new Node;
  node->x = n1;
  node->y = n2;
  if (!list_h) list_h = node;
  else list_t->next = node;
  list_t = node;
  list_t->next = NULL;
}

void CList::DisplayList(void)
{
  node = list_h;
  while (node)
  {
    cout << node->x << ',' << node->y << '\n';
    node = node->next;
  }
}

void CList::ClearList()
```

```
{
  while (list_h)
  {
    node = list_h;
    list_h = list_h->next;
    delete node;
  }
}

void CList::TransferList(CList &list2)
{
  list2.ClearList();
  list2.list_h = list_h;
  list2.list_t = list_t;
  list_h = NULL;
  list_t = NULL;
}

int CList::HasNodes()
{
  return ( list_h != NULL );
}

void CList::GetNode(int &c, int &r)
{
  if (list_h)
  {
    node = list_h;
    c = node->x;
    r = node->y;
    list_h = list_h->next;
    if (!list_h) list_t = NULL;
    delete node;
  }
}
```

The Life Program

Y ou now know how to handle linked lists. You've even created a handy cell-list class that you can use in your program to track cells as they are created and killed. It's time to put your knowledge of linked lists to work, by examining the full Life program. This program's lengthy listing is explored a piece at a time, in the order in which it is executed. But first, run the program and see what it does.

When you compile and run Life, the main screen appears, as shown in Figure 5.7. Most of the screen is made up of the grid in which your cells live and die. Below the grid is the button bar, which contains several command buttons used to control the program. Also at the bottom of the screen, on the right, is the generation count. Before the simulation starts, this readout shows the current setting for the number of generations (the default is 100). While the simulation is running, the readout shows the number of the current generation.

 Note: Remember when you compile programs that use Borland's graphics library, you must enable that library by turning on the Graphics library selection in the Libraries dialog box. You can display this dialog box by selecting the Options/Linker/Libraries menu item.

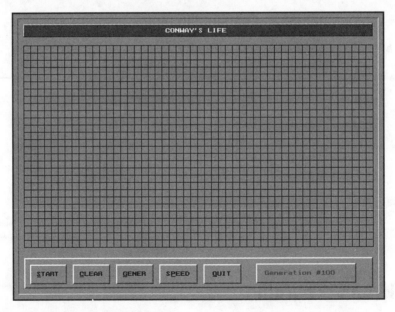

Figure 5.7. The main screen of Life.

160

To get started, you must first seed the grid with cells. To do this, place your mouse pointer where you want to place a cell and click the left button. A green cell appears where you clicked. If you want to place cells quickly, you can paint them to the grid by holding down the left mouse button as you sweep the pointer across the screen.

When you've placed your cells, activate the simulation by selecting the START button, either by clicking the button or by pressing Ctrl-S. When you select START, the simulation springs into life, with cells living and dying as they speed through their life cycles. To stop the simulation before the generations run out, click the mouse or press any key.

Next to the START button is the CLEAR button, which removes all cells from the grid. The GENER button sets the generation count. When you select this button, the Generations dialog box appears, as shown in Figure 5.8. To change the generation setting, type a number from 1 to 10,000. Invalid entries yield the default value of 100.

Figure 5.8. The Generations dialog box.

You may want to view the simulation at slower speeds so you can see more clearly the patterns that emerge from specific cell configurations. You can set the simulation to one of 10 speeds by selecting the SPEED button. The Simulation Speed dialog box then appears, as shown in Figure 5.9. Enter a value from 1 to 10. (1 is the slowest and 10 is the fastest.) Invalid entries yield the default value of 10.

Figure 5.9. The Simulation Speed dialog box.

To quit the simulation, select the QUIT button. A Yes/No box appears, asking whether you really want to quit. Select Yes to exit the program or No to return to the simulation.

Examining Life

N ow that you know how the program operates, take a look at the code, starting with the #include and #define statements:

```
#include <graphics.h>
#include <conio.h>
#include <iostream.h>
#include <stdlib.h>
#include <stdio.h>
#include <dos.h>

// Use mouse, window, and list classes.
#include "mous.h"
#include "windw.h"
#include "clist.h"
#include "event.h"

// Define global constants.
#define TRUE 1
#define FALSE 0
#define DEAD 0
#define ALIVE 1
#define MAXCOL 50
#define MAXROW 28
```

Most of this should be familiar territory. The files in the angle brackets are Borland C++'s system header files, which give you access to the libraries you need. Then come the header files for your own classes, enabling you to use the Mouse, Windw, and CList classes in the program. The event handler is also #included here. Finally, the program constants are defined. Of particular interest are DEAD and ALIVE, which are the status values for cells, and MAXCOL and MAXROW, which specify the size of the grid map.

After including the necessary header files, the data for the program is declared:

```
int mousex, mousey, // Mouse coordinates.
    repeat;         // Main program loop controller.
```

```
int generations,      // # of life generations.
    speed;            // Speed of simulation.

int world[MAXROW][MAXCOL], // Cell map.
    nbrs[MAXROW][MAXCOL];  // Neighbor count map.
```

It's obvious from the comments what this data is used for. But pay special attention to the world and nbrs arrays; these arrays were described when the algorithm for the program was developed.

After declaring this global data, the linked lists you use in the program are declared:

```
// Linked lists.
CList live, die, nextlive, nextdie;
```

The live and die lists hold the cells that live and die in a given generation. The nextlive and nextdie lists are used as temporary storage for cells that are eventually transferred to the live and die lists. You see how this works when you get further into the program's code.

The Life program uses many types of windows to draw its display. These windows are defined and created next:

```
// Windows and controls for main screen.
CapWindw wnd1(0, 0, 639, 479, TRUE, FALSE, "CONWAY'S LIFE");
Windw wnd2(20, 409, 599, 50, FALSE, FALSE);
Windw wnd3(420, 419, 170, 32, FALSE, FALSE);;
Button startbut(30, 420, "^START");
Button clearbut(105, 420, "^CLEAR");
Button generatebut(180, 420, "^GENER");
Button speedbut(255, 420, "S^PEED");
Button quitbut(330, 420, "^QUIT");
```

Note that these windows are defined, but not yet drawn on-screen. They are drawn later in the program by calling each window's DrawWindow() function.

Finally, before getting to the program code, the event-message structure is declared, and prototypes for all functions in the program are listed:

```
// Event message structure.
EvntMsg evntmsg;

// Function prototypes.
int KeyEvent(void);
void GetEvent(EvntMsg &evntmsg);
```

163

```
void DispatchEvent(EvntMsg evntmsg);
void Life(void);
void CreateLists(void);
void ClearWorld(void);
void GetGens(int &generations);
void GetSpeed(int &speed);
void PlaceCell(EvntMsg evntmsg);
void Live(void);
void Die(void);
void AddNbrs(void);
void SubNbrs(void);
void CalcLimits(int c, int r, int &xlow, int &xhigh,
          int &ylow, int &yhigh);
void UpdateGens(int g);
void Init(void);
void ReleaseNodes(void);
void DrawScreen(void);
void InitMouse(void);
void Cleanup(void);
```

Now you're ready to see what makes this program tick. As always, program execution begins at main():

```
void main(void)
{
  // Initialize game, mouse, and screen.
  Init();
  DrawScreen();
  InitMouse();

  // Repeat event loop until Quit.
  repeat = 1;
  while (repeat)
  {
    GetEvent(evntmsg);
    DispatchEvent(evntmsg);
  }

  closegraph();
}
```

This function initializes the program, draws the display, handles the event loop, and finally closes the program. Its first step is to call Init() to initialize the graphics display and the global program variables:

```
void Init(void)
{
  int gdriver = VGA, gmode = VGAHI, errorcode;

  errorcode = registerbgidriver(EGAVGA_driver);
  if (errorcode < 0)
  {
    cout << "Graphics not initialized: " << errorcode << '\n';
    cout << "Press any key.";
    getch();
    abort();
  }

  initgraph(&gdriver, &gmode, "");
  if ( (errorcode = graphresult()) != grOk)
  {
    cout << "Graphics not initialized: " << errorcode << '\n';
    cout << "Press any key.";
    getch();
    abort();
  }
  for (int r=0; r<MAXROW; ++r)
    for (int c=0; c<MAXCOL; ++c)
      world[r](c) = DEAD;
  generations = 100;
  speed = 1;
}
```

This function starts by initializing the graphics driver. In previous programs, you did this by loading the EGAVGA.BGI graphics driver from the disk at runtime. This program links the graphics driver with the program so the user doesn't have to worry about it being a separate file.

To do this, you first run Borland's BGIOBJ.EXE program to convert the EGAVGA.BGI driver to object-file format. When the driver is converted, you can link it into your program by adding the EGAVGA.OBJ file to your project list. That takes care of the linking, but in your program, you must inform the system that the driver is present. You do this with the `registerbgidriver()` function, as shown in the preceding code. After you register the driver, you initialize it as usual. (For more information on linking graphics drivers, consult the *Borland C++ Library Reference* or the UTIL.DOC file, which is included on your C++ disks.)

After initializing the graphics driver, `Init()` sets the status of every cell in the grid to `DEAD` and sets the default speed and generation count.

The `DrawScreen()` function draws the main display:

```
void DrawScreen(void)
{
  wnd1.DrawWindow();
  wnd2.DrawWindow();
  wnd3.DrawWindow();
  startbut.DrawWindow();
  clearbut.DrawWindow();
  generatebut.DrawWindow();
  speedbut.DrawWindow();
  quitbut.DrawWindow();
  setcolor(BLUE);
    for (int y=55; y<400; y+=12)
    {
      moveto(20, y); lineto(getmaxx()-20, y);
    }
    for (int x=20; x<630; x+=12 )
    {
      moveto(x, 55); lineto(x, 391);
    }
  setcolor(BROWN);
  outtextxy(435, 431, "Generation #100");
}
```

This function calls each window's `DrawWindow()` member function, which displays each window on-screen. After drawing the windows, it adds the grid to the main window using Borland's `moveto()` and `lineto()` graphics functions. Finally, it prints the generation readout at the bottom right of the screen, using Borland's `outtextxy()` function.

The last thing you must do before turning control over to the user is initialize the mouse:

```
void InitMouse(void) {
  if (!mouse.GotMouse()) {
    cout << "You have no mouse.\n";
    cout << "Press any key.";
    getch();
  }
  mouse.SetLimits(0,getmaxx(),0,getmaxy());
  mouse.ShowMouse();
}
```

You've seen this code before.

Now that the initialization is complete, the program enters the event loop, where it waits for the user to select a command. When the user presses a key or clicks a mouse button, the event loop passes the event message to `DispatchEvent()`:

```
void DispatchEvent(EvntMsg evntmsg)
{
  if ( startbut.Clicked(evntmsg) )
    Life();
  else if ( clearbut.Clicked(evntmsg) )
    ClearWorld();
  else if ( generatebut.Clicked(evntmsg) )
    GetGens(generations);
  else if ( speedbut.Clicked(evntmsg) )
    GetSpeed(speed);
  else if ( quitbut.Clicked(evntmsg) )
  {
    YesNoWindw wndw("QUIT", "Are you sure you",
             "want to quit?");
    wndw.DrawWindow();
    wndw.RunWindow();
    if (wndw.GetButton() == YES) repeat = 0;
  }
  else PlaceCell(evntmsg);
}
```

This function simply checks each button control to see whether it has been selected and sends program execution to the appropriate function. If the user clicks the mouse button without selecting a control button, the `PlaceCell()` function checks whether the mouse click was in the grid:

```
void PlaceCell(EvntMsg evntmsg)
{
  if ((evntmsg.mx > 20) && (evntmsg.mx < 620) &&
      (evntmsg.my > 56) && (evntmsg.my < 390))
  {
    mouse.HideMouse();
    int col = (evntmsg.mx - 20) / 12;
    int row = (evntmsg.my - 56) / 12;
    if (!world[row][col])
    {
      setfillstyle(SOLID_FILL, GREEN);
      setcolor(RED);
```

167

```
        fillellipse(col*12+26, row*12+61, 4, 4);
        world[row][col] = ALIVE;
      }
      mouse.ShowMouse();
    }
}
```

If the click was in the grid, this function draws a cell in the appropriate location and sets that cell to ALIVE in the world array. Notice that the function turns off the mouse pointer before drawing on-screen.

 Note: You must always hide the mouse pointer before drawing to the screen, then restore the pointer immediately after the drawing is done.

If the user has selected the START button, the Life function, which is the main simulation loop, takes over:

```
void Life(void)
{
  mouse.ButtonUp();
  CreateLists();
  for (int g=0; g<generations; ++g)
  {
    delay(speed);
    UpdateGens(g);
    Live();
    Die();
    AddNbrs();
    SubNbrs();
    nextlive.TransferList(live);
    nextdie.TransferList(die);
    if (KeyEvent() ¦¦ mouse.Event())
    {
      mouse.ButtonUp();
      break;
    }
  }
}
```

This function performs the simulation by calling the functions that count cell neighbors, create cells, and kill cells. To get started, it waits for the user to release the mouse button (this prevents button *drop-throughs,* in which holding the button down too long causes new event messages to be sent), then calls CreateLists():

```
void CreateLists(void)
{
  int c, r;

  ReleaseNodes();
  for (c=0; c<MAXCOL; ++c)
    for (r=0; r<MAXROW; ++r)
    {
      nbrs[r](c) = 0;
      if (world[r](c) == ALIVE)
      live.MakeNewNode(c, r);
    }
  AddNbrs();
  for (c=0; c<MAXCOL; ++c)
    for (r=0; r<MAXROW; ++r)
      if (((nbrs[r](c) < 2) ¦¦ (nbrs[r](c) > 3))
          && (world[r](c) == ALIVE))
      nextdie.MakeNewNode(c, r);
  nextlive.TransferList(live);
  nextdie.TransferList(die);
}
```

This function is responsible for initializing live and die, the two linked lists that the simulation has to get started, as well as initializing the starting neighbor counts. The function first calls ReleaseNodes(), which simply makes sure that all lists are empty. (When the program begins, the lists are empty. But in subsequent calls to Life(), your linked lists probably won't be empty, because it is rare for every cell on-screen to be dead after the generations run out.):

```
void ReleaseNodes(void)
{
  live.ClearList();
  die.ClearList();
  nextlive.ClearList();
  nextdie.ClearList();
}
```

After clearing the lists, CreateLists() scans the newly created world array, creating a new node for each living cell in the array. As CreateLists() scans the world array, it also takes advantage of the loop to initialize all the neighbor counts in the nbrs array to zero. After creating the live linked list, it calls the AddNbrs() function, which updates the neighbor counts and creates a nextlive and nextdie array for cells that may (or may not) live and die in the next generation:

```
void AddNbrs(void)
{
  int xlow, xhigh, ylow, yhigh;
  int c, r;

  while (live.HasNodes())
  {
    live.GetNode(c, r);
    CalcLimits(c, r, xlow, xhigh, ylow, yhigh);
    for (int x=xlow; x<=xhigh; ++x)
      for (int y=ylow; y<=yhigh; ++y)
      if ((x != c) ¦¦ (y != r))
      {
        nbrs[y][x] += 1;
        switch (nbrs[y][x])
        {
          case 1, 2: break;
          case 3:
            if (world[y][x] == DEAD)
            nextlive.MakeNewNode(x, y);
            break;
          case 4:
            if (world[y][x] == ALIVE)
            nextdie.MakeNewNode(x, y);
            break;
          case 5, 6, 7, 8: break;
        }
      }
  }
}
```

As you can see, AddNbrs() scans the live list, which contains all the cells that have just come to life. The while loop iterates until this list has been emptied. It first gets the cell's coordinates by calling the list's GetNode() member function. (Remember: GetNode() also deletes the node.) It then calls the CalcLimits() function, which determines the minimum and maximum coordinates for cells adjacent to the live cell:

```
void CalcLimits(int c, int r, int &xlow, int &xhigh,
        int &ylow, int &yhigh)
{
  if (c == 0) xlow = 0;
    else xlow = c - 1;
  if (c == MAXCOL-1) xhigh = MAXCOL-1;
    else xhigh = c + 1;
  if (r == 0) ylow = 0;
    else ylow = r - 1;
  if (r == MAXROW-1) yhigh = MAXROW-1;
    else yhigh = r + 1;
}
```

This calculation must be done because cells on any edge of the grid do not have eight adjacent cells.

After calculating the coordinates, nested for loops increment the neighbor count for every adjacent cell. After incrementing a cell's neighbor count, the switch statement checks the count, adding new nodes to the nextlive or nextdie list, as appropriate. Keep in mind that the nodes on the list are only "maybes." That is, by adding nodes to these two lists, you are saying, "When I finish counting all neighbors, I will check these cells again to see whether they actually live or die." Not every cell on the nextlive list comes to life, and not every cell on the nextdie list dies. Some cells may appear in both lists at the same time. Using these temporary lists, you can keep track of cells that might change—without changing the grid, which, as you learned, can really mess up the simulation.

Getting back to CreateNodes(), after the call to AddNbrs(), the function must scan the neighbor counts, looking for cells with fewer than two neighbors. It adds these cells to the nextdie list that AddNbrs() started. Unfortunately, AddNbrs() finds only cells that are being crowded to death (have four or more neighbors), not those that are about to die of loneliness, which is why you must look for lonely cells in CreateNodes(). After building the nextlive and nextdie lists, CreateNodes() finally transfers them to the live and die lists, where Life() expects to find them.

When CreateLists() has finished initializing the starting lists, program execution goes back to Life() and enters the main simulation loop. This loop is controlled by a for statement that compares its loop variable against generations, which is the number of generations that the simulation runs. Inside the loop, Borland's delay() function is called using speed as its parameter. This single function call is all that's required to control the speed of the simulation. Life() then calls UpdateGens() to draw the new generation count on-screen.

At last you get to the meat of the simulation. After updating the generation count, Life() calls the Live() function (not to be confused with Life() or the live linked list), which checks all the nodes on the live list, bringing to life only the nodes that meet the requirements for life:

```
void Live(void)
{
  CList temp;
  int r, c;

  live.TransferList(temp);
  while(temp.HasNodes())
  {
    temp.GetNode(c, r);
    if ((world[r](c) == DEAD) &&
     (nbrs[r](c) == 3))
    {
      world[r](c) = ALIVE;
      mouse.HideMouse();
      setcolor(RED);
      setfillstyle(SOLID_FILL, LIGHTRED);
      fillellipse(c*12+26, r*12+61, 4, 4);
      mouse.ShowMouse();
      live.MakeNewNode(c, r);
    }
  }
}
```

Here, Live() takes that "maybe" list and separates the wheat from the chaff, as it were. Cells that don't meet the requirements for life are simply deleted from memory. Cells that do meet the requirements are added to the world array, drawn on-screen, and placed back on the live list so they can be counted in the next generation.

After calling Live() and handling the live list, Life() calls Die(), which is Live()'s counterpart:

```
void Die(void)
{
  CList temp;
  int c, r;

  die.TransferList(temp);
  while(temp.HasNodes())
```

```
    {
      temp.GetNode(c, r);
      if ((world[r](c) == ALIVE) &&
       (nbrs[r](c) != 2) &&
       (nbrs[r](c) != 3))
      {
        world[r](c) = DEAD;
        mouse.HideMouse();
        setcolor(LIGHTGRAY);
        setfillstyle(SOLID_FILL, LIGHTGRAY);
        fillellipse(c*12+26, r*12+61, 4, 4);
        mouse.ShowMouse();
        die.MakeNewNode(c, r);
      }
    }
}
```

Here, `Die()` checks the `die` list, killing the cells that meet the requirements for death and deleting from the list the cells that don't. Any cells that die are placed back on the `die` list, so they can be evaluated in the next generation.

Now that all the cells on the "maybe" lists have been processed, it's time to update the neighbor counts for all cells adjacent to any cells that were just created or killed, all of which are now in the `live` or `die` list. First, `Life()` handles the `live` list by calling `AddNbrs()`. You looked at this function already. Then, `Life()` calls `SubNbrs()`, which scans the `die` list, decrementing the neighbor counts for any cells adjacent to a cell that just died:

```
void SubNbrs(void)
{
  int xlow, xhigh, ylow, yhigh;
  int c, r;

  while (die.HasNodes())
  {
    die.GetNode(c, r);
    CalcLimits(c, r, xlow, xhigh, ylow, yhigh);
    for (int x=xlow; x<=xhigh; ++x)
      for (int y=ylow; y<=yhigh; ++y)
      if ((x != c) || (y != r))
      {
        nbrs[y][x] -= 1;
        switch (nbrs[y][x])
```

```
    {
      case 0: break;
      case 1:
        if (world[y][x] == ALIVE)
       nextdie.MakeNewNode(x, y);
        break;
      case 2: break;
      case 3:
        if (world[y][x] == DEAD)
       nextlive.MakeNewNode(x, y);
        break;
      case 4, 5, 6, 7: break;
    }
  }
 }
}
```

This function works similarly to its counterpart, `AddNbrs()`, except it processes the `die` list, adding to the `nextlive` list any cells that have three neighbors (even though the cells may not keep all three neighbors) and adding to the `nextdie` list any cells with fewer than two neighbors (even though the cell's final neighbor count may not qualify it to die). Remember, these are "maybe" lists.

After the neighbor counts are fully updated, `Life()` transfers the `nextlive` and `nextdie` lists to the `live` and `die` lists, respectively, and checks for a keyboard or mouse event. If an event is detected, the program breaks out of the loop with a `break` statement. Otherwise, execution goes back to the top of the loop for the next generation.

This leaves only three other functions to discuss: `GetGens()`, `GetSpeed()`, and `ClearWorld()`. The user activates any of these by clicking the appropriate command button on the button bar. Look at `GetGens()` first:

```
void GetGens(int &generations)
{
  InputWindw w("GENERATIONS", "Enter # of generations:",
              "(Max = 10,000)");;
  char inp[81];

  w.DrawWindow();
  w.RunWindow();
  if (w.GetButton() == 1)
  {
    w.GetInput(inp);
```

```
      generations = atoi(inp);
      if (generations < 1) generations = 100;
      if (generations > 10000) generations = 10000;
      sprintf(inp, "Generation #%d", generations);
      setfillstyle(SOLID_FILL, LIGHTGRAY);
      settextjustify(LEFT_TEXT, TOP_TEXT);
      bar(435, 431, 575, 441);
      setcolor(BROWN);
      outtextxy(435, 431, inp);
  }
}
```

This function is called when the user selects the GENER button. It creates and displays an input box for entering a new value for the maximum number of generations. The user's input is converted to an integer and compared against the generation's minimum and maximum values. Adjustments are made, if necessary, and the function displays the value on-screen. Notice that, because the w window is declared in the GetGens() function, it is deleted when the function ends, which is when the window goes out of scope and its destructor is called.

The function GetSpeed() works similarly:

```
void GetSpeed(int &speed)
{
  InputWindw w("SIMULATION SPEED", "Enter new speed:",
               "(Min=1  Max=10)");;
  char inp[81];

  w.DrawWindow();
  w.RunWindow();
  if (w.GetButton() == 1)
  {
    w.GetInput(inp);
    speed = atoi(inp);
    if (speed < 1) speed = 10;
    if (speed > 10) speed = 10;
    speed = (10 - speed) * 100;
  }
}
```

Using this function, which is called by selecting the SPEED button, the user can change the simulation's speed. Unlike GetGens(), the final chosen value is not displayed on-screen.

175

The last function is `ClearWorld()`:

```
void ClearWorld(void)
{
  mouse.HideMouse();
  for (int c=0; c<MAXCOL; ++c)
    for (int r=0; r<MAXROW; ++r)
      if (world[r](c) == ALIVE)
      {
    world[r](c) = DEAD;
    setfillstyle(SOLID_FILL, LIGHTGRAY);
    setcolor(LIGHTGRAY);
    fillellipse(c*12+26, r*12+61, 4, 4);
      }
  ReleaseNodes();
  mouse.ShowMouse();
}
```

This function returns the simulation to its start-up state, with all cells marked DEAD, the on-screen grid blank, and all cell lists emptied. This function is called when the user selects the CLEAR button.

Conclusion

The entire Life program is shown in Listing 5.7. Your author has spent far too many hours watching little creatures live and die on-screen. Time to get back to work.

There's probably much that can be done to speed up the simulation even more, but that's left to you. Experimenting with code, after all, is a great way to learn.

Listing 5.7. LIFE.CPP—Conway's Life program.

```
/////////////////////////////////////////////////////
// CONWAY'S LIFE
// by Clayton Walnum
// Written with Borland C++ 3.1
/////////////////////////////////////////////////////

#include <graphics.h>
#include <conio.h>
#include <iostream.h>
```

```
#include <stdlib.h>
#include <stdio.h>
#include <dos.h>

// Use mouse, window, and list classes.
#include "mous.h"
#include "windw.h"
#include "clist.h"
#include "event.h"

// Define global constants.
#define TRUE 1
#define FALSE 0
#define DEAD 0
#define ALIVE 1
#define MAXCOL 50
#define MAXROW 28

int mousex, mousey, // Mouse coordinates.
    repeat;         // Main program loop controller.
int generations,    // # of life generations.
    speed;          // Speed of simulation.

int world[MAXROW][MAXCOL], // Cell map.
    nbrs[MAXROW][MAXCOL];  // Neighbor count map.

// Linked lists.
CList live, die, nextlive, nextdie;

// Windows and controls for main screen.
CapWindw wnd1(0, 0, 639, 479, TRUE, FALSE, "CONWAY'S LIFE");
Windw wnd2(20, 409, 599, 50, FALSE, FALSE);
Windw wnd3(420, 419, 170, 32, FALSE, FALSE);;
Button startbut(30, 420, "^START");
Button clearbut(105, 420, "^CLEAR");
Button generatebut(180, 420, "^GENER");
Button speedbut(255, 420, "S^PEED");
Button quitbut(330, 420, "^QUIT");

// Event message structure.
EvntMsg evntmsg;
```

continues

177

Listing 5.7. Continued

```c
// Function prototypes.
int KeyEvent(void);
void GetEvent(EvntMsg &evntmsg);
void DispatchEvent(EvntMsg evntmsg);
void Life(void);
void CreateLists(void);
void ClearWorld(void);
void GetGens(int &generations);
void GetSpeed(int &speed);
void PlaceCell(EvntMsg evntmsg);
void Live(void);
void Die(void);
void AddNbrs(void);
void SubNbrs(void);
void CalcLimits(int c, int r, int &xlow, int &xhigh,
        int &ylow, int &yhigh);
void UpdateGens(int g);
void Init(void);
void ReleaseNodes(void);
void DrawScreen(void);
void InitMouse(void);
void Cleanup(void);

/////////////////////////////////////////////////////////
// Main program.
/////////////////////////////////////////////////////////
void main(void)
{
  // Initialize game, mouse, and screen.
  Init();
  DrawScreen();
  InitMouse();

  // Repeat event loop until Quit.
  repeat = 1;
  while (repeat)
  {
    GetEvent(evntmsg);
    DispatchEvent(evntmsg);
  }

  closegraph();
}
```

```
////////////////////////////////////////////////////////
// DispatchEvent()
//
// This function checks the current event message and
// branches to the function chosen by the user.
////////////////////////////////////////////////////////
void DispatchEvent(EvntMsg evntmsg)
{
  if ( startbut.Clicked(evntmsg) )
    Life();
  else if ( clearbut.Clicked(evntmsg) )
    ClearWorld();
  else if ( generatebut.Clicked(evntmsg) )
    GetGens(generations);
  else if ( speedbut.Clicked(evntmsg) )
    GetSpeed(speed);
  else if ( quitbut.Clicked(evntmsg) )
  {
    YesNoWindw wndw("QUIT", "Are you sure you",
             "want to quit?");
    wndw.DrawWindow();
    wndw.RunWindow();
    if (wndw.GetButton() == YES) repeat = 0;
  }
  else PlaceCell(evntmsg);
}


////////////////////////////////////////////////////////
// Life()
//
// This function is the simulation's main loop and is
// called when the user selects the Start button.
////////////////////////////////////////////////////////
void Life(void)
{
  mouse.ButtonUp();
  CreateLists();
  for (int g=0; g<generations; ++g)
  {
    delay(speed);
    UpdateGens(g);
    Live();
```

continues

179

Listing 5.7. Continued

```
      Die();
      AddNbrs();
      SubNbrs();
      nextlive.TransferList(live);
      nextdie.TransferList(die);
      if (KeyEvent() || mouse.Event())
      {
        mouse.ButtonUp();
        break;
      }
    }
}


/////////////////////////////////////////////////////////
// GetGens()
//
// This function creates a dialog box with which the
// user can change the number of generations to run
// in each cycle of the Life() function.
/////////////////////////////////////////////////////////
void GetGens(int &generations)
{
  InputWindw w("GENERATIONS", "Enter # of generations:",
              "(Max = 10,000)");;
  char inp[81];

  w.DrawWindow();
  w.RunWindow();
  if (w.GetButton() == 1)
  {
    w.GetInput(inp);
    generations = atoi(inp);
    if (generations < 1) generations = 100;
    if (generations > 10000) generations = 10000;
    sprintf(inp, "Generation #%d", generations);
    setfillstyle(SOLID_FILL, LIGHTGRAY);
    settextjustify(LEFT_TEXT, TOP_TEXT);
    bar(435, 431, 575, 441);
    setcolor(BROWN);
    outtextxy(435, 431, inp);
  }
}
```

```
/////////////////////////////////////////////////////
// GetSpeed()
//
// This function creates a dialog box with which the
// user can change the speed of the simulation.
/////////////////////////////////////////////////////
void GetSpeed(int &speed)
{
  InputWindw w("SIMULATION SPEED", "Enter new speed:",
               "(Min=1  Max=10)");;
  char inp[81];

  w.DrawWindow();
  w.RunWindow();
  if (w.GetButton() == 1)
  {
    w.GetInput(inp);
    speed = atoi(inp);
    if (speed < 1) speed = 10;
    if (speed > 10) speed = 10;
    speed = (10 - speed) * 100;
  }
}


/////////////////////////////////////////////////////
// ClearWorld()
//
// This function clears all cells from the map.
/////////////////////////////////////////////////////
void ClearWorld(void)
{
  mouse.HideMouse();
  for (int c=0; c<MAXCOL; ++c)
    for (int r=0; r<MAXROW; ++r)
      if (world[r](c) == ALIVE)
      {
      world[r](c) = DEAD;
      setfillstyle(SOLID_FILL, LIGHTGRAY);
      setcolor(LIGHTGRAY);
      fillellipse(c*12+26, r*12+61, 4, 4);
      }
  ReleaseNodes();
```

continues

181

Listing 5.7. Continued

```
  mouse.ShowMouse();
}


/////////////////////////////////////////////////////
// PlaceCell()
//
// This function places a cell on-screen where the
// user clicked the map.
/////////////////////////////////////////////////////
void PlaceCell(EvntMsg evntmsg)
{
  if ((evntmsg.mx > 20) && (evntmsg.mx < 620) &&
      (evntmsg.my > 56) && (evntmsg.my < 390))
  {
    mouse.HideMouse();
    int col = (evntmsg.mx - 20) / 12;
    int row = (evntmsg.my - 56) / 12;
    if (!world[row][col])
    {
      setfillstyle(SOLID_FILL, GREEN);
      setcolor(RED);
      fillellipse(col*12+26, row*12+61, 4, 4);
      world[row][col] = ALIVE;
    }
    mouse.ShowMouse();
  }
}


/////////////////////////////////////////////////////
// CreateLists()
//
// This function initializes the cell maps and linked
// lists for the Life() function.
/////////////////////////////////////////////////////
void CreateLists(void)
{
  int c, r;

  ReleaseNodes();
  for (c=0; c<MAXCOL; ++c)
    for (r=0; r<MAXROW; ++r)
```

```
        {
          nbrs[r](c) = 0;
          if (world[r](c) == ALIVE)
         live.MakeNewNode(c, r);
        }
      AddNbrs();
      for (c=0; c<MAXCOL; ++c)
        for (r=0; r<MAXROW; ++r)
          if (((nbrs[r](c) < 2) ¦¦ (nbrs[r](c) > 3))
              && (world[r](c) == ALIVE))
          nextdie.MakeNewNode(c, r);
      nextlive.TransferList(live);
      nextdie.TransferList(die);
    }


    ///////////////////////////////////////////////////////
    // Live()
    //
    // This function scans the live linked list and brings
    // to life any cell that fits the requirements for life.
    // Cells that come to life are placed back into the live
    // list. Cells that don't meet the requirements for life
    // are deleted.
    ///////////////////////////////////////////////////////
    void Live(void)
    {
      CList temp;
      int r, c;

      live.TransferList(temp);
      while(temp.HasNodes())
      {
        temp.GetNode(c, r);
        if ((world[r](c) == DEAD) &&
          (nbrs[r](c) == 3))
        {
          world[r](c) = ALIVE;
          mouse.HideMouse();
          setcolor(RED);
          setfillstyle(SOLID_FILL, LIGHTRED);
          fillellipse(c*12+26, r*12+61, 4, 4);
          mouse.ShowMouse();
```

continues

183

Listing 5.7. Continued

```
        live.MakeNewNode(c, r);
    }
  }
}


////////////////////////////////////////////////////////
// Die()
//
// This function scans the die linked list and kills
// any cell that fits the requirements for death.
// Cells that die are placed back into the die list.
// Cells that don't meet the requirements for death
// are deleted.
////////////////////////////////////////////////////////
void Die(void)
{
  CList temp;
  int c, r;

  die.TransferList(temp);
  while(temp.HasNodes())
  {
    temp.GetNode(c, r);
    if ((world[r](c) == ALIVE) &&
      (nbrs[r](c) != 2) &&
      (nbrs[r](c) != 3))
    {
      world[r](c) = DEAD;
      mouse.HideMouse();
      setcolor(LIGHTGRAY);
      setfillstyle(SOLID_FILL, LIGHTGRAY);
      fillellipse(c*12+26, r*12+61, 4, 4);
      mouse.ShowMouse();
      die.MakeNewNode(c, r);
    }
  }
}


////////////////////////////////////////////////////////
// AddNbrs()
//
// This function increments the neighbor count of every
```

```
// cell adjacent to a cell that has just come to life.
// Cells that might come to life in the next generation
// are added to the nextlive list, and cells that might
// die in the next generation are added to the nextdie
// list. This function leaves the live list empty.
/////////////////////////////////////////////////////
void AddNbrs(void)
{
  int xlow, xhigh, ylow, yhigh;
  int c, r;

  while (live.HasNodes())
  {
    live.GetNode(c, r);
    CalcLimits(c, r, xlow, xhigh, ylow, yhigh);
    for (int x=xlow; x<=xhigh; ++x)
      for (int y=ylow; y<=yhigh; ++y)
      if ((x != c) ¦¦ (y != r))
      {
        nbrs[y][x] += 1;
        switch (nbrs[y][x])
        {
          case 1, 2: break;
          case 3:
            if (world[y][x] == DEAD)
           nextlive.MakeNewNode(x, y);
            break;
          case 4:
            if (world[y][x] == ALIVE)
           nextdie.MakeNewNode(x, y);
            break;
          case 5, 6, 7, 8: break;
        }
      }
  }
}


/////////////////////////////////////////////////////
// SubNbrs()
//
// This function decrements the neighbor count of every
// cell adjacent to a cell that has just died. Cells
```

continues

185

Listing 5.7. Continued

```
// that might die in the next generation are added to
// the nextdie list, and cells that might come to life
// in the next generation are added to the nextlive list.
// This function leaves the die list empty.
//////////////////////////////////////////////////////////
void SubNbrs(void)
{
  int xlow, xhigh, ylow, yhigh;
  int c, r;

  while (die.HasNodes())
  {
    die.GetNode(c, r);
    CalcLimits(c, r, xlow, xhigh, ylow, yhigh);
    for (int x=xlow; x<=xhigh; ++x)
      for (int y=ylow; y<=yhigh; ++y)
      if ((x != c) || (y != r))
      {
        nbrs[y][x] -= 1;
        switch (nbrs[y][x])
        {
          case 0: break;
          case 1:
            if (world[y][x] == ALIVE)
            nextdie.MakeNewNode(x, y);
            break;
          case 2: break;
          case 3:
            if (world[y][x] == DEAD)
            nextlive.MakeNewNode(x, y);
            break;
          case 4, 5, 6, 7: break;
        }
      }
  }
}


//////////////////////////////////////////////////////////
// CalcLimits()
//
// This function calculates the beginning and ending
// columns and rows to be checked by the AddNbrs() and
```

```
// SubNbrs() functions.
///////////////////////////////////////////////////////////
void CalcLimits(int c, int r, int &xlow, int &xhigh,
          int &ylow, int &yhigh)
{
  if (c == 0) xlow = 0;
    else xlow = c - 1;
  if (c == MAXCOL-1) xhigh = MAXCOL-1;
    else xhigh = c + 1;
  if (r == 0) ylow = 0;
    else ylow = r - 1;
  if (r == MAXROW-1) yhigh = MAXROW-1;
    else yhigh = r + 1;
}


///////////////////////////////////////////////////////////
// UpdateGens()
//
// This function draws the generation count on the
// screen.
///////////////////////////////////////////////////////////
void UpdateGens(int g)
{
  char s[10];

  mouse.HideMouse();
  setcolor(BROWN);
  setfillstyle(SOLID_FILL, LIGHTGRAY);
  bar(531, 431, 580, 439);
  sprintf(s, "%d", g+1);
  outtextxy(531, 431, s);
  mouse.ShowMouse();
}


///////////////////////////////////////////////////////////
// Init()
//
// This function performs general program initialization,
// initializing the graphics driver, setting all cells
// in the map to their DEAD state, and setting the
// default simulation speed and number of generations.
///////////////////////////////////////////////////////////
```

continues

187

Listing 5.7. Continued

```cpp
void Init(void)
{
  int gdriver = VGA, gmode = VGAHI, errorcode;

  errorcode = registerbgidriver(EGAVGA_driver);
  if (errorcode < 0)
  {
    cout << "Graphics not initialized: " << errorcode << '\n';
    cout << "Press any key.";
    getch();
    abort();
  }

  initgraph(&gdriver, &gmode, "");
  if ( (errorcode = graphresult()) != grOk)
  {
    cout << "Graphics not initialized: " << errorcode << '\n';
    cout << "Press any key.";
    getch();
    abort();
  }
  for (int r=0; r<MAXROW; ++r)
    for (int c=0; c<MAXCOL; ++c)
      world[r](c) = DEAD;
  generations = 100;
  speed = 1;
}


//////////////////////////////////////////////////////
// DrawScreen()
//
// This function draws the main screen.
//////////////////////////////////////////////////////
void DrawScreen(void)
{
  wnd1.DrawWindow();
  wnd2.DrawWindow();
  wnd3.DrawWindow();
  startbut.DrawWindow();
  clearbut.DrawWindow();
  generatebut.DrawWindow();
  speedbut.DrawWindow();
```

```
  quitbut.DrawWindow();
  setcolor(BLUE);
    for (int y=55; y<400; y+=12)
    {
      moveto(20, y); lineto(getmaxx()-20, y);
    }
    for (int x=20; x<630; x+=12 )
    {
      moveto(x, 55); lineto(x, 391);
    }
  setcolor(BROWN);
  outtextxy(435, 431, "Generation #100");
}


//////////////////////////////////////////////////////
// InitMouse()
//
// This function initializes the user's mouse.
//////////////////////////////////////////////////////
void InitMouse(void) {
  if (!mouse.GotMouse()) {
    cout << "You have no mouse.\n";
    cout << "Press any key.";
    getch();
  }
  mouse.SetLimits(0,getmaxx(),0,getmaxy());
  mouse.ShowMouse();
}


//////////////////////////////////////////////////////
// ReleaseNodes()
//
// This function deletes all nodes from the linked
// lists.
//////////////////////////////////////////////////////
void ReleaseNodes(void)
{
  live.ClearList();
  die.ClearList();
  nextlive.ClearList();
  nextdie.ClearList();
}
```

6

An Introduction to Recursion

During your programming career, you've probably heard the words "divide and conquer" as often as a mouse hunts for food. This is because experienced programmers know that writing a large program can be a psychologically draining challenge. When you think about all that goes into a full-length program, it's easy to become overwhelmed by the magnitude of the job. So, just as you read a book page by page or clean a house room by room, you write a program one function at a time. In this way, you can understand a huge task that might otherwise be beyond your abilities to grasp as a whole.

You can adopt the divide-and-conquer strategy in several ways, including using object-oriented programming and structured programming. *Recursion,* the subject of this chapter, is another technique you can use to break complex tasks into their components. Using recursion, you can take a repetitive task and reduce it to a single step that is repeated again and again until you obtain the desired result.

In this chapter, you learn what recursion is and how it can be used to replace complex code with short and elegant functions. You also use recursion in a full-length program, thus applying what you've learned to a practical case. In this program (a game!), you also learn more about object-oriented program design by using inheritance with your window library to create a new kind of interactive button.

Recursion: Barrels Within Barrels

When I was a kid, one of my favorite toys was a bunch of nested plastic barrels. I'd unscrew the first barrel, only to find a smaller one inside. In that barrel was yet another smaller barrel, and so on. Finally, in the tiniest barrel, was a small plastic rabbit. I spent hours fascinated with those barrels.

Recursion fascinates me in the same way, probably because recursion is a lot like those nested barrels. With recursion, you work your way deeper and deeper into an operation until you finally find that little bunny—the result of the operation you're trying to perform. Using recursion, complex operations can be programmed in only a few lines of code.

But what exactly is recursion? In a program, recursion occurs when a function calls itself. This may sound a little crazy. Why would a function want to call itself? When you called a function in past programs, you expected the function to do its job and return. With recursion, though, you must think about functions differently. Rather than finishing a job, a recursive function does only a small portion of the task and passes what's left to another call to itself.

The simplest recursive function looks something like this:

```
void Recursive(void)
{
  Recursive();
}
```

This function accomplishes nothing. Worse, it's an infinite loop. The `Recursive()` function is called again and again, until, finally, you run out of stack space. For a recursive function to operate correctly, it needs some way to break out of the recursion. A more useful template for a recursive function is

```
void Recursive(void)
{
  if (condition) return;
```

```
    else Recursive();
}
```

Here, when `condition` equals true, you return immediately rather than call `Recursive()` again. After breaking out of the recursion, previous calls to `Recursive()`—all of which have already executed their last statement (the `else` statement)—also return, until you finally return to the original call to `Recursive()`.

This last example function doesn't accomplish much, but it does illustrate the most important elements of a recursive function, as follows:

- A recursive function calls itself.

- A recursive function must contain a conditional statement that breaks the recursive cycle.

A Real-World Example

Now, how about an example that does something? If you consider those little barrels mentioned in the last section, you might see how recursion can simplify a programming task. To get to the bunny in those barrels, a child must open barrels, one after another, until she or he reaches the last one. Opening a single barrel is only a small part of the entire task. After the first barrel is opened, the same function must be performed on the remaining barrels.

Think of barrel-opening as a function in a program. In fact, you can do more than think about it, you can learn how to write it. Listing 6.1 is a program that simulates the bunny-in-barrels toy.

Listing 6.1. BARRELS.CPP—the bunny-in-barrels program.

```cpp
#include <iostream.h>
#include <conio.h>

void OpenBarrel(int num)
{
  if (num == 0) cout << "Got the bunny!" << '\n';
  else
  {
```

continues

193

Listing 6.1. Continued

```
    cout << "Opening barrel #" << num << '\n';
    OpenBarrel(num-1);
  }
}

void main(void)
{
  OpenBarrel(10);
  getch();
}
```

When you compile and run the program, you see the following output:

```
Opening barrel #10
Opening barrel #9
Opening barrel #8
Opening barrel #7
Opening barrel #6
Opening barrel #5
Opening barrel #4
Opening barrel #3
Opening barrel #2
Opening barrel #1
Got the bunny!
```

In the main program, OpenBarrel() is called with a parameter of 10. (This parameter indicates the number of barrels and can be any integer.) In OpenBarrel(), the value of num is first checked to determine whether the program has reached the last barrel. If it has, it prints the Got the bunny! message. Otherwise, the program calls OpenBarrel() again with a parameter of num-1. This call invokes OpenBarrel() a second time—before the first invocation has ended—with a value of 9. This second invocation checks the value of num, finds it to be 9, and calls OpenBarrel() a third time, this time with a value of 8. This process continues until a call to OpenBarrel() gets a value of 0 for num.

 Note: Each invocation of OpenBarrel() has its own num variable. The num variable for the first invocation is not the same num you use in the second invocation. This is important to understand, because this series of values eventually breaks the program out of the recursion.

A Power Function

Although the bunny-in-barrels program illustrates recursion well by simulating an easy-to-grasp, real-world problem, it doesn't show how you might use recursion in your programs. It's unlikely that you'll ever need to write programs about bunnies and barrels. So, take a look at a recursive function that accomplishes something worthwhile, but is still as easy to understand as the barrel program.

Consider the value 10^3. The result of the exponentiation is calculated by multiplying 10 by itself three times: 10*10*10. You can use a `for` loop to calculate this value, but that's much too pedestrian for power programmers. Instead, you can perform this multiplication operation recursively. Listing 6.2 includes a recursive function, `Power()`, which calculates the value of any integer raised to a positive integer exponent.

Listing 6.2. POWER.CPP—a recursive exponentiation example.

```cpp
#include <iostream.h>
#include <conio.h>

int Power(int num, int exp)
{
  if (exp == 1) return num;
  else return num * Power(num, exp-1);
}

void main(void)
{
  cout << Power(10,3) << '\n';
  getch();
}
```

Examine this short program carefully. Although the `Power()` function is only a few lines long, a lot more is going on than may at first be apparent. Basically, this function repeatedly calls itself with smaller and smaller values of `exp`, until `exp` equals 1. At this point, instead of calling itself again, `Power()` simply returns the value `num`. (In the 10^3 example, `num` would be 10.) Notice that no calculations are performed until the recursion is as deep as it can go. Then it returns

10 to the previous invocation of Power(), which multiplies that return value by 10. The result (100) is passed to the first invocation, which also multiplies it by 10—the final result being 1000.

Confused? Figure 6.1 will help dispel the mystery. Starting at the top of the figure, Power() is called with the parameters 10 and 3. In the first call to Power(), the if statement examines exp and finds it to be 3, so the else statement executes. In the else statement, num is multiplied by the value returned from Power(num, exp-1).

The function can't perform the multiplication until it gets a return value from Power(), however, so it drops down to the second call to Power(), which gets the parameters 10 and 2. Again, the if statement is evaluated and program execution drops down to the else statement, which multiplies num by yet another call to Power(), this time with the parameters 10 and 1.

This brings the program to the third call to Power(), shown in the bottom box. This call gets the parameters 10 and 1. This time the if statement finds that exp is 1, so it immediately returns the value of num, which in this case is 10.

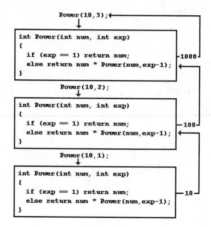

Figure 6.1. Solving 10^3 recursively.

Notice that the program has performed no multiplication operations, because it has had no result from Power(). Instead, it has simply called Power() exp times. The multiplication takes place as the program works its way back out of the recursions. The third recursion returns 10 to the second recursion, where this 10 is multiplied by num. The result of 100 is returned to the first call to Power(), which also multiplies the result by num. The result of 1000 is finally returned to your original call.

Recursion and the Stack

As you shall soon see, recursion is useful for more than solving simple mathematical problems. Recursion is also used in sorting routines, tree-traversal routines, parsing and solving complex mathematical expressions, disk directory management, and much more. In this chapter, you examine a tree-traversal routine. In Chapter 7, you use recursion to parse and evaluate formulas. But first you have to know how recursive routines affect the stack and how this can get you into trouble.

Earlier in this chapter, you looked at a simple recursive function that ran endlessly because there was no way to break out of the recursion. This function called itself repeatedly until it ran out of stack space. What does the stack have to do with recursion?

Every time a function is called, certain values are placed on the stack. These values are part of something called a *stack frame*. They include the parameters being passed to the particular function and the address to which the program should return after the function ends. The stack has only a limited amount of space, so it can hold only so many stack frames. When a recursive function calls itself too often, the stack fills with stack frames, until no space is left. And when the stack overflows, the program drops dead.

Listing 6.3 is a program that calls a recursive function containing no conditional with which to break out of the recursion. Each invocation of the `Recursive()` function prints the call number on-screen, so you can see that the program is actually doing something.

Listing 6.3. STACK1.CPP—version 1 of the stack-overflow program.

```cpp
#include <iostream.h>

void Recursive(int c)
{
  cout << c << ' ';
  Recursive(c+1);
}

void main(void)
{
  Recursive(1);
}
```

If you run this program, you see that it calls `Recursive()` approximately 8000 times before it runs out of stack space.

 Caution: You should compile this program with stack-overflow checking turned on. You can find this option in the Options/Compiler/Entry Exit menu. If you run the program without stack checking, you will have to reboot your computer.

Listing 6.4 is the same program, only this time the `Recursive()` function takes three parameters instead of one. By having more parameters, a call to `Recursive()` generates larger stack frames. Each call uses more stack space, so this program can call the function only about 5000 times before it runs out of stack space.

Listing 6.4. STACK2.CPP—version 2 of the stack-overflow program.

```
#include <iostream.h>

void Recursive(int c, int c2, int c3)
{
  cout << c << ' ';
  Recursive(c+1, c2, c3);
}

void main(void)
{
  Recursive(1, 1, 1);
}
```

As you already know, every recursive function needs a conditional statement that eventually ends the recursion, something Listings 6.3 and 6.4 are missing. Listing 6.5 adds a conditional statement that allows only 5000 recursions.

Listing 6.5. STACK3.CPP—version 3 of the stack-overflow program.

```
#include <iostream.h>

void Recursive(int c, int c2, int c3)
{
  cout << c << ' ';
```

```
  if (c==5000) return;
  Recursive(c+1, c2, c3);
}

void main(void)
{
  Recursive(1, 1, 1);
}
```

Does this solve your stack problem? Yes and no. As long as you don't change the size of the stack or add additional parameters to the `Recursive()` function, you should have no trouble with the stack. Listing 6.6 shows that adding even a single integer parameter can get you into trouble by overflowing the stack.

Listing 6.6. STACK4.CPP—version 4 of the stack-overflow program.

```
#include <iostream.h>

void Recursive(int c, int c2, int c3, int c4)
{
  cout << c << ' ';
  if (c>5000) return;
  Recursive(c+1, c2, c3, c4);
}

void main(void)
{
  Recursive(1, 1, 1, 1);
}
```

 Caution: Always be aware that you place a lot of data on the stack when using recursive routines. Moreover, the more parameters required by the recursive routines, the fewer number of stack frames fit on the stack, which limits even further the number of recursive calls you can make. To avoid stack problems, recursive functions should use as few parameters as possible. Be especially careful of passing large data structures such as arrays as parameters in a recursive function. If you have to use a large data structure as a parameter to a recursive function, pass it *by reference* (which passes only the data's address), not *by value* (which passes the contents of the entire data structure).

199

An Example Application: Trap Hunt

That takes care of all the work. Now you can have a little fun. Listing 6.7 is a puzzle game called *Trap Hunt*, shown in Figure 6.2. When you compile and run the program, the main screen appears with 400 buttons in a 25x16 grid. To win the game, you must find the 60 traps hidden under these buttons.

Figure 6.2. The Trap Hunt game board.

Listing 6.7. TRAPHUNT.CPP—the Trap Hunt program.

```
/////////////////////////////////////////////////////////
// TRAP HUNT
// by Clayton Walnum
// Written with Borland C++ 3.1
/////////////////////////////////////////////////////////

#include <stdlib.h>
#include <graphics.h>
#include <iostream.h>
#include <conio.h>
#include <dos.h>
```

```
#include "windw.h"
#include "event.h"
#include "mous.h"
#include "butn.h"

#define TRUE        1
#define FALSE       0
#define TRAP        -1   // Value for a trap square.
#define BLANK       0    // Value for a blank square.
#define TRAP_CNT    60   // # of traps on the board.
#define MAXCOLS     25   // # of columns on the board.
#define MAXROWS     16   // # of rows on the board.
#define XOFF        44   // Offset from left of first button.
#define YOFF        60   // Offset from top of first button.

// Game board array.
int board[MAXROWS][MAXCOLS];

// Numbers for marking numbered squares.
char *numbrs[5] = {"1", "2", "3", "4"};

int repeat,        // Controls main game loop.
    buttons_left,  // # of unpressed buttons on the board.
    butn_num,      // Total # of buttons on the board
    mark_cnt,      // # of marked buttons.
    good_marks;    // # of correctly marked buttons.

EvntMsg evntmsg;

// Function prototypes.
int KeyEvent(void);
void GetEvent(EvntMsg &evntmsg);
void DispatchEvent(EvntMsg evntmsg);
void CheckButton(EvntMsg evntmsg);
void ShowSquare(int x, int y);
void DoBlanks(int x, int y);
void Check4Blank(int x, int y);
void Init(void);
void Start(void);
void InitMouse(void);
void DrawScreen(void);
```

continues

Listing 6.7. Continued

```
void PlaceTraps(void);
void PlaceCounts(void);
void DrawNumbers (int x, int y);
void DeleteButns(void);
void FallIntoTrap(int x, int y);
void ShowBoard(void);
void GameOver(void);
void DrawTrap(int c, int r);
void DrawNoTrap(int c, int r);
void MarkButn(int x, int y);
int CountTraps(int c, int r);

// Array of button pointers for game board.
Butn *butn[MAXCOLS*MAXROWS];

// Display windows and buttons.
CapWindw wnd1(0, 0, 639, 479, TRUE, FALSE, "TRAP HUNT");
Button butn1(528, 425, "^QUIT");
Button butn2(450, 425, "^START");

/////////////////////////////////////////////////////
// Main program.
/////////////////////////////////////////////////////
void main(void)
{
  // Initialize game, mouse, and screen.
  Init();

  // Repeat event loop until Quit.
  repeat = TRUE;
  while (repeat)
  {
    if ((buttons_left == 0) || (mark_cnt == TRAP_CNT))
      GameOver();
    GetEvent(evntmsg);
    DispatchEvent(evntmsg);
  }
  DeleteButns();
  closegraph();
}
```

```
////////////////////////////////////////////////////
// Init()
//
// This function performs general program initialization.
// It initializes the graphics driver and mouse, then
// calls the Start() function, which initializes a
// new game.
////////////////////////////////////////////////////
void Init(void)
{
  int gdriver = VGA, gmode = VGAHI, errorcode;

  errorcode = registerbgidriver(EGAVGA_driver);
  if (errorcode < 0)
  {
    cout << "Graphics not initialized: " << errorcode << '\n';
    cout << "Press any key.";
    getch();
    abort();
  }
  initgraph(&gdriver, &gmode, "");
  if ( (errorcode = graphresult()) != grOk)
  {
    cout << "Graphics not initialized: " << errorcode << '\n';
    cout << "Press any key.";
    getch();
    abort();
  }
  InitMouse();
  Start();
}


////////////////////////////////////////////////////
// DispatchEvent()
//
// This function checks the current event message and
// branches to the function chosen by the user.
////////////////////////////////////////////////////
void DispatchEvent(EvntMsg evntmsg)
{
  mouse.ButtonUp();
```

continues

Listing 6.7. Continued

```
// Check whether START button was clicked.
if (butn1.Clicked(evntmsg))
  repeat = FALSE;

// Check whether QUIT button was pressed.
else if (butn2.Clicked(evntmsg))
{
  DeleteButns();
  Start();
}

// Cycle through all the buttons on the board
// to check whether one has been pressed.
else
  for (int bn=0; bn<butn_num; ++bn)
    if ( !butn[bn]->Pressed())
    if (butn[bn]->Clicked(evntmsg))
      CheckButton(evntmsg);
}


//////////////////////////////////////////////////////
// GameOver()
//
// This function is called when the player finds all
// the traps on the board or marks the maximum number
// of buttons allowed. It displays a dialog box and
// then resets the variables buttons_left and mark_cnt
// to prevent main() from calling GameOver() again.
//////////////////////////////////////////////////////
void GameOver(void)
{
  // If all the buttons have been pressed or the number
  // of correctly marked buttons matches the number of
  // traps, the player has won the game.
  if ((buttons_left == 0) ¦¦ (good_marks == TRAP_CNT))
  {
    OKWindw wndw("YOU WIN!", "Congratulations! You",
                 "found all the traps.");
    wndw.DrawWindow();
    wndw.RunWindow();
  }
```

```
    // Otherwise, the player loses, because he or she
    // has used up all marks without marking the
    // correct buttons.
    else
    {
      OKWindw *wndw = new OKWindw ("YOU LOSE",
             "You've marked the maximum",
             "number of buttons.");
      wndw->DrawWindow();
      wndw->RunWindow();
      delete wndw;
      ShowBoard();
    }

    // These variables are reset so the main game
    // loop will not recall this function.
    buttons_left = MAXCOLS * MAXROWS;
    mark_cnt = 0;
}

///////////////////////////////////////////////////////
// Start()
//
// This function initializes all variables needed to
// begin a new game, including setting the playing board
// to all blanks, calling the functions that place and
// count the traps, and calling the function that draws
// the main screen.
///////////////////////////////////////////////////////
void Start(void)
{
  // Initialize the random-number generator.
  randomize();

  // Set the entire game board to blanks.
  for ( int col=0; col<MAXCOLS; ++col )
    for ( int row=0; row<MAXROWS; ++row )
      board[row][col] = BLANK;

  // Place traps and numbers on game board.
  PlaceTraps ();
  PlaceCounts ();
```

continues

Listing 6.7. Continued

```
  // Draw game screen and init some variables.
  DrawScreen();
  buttons_left = MAXCOLS * MAXROWS;
  mark_cnt = good_marks = 0;
}


/////////////////////////////////////////////////////
// CheckButton()
//
// This function checks to see what is beneath the
// selected button, calling the appropriate function
// to display the part of the puzzle chosen.
/////////////////////////////////////////////////////
void CheckButton(EvntMsg evntmsg)
{
  // Translate mouse-button coords to column and
  // row coords for the playing board.
  int x = (evntmsg.mx - XOFF) / 22;
  int y = (evntmsg.my - YOFF) / 22;

  // If right mouse button pressed, mark
  // clicked button for a trap...
  if (evntmsg.button == RIGHT)
  {
    butn[y*MAXCOLS+x]->MarkButton();
    buttons_left -= 1;
    mark_cnt += 1;
    if (board[y][x] == TRAP)
      good_marks += 1;
  }

  // ...or if button pressed hides a trap, end game...
  else if (board[y][x] == TRAP)
    FallIntoTrap(x, y);

  // ...or else show what's under the square.
  else ShowSquare(x, y);
}


/////////////////////////////////////////////////////
// FallIntoTrap()
//
```

```
// This function is called when the player selects a
// button hiding a trap. It first displays a dialog
// box, informing the player of the mistake, then
// reveals all the squares on the board.
////////////////////////////////////////////////////
void FallIntoTrap(int x, int y)
{
  // Draw trap image.
  DrawTrap(x, y);

  // Display and run dialog box.
  OKWindw *wndw = new OKWindw ("YOU LOSE",
        "Whoops! You fell", "into a trap!");
  wndw->DrawWindow();
  wndw->RunWindow();
  delete wndw;

  // Reveal all the squares on the board.
  ShowBoard();
}


////////////////////////////////////////////////////
// ShowSquare()
//
// This function shows the contents of the selected
// square. If the square is blank, the recursive
// function DoBlanks() is called to show all the blank
// squares connected to the selected square.
////////////////////////////////////////////////////
void ShowSquare (int x, int y)
{
  int b = board[y][x];

  // If the square contains a blank, call the
  // function to show all connecting blanks.
  if (!b) DoBlanks(x, y);

  // Otherwise show the square's number.
  else DrawNumbers(x, y);
}
```

continues

207

Listing 6.7. Continued

```
////////////////////////////////////////////////////////
// ShowBoard()
//
// This function reveals all the squares on the board.
////////////////////////////////////////////////////////
void ShowBoard(void)
{
  // Cycle through all the buttons on the board.
  for (int c=0; c<MAXCOLS; ++c)
    for (int r=0; r<MAXROWS; ++r)
    {
      // If the square contains a trap and the
      // button was not marked, show the trap.
      if ((board[r](c)==TRAP) && (!butn[r*MAXCOLS+c]->Marked()))
      DrawTrap(c, r);

      // If the button is marked, but the square doesn't
      // contain a trap, display the error symbol.
      else if ((butn[r*MAXCOLS+c]->Marked()) &&
              (board[r](c)!=TRAP))
      DrawNoTrap(c, r);

      // If the square contains a number, show it.
      else if (board[r](c) > 0)
      DrawNumbers(c, r);

      // If the square contains a blank, show it.
      else if (board[r](c) == 0)
      butn[r*MAXCOLS+c]->PressButton();
    }
}


////////////////////////////////////////////////////////
// DoBlanks()
//
// This function reveals all the blank squares
// connected to a selected square.
////////////////////////////////////////////////////////
void DoBlanks (int x, int y)
{
  butn[y*MAXCOLS+x]->PressButton();
  buttons_left -= 1;
```

```
  // Move one square up.
  if (y != 0)
    Check4Blank(x, y-1);

  // Move one square up and to the right.
  if ((y != 0) && (x != MAXCOLS-1))
    Check4Blank(x+1, y-1);

  // Move one square right.
  if (x != MAXCOLS-1)
    Check4Blank(x+1, y);

  // Move one square down and to the right.
  if ((y != MAXROWS-1) && (x != MAXCOLS-1))
    Check4Blank(x+1, y+1);

  // Move one square down.
  if (y != MAXROWS-1)
    Check4Blank(x, y+1);

  // Move one square down and to the left.
  if ((y != MAXROWS-1) && (x != 0))
    Check4Blank(x-1, y+1);

  // Move one square left.
  if (x != 0)
    Check4Blank(x-1, y);

  // Move one square up and to the left.
  if ((y != 0) && (x != 0))
    Check4Blank(x-1, y-1);
}


/////////////////////////////////////////////////
// Check4Blank()
//
// This function checks the square at x,y for a blank.
// If it finds one, it makes a recursive call to
// DoBlanks() to traverse all the blank squares in the
// current direction. If the square is not a blank, it
// calls DrawNumbers() to reveal the contents of the
// square.
/////////////////////////////////////////////////
void Check4Blank(int x, int y)
```

continues

Listing 6.7. Continued

```
{
  if ((board[y][x] == BLANK) &&
      (!butn[y*MAXCOLS+x]->Pressed()))
    DoBlanks (x, y);
  else if ((!butn[y*MAXCOLS+x]->Pressed()) &&
        (!butn[y*MAXCOLS+x]->Marked()))
    DrawNumbers (x, y);
}


////////////////////////////////////////////////////
// DrawTrap()
//
// This function draws the image that represents a trap.
////////////////////////////////////////////////////
void DrawTrap(int c, int r)
{
  butn[r*MAXCOLS+c]->PressButton();
  setcolor(RED);
  setfillstyle(SOLID_FILL, BLACK);
  setlinestyle(SOLID_LINE, 0, NORM_WIDTH);
  int sx = c*22+XOFF;
  int sy = r*22+YOFF;
  mouse.HideMouse();
  fillellipse(sx+10, sy+10, 6, 6);
  mouse.ShowMouse();
}


////////////////////////////////////////////////////
// DrawNoTrap()
//
// This function draws the image that represents an
// incorrect trap-marked square.
////////////////////////////////////////////////////
void DrawNoTrap(int c, int r)
{
  butn[r*MAXCOLS+c]->PressButton();
  setlinestyle(SOLID_LINE, 0, THICK_WIDTH);
  setcolor(RED);
  int sx = (c*22)+XOFF;
  int sy = (r*22)+YOFF;
  circle(sx+10, sy+10, 8);
  moveto(sx+4, sy+4);
  lineto(sx+16, sy+17);
}
```

210

```
/////////////////////////////////////////////////////
// DrawNumbers()
//
// This function is called when the player selects a
// square containing a number. It draws the square and
// its number.
/////////////////////////////////////////////////////
void DrawNumbers (int x, int y)
{
  butn[y*MAXCOLS+x]->PressButton();
  setcolor(BLUE);
  int n = board[y][x];
  int sx = (x*22) + XOFF;
  int sy = (y*22) + YOFF;
  mouse.HideMouse();
  outtextxy(sx+7, sy+7, numbrs[n-1]);
  mouse.ShowMouse();
  buttons_left -= 1;
}


/////////////////////////////////////////////////////
// DrawScreen()
//
// This function draws the main screen.
/////////////////////////////////////////////////////
void DrawScreen(void)
{
  // Draw main display.
  wnd1.DrawWindow();
  butn1.DrawWindow();
  butn2.DrawWindow();

  // Create and display all the game-board buttons.
  butn_num = 0;
  for (int y=0; y<MAXROWS; ++y)
    for (int x=0; x<MAXCOLS; ++x)
    {
      butn[butn_num] = new Butn(x*22+XOFF, y*22+YOFF);
      butn[butn_num]->DrawWindow();
      ++butn_num;
    }
}
```

continues

211

Listing 6.7. Continued

```
///////////////////////////////////////////////////////
// PlaceTraps()
//
// This function places traps on an empty playing board.
// The traps are placed so that no more than four traps
// are adjacent to any square.
///////////////////////////////////////////////////////
void PlaceTraps(void)
{
  int n;

  // Loop for each trap on the board.
  for ( int z=0; z<TRAP_CNT; ++z )
  {
    int okay = FALSE;

    // The while loop will repeat until the
    // trap is properly placed.
    while (!okay)
    {
      // Get a random column and row for the trap.
      int c = random(MAXCOLS);
      int r = random(MAXROWS);

      // If there isn't already a trap at this
      // location, calculate the maximum and minimum
      // coordinates for every square adjacent to
      // this one.
      if (board[r](c) != TRAP)
      {
      int yl = r - 1;
      int yh = r + 1;
      int xl = c - 1;
      int xh = c + 1;
      if (xl == -1) xl = 0;
      if (xh == MAXCOLS) xh = MAXCOLS-1;
      if (yl == -1) yl = 0;
      if (yh == MAXROWS) yh = MAXROWS-1;

      okay = TRUE;
```

```
        // Count the traps surrounding every adjacent
        // square to be sure that no trap count goes
        // over four.
        for (int y=yl; y<yh+1; ++y )
          for (int x=xl; x<xh+1; ++x )
          {
            n = CountTraps(x, y);
            if (n > 3) okay = FALSE;
          }

          // If all trap counts are low enough,
          // place the trap.
          if (okay) board[r](c) = TRAP;
      }
    }
  }
}


///////////////////////////////////////////////////////
// PlaceCounts()
//
// This function counts the number of traps adjacent to
// each square on the board.
///////////////////////////////////////////////////////
void PlaceCounts(void)
{
   // Cycle through every square on the board,
   // counting adjacent traps.
   for ( int row=0; row<MAXROWS; ++row )
     for ( int col=0; col<MAXCOLS; ++col )
       if ( board[row][col] != TRAP )
         board[row][col] = CountTraps(col, row);
}


///////////////////////////////////////////////////////
// CountTraps()
//
// This function counts the traps adjacent to the square
// located at c,r.
///////////////////////////////////////////////////////
int CountTraps(int c, int r)
{
```

continues

213

Listing 6.7. Continued

```
  // Calculate the minimum and maximum coords
  // for every square adjacent to the one you're
  // checking.
  int yl = r - 1;
  int yh = r + 1;
  int xl = c - 1;
  int xh = c + 1;
  if (xl == -1) xl = 0;
  if (xh == MAXCOLS) xh = MAXCOLS-1;
  if (yl == -1) yl = 0;
  if (yh == MAXROWS) yh = MAXROWS-1;

  // Count all traps in adjacent squares.
  int count = 0;
  for (int y=yl; y<yh+1; ++y)
    for (int x=xl; x<xh+1; ++x)
      if (((x != c) || (y != r)) &&
          (board[y][x] == TRAP))
      ++count;
  return count;
}


////////////////////////////////////////////////////////
// DeleteButns()
//
// This function deletes all buttons from the playing
// board.
////////////////////////////////////////////////////////
void DeleteButns()
{
  for (int x=0; x<butn_num; ++x)
    if (butn[x] != NULL)
      delete butn[x];
 }


////////////////////////////////////////////////////////
// InitMouse()
//
// This function initializes the user's mouse.
////////////////////////////////////////////////////////
void InitMouse(void) {
```

214

```
if (!mouse.GotMouse()) {
  cout << "You have no mouse.\n";
  cout << "Press any key.";
  getch();
}
mouse.SetLimits(0,getmaxx(),0,getmaxy());
mouse.ShowMouse();
}
```

Each square on the game board contains one of three things: a trap, a number, or a blank. To start, click a button on the game board with your left mouse button (*not* the right button). If the button you choose reveals a trap, you lose the game (whew, that was fast!), and the entire game board is revealed. If the button reveals a blank square, every blank square connected to it is shown, up to and including bordering number squares. If a button reveals a number, this number informs you of the number of traps adjacent to the selected button.

Try to locate all the traps by using the number clues. When you locate a trapped button, click it with the right mouse button (*not* the left button). This marks the button with a red X and locks the button so it can no longer be clicked. You are apportioned only 60 markers, exactly enough for the traps, so you can't waste even one. If you use your markers before you've located all the traps, the game ends.

At the bottom of the screen are the START and QUIT buttons. You can start a new game any time by clicking the START button, and you can exit the program any time by clicking the QUIT button. Neither button warns you before it performs its function, so you can't undo your action if you accidentally click one during a game.

Trap Hunt and Inheritance

Look at the top of the Trap Hunt listing (Listing 6.7). See the `#include "butn.h"` line? If you looked at the program code already, you probably suspect that `Butn` is a new type of interactive screen object—and you're right. But more important, a `Butn` object is a new type of button derived from the `Button` class in your window library. All the buttons on the game board (except the START and QUIT buttons at the bottom of the screen) are objects of the `Butn` class.

Why do these buttons look and act so differently than the buttons you've used before? The original buttons' behavior has been modified to suit this program.

215

Rather than rewrite the original `Button` class or write a new class, however, *inheritance* adds to this new class all the things about the `Button` class you can use. Then, one only has to add the code to handle the differences between a `Butn` class and a `Button` class.

Now look at how this works. Listing 6.8 is the header file for the new `Butn` class.

Listing 6.8. BUTN.H—the *Butn* class header file.

```
#ifndef _BUTN_H
#define _BUTN_H

#include "windw.h"

class Butn: public Button
{
  int pressed, marked;

public:
  Butn(int x, int y);
  void PressButton(void);
  void MarkButton(void);
  int Pressed(void) { return pressed; }
  int Marked(void) { return marked; }
};

#endif
```

You can see from this listing that the `Butn` class is derived from `Button`. In addition, `Butn` has two private data members (besides those inherited from `Button`), `pressed` and `marked`, which keep track of whether the button has been pressed or marked. This class also has a constructor and four member functions (again, besides those inherited from `Button`). These functions perform the actions of pressing or marking a button, and returning the value of the `pressed` and `marked` private variables, so your program can read the button's status.

Now examine each of these functions, starting with the class' constructor:

```
Butn::Butn(int x, int y): Button(x, y, "")
{
  ww = wh = 20;
  pressed = FALSE;
  marked = FALSE;
}
```

Here, because a `Butn` is a type of `Button`, the program first calls `Button`'s constructor. But, because you don't want the game board buttons to have a label, this constructor is sent an empty string. `Button`'s constructor does everything required to create a functional screen button, except display it. Buttons of the `Button` class are always 64 pixels wide and 32 pixels high, but the buttons used on the game board are much smaller than this. Luckily, you can change the button's size by modifying its `ww` and `wh` data members, both of which are inherited from the `Button` class, which in turn inherits them from the `Windw` class. (My, what a tangled web.) In the `Butn` constructor, the program sets both `ww` and `wh` to 20. Finally, it initializes the `pressed` and `marked` data members to false, which indicate that the button has not been pressed or marked.

That's all you have to do to create a new button type. Are you surprised that it was so easy? You shouldn't be. Inheritance is one of object-oriented programming's most powerful features. If you've never used object-oriented programming techniques before, you're now getting a good idea of why modern programmers love them.

Now that you've created an object of the `Butn` class, how do you use it? Here's the `DispatchMessage()` function from Listing 6.7:

```
void DispatchEvent(EvntMsg evntmsg)
{
  mouse.ButtonUp();

  // Check whether START button was clicked.
  if (butn1.Clicked(evntmsg))
    repeat = FALSE;

  // Check whether QUIT button was pressed.
  else if (butn2.Clicked(evntmsg))
  {
    DeleteButns();
    Start();
  }

  // Cycle through all the buttons on the board
  // to check whether one has been pressed.
  else
    for (int bn=0; bn<butn_num; ++bn)
      if ( !butn[bn]->Pressed())
        if (butn[bn]->Clicked(evntmsg))
          CheckButton(evntmsg);
}
```

Look near the bottom of the function. Here, nested for loops cycle through an array of pointers to Butns. As you can see, this function checks the new buttons the same way you checked your old buttons, by calling their Clicked() function. You can do this because a button of the Butn class inherits all the functions of its ancestor class, Button.

Notice also that, before the program calls Clicked() for a button, it first calls the button's Pressed() member function. If this function returns false, the program knows that the button has not been clicked. If the function returns true, the program shouldn't call Clicked(), because that would animate a button that has already been pressed and erased. (The button object still exists in memory even though it's been erased from the screen.)

When the player clicks a button, its ClickButton() function (inherited from Button and called automatically by the Clicked() function) animates the button. However, when the button is clicked in Trap Hunt, the program must reveal what's beneath it. To do this, it first calls the class' PressButton() function:

```
void Butn::PressButton(void)
{
  pressed = TRUE;
  sound(500);
  delay(10);
  nosound();
  setlinestyle(SOLID_LINE, 0, NORM_WIDTH);
  setfillstyle(SOLID_FILL, LIGHTGRAY);
  mouse.HideMouse();
  bar(wx, wy, wx+ww, wy+wh);
  setcolor(BLUE);
  rectangle(wx, wy, wx+ww, wy+wh);
  mouse.ShowMouse();
}
```

This function first sets the button's pressed data member to true. After setting pressed, the program adds some extra sound to make things interesting. You hear this new beep immediately after the beep normally generated by the button's ClickButton() function. After the beep, the program erases the button by drawing a gray rectangle with a blue border. The Trap Hunt program decides whether to leave this square blank, draw a number in it, or reveal a trap.

Your new type of button behaves differently when it's clicked with the right mouse button. In this case, the program must mark the button with a red X. This task is handled by the class' MarkButton() function:

```
void Butn::MarkButton(void)
{
  PressButton();
  DrawWindow();
  setcolor(RED);
  mouse.HideMouse();
  outtextxy(wx+7, wy+7, "X");
  mouse.ShowMouse();
  marked = TRUE;
}
```

Here, the program calls `PressButton()` to record the button press and get the beep sound. Then it redraws the button (because `PressButton()` has the side effect of erasing it) by calling its `DrawWindow()` member function. Finally, the red X is drawn on the button.

Look over the Trap Hunt listing carefully to be sure you understand how the new `Butn` class works. In your future programming projects, you can make use of inheritance to quickly create new classes based on classes that contain some characteristics you need. To practice with inheritance, experiment further with the window library, creating new kinds of windows and buttons. How about a button that can hold longer labels? Or a dialog box that enables the user to select a file from a list?

The full `Butn` class implementation is shown in Listing 6.9.

Listing 6.9. BUTN.CPP—the *Butn* class implementation.

```
#include "butn.h"
#include "dos.h"
#include "mous.h"
#include "graphics.h"

Butn::Butn(int x, int y): Button(x, y, "")
{
  ww = wh = 20;
  pressed = FALSE;
  marked = FALSE;
}

void Butn::PressButton(void)
{
  pressed = TRUE;
```

continues

219

Listing 6.9. Continued

```
    sound(500);
    delay(10);
    nosound();
    setlinestyle(SOLID_LINE, 0, NORM_WIDTH);
    setfillstyle(SOLID_FILL, LIGHTGRAY);
    mouse.HideMouse();
    bar(wx, wy, wx+ww, wy+wh);
    setcolor(BLUE);
    rectangle(wx, wy, wx+ww, wy+wh);
    mouse.ShowMouse();
}

void Butn::MarkButton(void)
{
    PressButton();
    DrawWindow();
    setcolor(RED);
    mouse.HideMouse();
    outtextxy(wx+7, wy+7, "X");
    mouse.ShowMouse();
    marked = TRUE;
}
```

Programming with Trees

The Trap Hunt program contains an excellent example of recursion that you can study to get further insight into this handy and interesting programming technique. In a previous discussion of ways to use recursion, tree-traversal routines were mentioned. This is the type of recursion used in Trap Hunt.

What's a *tree*? A tree is a data structure that connects a collection of items, called *nodes*. A tree starts with a root node. Connected to the root are any number of child nodes. Each child node, too, can have any number of its own child nodes. This hierarchy continues down the tree until a child node has no children of its own.

Figure 6.3 shows a binary tree, which is a special type of tree that has left and right children for every node except the base nodes. Node A is the root node. Nodes B and C, which are called siblings because they are on the same level of the tree, are A's child nodes. Nodes B and C also have two child nodes each, the base nodes D, E, F, and G.

220

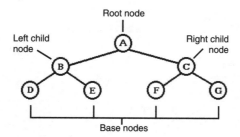

Figure 6.3. A binary tree.

Recursion is particularly useful for traversing trees—that is, for following every path in the tree from the root to the base nodes. Listing 6.10 creates and traverses the binary tree shown in Figure 6.4. The program's output follows:

```
At node A
At node B
At node D
At node E
At node C
At node F
At node G
```

Listing 6.10. TREE.CPP—creating the binary tree shown in Figure 6.3.

```cpp
#include <stdlib.h>
#include <iostream.h>
#include <conio.h>

struct Node
{
  char name;
  Node *left, *right;
};

Node *tree;

void AddNodes(Node *node, char c1, char c2);
void TraverseTree(Node *n);

void main(void)
```

continues

Listing 6.10. Continued

```cpp
{
  tree = new Node;
  tree->name = 'A';
  AddNodes(tree, 'B', 'C');
  AddNodes(tree->left, 'D', 'E');
  AddNodes(tree->right, 'F', 'G');
  TraverseTree(tree);
  delete tree;
  getch();
}

void AddNodes(Node *node, char c1, char c2)
{
  Node *n = new Node;
  n->name = c1;
  n->left = NULL;
  n->right = NULL;
  node->left = n;
  n = new Node;
  n->name = c2;
  n->left = NULL;
  n->right = NULL;
  node->right = n;
}

void TraverseTree(Node *n)
{
  cout << "At node " << n->name << '\n';
  if (n->left)
  {
    TraverseTree(n->left);
    delete n->left;
  }
  if (n->right)
  {
    TraverseTree(n->right);
    delete n->right;
  }
}
```

The program implements a node as a `struct` containing the node's label and pointers to the node's left and right children. In `main()`, the program first creates the tree's root node, which is appropriately named `tree`. Then it calls the `AddNodes()` function to create two child nodes for `tree`. The program also calls `Addnodes()` (indirectly by way of the `tree->left` and `tree->right` pointers) for each of `tree`'s child nodes to create their child nodes. The operations here are similar to those you learned when studying linked lists.

There should be no need to go into the details of the tree construction. What you must examine closely, though, is the recursive procedure that traverses the tree structure. In Listing 6.10, that function is `TraverseTree()`.

Here's how the recursion works:

1. The program calls `TraverseTree()` from `main()` with `tree`, which is a pointer to the tree's root node.

2. In `TraverseTree()`, the function first prints a message, showing which node it's currently examining. In this case, the node is A.

3. Then the function checks node A's `left` pointer. If it's not NULL, A has a left child, so the function calls `TraverseNode()` recursively to check that left child, which is B.

4. This call initiates a second invocation of `TraverseNode()`, in which a message for node B is printed and node B's `left` pointer is checked.

5. Because node B also has a left child, the program calls `TraverseNode()` yet again, this time for node D. In this third invocation of `TraverseTree()`, the program prints D's message and checks its `left` pointer.

6. D has no left child, so the program drops out of the first `if` and checks D's `right` pointer. D has no right child either. So, the third invocation of `TraverseTree()` ends, and the program is back to the second, where it last checked B's `left` pointer.

7. The program is now finished with B's left child, D, so it deletes it and checks B's `right` pointer, only to discover that it has a right child, E. This means the program must call `TraverseTree()` to examine node E.

8. Because node E, like node D, has no left or right children, the program promptly returns to B, where it deletes E and steps back to the first invocation of `TraverseTree()`.

9. The program had last checked A's `left` pointer, so it can delete that left child and move to A's right child, C.

10. The right side of the tree is traversed the same way the left side was, by visiting C, F, and finally G.

11. At the end of the traversal, the program returns to A with all nodes examined and all nodes deleted, except the root node. The root node, `tree`, is deleted in `main()`.

Trap Hunt's Trees

Trap Hunt uses trees. How? When the player selects a blank square, the program must reveal all blank squares connected to it, as well as any number squares adjacent to blank squares. It does this by forming a tree and traversing the tree recursively.

The first step in forming the tree is to select the tree's root. Trap Hunt makes the selected square the root of the tree. When the program has selected this root node, all other squares on the board fall logically into a tree pattern (not a binary tree), as you soon see. No matter which square the user selects, the remaining squares can be thought of as a tree structure with the selected square as the root.

The program then calls a recursive routine to traverse the tree, starting at the root. Any node in the tree can have as many as seven child nodes. A child node, in this case, is an unpressed button covering either another blank square or a number. Number squares are the tree's base nodes—that is, the traversal never goes past a number square.

This tree traversal is more complex than the first example. In the binary tree, the program had to examine only left and right pointers for each node in a tree. In the game-board tree, the program must examine nodes in *eight* directions: up, up-right, right, right-down, down, left-down, left, and left-up. Still, except for extra recursive calls to the additional directions, the process is identical to the one used for binary trees.

Two functions in the Trap Hunt program accomplish the tree traversal. They are `DoBlanks()` and `Check4Blank()`:

```
void DoBlanks (int x, int y)
{
  butn[y*MAXCOLS+x]->PressButton();
  buttons_left -= 1;
```

```
  // Move one square up.
  if (y != 0)
    Check4Blank(x, y-1);

  // Move one square up and to the right.
  if ((y != 0) && (x != MAXCOLS-1))
    Check4Blank(x+1, y-1);

  // Move one square right.
  if (x != MAXCOLS-1)
    Check4Blank(x+1, y);

  // Move one square down and to the right.
  if ((y != MAXROWS-1) && (x != MAXCOLS-1))
    Check4Blank(x+1, y+1);

  // Move one square down.
  if (y != MAXROWS-1)
    Check4Blank(x, y+1);

  // Move one square down and to the left.
  if ((y != MAXROWS-1) && (x != 0))
    Check4Blank(x-1, y+1);

  // Move one square left.
  if (x != 0)
    Check4Blank(x-1, y);

  // Move one square up and to the left.
  if ((y != 0) && (x != 0))
    Check4Blank(x-1, y-1);
}

void Check4Blank(int x, int y)
{
  if ((board[y][x] == BLANK) &&
      (!butn[y*MAXCOLS+x]->Pressed()))
    DoBlanks (x, y);
  else if ((!butn[y*MAXCOLS+x]->Pressed()) &&
       (!butn[y*MAXCOLS+x]->Marked()))
    DrawNumbers (x, y);
}
```

225

Although this code performs a recursive traversal of your game board's tree, there are no calls to `DoBlanks()` inside `DoBlanks()` and no calls to `Check4Blank()` inside `Check4Blank()`. How, then, is this routine recursive? Easy! `DoBlanks()` calls `Check4Blank()`, which then calls `DoBlanks()`. This circular pattern is recursive because new calls to `DoBlanks()` are made before previous invocations of `DoBlanks()` have ended. Neither of these functions is recursive, but together they form a recursive routine.

The `if` statements in the `DoBlanks()` function check that the recursion doesn't overrun the boundary of the game board. `DoBlanks()` also makes sure that all eight directions are checked. `DoBlanks()` selects the next square in the traversal and passes it to `Check4Blank()`, which decides what to do with the square. If the square is a blank and its button hasn't been pressed, `Check4Blank()` calls `DoBlanks()` recursively for the new blank square. Otherwise, if the square's button hasn't been pressed or marked, `Check4Blank()` calls `DrawNumbers()` to reveal the square's number.

This is probably very confusing, not because the concept is difficult to understand, but because it is difficult to follow the many recursions needed to traverse the tree. To help you understand Trap Hunt's tree-traversal routine, try the exercise in Figure 6.4, which shows the Trap Hunt game screen immediately after the player has selected a blank square.

At the point shown in the figure, the program has traversed the game-board tree, revealing blank squares and bordering number squares. The large black rectangle is the square the player originally chose. (During the game, there is no black rectangle. It was added to the figure for the exercise.) Get a pencil and draw the path that the traversal took to reveal the squares, using the source code for the `DoBlanks()` and `Check4Blank()` functions.

 Note: Start the traversal by moving upward from the selected square. If you run into a numbered square, back up and try the next direction. Every new blank square you run into starts the process over again, because it results in a recursive call to `DoBlanks()`.

To get you started, Figure 6.5 shows the first 14 squares in the traversal. The entire traversal is shown in Figure 6.6.

Figure 6.4. Tree-traversal exercise.

Figure 6.5. The first 14 steps in the tree traversal.

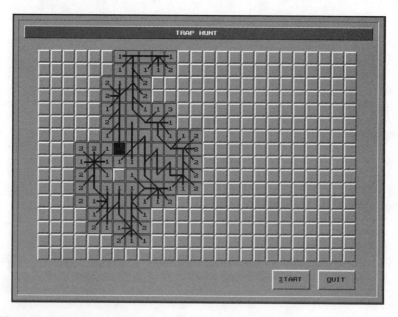

Figure 6.6. The complete tree traversal.

Conclusion

The exercise in Figure 6.4 may look like an immense task, but after you get the hang of it, you will be able to trace the traversal without even looking at the source code. When you can do that, you will have a good understanding of how recursive tree-traversal works (which is the whole point). And when you have that understanding, you'll be ready to tackle Chapter 7, which shows how recursion can be used to parse and evaluate mathematical formulas.

7

Using Recursion to Parse Formulas

Anyone who has ever written a program that must accept elaborate text input from a user knows how difficult it can be to change that input into usable data. *Parsing*—the process of analyzing text input and translating it into something the computer can understand—is a complex task. A complete tutorial on the subject of parsing could probably fill an encyclopedia. Unfortunately, this book doesn't have that much space to dedicate to this important topic. This chapter, however, looks at one of the most useful forms of parsing: recursive-descent parsing.

In this chapter, you learn to translate complex formulas entered from the keyboard into data with which the computer can work. Moreover, you learn to solve these formulas and return the results to the user. The techniques presented here can be the basis for any type of math program, from a simple text-based calculator to a full-blown spreadsheet application.

A Difficult Task?

Look at this formula:

```
AVG(SQRT(7*ABS(AVG(-15,-20,-32.5))),SQRT(999))
```

What if your job was to write a program that could solve expressions like this? How would you go about it? Your first inclination might be to scan the characters comprising the formula, starting at the left and working your way to the right. However, because formulas like the preceding can contain any number of nested functions or operations, the process of keeping track of parentheses, not to mention the results of the operations within parentheses, would be clumsier than a blind date.

One solution to working with nested functions is to use a data structure like a stack as a temporary holding place, storing values to be used after operations with higher precedence have been solved. But there's a more elegant solution. Think about the structure of the example formula. It has formulas within formulas within formulas. Looks a lot like the old bunny-in-barrels problem, doesn't it? And as you did when finding that little bunny (see Chapter 6), you can use recursion to work your way to the deepest level of the formula, then solve the formula a step at a time as you work your way back out of the recursion.

Before you can solve a formula, though, you have to define exactly what a formula is.

Formulas as a Grammar

Your formulas can contain many types of functions and operations. This means you must develop a grammar for your formulas so the user knows how your program expects a formula to be constructed. For example, if you were writing a spreadsheet program, your program, as well as the user, must know not only how basic mathematical operations are entered from the keyboard, but also what built-in functions are available. Trying to write a parser without this information is like trying to make a cake without a recipe.

To define the syntax for formulas, you must think of formulas as language constructions. Just as a sentence is the expression of a concept in the English language, so a formula is the expression of a concept in a mathematical language. It's up to you, the author of the parser, to decide the rules of this mathematical language. To do this, you must identify the elements of the language and its hierarchical structure. After you've identified these important characteristics, you can define your language's formal rules, or *grammar*.

Think about what makes up a formula like the one you saw previously. First, it has a few built-in functions. AVG returns the average of a list of numbers, SQRT returns the square root of a number, and ABS returns the absolute value of a number. Besides these functions, the example formula has multiplication (*), one of the basic mathematical operations that also include addition, subtraction, and division (+, −, and /, respectively). The formula also contains parentheses for specifying operation precedence and enclosing function arguments. And, finally, the formula contains values, which are expressed using a combination of digits, decimal points, and minus signs.

All these items are the building blocks of a formula, but knowing them is not enough to define a grammar. You must know the proper way in which these elements can be combined to form valid expressions. In short, you must know the language's *syntax*. This syntax can be expressed in top-down form by using something called the Backus-Naur Form.

Defining Grammar Syntax

E very language is defined by its grammar. In the English language, you use letters to form words, words to form sentences, and sentences to form paragraphs. In addition, to organize these constructions, you use syntactical rules that define the way the elements of the language can be combined. Your mathematical language can also be defined as a grammar. You can identify the elements of your language and organize these elements into a hierarchy. Finally, you can develop rules for combining these language elements into formulas.

Assume that a formula is the mathematical equivalent of a paragraph in English. But instead of calling a formula a paragraph, you call it an *expression*. An expression, then, is the top of your grammatical hierarchy. Unfortunately, your formulas are not written in anything much like English—they don't have sentences or words. You must think of your grammar in mathematical terms before you can fully represent it in hierarchical form.

So, if an English paragraph contains sentences and punctuation, what does a mathematical expression contain? The answer is one or more terms combined with the + and – additive operators. An example of an expression, then, might be

```
term + term - term
```

Guess what? You've just developed the first rule for your grammar. But before you define the complete syntax, you have to develop many similar rules. This means you must have a notation for specifying the rules of your grammar. There are many forms of grammar notation; this book uses the Backus-Naur Form.

Backus-Naur Form

With *Backus-Naur* Form, or BNF, a grammar is broken into a set of rules. These rules—each of which defines one element of the grammar—are developed using a top-down approach. The first rule describes the entire grammar in general, the same way the `main()` function in a well-structured C program describes a program in general. Each subsequent rule is more specific, with the last rules defining grammar elements that can no longer be described generally.

For example, a grammar describing a simplified version of the Pascal programming language would begin with a rule that defines a program. This rule might state that a program is the keyword `PROGRAM`, followed by a program name, the keyword `VAR`, a variable-declaration list, the keyword `BEGIN`, a statement list, and the keyword `END`. Program elements such as the variable-declaration list and the statement list would be defined in their own rules. Likewise, general elements of the variable-declaration list and the statement list would be defined in their own rules. And so on until the entire grammar has been described.

To describe rules clearly and concisely, BNF grammars use special symbols, some of which (the ones you need for your formulas) are listed in Table 7.1. Basically, BNF rules consist of terminal symbols and nonterminal symbols organized using the symbols listed in the table.

- *Terminal symbols* are elements of the grammar that cannot be described in general terms. In other words, they have been described as specifically as possible. In the simplified Pascal grammar, the keywords `PROGRAM`, `VAR`, `BEGIN`, and `END` are all terminal symbols.

- *Nonterminal symbols* are the elements of the grammar that have to be further defined in other rules. In the Pascal example, the nonterminal symbols are the program name, the variable-declaration list, and the statement list. A nonterminal symbol is always enclosed in angle brackets, so it can't be confused with terminal symbols or other symbols used to define the grammar.

Table 7.1. BNF symbols used in a formula grammar.

Symbol	Definition
<>	Identifies a nonterminal symbol (e.g. *<strg>*)
::=	Is defined as
{}	Identifies an item that is repeated 0 or more times (e.g. { *item* })
¦	Or

So, the first rule in the simplified Pascal grammar might look like this:

```
<program> ::= PROGRAM <prgname> VAR <decl-list>
              BEGIN <stmt-list> END.
```

Here, the nonterminal symbol `<program>` is on the left of the `::=` symbol, so it is the symbol being defined by the rule. (The `::=` is read as "is defined as".) The nonterminal symbols on the right side of the `::=` symbol (in this case, `<prgname>`, `<decl-list>`, and `<stmt-list>`) are defined elsewhere in the grammar.

Defining an Expression

Now, getting back to your formula, the first grammar rule looks like this in Backus-Naur notation:

```
<expr> ::= <term> { <addop> <term> }
```

In this rule, the nonterminal symbol `<expr>` (expression) is being defined by the rule. Now, although you have a definition for `<expr>`, you don't have definitions for `<term>` and `<addop>` (additive operator). These nonterminal symbols must be defined in other rules, as you will do soon.

In a BNF rule, the items enclosed in the braces may be repeated zero or more times, but always as a complete set. In other words, based on the preceding rule, if you place an `<addop>` after the first `<term>` in an `<expr>`, you must follow that `<addop>` with another `<term>`. So, an `<expr>` is defined as a `<term>`, which may be followed by one or more sets of `<addop>` and `<term>`.

You've taken a step down your grammar's hierarchy, but you're a long way from finished. You now must define both `<term>` and `<addop>`. Defining `<addop>` is easy:

```
<addop> ::= + ¦ -
```

This rule is read as "an additive operator is defined to be a plus or minus symbol." The plus and minus symbols in this rule are terminal symbols, because they require no further definition. The single vertical line separating the terminal symbols (¦) is the symbol for *or*. A nonterminal symbol can have more than one definition, as long as you use the ¦ symbol to separate each definition.

Defining a Term

Now you can tackle `<term>`. If an `<expr>` is any number of `<term>`s combined with additive operators, it's logical to say that a `<term>` can be any number of `<factor>`s combined with multiplicative operators. When you define the basic mathematical operations in this order, you retain the standard operator precedence, in which multiplication and division must be performed before addition and subtraction.

 Note: In your recursive routines, you first find your way to the formula's deepest level, then work your way back up, solving expressions as you go. That is, the lowest items in the hierarchy are solved before higher ones. This is why placing the multiplicative operators lower in precedence than the additive operators assures that operator precedence is maintained.

Here's your rule for a `<term>`:

```
<term> ::= <factor> { <multop> <factor> }
```

This rule is similar to the one for an `<expr>`, except here `<factor>` and `<multop>` are used instead of `<term>` and `<addop>`. The `<multop>` (multiplicative operator) nonterminal is easily defined as

```
<multop> ::= * ¦ /
```

Defining a Factor

Now look at a <factor>. It must be something that yields a value you can multiply, divide, add, or subtract. So, the most obvious way to define a <factor> is to say that it is a constant value, such as 0, 10, or 54.6746. If you were to stop there, however, you could parse only formulas that contain constant values and mathematical operations.

Luckily, a <factor> can be anything that results in a value, including functions. In addition, remember that your formulas can have nested functions. More-over, you can use parentheses not only to enclose a function's arguments, but also to change the standard operator precedence. Somehow, you have to add a recursive element to your definition of a <factor>, one that includes parentheses and, more important, brings you back to the top of the hierarchy. So, assume that a <factor> can also be an <expr> enclosed in parentheses. Your rule for a factor then is

```
<factor> ::= value ¦ <func> ¦ ( <expr> )
```

As you can see, this is where the recursion is necessary. A formula that starts with <expr> (as all formulas must) can lead you back to <expr> any number of times. That is, an <expr> is a <term>, a <term> is a <factor>, a <factor> is an <expr>, an <expr> is a <term>, a <term> is a <factor>, a <factor> is an <expr>, and so on, until <factor> finally evolves into something other than an <expr>. This rule enables you to describe expressions that are nested any number of levels. This process is summarized in Figure 7.1, using the expression (3) as an example.

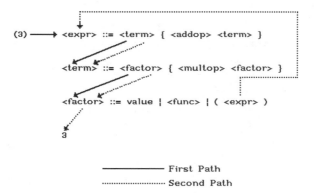

Figure 7.1. Recursion in a formula.

Now you can define a `<func>` (function). Because you have two types of functions—one that takes only a single argument and one that takes a list of arguments—a `<func>` is defined as

```
<func> ::= <func1> ¦ <func2>
```

in which the following is true:

```
<func1> ::= <fname1> ( <expr> )
<func2> ::= <fname2> ( <expr> { , <expr> } )
```

Notice that, even if a `<factor>` evolves into a `<func>`, you still can end up back at `<expr>` because any argument for a function is an `<expr>`!

Finally, to finish your grammar definition:

```
<fname1> ::= ABS ¦ SQRT
<fname2> ::= AVG
```

You really don't need a separate rule for `<fname2>`, because you could have used the AVG terminal in the rule for `<func2>`. But by defining the single function name this way, you are remaining consistent with the definition for `<func1>`, and you can add a new function easily, by adding the ¦ symbol and another function name.

The Finished Grammar

Here's the entire grammar in Backus-Naur Form. Look it over to be sure you understand how it works. Write a few formulas of your own, and trace them through the rules to see how they are derived.

```
<expr> ::= <term> { <addop> <term> }
<term> ::= <factor> { <multop> <factor> }
<factor> ::= value ¦ <func> ¦ ( <expr> )
<func> ::= <func1> ¦ <func2>
<func1> ::= <fname1> ( <expr> )
<func2> ::= <fname2> ( <expr> { , <expr> } )
<fname1> ::= ABS ¦ SQRT
<fname2> ::= AVG
<addop> ::= + ¦ -
<multop> ::= * ¦ /
```

A Recursive-Descent Parser

D eveloping the grammar for formulas, or for any type of language (especially programming languages), is a lot of work. The good news is that after the grammar is written, it can be used as an outline for the actual parser program.

To write the code for your parser, you need only follow the map you've developed. Each nonterminal in the grammar has a corresponding function. In other words, you start evaluating a formula with a function called `Expr()`. This function calls a function called `Term()`, `Term()` calls a function called `Factor()`, and so on down the hierarchy, until you have a function for every nonterminal in the grammar. (See Figure 7.2.) This type of program is called a *recursive-descent parser* because it uses recursion to descend to the deepest level of the grammar it's parsing.

```
<expr>    ::= <term> { <addop> <term> }          ──────▶   Expr()
<term>    ::= <factor> { <multop> <factor> }     ──────▶   Term()
<factor>  ::= value | <func> | ( <expr> )        ──────▶   Factor()
<func>    ::= <func1> | <func2>                   ──────▶   Func()
<func1>   ::= <fname1> ( <expr> )                 ──────▶   Func1()
<func2>   :=  <fname2> ( <expr> { , <expr> } )   ──────▶   Func2()
<fname1>  ::= ABS | SQRT                           ──────▶   FName1()
<fname2>  ::= AVG                                  ──────▶   FName2()
<addop>   ::= + | -                                ──────▶   AddOp()
<multop>  ::= * | /                                ──────▶   MultOp()
```

Figure 7.2. Changing grammar rules to functions.

Listing 7.1 is the recursive-descent parser for the grammar you just developed. If you start at the top of the listing and work your way down, you see all the functions that represent the nonterminals in your grammar. Following these functions are several utility functions that help the nonterminal functions do their jobs. Notice that the comments at the beginning of each nonterminal function include the rule for the appropriate nonterminal.

Listing 7.1. PARSER.CPP—a parser for mathematical formulas.

```
#include <math.h>
#include <string.h>
#include "strng.h"

#define TRUE        1
#define FALSE       0
```

continues

237

Listing 7.1. Continued

```
void Expr(String &s, float &v);
void Term(String &s, float &v);
void Factor(String &s, float &v);
void Func(String &s, float &v);
int Func1(String &s, float &v);
int Func2(String &s, float &v);
int FName1(String &s, String &name);
int FName2(String &s, String &name);
int AddOp(String &s, String &op);
int MultOp(String &s, String &op);
int FindValue(String &s, float &v);
int GetFuncName(String &s, String &name);
float CalcValues(String &name, float *values, int indx);
int NumChar(String s, int indx);
float Do_SQRT(float v);
float Do_ABS(float v);
float Do_AVG (float *values, int indx);
int Expect(String &s, char *c);
float Evaluate(String formula);

/////////////////////////////////////////////////////
// Expr()
//
// <expr> ::= <term> { <addop> <term> }
/////////////////////////////////////////////////////
void Expr(String &s, float &v)
{
  Term(s, v);
  float v1 = v;
  String op("");
  while (AddOp(s, op))
  {
    Term(s, v);
    if (op == "+")
      v += v1;
    else
      v = v1 - v;
    v1 = v;
  }
}
```

```
//////////////////////////////////////////////////////
// Term()
//
// <term> ::= <factor> { <multop> <factor> }
//////////////////////////////////////////////////////
void Term(String &s, float &v)
{
  Factor(s, v);
  float v1 = v;
  String op("");
  while (MultOp(s, op))
  {
    Factor(s, v);
    if (op == "*")
      v *= v1;
    else v = v1 / v;
    v1 = v;
  }
}


//////////////////////////////////////////////////////
// Factor()
//
// <factor> ::= value ¦ <func> ¦ ( <expr> )
//////////////////////////////////////////////////////
void Factor(String &s, float &v)
{
  if (s.GetSubStr(1,1) == "(")
  {
    Expect(s, "(");
    Expr(s, v);
    Expect(s, ")");
  }
  else
    if (!FindValue(s, v))
      Func(s, v);
}


//////////////////////////////////////////////////////
// Func()
//
// Func ::= <func1> ¦ <func2>
//////////////////////////////////////////////////////
```

continues

239

Listing 7.1. Continued

```
void Func(String &s, float &v)
{
  if (!Func1(s, v))
    Func2(s, v);
}


//////////////////////////////////////////////////////////
// Func1()
//
// <func1> ::= <fname1> ( <expr> )
//////////////////////////////////////////////////////////
int Func1(String &s, float &v)
{
  int result = FALSE;

  String name("");
  if (FName1(s, name))
  {
    result = TRUE;
    Expect(s, "(");
    Expr(s, v);
    Expect(s, ")");
    if (name == "ABS")
      v = Do_ABS(v);
    else
      v = Do_SQRT(v);
  }
  return result;
}


//////////////////////////////////////////////////////////
// Func2()
//
// <func2> ::= <fname2> ( <expr> { , <expr> } )
//////////////////////////////////////////////////////////
int Func2(String &s, float &v)
{
  float values[10];
```

```
    int result = FALSE;
    String name("");
    if (FName2(s, name))
    {
      result = TRUE;
      Expect(s, "(");
      s.Insert(",",1);
      int indx = 0;
      while (s.GetSubStr(1,1) == ",")
      {
        Expect(s, ",");
        Expr(s, v);
        values[indx++] = v;
      }
      Expect(s, ")");
      v = Do_AVG(values, indx-1);
    }
    return result;
}


///////////////////////////////////////////////////////
// FName1()
//
// <fname1> ::= ABS ¦ SQRT
///////////////////////////////////////////////////////
int FName1(String &s, String &name)
{
  GetFuncName(s, name);
  if ((name != "ABS") && (name != "SQRT"))
  {
    s.Insert(name, 1);
    return FALSE;
  }
  else
    return TRUE;
}


///////////////////////////////////////////////////////
// FName2()
//
// <fname2> ::= AVG
///////////////////////////////////////////////////////
```

continues

241

Listing 7.1. Continued

```
int FName2(String &s, String &name)
{
  GetFuncName(s, name);
  if (name != "AVG")
  {
    s.Insert(name, 1);
    return FALSE;
  }
  else
    return TRUE;
}


//////////////////////////////////////////////////////
// AddOp()
//
// <addop> ::= + ¦ -
//////////////////////////////////////////////////////
int AddOp(String &s, String &op)
{
  op = s.GetSubStr(1,1);
  if ((op == "+") ¦¦ (op == "-"))
  {
    s = s.GetSubStr(2, s.Length()-1);
    return TRUE;
  }
  else
    return FALSE;
}


//////////////////////////////////////////////////////
// MultOp()
//
// <multop> ::= * ¦ /
//////////////////////////////////////////////////////
int MultOp(String &s, String &op)
{
  op = s.GetSubStr(1,1);
  if ((op == "*") ¦¦ (op == "/"))
  {
    s = s.GetSubStr(2, s.Length()-1);
    return TRUE;
  }
```

```
    else
      return FALSE;
}


///////////////////////////////////////////////////
// Expect()
///////////////////////////////////////////////////
int Expect(String &s, char *c)
{
  String chr(c);
  if (s.GetSubStr(1,1) != chr)
    return FALSE;
  else
  {
    s = s.GetSubStr(2, s.Length()-1);
    return TRUE;
  }
}


///////////////////////////////////////////////////
// FindValue()
///////////////////////////////////////////////////
int FindValue (String &s, float &v)
{
  int result;

  result = TRUE;
  int indx = 1;
  if (s.GetSubStr(1,1) == "-")
    indx = 2;
  while ((indx <= s.Length()) && (NumChar(s, indx)))
    ++indx;
  if (indx == 1)
    result = FALSE;
  else
  {
    String ts = s.GetSubStr(1, indx-1);
    char c[81];
    ts.GetStr(c, sizeof(c));
    v = atof(c);
    s = s.GetSubStr(indx, s.Length()-indx+1);
  }
```

continues

243

Listing 7.1. Continued

```
  return result;
}


///////////////////////////////////////////////////////
// GetFuncName()
///////////////////////////////////////////////////////
int GetFuncName(String &s, String &name)
{
  int found_open_paren = FALSE;
  int indx = 1;
  while ((indx <= s.Length()) && (!found_open_paren))
  {
    if (s.GetSubStr(indx, 1) != "(")
      ++indx;
    else found_open_paren = TRUE;
  }

  int result;
  if (indx > s.Length()) result = FALSE;
  else
  {
    name = s.GetSubStr(1, indx-1);
    s = s.GetSubStr(indx, s.Length()-indx+1);
    result = TRUE;
  }
  return result;
}


///////////////////////////////////////////////////////
// NumChar()
///////////////////////////////////////////////////////
int NumChar(String s, int indx)
{
  if (((s.GetSubStr(indx, 1) >= "0") &&
       (s.GetSubStr(indx, 1) <= "9")) ||
      (s.GetSubStr(indx, 1) == "."))
    return TRUE;
  else
    return FALSE;
}
```

```
////////////////////////////////////////////////////
// Do_ABS()
////////////////////////////////////////////////////
float Do_ABS(float v)
{
  return fabs(v);
}


////////////////////////////////////////////////////
// Do_AVG()
////////////////////////////////////////////////////
float Do_AVG (float *values, int indx)
{
  float sum = 0;
  for (int x=0; x<=indx; ++x)
    sum += values[x];
  return sum / (indx+1);
}


////////////////////////////////////////////////////
// Do_SQRT()
////////////////////////////////////////////////////
float Do_SQRT(float v)
{
  if (v > 0)
    return sqrt(v);
  else
    return 0;
}


////////////////////////////////////////////////////
// Evaluate
////////////////////////////////////////////////////
float Evaluate(String formula)
{
  String s(formula);
  float v;

  v = 0;
  Expr(s, v);
  return v;
}
```

continues

245

Listing 7.1. Continued

```
/////////////////////////////////////////////////////
// Main program
/////////////////////////////////////////////////////
void main(void)
{
  char s[81];
  String formula("");

  while (formula != "QUIT")
  {
    cout << "Type Formula: ";
    cin >> s;
    formula = s;
    float answer = Evaluate(formula);
    cout << "Answer: " << answer << '\n';
  }
}
```

Run the program and try it out. Enter a formula, and the parser returns the answer. The parser isn't smart enough to handle lowercase characters, so enter all function names in uppercase. To exit the program, type QUIT when prompted for a formula. Table 7.2 shows the steps involved in parsing a formula. Refer to this table as you learn how the program works.

 Caution: Be extra careful not to make a mistake when entering your formula in Listing 7.1. To keep the workings of the parser as clear as possible, there is no error-checking in this program. If, for example, you enter a formula that results in a division-by-zero error, you crash the program. Ditto for something like requesting the square root of a negative number.

Table 7.2. Parsing a formula.

Contents of *s* Before Function Call	Function Trace	Terminals Extracted	Value of *v*
4*(SQRT(10+15))	Enter Expr()1		0
4*(SQRT(10+15))	Enter Term()1		0
4*(SQRT(10+15))	Enter Factor()1	4	4
*(SQRT(10+15))	Exit Factor()1		4
*(SQRT(10+15))	Return to Term()1	*	4
(SQRT(10+15))	Enter Factor()2	(	4
SQRT(10+15))	Enter Expr()2		4
SQRT(10+15))	Enter Term()2		4
SQRT(10+15))	Enter Factor()3		4
SQRT(10+15))	Enter Func()1		4
SQRT(10+15))	Enter Func1()1		4
SQRT(10+15))	Enter FName1()1	SQRT	4
(10+15))	Exit FName1()1		4
(10+15))	Return to Func1()1	(	4
10+15))	Exit Func1()1		4
10+15))	Enter Expr()3		4
10+15))	Enter Term()3		4
10+15))	Enter Factor()4	10	10
+15))	Exit Factor()4		10
+15))	Exit Term()3		10
+15))	Return to Expr()3	+	10
15))	Enter Term()4		10
15))	Enter Factor()5	15	15

continues

247

Table 7.2. Parsing a Formula *(continued)*.

Contents of *s* Before Function Call	Function Trace	Terminals Extracted	Value of *v*
))	Exit Factor()5		15
))	Exit Term()4		15
))	Return Expr()3		25
))	Exit Expr()3		25
))	Return to Func1()1	)	5
)	Exit Func1()1		5
)	Exit Factor()3		5
)	Return to Term()2		5
)	Exit Term()2		5
)	Exit Expr()2		5
)	Return to Factor()2	)	5
	Exit Factor()2		5
	Return to Term()1		5
	Exit Term()1		20
	Exit Expr()1		20

Note: *The numbers following the functions identify the specific function call. For example,* Factor()1 *is the first call to* Factor()*, and* Factor()2 *is the second call to* Factor()*. This numbering scheme helps track recursive calls.*

Now, you can see what makes the program tick. (Somewhere along the line, you might want to trace through Table 7.2, which shows a formula going through the parsing process.) Look at the main program first:

```
void main(void)
{
  char s[81];
  String formula("");
```

```
  while (formula != "QUIT")
  {
    cout << "Type Formula: ";
    cin >> s;
    formula = s;
    float answer = Evaluate(formula);
    cout << "Answer: " << answer << '\n';
  }
}
```

As you can see from Listing 7.1, there's a lot of string handling in this program, so the `String` class you developed in Chapter 2 is included in the program. Using this class greatly simplifies the parsing process. In the main program, the `String formula` holds the formula to be parsed. However, because the `String` class doesn't include functions for accepting a string from an input stream, an 81-element character array is used to get the formula from the user. This character array is then converted to a `String` and passed to the function `Evaluate()`:

```
float Evaluate(String formula)
{
  String s(formula);
  float v;

  v = 0;
  Expr(s, v);
  return v;
}
```

`Evaluate()` initializes the data needed by the parser, then calls `Expr()`, which begins the parsing process. See the `String` s and the floating point value v? At any point in the parsing process, s contains the portion of `formula` that has yet to be parsed. Each time a part of s is parsed, that part is removed from s. At the end of the parsing process, s contains an empty `String`. The value v is used to pass the value of the most recently evaluated expression between functions.

Now you can see how your grammar is converted into C++ functions, starting at the top of the hierarchy. As you examine these functions, you should compare them to the grammar you developed earlier.

```
void Expr(String &s, float &v)
{
  Term(s, v);
  float v1 = v;
  String op("");
```

```
while (AddOp(s, op))
{
  Term(s, v);
  if (op == "+")
    v += v1;
  else
    v = v1 - v;
  v1 = v;
}
}
```

According to the grammar rules, an <expr> must start with a <term>, so the first thing Expr() does is call Term(). After returning from Term(), there is a value in v, which is the result of parsing the first term in the expression. For example, if the first term were 10, v would be 10. If the first term were AVG(10,30,5), v would be 15.

Because it might use the result of the first term in an addition or subtraction operation, Expr() saves it in v1. (The variable v changes the next time you call Term().) Expr() then creates a String to hold the additive operator, if there is one. Because, according to the grammar, the program must allow any number of <term> and <addop> pairs, Expr() sets up a while loop that iterates until there are no additive operators in the expression. The function AddOp(), which is the loop's conditional expression, returns true if the next character in the formula is a plus or minus sign. It also returns the character in the op String:

```
int AddOp(String &s, String &op)
{
  op = s.GetSubStr(1,1);
  if ((op == "+") ¦¦ (op == "-"))
  {
    s = s.GetSubStr(2, s.Length()-1);
    return TRUE;
  }
  else
    return FALSE;
}
```

If AddOp() returns true, Expr() must call Term() to get a value for the next term in the expression. When Term() returns, the operator in op is checked. If it's a plus sign, v1 is added to the new v. Otherwise, v is subtracted from v1. In any case, the result is stored in v, after which the program returns to the top of the loop and checks AddOp() again. As long as AddOp() returns true, Expr() continues to add or subtract new terms.

Now, look at `Term()`:

```
void Term(String &s, float &v)
{
  Factor(s, v);
  float v1 = v;
  String op("");
  while (MultOp(s, op))
  {
    Factor(s, v);
    if (op == "*")
      v *= v1;
    else v = v1 / v;
    v1 = v;
  }
}
```

The `Term()` function is similar to `Expr()`, just as the rule for `<term>` is similar to the rule for `<expr>`. In fact, `Term()` works exactly like `Expr()`, except it evaluates factors and performs multiplication and division. To check mathematical operations, `Term()` calls `MultOp()` instead of `AddOp()`.

`Factor()`, on the other hand, is very different from `Expr()` and `Term()`:

```
void Factor(String &s, float &v)
{
  if (s.GetSubStr(1,1) == "(")
  {
    Expect(s, "(");
    Expr(s, v);
    Expect(s, ")");
  }
  else
    if (!FindValue(s, v))
      Func(s, v);
}
```

`Factor()` must allow for three types of factors: constant values, functions, or expressions enclosed in parentheses. First, `Factor()` checks whether the first character of the `String` s is an open parenthesis. If it is, `Expect()` is called, which checks for a specific character and, if found, removes the character from the `String`. (`Expect()` also returns true or false, depending on whether it found the expected character. The return value isn't used here, but it is discussed in the "Returning Syntax Errors" section.):

```
int Expect(String &s, char *c)
{
  String chr(c);
  if (s.GetSubStr(1,1) != chr)
    return FALSE;
  else
  {
    s = s.GetSubStr(2, s.Length()-1);
    return TRUE;
  }
}
```

Then, `Factor()` calls `Expr()` recursively to evaluate the expression enclosed in the parentheses. After `Expr()` returns, `Factor()` checks for the closing parenthesis.

If the first character in s is not a parenthesis, `Factor()` must check for a value or a function. Because a value is a terminal, there is no function called `Value()`. However, there is a utility function called `FindValue()` that returns true if the next characters in s form a constant. Also, the value of the constant is returned in v.

```
int FindValue (String &s, float &v)
{
  int result;

  result = TRUE;
  int indx = 1;
  if (s.GetSubStr(1,1) == "-")
    indx = 2;
  while ((indx <= s.Length()) && (NumChar(s, indx)))
    ++indx;
  if (indx == 1)
    result = FALSE;
  else
  {
    String ts = s.GetSubStr(1, indx-1);
    char c[81];
    ts.GetStr(c, sizeof(c));
    v = atof(c);
    s = s.GetSubStr(indx, s.Length()-indx+1);
  }
  return result;
}
```

Here, s is scanned one character at a time, until a character that is not part of a value is found (that is, it is not a decimal point or a digit from 0 to 9). The NumChar() function does this checking, returning true if it finds an appropriate character or false if it does not.

If no value is found, FindValue() returns false. If it does find a value, it not only returns true, but also converts the ASCII characters to a floating point value and removes the converted characters from s.

Getting back to Factor()—if a value isn't found, the only possible factor left is a function. Factor() checks for this with the Func() nonterminal function:

```
void Func(String &s, float &v)
{
  if (!Func1(s, v))
    Func2(s, v);
}
```

Just as with the rule for <func>, Func() first checks for a function of type <func1>. If it doesn't find one, it looks for a function of type <func2>. Both functions return true or false, as appropriate. Notice, however, that the program doesn't use the return value from Func2(). This is because this stripped-down parser doesn't check for errors and instead assumes that if it doesn't have a <func1>, it must have a <func2>. In a full program, you'd want to generate an error if both Func1() and Func2() returned false.

Now, move on to Func1():

```
int Func1(String &s, float &v)
{
  int result = FALSE;
  String name("");
  if (FName1(s, name))
  {
    result = TRUE;
    Expect(s, "(");
    Expr(s, v);
    Expect(s, ")");
    if (name == "ABS")
      v = Do_ABS(v);
    else
      v = Do_SQRT(v);
  }
  return result;
}
```

Here, the FName1() nonterminal function is first called, which checks for the function names ABS and SQRT. If it finds either, it returns true. FName1() also returns the function name in the name reference variable. If a function name is found, Func1() then calls Expect() to get the function's opening parenthesis. It then makes a recursive call to Expr() to evaluate the function's argument, after which another call to Expect() gets the closing parenthesis. Finally, the function's value is calculated by calling Do_ABS() or Do_SQRT(), as appropriate.

Func2() works similarly, except it must handle an unknown number of arguments:

```
int Func2(String &s, float &v)
{
  float values[10];

  int result = FALSE;
  String name("");
  if (FName2(s, name))
  {
    result = TRUE;
    Expect(s, "(");
    s.Insert(",",1);
    int indx = 0;
    while (s.GetSubStr(1,1) == ",")
    {
      Expect(s, ",");
      Expr(s, v);
      values[indx++] = v;
    }
    Expect(s, ")");
    v = Do_AVG(values, indx-1);
  }
  return result;
}
```

As Func2() is written, you can have a maximum of 10 arguments for a <func2> function. If you like, you can increase this maximum by changing the declaration of the values[] array.

Func2() checks for function names just as Func1() did, except it calls the FName2() nonterminal function instead of FName1(). If it finds a function name of type <fname2>, it checks for and removes the open parenthesis, then inserts a comma into the beginning of s. The comma is added only so the function can get into the `while` loop, which iterates as long as it finds a comma in the first character of `s`.

 Note: In the parser presented in Listing 7.1, `<fname2>` can only be `AVG`, but you can add other functions of this type if you like. How about `MIN` and `MAX`, which return the minimum and maximum value, respectively, in a list of values?

In the loop, a call to `Expect()` gets the comma, after which `Expr()` is called recursively to evaluate the current argument. The value returned in `v` is saved in the `values` array. Finally, after processing all the arguments, the program breaks from the loop, checks for the closing parenthesis, and calls `Do_AVG()` to average the values stored in the `values[]` array.

The `FName1()` nonterminal function looks for function names of the type `<fname1>`:

```
int FName1(String &s, String &name)
{
  GetFuncName(s, name);
  if ((name != "ABS") && (name != "SQRT"))
  {
    s.Insert(name, 1);
    return FALSE;
  }
  else
    return TRUE;
}
```

First, the `GetFuncName()` utility function is called, which scans `s`, looking for and removing the function name. The name is returned in the `name` reference variable. This variable is checked against the function names `ABS` and `SQRT`. If it doesn't match, `s` is restored to its original state by reinserting `name` into the beginning of `String`, after which the function returns false. If an appropriate function name is found, `FName1()` returns true, with the function name stored in `name`.

The `FName2()` function is similar. The main difference is that this function looks for the name `AVG`, rather than `ABS` or `SQRT`:

```
int FName2(String &s, String &name)
{
```

255

```
GetFuncName(s, name);
if (name != "AVG")
{
  s.Insert(name, 1);
  return FALSE;
}
else
  return TRUE;
}
```

The remaining functions in the program are fairly self-explanatory, so there's no need to explore them in any detail. However, before closing up shop for this chapter, you have to consider an important parsing topic: *syntax errors.*

Returning Syntax Errors

The program in Listing 7.1 does no error checking. It is assumed that the formula the parser receives follows the rules of the grammar. More important, there is no checking for illegal mathematical operations, which could crash the program if they sneak through. The error checking was left out because the extra code would have made the source code much more difficult to follow.

Before you use a parser like Listing 7.1, you must add enough error checking to ensure that the program doesn't crash and that the values returned from the parser are always accurate. As the parser stands now, a return value of 0 may be the formula's result or may indicate an error in the formula. Obviously, this ambiguity cannot be tolerated in a finished program.

Where should you add the error checking? The first place to look is any function that performs mathematical operations. For example, in the `Term()` function, the statement `v = v1 / v` won't get far if `v` happens to be zero. You should not only check for this illegal value, but also display an error message and, probably, stop the parsing. Exiting the parser early is tricky, because you have to back out of the recursion first. You could do this by setting an error flag that can be checked by each function. If an error is detected, each function does nothing but return.

Another type of error arises when the user types a formula that doesn't follow the rules of the grammar. For example, what if every open parenthesis can't be matched with a closed parenthesis? One place to check for an error like this is in the `Expect()` function. If the character that `Expect()` is expecting doesn't exist, the function could return an error.

The error message you return to the user should be as helpful as possible. For example, if your error message indicates that a parenthesis is missing, the user knows at least what type of problem for which to look.

This is how you might rewrite the `Factor()` function with error checking:

```
void Factor(String &s, float &v)
{
  if (s.GetSubStr(1,1) == "(")
  {
    Expect(s, "(");
    Expr(s, v);
    if (!error)
      if (!Expect(s, ")"))
        error = MISSINGPAREN;
  }
  else
    if (!FindValue(s, v))
      if (!Func(s, v))
        error = NOSUCHFUNC;
}
```

In this new version of `Factor()`, the function first checks for an open parenthesis. If it finds one, it calls `Expect()` to remove the parenthesis from s. `Expect()`'s return value is ignored because, if the program got past the `if` statement, it already knows it has the open parenthesis.

Next, `Expr()` is called to evaluate the expression enclosed in the parentheses. By the time `Expr()` returns, an error condition may have been detected. So, before continuing, the program checks the `error` flag. If there is no error, it calls `Expect()` to look for the close parenthesis. If the parenthesis is missing, `error` is set to a constant that indicates the type of error discovered. At the end of the parsing process, the program can check `error`. If it's not zero, an appropriate error message should be printed rather than the value returned from the parser.

If the first `if` statement doesn't find an open parenthesis, it's safe to assume that the factor is a value or a function. Therefore, `FindValue()` is called. If `FindValue()` returns true, the constant value is in v. If `FindValue()` returns false, the only thing left to check for is a function. If `Func()` returns true, the value returned from the function is in v. If `Func()` returns false, the program has discovered an error, because there is no other type of factor for which to check. To flag this error, `error` is set to `NOSUCHFUNC`.

You can check for other error conditions throughout the parser by adding similar code to the other functions. As you beef up the parser with error-checking routines, you discover why the errors you get from your C++ compiler don't always seem to make sense. Because C++ includes no mind-reading functions, it's often impossible to know exactly why something is wrong. All you can do is make an educated guess and hope the user can find the problem from the clues you supply.

Conclusion

Recursive-descent parsing is an excellent way to evaluate mathematical formulas. It can also be used for many other tasks. For example, many compilers use recursive-descent parsing to check the syntax of source code. Before the compiler is written, the entire programming language must be reduced to a grammar, which is then used as a model for the parser. In a way, the parser is a mini-compiler. Isn't that clever?

8

Writing Interrupt Handlers and TSR Programs

These days, the word *multitasking* gets a lot of attention. Products like Microsoft Windows 3.1 and IBM OS/2 2.0 boast multitasking capability, which enables you to run more than one program simultaneously. But you may be surprised to learn that your computer has always been capable of multitasking, although in a very limited way. Without this capability, in fact, your computer would be little more than a big paperweight. Think about what goes on inside your computer. Data travels its data buses, clocks tick, keystrokes are gathered from the keyboard, the screen is continually refreshed, and on and on. All this activity is apparently happening simultaneously, thanks to things called *interrupts*.

The key word in the preceding sentence is *apparently*. The truth is that a computer with only a single CPU can never do more than one thing at a time. Because the CPU operates so quickly, however, it can divide its attention between several tasks, switching between them so fast that it seems as though the tasks are running simultaneously. This is the way Windows and OS/2 perform their magic. It's also the way interrupts keep your computer running.

In this chapter, you learn how to use interrupts to change the way the operating system responds to certain events. Your knowledge of interrupts will enable you to write TSR (terminate and stay resident) programs, which sit in the background, unaffected by any other program you may run. You put this knowledge to the test by writing a TSR clock that displays the time in the corner of the screen.

What's an Interrupt?

As mentioned, computers must do a great deal of work to keep the operating system active and responding to input. For example, what good would a word processor be if the computer's operating system didn't have a way to gather keystrokes from the keyboard without interfering with the word processor? Likewise, if the computer's monitor was not continually refreshed with new information, you couldn't see your keystrokes. That would be a tough way to produce a document! Thanks to interrupts, the computer's operating system can perform dozens of these little tasks without affecting the currently running program.

Because a single CPU can work on only one task at a time, it must be continually interrupted to perform all operating system tasks. Each operating system task has its own interrupt. For example, when you press a key, a keyboard interrupt is sent to the CPU. The CPU stops what it's doing, grabs the keystroke, then picks up where it left off with the task that was interrupted. These interrupts occur constantly. A timer interrupt alone occurs about 18 times a second. When you consider that the CPU can service hundreds of different interrupts, it's a wonder that your programs can run at all.

You may wonder how the CPU knows what to do when it receives an interrupt. Each interrupt is handled by a small program called an *interrupt handler*. When the CPU receives a keyboard interrupt, for example, it runs the keyboard handler, which gets the keystroke. Although every interrupt has a handler, some interrupt handlers do nothing. Later, you see how such an apparently pointless handler can perform a useful task.

Each interrupt in the system owns an entry in a table of addresses, or vectors, in low memory. When the CPU must find an interrupt handler, it uses the interrupt number to index the interrupt vector table, using the address it finds there to run the handler. Luckily for people who write interrupt handlers and TSR programs, the addresses in the interrupt vector table can be changed to point to any place in memory. By changing a vector to point to your custom-written interrupt handler, you can change the way the operating system responds to a specific interrupt.

Writing an Interrupt Handler

There are two ways to take over an interrupt, by chaining one and by hooking one. They are defined as follows:

- By *chaining* to an interrupt. Chaining, which allows many interrupt handlers to run off the same interrupt, is discussed later in this chapter because it's the more complicated method.

- By *hooking* an interrupt. Hooking an interrupt is a fairly straightforward process: You simply place the address of your custom interrupt handler into the interrupt vector table. When the interrupt occurs, the CPU runs your handler instead of the original one. This may sound high-tech, but modifying the interrupt vector table is a snap because Borland C++ provides many handy functions for dealing with interrupts.

Listing 8.1 contains an interrupt handler that takes over the control-break interrupt, which occurs when you try to exit a program by pressing Ctrl-C. When you run the program, it installs the interrupt handler and continually prints the message `Waiting...` on-screen. When you press Ctrl-C, the interrupt handler takes over and prints the message `*** Ctrl-C caught! ***`.

Listing 8.1. CTRLC.CPP—Control-C interrupt program.

```
#include <dos.h>
#include <iostream.h>
#include <string.h>

#define CTRLC 0x23

extern unsigned _heaplen = 1024;
extern unsigned _stklen = 512;

void interrupt (*old_ctrlc)(...);
```

continues

Listing 8.1. Continued

```
void interrupt ctrlc(...)
{
  char s[] = {"*** Ctrl-C caught! ***\r\n"};
  for (int i=0; i<strlen(s); ++i)
    bdos(0x02, s[i], 0);
}

void main(void)
{
  old_ctrlc = getvect(CTRLC);
  setvect(CTRLC, ctrlc);
  for (int x=0; x<300; ++x)
  {
    cout << "Waiting...\n";
    for (long x=0; x<60000; ++x);
  }
  setvect(CTRLC, old_ctrlc);
}
```

Ordinarily, when there is a control-break interrupt, its handler terminates the running program and exits to the DOS prompt. However, this interrupt is often disabled in commercial programs so users don't accidentally exit the application. Remember the mention of interrupt handlers that do nothing? Handlers that hook the control-break interrupt are often in this category, being composed of nothing more than the IRET (return from interrupt) instruction. With this type of handler, the Ctrl-C keystroke does nothing. The previous handler, however, prints a message to the screen when Ctrl-C is pressed to show that the handler is working.

How does the program work? First, near the top is the line #define CTRLC 0x23. The value 0x23 is the control-break interrupt number. Every interrupt is identified by a unique interrupt number that you use when you change the interrupt vector table. The CPU uses this number to index the interrupt vector table and find the right address. After the interrupt number definition are these lines:

```
extern unsigned _heaplen = 1024;
extern unsigned _stklen = 512;
```

The first line sets the maximum size of the heap to 1024 bytes (normally this is around 64K), and the second sets the size of the stack to 512 bytes (which is normally around 4K). Because interrupt handlers and TSR programs stay in memory while other programs are running, they should be as small as possible. The less memory they consume, the less likely they are to prevent larger programs from loading.

The next line, `void interrupt (*old_ctrlc)(...)`, declares `old_ctrlc` as a pointer to an interrupt function. The address of the old control-break handler is stored in this pointer. Now examine `main()`:

```
void main(void)
{
  old_ctrlc = getvect(CTRLC);
  setvect(CTRLC, ctrlc);
  for (int x=0; x<300; ++x)
  {
    cout << "Waiting...\n";
    for (long x=0; x<60000; ++x);
  }
  setvect(CTRLC, old_ctrlc);
}
```

First, Borland's `getvect()` function gets the address of the old control-break interrupt handler. Notice that `getvect()` needs the interrupt number, which is used by the CPU to index the interrupt vector table. After saving the address of the old interrupt handler, Borland's `setvect()` function installs the new handler. The function's parameters are the interrupt number and the address of your interrupt handler. Believe it or not, after these two simple calls, the new handler is installed and ready to go.

In the `for` loop, the message `Waiting...` is printed and another `for` loop acts as a delay. After printing the message 300 times (to give you plenty of time to experiment with the Ctrl-C key), `setvect()` is called to reinstall the old handler, using the address saved in `old_ctrlc`. (Actually, the old handler is supposedly reinstalled automatically when the program terminates, but why take a chance?)

You can see that the message `*** Ctrl-C captured! ***` is nowhere in the main program, nor is there any call in the program to any function containing the message. The message is, instead, in the interrupt handler, which is called by the CPU whenever it detects a Ctrl-C keystroke:

```
void interrupt ctrlc(...)
{
  char s[] = {"*** Ctrl-C caught! ***\r\n"};
  for (int i=0; i<strlen(s); ++i)
    bdos(0x02, s[i], 0);
}
```

First, notice the `interrupt` keyword used in this function's declaration. When programmers wrote interrupt handlers in the old days, they had to write assembly-language code that saved the contents of all the registers before their handler ran. They had to do this to restore the machine to its original state after the handler exited. To avoid all this assembly-language programming, Borland created a special type of function for interrupt handlers. When the Borland compiler sees the `interrupt` keyword in a function's definition, it automatically generates the code needed to save and restore the registers.

 Caution: An interrupt doesn't care what a program is doing when it takes over. The interrupted program's state is represented only by the contents of the registers. Changing those registers without restoring them to their original state leads to disastrous results when the interrupted program tries to take up where it left off.

Now look at the body of the function. In the first line, the function declares and initializes a string for the message. Then, in the `for` loop, the 0x02 DOS function prints the message to the screen, one character at a time. When you run the program and press Ctrl-C, notice that the interrupt handler's message interrupts whatever the main program is printing to the screen. Such is the nature of an interrupt: It takes over immediately and returns control to the main program only after it has finished doing its thing.

In a real program, you wouldn't print a message when the user pressed Ctrl-C. Instead, you would probably ignore the keystroke. You might do this by creating a control-break interrupt handler that does nothing:

```
void interrupt ctrlc(...)
{
}
```

264

Writing a TSR Program

A TSR program is a lot like an interrupt handler because it relies on interrupts to interact with the user and the system. When a user loads a TSR, it first runs like any other program, executing the code in `main()`, which usually contains the TSR's initialization. After `main()` ends, however, the program doesn't terminate in the same way a conventional program does. Instead, it stays in memory, waiting to be reactivated by the user or by a system interrupt. When the TSR receives its appropriate signal, it "wakes up," does what it is designed to do, then becomes dormant until it's needed again.

Some TSR programs, like the on-screen clock in this chapter, require no user input. The user runs the program and then forgets about it. This type of TSR, like any TSR, gets its wake-up call through an interrupt. (For example, the clock TSR presented later in this chapter is activated by the timer interrupt.) Other TSR programs, like Borland's famous SideKick, are activated when the user types a specific hot key. This type of TSR works by chaining to the keyboard interrupt, which occurs when you press a key. This interrupt actually takes place twice for every keystroke, once when the key is pressed and once when the key is released. A TSR can look for its own hot key by examining the keys that are pressed.

Listing 8.2 contains an interrupt handler that chains to the keyboard interrupt. After you run this program, you hear a beep when you press a key and also when you release it. This magical, yet annoying, special effect continues until you reboot your computer.

Listing 8.2. TSR1.CPP—key beep program, version 1.

```
#include <dos.h>
#include <iostream.h>
#include <string.h>

#define KEYBRD 0x09

extern unsigned _heaplen = 1024;
extern unsigned _stklen = 512;

void interrupt (*old_keybrd)(...);

void interrupt keybrd(...)
```

continues

265

Listing 8.2. Continued

```
{
  old_keybrd();
  sound(500);
  delay(30);
  nosound();
}

void main(void)
{
  old_keybrd = getvect(KEYBRD);
  setvect(KEYBRD, keybrd);
  keep(0, (_SS + (_SP/16) - _psp));
}
```

Look at main():

```
void main(void)
{
  old_keybrd = getvect(KEYBRD);
  setvect(KEYBRD, keybrd);
  keep(0, (_SS + (_SP/16) - _psp));
}
```

Here, the program first gets the old keyboard interrupt vector and saves it in old_keybrd. Then it changes the interrupt vector table to point to the new handler. You saw this in Listing 8.1, so you should know what's going on here. One big difference between Listings 8.1 and 8.2 is that, in Listing 8.1, main() prints messages, but in Listing 8.2 main() only sets up the new interrupt. The second difference is that strange last line in main(), the one that calls the keep() function.

The keep() function is the magician that allows TSR programs to be written with Borland C. It's the command that informs DOS to keep your program in memory when main() has terminated, which is what is meant by "terminate and stay resident." When you call keep(), the first argument should be 0, which is the status code returned by DOS. The second argument is the size of the program. This is calculated by the formula (_SS + (_SP/16) - _psp).

This formula finds the program's highest address by determining the address of the end of the stack (using the SS and SP pseudo-variables, which contain the contents of the stack-segment and stack-pointer registers). It then subtracts the address of the program segment prefix (stored in the psp global variable) from the address of the top of the stack. Because the address of the PSP is also the starting address of the program, this subtraction yields the size of the program. If all this has your head spinning, don't worry—simply use the formula as it's shown.

Now look at the interrupt handler:

```
void interrupt keybrd(...)
{
  old_keybrd();
  sound(500);
  delay(30);
  nosound();
}
```

First, the old keyboard handler is called. (Remember: old_keybrd is defined as a pointer to an interrupt function, so you can call it like any other function.) This calling of the old interrupt is what is meant by chaining to the interrupt. You have to do this because the keyboard interrupt must be allowed to perform its usual function, unlike the control-break interrupt, which performs no essential services for the operating system. If the regular keyboard interrupt doesn't run, your computer stops responding to the keyboard, a predicament to which the only solution is a reboot.

 Note: When writing an interrupt handler for an interrupt that performs essential services, you must *chain* to the interrupt. That is, you must allow the old interrupt handler to run either before or after your own handler. You can *hook* an interrupt (take it over completely) only when the old interrupt handler can be ignored.

After the old keyboard handler runs, it returns control to the new interrupt handler, which sounds a short beep and exits. In this case, it doesn't matter whether you call the original interrupt handler before or after the beep. But with critical interrupts like the keyboard handler, it's usually a good idea to let them run first.

Chaining to an interrupt is important for interrupts that perform critical operating system functions. But it's also a good idea for most other types of interrupts. Why? Suppose a user loads a TSR that chains to the timer interrupt. Now suppose the user loads another TSR that also uses the timer interrupt, but it only hooks the interrupt, rather than chains to it (which is dumb, but ignore that for now). The second TSR disables the first TSR, because the first TSR's entry in the interrupt vector table was wiped out by the second TSR. By chaining to an interrupt, you ensure that critical operating system functions work properly and that other custom interrupt handlers and TSR programs continue to run properly.

In the "key beeper," you can see that the chaining is working because the keyboard continues to work along with the beeps. You can test this further by running yet another TSR that chains to the keyboard interrupt. Listing 8.3 is a version of the key beeper TSR that produces a higher beep. Run the first beeper and then run the second. Every time you press a key, you hear both types of beeps, which proves that all three interrupts—beep one, beep two, and the original keyboard handler—are running off the single keyboard interrupt.

Listing 8.3. TSR2.CPP—key beep program, version 2.

```
#include <dos.h>
#include <iostream.h>
#include <string.h>

#define KEYBRD 0x09

extern unsigned _heaplen = 1024;
extern unsigned _stklen = 512;

void interrupt (*old_keybrd)(...);

void interrupt keybrd(...)
{
  old_keybrd();
  sound(1000);
  delay(10);
  nosound();
}

void main(void)
{
  old_keybrd = getvect(KEYBRD);
```

```
    setvect(KEYBRD, keybrd);
    keep(0, (_SS + (_SP/16) - _psp));
}
```

An On-Screen Clock

N ow that you know the basics of writing interrupt handlers and TSR programs, how about writing something useful? Listing 8.4 combines everything you've learned to produce an on-screen clock. When you run the clock TSR, the clock display appears in the upper-right corner of your screen. It's a tenacious little critter; as long as the computer stays in text mode, the clock should stay on your screen.

Listing 8.4. CLOCK1.CPP—on-screen clock TSR program.

```
////////////////////////////////////////////////////////
// ON-SCREEN CLOCK TSR, VERSION 1
// by Clayton Walnum
// Written with Borland C++ 3.1
////////////////////////////////////////////////////////

#include <dos.h>

#define CLOCK 0x1c
#define ATTR 0x7900
#define FALSE 0
#define TRUE 1

// Reduce size of TSR.
extern unsigned _heaplen = 1024;
extern unsigned _stklen = 512;

// Define pointer to hold old vector.
void interrupt (*oldclock)(...);

// Define a pointer to screen memory.
unsigned int (far *screen);
```

continues

269

Listing 8.4. Continued

```
// Define some global data.
struct time t;        // Struct for gettime().
int hour, min, sec;   // Counters for time.
int count,            // Interrupt counter.
    tick,             // Another interrupt counter.
    colon;            // Flag for colon visibility.
char clockstr[] = {"00:00"}; // Clock display string.

// Function prototypes.
void FormatClockStr();
void HandleColon();
void HandleTime();
void interrupt ClockIntr(...);

//////////////////////////////////////////////////////////
// FormatClockStr()
//
// This function uses the hour and minute counters to
// construct the clock's display.
//////////////////////////////////////////////////////////
void FormatClockStr()
{
  // Format hour portion of string.
  if (hour < 10)
  {
    clockstr[0] = '0';
    clockstr[1] = hour + '0';
  }
  else
  {
    clockstr[0] = hour/10 + '0';
    clockstr[1] = hour%10 + '0';
  }

  // Format minute portion of string.
  if (min < 10)
  {
    clockstr[3] = '0';
    clockstr[4] = min + '0';
  }
```

```
    else
    {
      clockstr[3] = min/10 + '0';
      clockstr[4] = min%10 + '0';
    }
}


//////////////////////////////////////////////////////////
// HandleColon()
//
// This function is responsible for the blinking colon
// in the clock display. Every 9 ticks (1/2 second), the
// colon is added to or deleted from the string, which
// causes the colon to blink in 1-second intervals.
//////////////////////////////////////////////////////////
void HandleColon()
{
  // Increment counter.
  ++tick;

  // If a half second has passed, set counter back
  // to zero, and then add or remove the colon.
  if (tick == 9)
  {
    tick = 0;

    // If colon is in the string, remove it.
    if (colon)
    {
      clockstr[2] = ' ';
      colon = FALSE;
    }

    // If colon is not in the string, add it.
    else
    {
      clockstr[2] = ':';
      colon = TRUE;
    }
  }
}
```

continues

Listing 8.4. Continued

```
/////////////////////////////////////////////////////////
// HandleTime()
//
// This function calculates when a minute has passed,
// at which time it updates the time counters to
// reflect the current time.
/////////////////////////////////////////////////////////
void HandleTime()
{
  // Increment timer.
  ++count;

  // If count == 1092, a minute has passed.
  // (18.2 ticks per second times 60.)
  if (count == 1092)
  {
    // Reset counter.
    count = 0;

    // Increment minutes.
    ++min;

    // If min == 60, reset min and increment hour.
    if (min == 60)
    {
      min = 0;
      ++hour;

      // If hour == 24, recycle back to 0 to
      // simulate 24-hour clock.
      if (hour == 24)
      hour = 0;
    }
    // Create new display string from new times.
    FormatClockStr();
  }
}
```

```
//////////////////////////////////////////////////////
// ClockIntr()
//
// This is the interrupt handler. It displays the
// current clock string, checks the counters, and
// finally chains to the old interrupt.
//////////////////////////////////////////////////////
void interrupt ClockIntr(...)
{
  // Get the screen address.
  screen = (unsigned int far *) MK_FP(0xb800,0);

  // Get address of clock position on first screen line.
  screen += 75;

  // Write clock display string directly to screen memory.
  for (int x= 0; x<5; ++x)
    *screen++ = clockstr[x] + ATTR;

  // Update counters.
  HandleColon();
  HandleTime();

  // Chain to old handler.
  _chain_intr(oldclock);
}


//////////////////////////////////////////////////////
// Main program.
//////////////////////////////////////////////////////
void main(void)
{
  // Get old vector and set new vector.
  oldclock = getvect(CLOCK);
  setvect(CLOCK, ClockIntr);

  // Initialize time counters and colon flag.
  gettime(&t);
  min = t.ti_min;
  hour = t.ti_hour;
  count = t.ti_sec * 18;
  tick = 0;
  colon = FALSE;
```

continues

Listing 8.4. Continued

```
// Initialize display string.
FormatClockStr();

// Go TSR.
keep(0, (_SS + (_SP/16) - _psp));
}
```

Although the clock TSR is a bit more sophisticated than the keyboard beeper, you should be delighted to know that it's still a fairly simple program. The following discusses the program function by function, starting with `main()`:

```
void main(void)
{
  // Get old vector and set new vector.
  oldclock = getvect(CLOCK);
  setvect(CLOCK, ClockIntr);

  // Initialize time counters and colon flag.
  gettime(&t);
  min = t.ti_min;
  hour = t.ti_hour;
  count = t.ti_sec * 18;
  tick = 0;
  colon = FALSE;

  // Initialize display string.
  FormatClockStr();

  // Go TSR.
  keep(0, (_SS + (_SP/16) - _psp));
}
```

In a TSR, most program initialization takes place in `main()`, which executes once when the program is initially loaded. Here, the program first gets and saves the old timer vector, then installs the new handler. Next, a call to `gettime()` gets the current time, which is saved in the `min`, `hour`, and `count` time counters. Because `count` counts timer ticks (each timer interrupt represents one tick and occurs 18.2 times a second), `count` is initialized by multiplying `t.ti_sec` by 18. After initializing the remaining variables and the starting clock string, the program calls `keep()` to exit the program and to leave it resident in memory.

After `main()` finishes its tasks, it's finished forever (or at least until the next time the program is loaded). However, the TSR, which is represented by the interrupt handler and the functions it calls, stands ready to spring into action whenever it detects a timer interrupt, which is 18.2 times a second:

```
void interrupt ClockIntr(...)
{
  // Get the screen address.
  screen = (unsigned int far *) MK_FP(0xb800,0);

  // Get address of clock position on first screen line.
  screen += 75;

  // Write clock display string directly to screen memory.
  for (int x= 0; x<5; ++x)
    *screen++ = clockstr[x] + ATTR;

  // Update counters.
  HandleColon();
  HandleTime();

  // Chain to old handler.
  _chain_intr(oldclock);
}
```

The handler first calculates the address of screen memory. It then adds 75 to the resulting address, yielding an address near the end of the first screen line (80 characters to a line). After calculating the screen address, the handler writes the clock display string directly into screen memory.

Why print directly to screen memory? First, if the handler prints to the screen using standard stream I/O (`cout`) or a string-display function like `cputs()`, it changes the location of the text cursor, which messes up the user's screen. (You could get around this problem by saving the location of the cursor, printing your string, and then restoring the cursor's location.)

There's another, more important reason why the handler must write directly to screen memory. When the handler wants to print your clock display, MS-DOS may be busy with another task, so it cannot call MS-DOS safely.

Caution: Your TSR is running in the background; a foreground application, or even another TSR, may be running as well. MS-DOS can handle only one task at a time; to ask it to do more is courting disaster. Imagine, for example, trying to save two files to disk simultaneously. Ouch!

Unless you know what you're doing, calling MS-DOS from a TSR can yield unpredictable behavior, anything from locking up the keyboard to destroying data on a hard disk. The next section shows some ways to determine whether MS-DOS is busy. For now, however, keep things simple. (Note that the program can call the MS-DOS `gettime()` function in `main()` because, when `main()` is running, the program is not yet a TSR program. When `main()` is running, the clock program is like any other program. There can be no conflict with MS-DOS, because no other program can call MS-DOS until `main()` is finished.)

After the handler displays the clock string, it calls the `HandleColon()` and `HandleTime()` functions, which implement the blinking colon in the display and update the time counters, respectively. Finally, the handler chains to the old timer interrupt by calling `_chain_intr()` with the address of the old handler. This function turns control over to the old handler without returning to the handler that called it. For this reason, call `_chain_intr()` only as the last line of a handler. If you must call the original handler before executing your own, use the method shown in Listing 8.3.

The `HandleColon()` function implements the blinking colon that marks the passing seconds:

```
void HandleColon()
{
  // Increment counter.
  ++tick;

  // If a half second has passed, set counter back
  // to zero, and then add or remove the colon.
  if (tick == 9)
  {
    tick = 0;

    // If colon is in the string, remove it.
    if (colon)
    {
      clockstr[2] = ' ';
      colon = FALSE;
    }

    // If colon is not in the string, add it.
    else
    {
      clockstr[2] = ':';
```

```
        colon = TRUE;
    }
  }
}
```

This function first increments the `tick` counter. Because the timer interrupt occurs 18.2 times a second, a half second has passed when this counter reaches nine. In that case, the counter is set back to 0, and the colon character is added to or removed from the string. Which is done depends on the value of the `colon` flag. By adding or removing the colon every half second, the colon appears to blink.

The next function, `HandleTime()`, is responsible for keeping the clock up to date:

```
void HandleTime()
{
  // Increment timer.
  ++count;

  // If count == 1092, a minute has passed.
  // (18.2 ticks per second times 60.)
  if (count == 1092)
  {
    // Reset counter.
    count = 0;

    // Increment minutes.
    ++min;

    // If min == 60, reset min and increment hour.
    if (min == 60)
    {
      min = 0;
      ++hour;

      // If hour == 24, recycle back to 0 to
      // simulate 24-hour clock.
      if (hour == 24)
     hour = 0;
    }
    // Create new display string from new times.
    FormatClockStr();
  }
}
```

This function works similarly to `HandleColon()`, except its counter can count up to 1092, which is the number of timer interrupts per minute (60 * 18.2). When the counter reaches 1092, it's time to update the clock string with a new minute, and maybe even a new hour. After resetting the counter, `min` is incremented. If `min` is 60, another hour has passed, so `min` is reset to 0 and `hour` is incremented. If `hour` is 24, it's reset to 0, which simulates a 24-hour clock. Finally, `FormatClockStr()` builds the clock's display string:

```
void FormatClockStr()
{
  // Format hour portion of string.
  if (hour < 10)
  {
    clockstr[0] = '0';
    clockstr[1] = hour + '0';
  }
  else
  {
    clockstr[0] = hour/10 + '0';
    clockstr[1] = hour%10 + '0';
  }

  // Format minute portion of string.
  if (min < 10)
  {
    clockstr[3] = '0';
    clockstr[4] = min + '0';
  }
  else
  {
    clockstr[3] = min/10 + '0';
    clockstr[4] = min%10 + '0';
  }
}
```

There's not much to talk about here. This function simply uses the values in `min` and `hour` to construct the display string.

The MS-DOS Busy Flag

When the designers of MS-DOS knew that folks like you and me would be writing interrupt handlers and TSR programs, they provided a way for these programs to find out whether MS-DOS is busy. After all, if MS-DOS isn't servicing some other program, there's no reason why you can't call it in your interrupt handlers and TSR programs. To provide this extra service, the designers of MS-DOS added the InDos flag.

The InDos flag is nothing more than a location in memory that marks whether MS-DOS is currently servicing a function request. When MS-DOS is busy, this flag is set to 1. When MS-DOS is idle, the InDos flag is cleared to 0. So, to use MS-DOS in your TSR programs, you need only check the value of InDos. If it's 0, you can go ahead and do what you like. Right?

Well, 99.9 percent of the time you would be right. Unfortunately, MS-DOS' critical error handler (that's the handler that displays the infamous Abort, Retry, Fail? prompt) complicates matters. The details of this complication are beyond the scope of this book; simply put, to safely call MS-DOS, you must check both the InDos flag and another flag called CritErr (Critical Error). If both these flags are clear, you can use MS-DOS without worry.

Listing 8.5 is a new version of the clock TSR that relies on the InDos and CritErr flags to determine whether it can call MS-DOS. In this version, the call to gettime() is moved from main() to the interrupt handler. Doing this means the handler can get the current time at every timer interrupt, without keeping track of minute and hour counters. Because the handler no longer needs the time counters, the entire HandleTime() function has been deleted.

Listing 8.5. CLOCK2.CPP—on-screen clock TSR program, version 2.

```
/////////////////////////////////////////////////////
// ON-SCREEN CLOCK TSR, VERSION 2
// by Clayton Walnum
// Written with Borland C++ 3.1
/////////////////////////////////////////////////////

#include <dos.h>

#define CLOCK 0x1c
#define ATTR 0x7900
#define FALSE 0
#define TRUE 1

// Reduce size of TSR.
extern unsigned _heaplen = 1024;
extern unsigned _stklen = 512;
```

continues

279

Listing 8.5. Continued

```c
// Define pointer to hold old vector.
void interrupt (*oldclock)(...);

// Define a pointer to screen memory.
unsigned int (far *screen);

// Define some global data.
struct time t;          // Struct for gettime().
int tick,               // Interrupt counter.
    colon;              // Flag for colon visibility.
char clockstr[] = {"00:00"}; // Clock display string.

// Declare pointers to InDOS and CritErr flags.
char far *indos;
char far *criterr;

// Function prototypes.
void FormatClockStr();
void HandleColon();
void interrupt ClockIntr(...);

/////////////////////////////////////////////////////
// FormatClockStr()
//
// This function uses the hour and minute counters to
// construct the clock's display.
/////////////////////////////////////////////////////
void FormatClockStr()
{
  // Format hour portion of string.
  if (t.ti_hour < 10)
  {
    clockstr[0] = '0';
    clockstr[1] = t.ti_hour + '0';
  }
  else
  {
    clockstr[0] = t.ti_hour / 10 + '0';
    clockstr[1] = t.ti_hour % 10 + '0';
  }

  // Format minute portion of string.
```

```
    if (t.ti_min < 10)
    {
      clockstr[3] = '0';
      clockstr[4] = t.ti_min + '0';
    }
    else
    {
      clockstr[3] = t.ti_min / 10 + '0';
      clockstr[4] = t.ti_min % 10 + '0';
    }
}


//////////////////////////////////////////////////////
// HandleColon()
//
// This function is responsible for the blinking colon
// in the clock display. Every 9 ticks (1/2 second), the
// colon is added to or deleted from the string, which
// causes the colon to blink in 1-second intervals.
//////////////////////////////////////////////////////
void HandleColon()
{
  // Increment counter.
  ++tick;

  // If a half second has passed, set counter back
  // to zero, and then add or remove the colon.
  if (tick == 9)
  {
    tick = 0;

    // If colon is in the string, remove it.
    if (colon)
    {
      clockstr[2] = ' ';
      colon = FALSE;
    }

    // If colon is not in the string, add it.
    else
    {
      clockstr[2] = ':';
      colon = TRUE;
```

continues

281

Listing 8.5. Continued

```
      }
    }
}


//////////////////////////////////////////////////////
// ClockIntr()
//
// This is the interrupt handler. It displays the
// current clock string, checks the counters, and
// finally chains to the old interrupt.
//////////////////////////////////////////////////////
void interrupt ClockIntr(...)
{
  // Handle the blinking colon.
  HandleColon();

  // Is it safe to call MS-DOS?
  if (!*indos && !*criterr)
  {
    // Use MS-DOS to get current time.
    gettime(&t);

    // Build clock display string.
    FormatClockStr();

    // Get the screen address.
    screen = (unsigned int far *) MK_FP(0xb800,0);

    // Get address of clock position on first screen line.
    screen += 75;

    // Write clock display string directly to screen memory.
    for (int x= 0; x<5; ++x)
      *screen++ = clockstr[x] + ATTR;
  }

  // Chain to old handler.
  _chain_intr(oldclock);
}
```

```
///////////////////////////////////////////////////
// Main program.
///////////////////////////////////////////////////
void main(void)
{
  // Get address of inDOS flag.
  _AH = 0x34;
  geninterrupt(0x21);

  // Initialize InDOS and CritErr pointers.
  unsigned int seg = _ES;
  unsigned int off = _BX;
  indos = (char far *) MK_FP(seg, off);
  criterr = indos - 1;

  // Get old vector and set new vector.
  oldclock = getvect(CLOCK);
  setvect(CLOCK, ClockIntr);

  // Initialize time counters and colon flag.
  tick = 0;
  colon = FALSE;

  // Go TSR.
  keep(0, (_SS + (_SP/16) - _psp));
}
```

Now you can see what else has changed in this version, starting with main():

```
void main(void)
{
  // Get address of inDOS flag.
  _AH = 0x34;
  geninterrupt(0x21);

  // Initialize InDOS and CritErr pointers.
  unsigned int seg = _ES;
  unsigned int off = _BX;
  indos = (char far *) MK_FP(seg, off);
  criterr = indos - 1;
```

283

```
// Get old vector and set new vector.
oldclock = getvect(CLOCK);
setvect(CLOCK, ClockIntr);

// Initialize time counters and colon flag.
tick = 0;
colon = FALSE;

// Go TSR.
keep(0, (_SS + (_SP/16) - _psp));
}
```

First, the program gets the address of the InDos flag by calling the MS-DOS function 34 (Int 21). This function call returns the segment portion of the address in ES and the offset portion of the address in BX. To create a far pointer from these values, use Borland's MK_FP() macro. The CritErr flag is a little easier to calculate. In MS-DOS Version 3.0 or greater, it's located at InDos-1.

After getting these all-important pointers, the program chains into the timer interrupt, initializes a few variables, and exits, leaving the program resident in memory. Because more of the work is done in the interrupt handler, main() is much smaller, and does little more than get the TSR going.

As with the first version of the clock program, after main() finishes, the interrupt handler is installed and starts responding to timer interrupts:

```
void interrupt ClockIntr(...)
{
  // Handle the blinking colon.
  HandleColon();

  // Is it safe to call MS-DOS?
  if (!*indos && !*criterr)
  {
    // Use MS-DOS to get current time.
    gettime(&t);

    // Build clock display string.
    FormatClockStr();

    // Get the screen address.
    screen = (unsigned int far *) MK_FP(0xb800,0);
```

```
    // Get address of clock position on first screen line.
    screen += 75;

    // Write clock display string directly to screen memory.
    for (int x= 0; x<5; ++x)
      *screen++ = clockstr[x] + ATTR;
  }

  // Chain to old handler.
  _chain_intr(oldclock);
}
```

Here, `HandleColon()` updates the interrupt count and modifies the clock display string each half second (nine ticks). This is done before anything else to ensure that the counter remains accurate. The colon in the display string does not blink at the proper interval if the counter is not kept up to date.

After taking care of the colon, the handler checks the `indos` and `criterr` flags to determine whether it's safe to call MS-DOS. If MS-DOS is busy, the bulk of the handler is skipped, and control is given to the old handler. (This is why the `HandleColon()` call wasn't placed here. When MS-DOS is busy, the interrupt counter would not be updated properly.) If it's safe to request MS-DOS services, the handler calls `gettime()` to get the current time and uses the values it returns to format the clock display string. Finally, the clock's display string is written to the screen. After the code inside the `if` statement concludes, the program chains to the old handler.

Note: Whether or not MS-DOS is busy, the old timer handler in Listing 8.5 is always called. If the program didn't do this, results would be unpredictable and other TSR programs chained to the interrupt might not run properly.

The other functions in version 2 of the clock program (Listing 8.5) are similar or identical to version 1 (Listing 8.4). The only difference is that the `FormatClockStr()` function no longer uses the values of the timer counters to construct the display string; it uses the time data in the `t` structure, which contains the values returned from `gettime()`.

To see that the `indos` and `criterr` flags are really doing their job, try this experiment: After resetting your machine (to be sure that all versions of the clock TSR are erased from memory), run CLOCK1 (Listing 8.4). Now, watching the clock display, copy a file to a diskette. Although MS-DOS is busy copying the file, the clock continues to function. Now, after resetting your machine again, load CLOCK2 (Listing 8.5) and repeat the experiment. This time when you copy a file, the clock stops working until MS-DOS finishes its task. This proves that your TSR now knows when to leave MS-DOS alone.

One final note about the InDos flag. When you're at the DOS prompt, your computer calls an MS-DOS function to poll the keyboard for input, so the InDos flag is continually set and cleared as your computer looks for keystrokes. You can see this in action by modifying the interrupt handler in Listing 8.5 so the HandleColon() function call comes after the if statement. When you run the clock, the colon blinks about half as fast because the interrupt counter isn't properly updated when the InDos flag is set.

This can be a problem for a TSR that relies on the InDos flag to get its work accomplished. Luckily, there's a solution. When your computer is polling for keystrokes, it continually generates interrupt 0x28, which is the idle loop interrupt. By chaining to this interrupt, you can determine when MS-DOS is polling for keystrokes. Moreover, this interrupt is issued only when it's safe to call MS-DOS, regardless of the InDos flag's state. When you detect interrupt 0x28, you can safely call MS-DOS functions from your TSR.

Conclusion

In this chapter, you explored the basics of writing interrupt handlers and TSR programs. However, this chapter didn't cover advanced topics, such as how to know when your TSR is already loaded, how to unload a TSR from memory, how to avoid TSR stack overflows, or how to communicate with your or other TSR programs. These and other advanced topics are best left to highly experienced programmers with a good knowledge of assembly-language programming.

However, such advanced topics cannot be overlooked by any programmer who plans to distribute her or his TSR programs. Because this chapter was meant as only an introduction to TSR programs for intermediate-level programmers, it does not confront many of the critical topics that a competent TSR programmer must know. Writing TSR programs is a complex subject that requires much study to master. Please don't assume that this humble introduction arms you with the knowledge you need to write commercial-quality TSR programs. It does not.

If you want to write TSR programs for general distribution, here are a few additional resources:

- A TSR standard has been developed by a group known as the TesSeRact Development Team. The TSR specifications included in this standard dictate a consistent way for TSR programs to communicate through interrupt 0x2f. For a copy of this standard, write to:

  TesSeRact Development Team
  1657 The Fairways, Suite 101
  Jenkintown, PA 19046

- You may find additional information about interrupts and TSR programs in advanced programming books. Two you might want to check out are *Using Borland C++,* Second Edition (published by Que Corporation) and *Advanced MS-DOS Programming* by Ray Duncan (published by Microsoft Press).

- You can obtain the source code for several working TSR programs from Borland's BBS at (408) 439-9096. One example program, TSR_C.ZIP, includes code for checking whether a TSR is already running and for unloading a TSR from memory.

II

Windows Topics

9

Creating Status Bars and Toolbars

L earning the basics of Windows programming is not particularly difficult, especially when you use a powerful class library like ObjectWindows. With ObjectWindows, it takes only a few lines of code to bring a window on-screen and only a few more lines to add menus, dialog boxes, and other Windows objects.

After you get past the basics, however, the Windows learning curve is steep. Simply finding the right function in the immense API is time-consuming and frustrating. In addition, there is seemingly no limit to the ways a particular task can be accomplished. In this chapter, you learn that, although there are many ways to solve a programming problem in Windows, the best method depends, as always, on your particular application.

One question new Windows programmers often ask is "How do I program toolbars and status bars?" The answer to that question varies depending on how you want the application to run. In this chapter, you examine three methods of adding these special windows to your applications:

1. Painting the status bar or toolbar directly into a main window.

2. Creating custom status bar and toolbar windows.

3. Creating custom status bar or toolbar windows in an MDI application.

Each of these methods is increasingly difficult to implement; but with the extra difficulty comes extra flexibility. Moreover, although it is much easier to implement method 1 than method 3, none of the methods requires inordinate programming skill. The most important consideration is not how difficult any particular method is to implement, but rather which method is most appropriate for your program.

Because the basic methods used for programming both status bars and toolbars are similar, you first learn methods for adding a status bar to an application. You create a toolbar only in the final example for MDI applications. The toolbar methods learned there, however, can be applied directly to method 1 or 2.

Before jumping into the main topics, a quick overview of Windows programming and Borland's ObjectWindows library is in order.

Windows and ObjectWindows

Earlier in this book, you developed an event-driven window library for DOS that you can use to create programs with captioned windows, dialog boxes, and animated button controls. Microsoft Windows, although many times more complex, is not unlike that DOS windows library. It, too, enables you to display windows, dialog buttons, and button controls. However, Windows allows many different types of windows and special features.

Although Windows is more complex than the DOS window library in Chapter 4, it is also a veritable workhorse that handles much of an application's activity automatically. Windows applications usually have a main window with a menu bar, scroll bars, sizing buttons, and other controls—all of which are handled to a great extent by Windows. For example, when you create a window with a menu bar, your program doesn't have to control the menu. Windows does this for you by sending your program a message whenever the user selects an item in the menu.

A Windows program can recieve hundreds of different messages while it's running. It's up to your application to decide whether to respond to these messages or to ignore them. If the user clicks her mouse pointer in your window, for example, your program gets a message (WM_LBUTTONDOWN). If you determine that the user clicked something important, you can handle the message, performing the function the user requested. On the other hand, you can simply ignore the message. It's up to you.

All this sounds terrific until you get your first look at a Windows programming manual and see the almost 1,000 function calls included in the Application Program Interface (API). Surely there must be an easier way to program Windows than to plow through thousands of pages of documentation. Isn't there?

Yes and no. No matter what route you take, learning to program Windows, while not especially difficult, takes time and practice. Before you program your first application, you should be familar with the most frequently used functions in the API, so you know the tools you have at your disposal.

Borland's ObjectWindows library goes a long way toward simplifing the process of writing Windows applications by hiding much of the details inside custom window classes. Using ObjectWindows, you can create a fully operational window in a little more than a dozen lines of code. Compare this to the over 80 lines of C code required to produce the same window without ObjectWindows.

Learning to use ObjectWindows is no picnic, either. It has its own set of rules and requirements, in addition to Windows. Even once you've learned the basics of Windows and ObjectWindows programming, you'll undoubtedly have many questions about how to do some of the things you see every day in Windows applications. This section of *Borland C++ Power Programming* was designed to help answer some of those questions.

 Caution: The bottom line is, if you've had no experience with Windows or ObjectWindows programming, put this book down for a couple of days and pick up the *ObjectWindows for C++ User's Guide* that came with your copy of Borland C++. Read the book and practice with the coding examples you find there. When you get to the end of the user's guide, you should be ready to continue with this book.

By reading this book, you learn some of the tricks of professional Windows programmers. And speaking of tricks, how can you add a status bar to your windows? Read on, and see.

Painting a Status Bar

When you create a main window for your Windows application, you must make sure that the window is properly updated with the data it should display. You can display any type of data in the window, in any manner you choose. Windows simply presents a blank slate.

Although most of the data you display in a main window is textual, graphics can also be displayed. (Text displayed in a window is actually graphics text. Everything in Windows is drawn graphically.) The Windows Graphics Device Interface (GDI) provides a rich set of graphics functions upon which you can draw (yes, that's a pun) to create the contents of a window. Using these functions, you can draw anything from a simple text display to a complex graphical display.

Although Windows won't update your windows for you, it does inform you when it is time to update them. Like everything else in Windows, this notification comes in the form of a window message. Specifically, when your application receives a WM_PAINT message, it knows it's time to redraw the window that generated the message. Luckily for Borland C++ programmers, ObjectWindows automatically routes these messages to the window's Paint() function. You provide this function, which draws the contents of the window.

In the first status bar program, the WM_PAINT message is used to draw a status bar at the bottom of the main window. Listings 9.1 through 9.4 show the files needed for this program.

Listing 9.1. STATAPP1.CPP—version 1 of the status bar application.

```
// STATAPP1.CPP: Status bar application, version 1.

#include <owl.h>
#include "statwnd1.h"


// Application class declaration.
class TStatbarApp: public TApplication {
public:
```

```
    TStatbarApp(LPSTR AName, HINSTANCE AnInstance,
          HINSTANCE APrevInstance, LPSTR ACmdLine,
          int ACmdShow): TApplication(AName,
          AnInstance, APrevInstance, ACmdLine,
          ACmdShow) {};
  virtual void InitMainWindow();
};


/////////////////////////////////////////////////////
// TStatbarApp::InitMainWindow()
//
// This function creates the application's main window.
/////////////////////////////////////////////////////
void TStatbarApp::InitMainWindow()
{
  MainWindow = new TStatbarWnd(
                      NULL, "Status Bar Window 1");
}


/////////////////////////////////////////////////////
// WinMain()
/////////////////////////////////////////////////////
int PASCAL WinMain(HINSTANCE hInstance, HINSTANCE hPrevInstance,
                LPSTR lpszCmdLine, int nCmdShow)
{
  TStatbarApp StatbarApp("StatbarApp1", hInstance,
                      hPrevInstance, lpszCmdLine, nCmdShow);
  StatbarApp.Run();
  return StatbarApp.Status;
}
```

Listing 9.2. STATWND1.H—the main window's header file.

```
// STATWND1.H: Header file for the main window.

#ifndef _STATWND1_H
#define _STATWND1_H

_CLASSDEF(TStatbarWnd)
class TStatbarWnd: public TWindow {
```

continues

295

Listing 9.2. Continued

```
public:
  TStatbarWnd(PTWindowsObject AParent, LPSTR ATitle);
  virtual void Paint(HDC DC, PAINTSTRUCT&);
};


#endif
```

Listing 9.3. STATWND1.CPP—the main window's implementation.

```
// STATWND1.CPP: Implementation for the main window.

#include <owl.h>
#include "statwnd1.h"


////////////////////////////////////////////////////////
// TStatbarWnd::TStatbarWnd()
//
// This is the main window's constructor.
////////////////////////////////////////////////////////
TStatbarWnd::TStatbarWnd(PTWindowsObject AParent,
              LPSTR ATitle): TWindow(AParent, ATitle)
{
  // Set the window's size.
  Attr.X = 40;
  Attr.Y = 40;
  Attr.H = GetSystemMetrics(SM_CYSCREEN) / 1.5;
  Attr.W = GetSystemMetrics(SM_CXSCREEN) / 1.5;
}


////////////////////////////////////////////////////////
// TStatbarWnd::Paint()
//
// This function paints the status bar into the window.
////////////////////////////////////////////////////////
void TStatbarWnd::Paint(HDC DC, PAINTSTRUCT&)
{
  RECT r;

  // Get the size of the window's client area.
  GetClientRect(HWindow, &r);
```

```
    // Select a new brush and pen into the device context.
    HPEN new_pen = GetStockObject(BLACK_PEN);
    HPEN prev_pen = SelectObject(DC, new_pen);
    HBRUSH new_brush = GetStockObject(LTGRAY_BRUSH);
    HBRUSH prev_brush = SelectObject(DC, new_brush);

    // Draw a filled rectangle for status bar.
    Rectangle(DC, r.left, r.bottom - 22,
                  r.right, r.bottom);

    // Draw a 3-D outline in the status bar.
    MoveTo(DC, r.left+3, r.bottom-3);
    LineTo(DC, r.left+3, r.bottom-19);
    LineTo(DC, r.right-3, r.bottom-19);

    new_pen = GetStockObject(WHITE_PEN);
    SelectObject(DC, new_pen);
    MoveTo(DC, r.left+3, r.bottom-3);
    LineTo(DC, r.right-3, r.bottom-3);
    LineTo(DC, r.right-3, r.bottom-19);

    // Print info line into the status bar.
    char s[] = "Client Area Width:        ";
    wsprintf(&s[20], "%d", r.right - r.left);
    HANDLE prev_mode = SetBkMode(DC, TRANSPARENT);
    TextOut(DC, r.left+10, r.bottom-19, s, lstrlen(s));

    // Restore old pen, brush, and mode.
    SelectObject(DC, prev_pen);
    SelectObject(DC, prev_brush);
    SetBkMode(DC, prev_mode);
}
```

Listing 9.4. STATTOOL.DEF—definition file for the status bar application.

```
EXETYPE WINDOWS
CODE PRELOAD MOVEABLE DISCARDABLE
DATA PRELOAD MOVEABLE MULTIPLE
HEAPSIZE 4096
STACKSIZE 5120
```

When you run the program (which comprises all four listings), the window shown in Figure 9.1 appears. This window features a status bar that shows the width of the window's *client area* (the area in which you can draw). If you change the size of the window, the value displayed in the status bar changes to show the new width. (Go ahead; give it a try.)

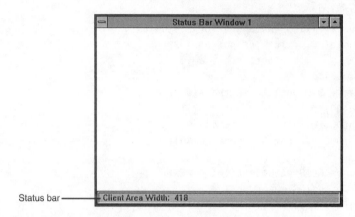

Status bar

Figure 9.1. The first version of the status bar application.

Now look at the code. As with all ObjectWindows programs, you must begin with an application class:

```
class TStatbarApp: public TApplication {
public:
  TStatbarApp(LPSTR AName, HINSTANCE AnInstance,
            HINSTANCE APrevInstance, LPSTR ACmdLine,
            int ACmdShow): TApplication(AName,
            AnInstance, APrevInstance, ACmdLine,
            ACmdShow) {};
  virtual void InitMainWindow();
};
```

Thanks to the power of ObjectWindows, there's not much to discuss here. The application object is a descendent of the `TApplication` class. Although the application class inherits many goodies from its ancestor, the only two function members with which you're directly concerned are the `TStatbarApp()` constructor and `InitMainWindow()`. The constructor is implemented in-line and does nothing more than pass parameters to the `TApplication()` constructor. `InitMainWindow()` creates the application's main window:

```
void TStatbarApp::InitMainWindow()
{
  MainWindow = new TStatbarWnd(
               NULL, "Status Bar Window 1");
}
```

Here, a new window is created on the heap and its address is assigned to the MainWindow pointer, which is a data member of the TApplication class. This new window is an object of the window class TStatbarWnd:

```
_CLASSDEF(TStatbarWnd)
class TStatbarWnd: public TWindow {
public:
  TStatbarWnd(PTWindowsObject AParent, LPSTR ATitle);
  virtual void Paint(HDC DC, PAINTSTRUCT&);
};
```

This custom window class, derived from the ObjectWindows class TWindow, includes a constructor and a Paint() function. In the constructor, TWindow() is called to construct the basic window. Then the window's position and size are set by assigning new values to each member of the Attr structure, which is a data member of the TWindow class:

```
TStatbarWnd::TStatbarWnd(PTWindowsObject AParent,
               LPSTR ATitle): TWindow(AParent, ATitle)
{
  // Set the window's size.
  Attr.X = 40;
  Attr.Y = 40;
  Attr.H = GetSystemMetrics(SM_CYSCREEN) / 1.5;
  Attr.W = GetSystemMetrics(SM_CXSCREEN) / 1.5;
}
```

The GetSystemMetrics() function returns various system settings, depending on the function's parameter. Here, the program is requesting the full screen's height (SM_CYSCREEN) and \width (SM_CXSCREEN). To get the height and width for the main window, the return values from GetSystemMetrics() are divided by 1.5. The divisor 1.5 yields a window height and width suitable for this example.

As mentioned, Paint() is called automatically when the window receives a WM_PAINT message:

```
void TStatbarWnd::Paint(HDC DC, PAINTSTRUCT&)
{
  RECT r;
```

299

```
// Get the size of the window's client area.
GetClientRect(HWindow, &r);

// Select a new brush and pen into the device context.
HPEN new_pen = GetStockObject(BLACK_PEN);
HPEN prev_pen = SelectObject(DC, new_pen);
HBRUSH new_brush = GetStockObject(LTGRAY_BRUSH);
HBRUSH prev_brush = SelectObject(DC, new_brush);

// Draw a filled rectangle for status bar.
Rectangle(DC, r.left, r.bottom - 22,
              r.right, r.bottom);

// Draw a 3-D outline in the status bar.
MoveTo(DC, r.left+3, r.bottom-3);
LineTo(DC, r.left+3, r.bottom-19);
LineTo(DC, r.right-3, r.bottom-19);

new_pen = GetStockObject(WHITE_PEN);
SelectObject(DC, new_pen);
MoveTo(DC, r.left+3, r.bottom-3);
LineTo(DC, r.right-3, r.bottom-3);
LineTo(DC, r.right-3, r.bottom-19);

// Print info line into the status bar.
char s[] = "Client Area Width:      ";
wsprintf(&s[20], "%d", r.right - r.left);
HANDLE prev_mode = SetBkMode(DC, TRANSPARENT);
TextOut(DC, r.left+10, r.bottom-19, s, lstrlen(s));

// Restore old pen, brush, and mode.
SelectObject(DC, prev_pen);
SelectObject(DC, prev_brush);
SetBkMode(DC, prev_mode);
}
```

This function isn't as complicated as it looks. It does little more than draw rectangles and lines to create a 3-D graphic. It first calls `GetClientRect()` to get the size of the window's client area. Then, it selects a new pen and brush into the device context. Any lines drawn are black, and any fill operations are performed with the light gray brush. After selecting the new pen and brush, the program draws a filled rectangle at the bottom of the window, using the coordinates stored in the structure r, which was filled by the call to

GetClientRect(). Next, a series of MoveTo() and LineTo() function calls (along with another pen change for white lines) draws the status bar's 3-D outline.

After drawing the 3-D outline, standard string-handling is used to build the status bar's display string, and then the TextOut() GDI function is called to display the string. Notice the call to SetBkMode(). If the background mode is not set to TRANSPARENT, the text's background, which is normally solid white, erases part of the status bar. Finally, the old pen, brush, and background mode are restored.

As you can see, displaying a status bar in this way is quick and easy. However, it suffers from at least two limitations.

First, this method works well only with windows that don't have scroll bars. When you add scroll bars to this type of window, the status bar scrolls along with the other data in the window. To see this in action, add the following lines to the end of the TStatbarWnd() constructor (isn't it amazing how much you can do in ObjectWindows with only two lines of code?):

```
Attr.Style |= WS_VSCROLL;
Scroller = new TScroller(this, 0, 15, 0, 100);
```

When you run the program after adding these lines, you see the window in Figure 9.2. Click the scroll arrows a few times, and the status bar scrolls with the rest of the window, as shown in Figure 9.3. The solution to this scrolling problem might be to write a function that responds to the WM_VSCROLL message (or the WM_HSCROLL message for horizontal scrollers). This function could then redraw the status window back at the bottom of the main window after it's been scrolled. This solution, however, leads to unattractive flickering and is a workaround, at best.

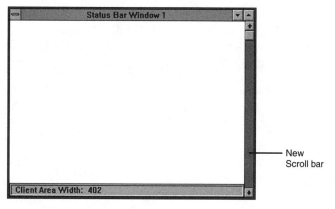

Figure 9.2. The status bar application with scroll bars.

301

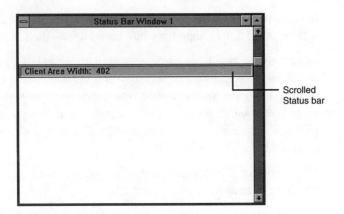

Figure 9.3. The status bar application after scrolling.

Another problem with this method of displaying a status bar is that it places the burden of updating the status bar on the main window. In a full application, the main window usually has enough to do. A main window's `Paint()` function can get unwieldy if it's overburdened. So, if your status bar is displaying data that must be updated often, create a new class for your status bar. Then you can manipulate it as a unique object, separate from your main window. You look at this method in the next section.

A Status Bar Object

To implement a more sophisticated status bar—one that can take care of itself without cluttering the code of your main window—you're better off, in the spirit of object-oriented programming, to create a separate status bar window. Implementing this method isn't much more difficult than implementing the previous one. You need do little more than move the code to handle the status bar out of the `TStatbarWnd` class and into its own `TStatbar` class.

Listings 9.5 through 9.9 are the program listings for creating the second version of the status bar application—minus the STATTOOL.DEF file, which is identical to Listing 9.4.

Listing 9.5. STATAPP2.CPP—version 2 of the status bar application.

```cpp
// STATAPP2.CPP: Status bar application, version 2.

#include <owl.h>
#include "statwnd2.h"
#include "statbar2.h"

class TStatbarApp: public TApplication {
public:
  TStatbarApp(LPSTR AName, HINSTANCE AnInstance,
           HINSTANCE APrevInstance, LPSTR ACmdLine,
           int ACmdShow): TApplication(AName,
           AnInstance, APrevInstance, ACmdLine,
           ACmdShow) {};
  virtual void InitMainWindow();
};


/////////////////////////////////////////////////////
// TStatbarApp::InitMainWindow()
//
// This function creates the application's main window.
/////////////////////////////////////////////////////
void TStatbarApp::InitMainWindow()
{
  MainWindow = new TStatbarWnd(
                       NULL, "Status Bar Window 2");
}


/////////////////////////////////////////////////////
// WinMain()
/////////////////////////////////////////////////////
int PASCAL WinMain(HINSTANCE hInstance,
                   HINSTANCE hPrevInstance,
                   LPSTR lpszCmdLine, int nCmdShow)
{
  TStatbarApp StatbarApp("StatbarApp2", hInstance,
              hPrevInstance, lpszCmdLine,
              nCmdShow);
  StatbarApp.Run();
  return StatbarApp.Status;
}
```

Listing 9.6. STATWND2.H—the main window's header file.

```
// STATWND2.H: Header file for the main window.

#ifndef _STATWND2_H
#define _STATWND2_H

#include "statbar2.h"

_CLASSDEF(TStatbarWnd)
class TStatbarWnd: public TWindow {
  PTStatbar pstatbar;
public:
  TStatbarWnd(PTWindowsObject AParent, LPSTR ATitle);
  virtual void WMSize(RTMessage)
      = [WM_FIRST + WM_SIZE];
};

#endif
```

Listing 9.7. STATWND2.CPP—the main window's implementation.

```
// STATWND2.CPP: Implementation for the main window.

#include <owl.h>
#include "statbar2.h"
#include "statwnd2.h"


//////////////////////////////////////////////////////
// TStatbarWnd::TStatbarWnd()
//
// This is the main window's constructor.
//////////////////////////////////////////////////////
TStatbarWnd::TStatbarWnd(PTWindowsObject AParent,
                LPSTR ATitle): TWindow(AParent, ATitle)
{
  // Set the window's size.
  Attr.X = 40;
  Attr.Y = 40;
  Attr.H = GetSystemMetrics(SM_CYSCREEN) / 1.5;
  Attr.W = GetSystemMetrics(SM_CXSCREEN) / 1.5;
```

```
  // Create the status bar object.
  pstatbar = new TStatbar(this);
}


/////////////////////////////////////////////////////
// TStatbarWnd::WMSize()
//
// This function ensures that the status bar window will
// correctly position itself whenever the main window
// is moved.
/////////////////////////////////////////////////////
void TStatbarWnd::WMSize(RTMessage msg)
{
  // Process WM_SIZE message.
  TWindow::WMSize(msg);

  // Send the move message to the status bar.
  pstatbar->MoveBar(msg.LP.Lo, msg.LP.Hi);
}
```

Listing 9.8. STATBAR2.H—the status bar class' header file.

```
// STATBAR2.H: Header file for the status bar class.

#ifndef _STATBAR2_H
#define _STATBAR2_H

_CLASSDEF(TStatbar)
class TStatbar: public TWindow {
public:
  TStatbar(PTWindowsObject AParent);
  virtual LPSTR GetClassName();
  virtual void GetWindowClass(WNDCLASS &AWndClass);
  virtual void Paint(HDC PaintDC, PAINTSTRUCT &);
  void MoveBar(int w, int h);
};

#endif
```

Listing 9.9. STATBAR2.CPP—the status bar class' implementation.

```cpp
// STATBAR2.CPP: Implementation for the status bar class.

#include <owl.h>
#include "statbar2.h"

/////////////////////////////////////////////////////////
// TStatbar::TStatbar()
//
// Status bar constructor.
/////////////////////////////////////////////////////////
TStatbar::TStatbar(PTWindowsObject AParent):
         TWindow(AParent, NULL)
{
  Attr.Style = WS_CHILD ¦ WS_VISIBLE ¦ WS_BORDER;
}


/////////////////////////////////////////////////////////
// TStatbar::GetWindowClass()
//
// Set attributes for registering a status bar window
// class.
/////////////////////////////////////////////////////////
void TStatbar::GetWindowClass(WNDCLASS &AWndClass)
{
  // Set the default registration attributes.
  TWindow::GetWindowClass(AWndClass);

  // Set the window background color to light gray.
  AWndClass.hbrBackground = GetStockObject(LTGRAY_BRUSH);
}


/////////////////////////////////////////////////////////
// TStatbar::GetClassName()
//
// Supply the class name for the status bar window.
/////////////////////////////////////////////////////////
LPSTR TStatbar::GetClassName()
{
  return "TStatbar2";
}
```

```
/////////////////////////////////////////////////////
// TStatbar::MoveBar()
//
// Respond to message from main window to move status
// bar to new location.
/////////////////////////////////////////////////////
void TStatbar::MoveBar(int w, int h)
{
  MoveWindow(HWindow, 0, h-22, w, 22, TRUE);
}


/////////////////////////////////////////////////////
// TStatbar::Paint()
//
// Draw 3-D outline and text into status bar.
/////////////////////////////////////////////////////
void TStatbar::Paint(HDC DC, PAINTSTRUCT&)
{
  RECT r;

  // Get the size of the client area.
  GetClientRect(HWindow, &r);

  // Draw a 3-D border.
  HPEN new_pen = GetStockObject(BLACK_PEN);
  HPEN prev_pen = SelectObject(DC, new_pen);
  MoveTo(DC, r.left+2, r.bottom-2);
  LineTo(DC, r.left+2, r.top+2);
  LineTo(DC, r.right-2, r.top+2);
  new_pen = GetStockObject(WHITE_PEN);
  SelectObject(DC, new_pen);
  MoveTo(DC, r.left+2, r.bottom-2);
  LineTo(DC, r.right-2, r.bottom-2);
  LineTo(DC, r.right-2, r.top+2);

  // Print info string.
  char s[] = "Client Area Width:     ";
  wsprintf(&s[20], "%d", Attr.W);
  HANDLE prev_mode = SetBkMode(DC, TRANSPARENT);
  TextOut(DC, r.left+10, r.top+2, s, lstrlen(s));

  // Restore old pen and mode.
  SelectObject(DC, prev_pen);
  SetBkMode(DC, prev_mode);
}
```

307

When you run this program, the window shown in Figure 9.4 appears. Except for the new window name, the differences between this version and the first one are not apparent on-screen. The changes are in the code, where you make the status bar a separate object.

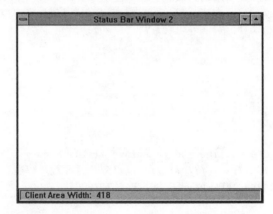

Figure 9.4. The second version of the status bar application.

The application class for this program and the first version are almost identical; the differences are that the window caption is now Status Bar Window 2 and the application's name is `StatbarApp2`. In addition, new versions of the `include` files are used.

Look at the main window class, `TStatbarWnd`:

```
_CLASSDEF(TStatbarWnd)
class TStatbarWnd: public TWindow {
  PTStatbar pstatbar;
public:
  TStatbarWnd(PTWindowsObject AParent, LPSTR ATitle);
  virtual void WMSize(RTMessage)
      = [WM_FIRST + WM_SIZE];
};
```

The first difference here is the `pstatbar` private data member, which is a pointer to this window's status bar object. Soon you see how this pointer fits in with the scheme of things. Another big difference is the conspicuous lack of a `Paint()` function. Because the status bar can now take care of itself, there's no need for the main window to paint it. (In a full application, you'd still need the `Paint()` function to draw the data the main window should display.)

Another difference in the new main window class is the WMSize() message-response member function. The WM_SIZE message is sent by Windows when the user changes the size of a window. If the user changes the size of the main window, the size of the status bar window must be changed, too. As you will see, the program can take care of this by responding to the WM_SIZE message.

The new TStatbarWnd constructor is similar to the first version:

```
TStatbarWnd::TStatbarWnd(PTWindowsObject AParent,
                LPSTR ATitle): TWindow(AParent, ATitle)
{
  // Set the window's size.
  Attr.X = 40;
  Attr.Y = 40;
  Attr.H = GetSystemMetrics(SM_CYSCREEN) / 1.5;
  Attr.W = GetSystemMetrics(SM_CXSCREEN) / 1.5;

  // Create the status bar object.
  pstatbar = new TStatbar(this);
}
```

Here, besides calling the TWindow() constructor and setting the position and size of the window, a new TStatbar object is created, a pointer to which is saved in the pstatbar data member. The program uses this pointer to call the status bar's member functions, as you can see in the WMSize() function:

```
void TStatbarWnd::WMSize(RTMessage msg)
{
  // Process WM_SIZE message.
  TWindow::WMSize(msg);

  // Send the move message to the status bar.
  pstatbar->MoveBar(msg.LP.Lo, msg.LP.Hi);
}
```

As mentioned, this function responds to WM_SIZE messages directed to the main window. When the window receives this message, the WMSize() message-response function is called. Here, the ancestor function is called to size the main window. Then the status bar's member function, MoveBar(), is called, which repositions the status bar at the bottom of the main window. The parameters to this function are the main window's new width and height as retrieved from the msg window message.

Most of the action in the program takes place in the status bar's class, `TStatbar`:

```
_CLASSDEF(TStatbar)
class TStatbar: public TWindow {
public:
  TStatbar(PTWindowsObject AParent);
  virtual LPSTR GetClassName();
  virtual void GetWindowClass(WNDCLASS &AWndClass);
  virtual void Paint(HDC PaintDC, PAINTSTRUCT &);
  void MoveBar(int w, int h);
};
```

This class includes the usual constructor and member functions to register a new window class, paint the status bar on-screen, and move the status bar to a new location. The constructor simply sets the new window's style:

```
TStatbar::TStatbar(PTWindowsObject AParent):
        TWindow(AParent, NULL)
{
  Attr.Style = WS_CHILD ¦ WS_VISIBLE ¦ WS_BORDER;
}
```

The program doesn't have to set the status bar's position here, because that is handled by the `MoveBar()` function. But before worrying about moving a status bar, you must create its Windows class.

 Note: Don't confuse a window's *Windows class* with a window's *object class*. A Windows class is the type of window that Windows displays on-screen and includes such attributes as its color, cursor type, and menu. The window's object class determines how it fits into the ObjectWindows object-oriented hierarchy.

To create a new Windows class, you must override the ObjectWindows `GetWindowClass()` function:

```
void TStatbar::GetWindowClass(WNDCLASS &AWndClass)
{
  // Set the default registration attributes.
  TWindow::GetWindowClass(AWndClass);

  // Set the window background color to light gray.
  AWndClass.hbrBackground = GetStockObject(LTGRAY_BRUSH);
}
```

Here, the program first calls the ancestor function to set the window's class attributes to the ObjectWindows default values. Then it modifies the class by changing the background brush to the light gray brush. The handle to this brush is stored in the hbrBackground member of the AWndClass structure, which is used to pass the class attributes to Windows when the new class is registered.

Besides setting the Windows class attributes, you must also give the new class a name. This is done by overriding the GetClassName() function:

```
LPSTR TStatbar::GetClassName()
{
  return "TStatbar2";
}
```

ObjectWindows calls this function when it registers the new Windows class. The program doesn't call the GetClassName() ancestor function because it only supplies the default class name OWLWindow. You want to use your new class name, not the default name supplied by ObjectWindows.

When the new status bar window is created (in the TStatbarWnd constructor), the window appears as a gray rectangle, thanks to your changing its background brush to a light gray brush. To fill the status bar with data that is updated as required, the status bar needs a Paint() function, just like any window:

```
void TStatbar::Paint(HDC DC, PAINTSTRUCT&)
{
  RECT r;

  // Get the size of the client area.
  GetClientRect(HWindow, &r);

  // Draw a 3-D border.
  HPEN new_pen = GetStockObject(BLACK_PEN);
  HPEN prev_pen = SelectObject(DC, new_pen);
  MoveTo(DC, r.left+2, r.bottom-2);
  LineTo(DC, r.left+2, r.top+2);
  LineTo(DC, r.right-2, r.top+2);
  new_pen = GetStockObject(WHITE_PEN);
  SelectObject(DC, new_pen);
  MoveTo(DC, r.left+2, r.bottom-2);
  LineTo(DC, r.right-2, r.bottom-2);
```

```
      LineTo(DC, r.right-2, r.top+2);

      // Print info string.
      char s[] = "Client Area Width:      ";
      wsprintf(&s[20], "%d", Attr.W);
      HANDLE prev_mode = SetBkMode(DC, TRANSPARENT);
      TextOut(DC, r.left+10, r.top+2, s, lstrlen(s));

      // Restore old pen and mode.
      SelectObject(DC, prev_pen);
      SetBkMode(DC, prev_mode);
}
```

This `Paint()` function is not unlike the one in the first version of `TStatbarWnd`. It draws the window's 3-D border and displays a string. The coordinates used in the drawing operations are different because now they're relative to the coordinates for the status bar window rather than to the entire main window.

The last function in the new status bar class repositions the status bar in its parent window:

```
void TStatbar::MoveBar(int w, int h)
{
  MoveWindow(HWindow, 0, h-22, w, 22, TRUE);
}
```

If you remember, this function is called by `TStatbarWnd`'s `WMSize()` function, which leaps into action when the user generates a `WM_SIZE` message by changing the size of the main window. The `MoveBar()` parameters are the new width and height of the main window. A call to the Windows API `MoveWindow()` function with these values sets the window's position and size.

That's all there is to creating a status bar window. Unfortunately, this type of status bar exhibits the same type of scrolling problems that the earlier version did: The status bar scrolls along with the rest of the main window's contents. One way around this problem is to place the status bar window into an application that takes advantage of the Multiple Document Interface (MDI). You do this in the next section.

Status Bars and MDI Applications

The Windows Multiple Document Interface (MDI) offers programmers a powerful way to control the objects—especially the document windows—that make up an application. An MDI application not only creates a sort of minidesktop on which the user can organize related windows and icons, but also provides the programmer with many easy-to-implement functions that automatically handle those windows. MDI applications require more effort to program, but their advantages far outweigh any extra labor involved.

Why should you care about MDI applications? First, MDI applications are an important part of learning to program in Windows. Specifically, by making your status bar program an MDI application, you can create status bars and toolbars that are unaffected by the main window, even if that window is scrollable. Could this finally be the cure for your status bar blues?

A Review of MDI Applications

MDI applications in Windows are as common as skid marks on a highway. You may not realize it, but if you use Windows, you use MDI applications. The Windows Program Manager and File Manager, for example, are MDI applications. Other MDI applications with which you may be familiar include Microsoft Works for Windows, Quicken for Windows, Windows System Configuration Editor, PageMaker 4.0, and Borland's Resource Workshop.

What exactly makes up an MDI application? Here's a list of the most important characteristics:

- An MDI application's main window is called a *frame window*. The frame window doesn't provide a workspace for the display of data like a conventional window; rather, it provides a desktop-like surface for the organization of *child* (document) windows.

- When a new file is opened in an MDI application, it is represented by a *document window,* which appears over the frame window's client area. An MDI application may have any number of document windows open simultaneously.

- An MDI frame window always has a *menu bar*, which includes, but is not limited to, a Window menu for controlling MDI document windows. From this menu, document windows can usually be selected, tiled, and cascaded, among other things.

- MDI document windows have no menus. They receive commands from the application's frame-window menu.

- MDI document windows cannot be moved outside the frame window.

- When an MDI document window is minimized, it's displayed as an icon at the bottom of the frame window.

313

- When an MDI document window is maximized, it takes over the entire frame window, and its controls merge with those of the frame window.

- An MDI application's frame window is covered by an *invisible client window,* which acts as a parent to windows and controls that appear over the frame window.

Most of this probably sounds familiar. If not, you should spend more time using Windows. But what's this invisible client window?

The Mysterious Client Window

Figure 9.5 shows the main elements of an MDI application. One element of particular interest is the *client window.* The client window is an invisible window (well, not always fully invisible, as you see later) that usually covers the frame window's entire client area. The client window is a child to the frame window, and MDI child windows are children to the client window. The client window controls most of what makes an MDI application work. You might think of it as an invisible container that holds many of the elements—including child windows, scroll bars, and icons—that have to work together in an MDI application.

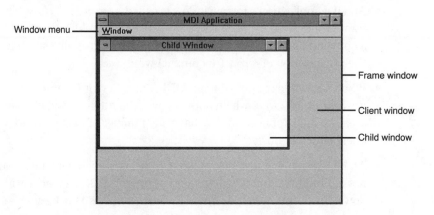

Figure 9.5. The main elements of an MDI application.

Although the client window seems mysterious, it is still nothing more exotic than a window. Like any window, you can manipulate it in various ways. For example, you can resize the client window so it no longer entirely covers the frame window's client area. Consider that MDI child windows have the client window (not the frame window) as their parent and cannot be moved outside the client window. When you reduce the size of the client window, you restrict the area in which the child windows can function. It is this characteristic of the client-window and child-window relationship that makes a scroll-proof status bar possible.

Reserving Space in the Frame Window

To place the status bar somewhere safe—where it can't be ravaged by inconsiderate controls such as scroll bars—you must reserve space for it in the application's frame window. Because the frame window is normally covered by the client window, you must first change the size and position of the client window. When you do this, you uncover sections of the frame window—sections that make perfect homes for windows that you want excluded from normal MDI activity. Listings 9.10 through 9.14 show how you can do this. When you compile and run the listings, they create an MDI application that has space reserved at the bottom of the frame window.

Listing 9.10. STATAPP3.CPP—version 3 of the status bar application.

```
// STATAPP3.CPP: Status bar application, version 3.

#include <owl.h>
#include <mdi.h>
#include "childwnd.h"
#include "statwnd3.h"

class TStatbarApp : public TApplication
{
public:
  TStatbarApp(LPSTR AName, HINSTANCE hInstance,
      HINSTANCE hPrevInstance, LPSTR lpCmdLine,
      int nCmdShow): TApplication(AName, hInstance,
      hPrevInstance, lpCmdLine, nCmdShow) {};
  virtual void InitMainWindow();
};
```

continues

Listing 9.10. Continued

```
/////////////////////////////////////////////////////
// TStatbarApp::InitMainWindow()
//
// This function creates the application's main window.
/////////////////////////////////////////////////////
void TStatbarApp::InitMainWindow()
{
  MainWindow = new TStatbarWnd(Name);
}


/////////////////////////////////////////////////////
// WinMain()
/////////////////////////////////////////////////////
int PASCAL WinMain(HINSTANCE hInstance,
                   HINSTANCE hPrevInstance,
            LPSTR lpCmdLine, int nCmdShow)
{
  TStatbarApp StatbarApp("Status Bar Window 3", hInstance,
                    hPrevInstance, lpCmdLine, nCmdShow);
  StatbarApp.Run();
  return StatbarApp.Status;
}
```

Listing 9.11. STATWND3.H—the frame window's header file.

```
// STATWND3.H -- Header file for the frame window.

#ifndef _STATWND3_H
#define _STATWND3_H

#include <owl.h>

_CLASSDEF(TStatbarWnd)
class TStatbarWnd: public TMDIFrame
{
public:
  TStatbarWnd(LPSTR ATitle);
  virtual void SetupWindow();
  virtual PTWindowsObject InitChild();
```

```
    virtual void WMSize(RTMessage msg)
        = [WM_FIRST + WM_SIZE];
};


#endif
```

Listing 9.12. STATWND3.CPP—the frame window's implementation.

```
// STATWND3.CPP -- Implementation for the frame window.

#include <stdio.h>
#include <owl.h>
#include <mdi.h>
#include "statwnd3.h"
#include "childwnd.h"


//////////////////////////////////////////////////////
// TStatbarWnd::TStatbarWnd()
//
// This is the frame window's constructor.
//////////////////////////////////////////////////////
TStatbarWnd::TStatbarWnd(LPSTR ATitle):
            TMDIFrame(ATitle, "STATMENU")
{
  // Set size and position of frame window.
  Attr.X = 40;
  Attr.Y = 40;
  Attr.H = GetSystemMetrics(SM_CYSCREEN) / 1.5;
  Attr.W = GetSystemMetrics(SM_CXSCREEN) / 1.5;
}


//////////////////////////////////////////////////////
// TStatbarWnd::SetupWindow()
//
// This function creates the starting child window for
// the application.
//////////////////////////////////////////////////////
void TStatbarWnd::SetupWindow()
{
  TMDIFrame::SetupWindow();
```

continues

317

Listing 9.12. Continued

```
  CreateChild();
}


////////////////////////////////////////////////////////
// TStatbarWnd::InitChild()
//
// This function creates a new child window.
////////////////////////////////////////////////////////
PTWindowsObject TStatbarWnd::InitChild()
{
  return (new TMyMDIChild(this));
}


////////////////////////////////////////////////////////
// TStatbarWnd::WMSize()
//
// This function sets the size and position of the
// client window whenever the frame window is moved.
// This assures that space at the bottom of the frame
// window is reserved for the status bar window.
////////////////////////////////////////////////////////
void TStatbarWnd::WMSize(RTMessage msg)
{
  // Process WM_SIZE message.
  TMDIFrame::WMSize(msg);

  // Set the size and position of the client window.
  MoveWindow(ClientWnd->HWindow, 0, 0,
        msg.LP.Lo, msg.LP.Hi-22, TRUE);
}
```

Listing 9.13. CHILDWND.H—the child window's header file.

```
// CHILDWND.H: Header file for the child window.

#ifndef _CHILDWND_H
```

```
#define _CHILDWND_H

_CLASSDEF(TMyMDIChild)
class TMyMDIChild : public TWindow
{
public:
  TMyMDIChild(PTWindowsObject AParent):
       TWindow(AParent, "Child Window") {}
};

#endif
```

Listing 9.14. STATTOOL.RC—resource file for an MDI status bar application.

```
#include <owlrc.h>

STATMENU MENU LOADONCALL MOVEABLE PURE DISCARDABLE
BEGIN
  POPUP "&Window"
  BEGIN
    MenuItem   "C&reate", CM_CREATECHILD
    MenuItem   "&Cascade", CM_CASCADECHILDREN
    MenuItem   "&Tile", CM_TILECHILDREN
    MenuItem   "C&lose All", CM_CLOSECHILDREN
  END
END
```

When you run the program, the screen appears as shown in Figure 9.6. If you examine this figure closely, you see that a client window isn't completely invisible—except in the sense that it has no controls. Its client area is visible because it is often a different color than the client area of the frame window, depending on how the colors for your Windows desktop are configured. If you have your application workspace set to a different color than your window background, you can see the client window (which really is the application workspace).

319

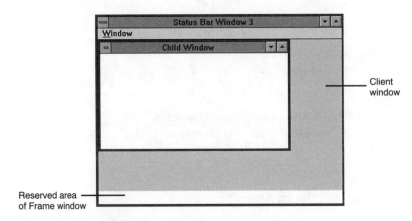

Figure 9.6. The client window exposed.

To see the difference between the frame and client windows more clearly, move the child window so it's off the screen at the left and bottom, as shown in Figure 9.7. Moving the child window this way forces the MDI application to display scroll bars. But because these scroll bar controls are owned by the client window, they do not intrude on the area you reserved in the frame window.

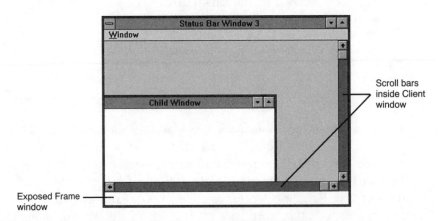

Figure 9.7. The scroll bars are owned by the client window.

As a final experiment, use the Create option of the Window menu to open several new child windows. Then tile them, using the Window menu's Tile option. Figure 9.8 shows the result. Because the child windows have as a parent the client window rather than the frame window, your reserved area is safe, even from the tiling operation.

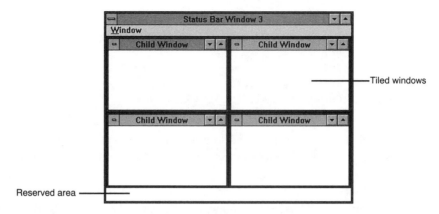

Figure 9.8. MDI child windows are children to the client window.

Now look over the program. The application object in this program is much like the application classes you already examined, so you don't have to spend time with it. The application's main window, however, has been modified extensively:

```
_CLASSDEF(TStatbarWnd)
class TStatbarWnd: public TMDIFrame
{
public:
  TStatbarWnd(LPSTR ATitle);
  virtual void SetupWindow();
  virtual PTWindowsObject InitChild();
  virtual void WMSize(RTMessage msg)
      = [WM_FIRST + WM_SIZE];
};
```

Notice that this window is no longer derived from TWindow. Rather, it is derived from TMDIFrame, which is a special class for MDI frame windows. By using this window class, the program automatically inherits all the power that goes with being an MDI application.

The main window is now a frame window, which means it must be able to create and manage child windows. The child windows display any data that your application has to display. To tackle window-creation duties, the InitChild() function is included.

You examine these functions soon, but first look at the class' constructor:

```
TStatbarWnd::TStatbarWnd(LPSTR ATitle):
          TMDIFrame(ATitle, "STATMENU")
```

321

```
{
  // Set the size and position of the frame window.
  Attr.X = 40;
  Attr.Y = 40;
  Attr.H = GetSystemMetrics(SM_CYSCREEN) / 1.5;
  Attr.W = GetSystemMetrics(SM_CXSCREEN) / 1.5;
}
```

At first glance, this constructor seems identical to the previous main-window constructors. But the ancestor constructor is now `TMDIFrame()`, which requires different parameters than the `TWindow()` constructor. When you derived a window from `TWindow()`, you had to supply the ancestor constructor with a pointer to the parent window, as well as the window's title. Because a `TMDIWindow` can never be a child window, its constructor does not need a pointer to a parent window. A `TMDIWindow` must have a menu, however, so its constructor needs a menu resource ID (in addition to a window title). This parameter may be an integer or a menu name. In this constructor, the program uses the menu name found in the menu's resource, STATAPP3.RC (Listing 9.14).

When an MDI frame window appears on-screen, it contains no child windows. It's up to the program to create those windows. Some applications require that the user select a file before a child window appears. Others automatically begin with a generic child window that is renamed when the user assigns a file to it. The application you're now studying is in the latter category. It creates a starting child window by overriding the `SetupWindow()` function:

```
void TStatbarWnd::SetupWindow()
{
  TMDIFrame::SetupWindow();
  CreateChild();
}
```

Because `SetupWindow()` performs vital services for the frame window, the program must first call the ancestor function, `TMDIFrame::SetupWindow()`. Afterwards, it can set up the specific frame window. In this case, the program creates the first child window by calling `CreateChild()`, which is a member function of the `TMDIFrame` class. This function calls `InitChild()`, which is overridden by `TStatbarWnd::InitChild()`:

```
PTWindowsObject TStatbarWnd::InitChild()
{
  return (new TMyMDIChild(this));
}
```

This function comprises a single line of code that performs two tasks. First, it calls new to create a new child-window object on the heap. Then, the pointer returned from new is returned from the function. Notice that, when the user selects the Create entry of the Window menu, CreateChild() is called automatically by TMDIFrame's member function CMCreateChild(). To get this service, you need only provide a menu item with the CM_CREATECHILD ID.

The final function, the WMSize() message-response function, handles the application's client window:

```
void TStatbarWnd::WMSize(RTMessage msg)
{
  // Process WM_SIZE message.
  TMDIFrame::WMSize(msg);

  // Set the size and position of the client window.
  MoveWindow(ClientWnd->HWindow, 0, 0,
            msg.LP.Lo, msg.LP.Hi-22, TRUE);
}
```

Here, the program first calls TMDIFrame's WMSize() function to properly process the WM_SIZE message. Then it resizes and repositions the client window with a call to MoveWindow(). Accessing the client window's handle, which is the first parameter in the call to MoveWindow(), is easy thanks to the ClientWnd data member, which contains a pointer to the frame window's client window. (This pointer is supplied by ObjectWindows as a data member of the TMDIFrame class. You needn't do anything to create or initialize it.)

As in previous versions of this program, the new window's width and height, supplied in the message structure, are used to calculate the new size of the child window. Here, the child window is not a status bar, but rather the client window. Notice that the height of the client window is set to 22 pixels shorter than the height of the frame window. This reserves space for the status bar, which you add in the next version of this program.

The only thing left to look at is the child window class:

```
_CLASSDEF(TMyMDIChild)
class TMyMDIChild : public TWindow
{
public:
  TMyMDIChild(PTWindowsObject AParent):
            TWindow(AParent, "Child Window") {}
};
```

A child-window class couldn't get much simpler than this. It has only a single, in-line constructor that creates a child window. Because the program doesn't use these windows, this is all the code you need. This simple class demonstrates the power of the ObjectWindows library. Imagine creating a window with a single line of code!

Now that you know how to handle the client window, the next sections show you how to add your status bar window and a toolbar.

Adding a Status Bar

In the preceding section, you learned to reserve space in an MDI application's frame window for screen objects that shouldn't be treated as MDI objects. Armed with this technique, you can now add a status bar to the MDI application. Listings 9.15 through 9.19 are the program listings needed to construct this application.

Listing 9.15. STATAPP4.CPP—version 4 of the status bar application.

```
// STATAPP4.CPP: Status bar application, version 4.

#include <owl.h>
#include <mdi.h>
#include "childwnd.h"
#include "statwnd4.h"

class TStatbarApp : public TApplication
{
public:
  TStatbarApp(LPSTR AName, HINSTANCE hInstance,
      HINSTANCE hPrevInstance, LPSTR lpCmdLine,
      int nCmdShow): TApplication(AName, hInstance,
      hPrevInstance, lpCmdLine, nCmdShow) {};
  virtual void InitMainWindow();
};


///////////////////////////////////////////////////////
// TStatbarApp::InitMainWindow()
//
// This function creates the application's main window.
///////////////////////////////////////////////////////
void TStatbarApp::InitMainWindow()
```

```
{
  MainWindow = new TStatbarWnd(Name);
}


/////////////////////////////////////////////////////
// WinMain()
/////////////////////////////////////////////////////
int PASCAL WinMain(HINSTANCE hInstance,
                   HINSTANCE hPrevInstance,
             LPSTR lpCmdLine, int nCmdShow)
{
  TStatbarApp StatbarApp("Status Bar Window 4", hInstance,
                      hPrevInstance, lpCmdLine, nCmdShow);
  StatbarApp.Run();
  return StatbarApp.Status;
}
```

Listing 9.16. STATWND4.H—the frame window's header file.

```
// STATWND4.H -- Header file for the frame window.

#ifndef _STATWND4_H
#define _STATWND4_H

#include <owl.h>
#include "statbar4.h"

_CLASSDEF(TStatbarWnd)
class TStatbarWnd: public TMDIFrame
{
private:
  PTStatbar pstatbar;

public:
  TStatbarWnd(LPSTR ATitle);
  virtual void SetupWindow(void);
  virtual PTWindowsObject InitChild();
  virtual void WMSize(RTMessage msg)
      = [WM_FIRST + WM_SIZE];
};

#endif
```

Listing 9.17. STATWND4.CPP—the frame window's implementation.

```
// STATWND4.CPP -- Implementation for the frame window.

#include <stdio.h>
#include <owl.h>
#include <mdi.h>
#include "statwnd4.h"
#include "childwnd.h"
#include "statbar4.h"


//////////////////////////////////////////////////////
// TStatbarWnd::TStatbarWnd()
//
// This is the frame window's constructor.
//////////////////////////////////////////////////////
TStatbarWnd::TStatbarWnd(LPSTR ATitle):
    TMDIFrame(ATitle, "STATMENU")
{
  // Set size and position of frame window.
  Attr.X = 40;
  Attr.Y = 40;
  Attr.H = GetSystemMetrics(SM_CYSCREEN) / 1.5;
  Attr.W = GetSystemMetrics(SM_CXSCREEN) / 1.5;

  // Create status bar object.
  pstatbar =  new TStatbar(this);
}


//////////////////////////////////////////////////////
// TStatbarWnd::SetupWindow()
//
// This function creates the starting child window for
// the application.
//////////////////////////////////////////////////////
void TStatbarWnd::SetupWindow(void)
{
  TMDIFrame::SetupWindow();
  CreateChild();
}
```

```
//////////////////////////////////////////////////////
// TStatbarWnd::InitChild()
//
// This function creates a new child window.
//////////////////////////////////////////////////////
PTWindowsObject TStatbarWnd::InitChild()
{
  return (new TMyMDIChild(this));
}


//////////////////////////////////////////////////////
// TStatbarWnd::WMSize()
//
// This function sets the size and position of the
// client window and the status bar whenever the frame
// window is moved.
//////////////////////////////////////////////////////
void TStatbarWnd::WMSize(RTMessage msg)
{
  // Process WM_SIZE message.
  TMDIFrame::WMSize(msg);

  // Set the size and position of the client window.
  MoveWindow(ClientWnd->HWindow, 0, 0, msg.LP.Lo,
          msg.LP.Hi-22, TRUE);

  // Set the size and position of the status bar.
  pstatbar->MoveBar(msg.LP.Lo, msg.LP.Hi);
}
```

Listing 9.18. STATBAR4.H—the status bar's header file.

```
// STATBAR4.H -- Header file for status bar class.

#ifndef _STATBAR4_H
#define _STATBAR4_H

_CLASSDEF(TStatbar)
class TStatbar: public TWindow {
```

continues

327

Listing 9.18. Continued

```
public:
  TStatbar(PTWindowsObject AParent);
  virtual LPSTR GetClassName();
  virtual void GetWindowClass(WNDCLASS &AWndClass);
  virtual void Paint(HDC PaintDC, PAINTSTRUCT &);
  void MoveBar(int w, int h);
};


#endif
```

Listing 9.19. STATBAR4.CPP—the status bar class' implementation.

```
// STATBAR4.CPP: Implementation for status bar class.

#include <owl.h>
#include "statbar4.h"

//////////////////////////////////////////////////////
// TStatbar::TStatbar()
//
// Status bar constructor.
//////////////////////////////////////////////////////
TStatbar::TStatbar(PTWindowsObject AParent):
        TWindow(AParent, NULL)
{
  SetFlags(WB_MDICHILD, FALSE);
  Attr.Style = WS_CHILD | WS_VISIBLE | WS_BORDER;
}


//////////////////////////////////////////////////////
// TStatbar::GetWindowClass()
//
// Initialize a window class for the status bar.
//////////////////////////////////////////////////////
void TStatbar::GetWindowClass(WNDCLASS &AWndClass)
{
  // Allow normal processing.
  TWindow::GetWindowClass(AWndClass);

  // Set the window background color to light gray.
```

```
      AWndClass.hbrBackground = GetStockObject(LTGRAY_BRUSH);
}


/////////////////////////////////////////////////////
// TStatbar::GetClassName()
//
// Supply the class name for the status bar window.
/////////////////////////////////////////////////////
LPSTR TStatbar::GetClassName()
{
  return "TStatbar4";
}


/////////////////////////////////////////////////////
// TStatbar::MoveBar()
//
// Respond to the message from main window to move the
// status bar to a new location.
/////////////////////////////////////////////////////
void TStatbar::MoveBar(int w, int h)
{
  MoveWindow(HWindow, 0, h-22, w, 22, TRUE);
}


/////////////////////////////////////////////////////
// TStatbar::Paint()
//
// Draw a 3-D outline and text into status bar.
/////////////////////////////////////////////////////
void TStatbar::Paint(HDC DC, PAINTSTRUCT&)
{
  RECT r;

  // Get the size of the client area.
  GetClientRect(HWindow, &r);

  // Draw a 3-D border.
  int new_pen = GetStockObject(BLACK_PEN);
  int prev_pen = SelectObject(DC, new_pen);
  MoveTo(DC, r.left+2, r.bottom-2);
  LineTo(DC, r.left+2, r.top+2);
```

continues

329

Listing 9.19. Continued

```
LineTo(DC, r.right-2, r.top+2);
new_pen = GetStockObject(WHITE_PEN);
SelectObject(DC, new_pen);
MoveTo(DC, r.left+2, r.bottom-2);
LineTo(DC, r.right-2, r.bottom-2);
LineTo(DC, r.right-2, r.top+2);

// Print info string.
char s[] = "Client Area Width:      ";
wsprintf(&s[20], "%d", Attr.W);
int prev_mode = SetBkMode(DC, TRANSPARENT);
TextOut(DC, r.left+10, r.top+2, s, lstrlen(s));

// Restore the old pen and mode.
SelectObject(DC, prev_pen);
SetBkMode(DC, prev_mode);
}
```

When you run the program, the application's main window appears with your status bar drawn at the bottom, as shown in Figure 9.9. No matter what you do with the window's controls, the status window is unaffected. For example, Figure 9.10 shows the application when the child window has been maximized.

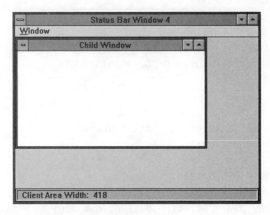

Figure 9.9. The final status bar application.

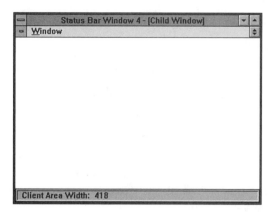

Figure 9.10. Even maximizing a child window does not affect the status bar.

As you've probably guessed, the application class for this program is similar to previous versions. Likewise, the frame window class has undergone only minimal adjustments. One change can be found in the class' constructor:

```
TStatbarWnd::TStatbarWnd(LPSTR ATitle):
          TMDIFrame(ATitle, "STATMENU")
{
  // Set the size and position of the frame window.
  Attr.X = 40;
  Attr.Y = 40;
  Attr.H = GetSystemMetrics(SM_CYSCREEN) / 1.5;
  Attr.W = GetSystemMetrics(SM_CXSCREEN) / 1.5;

  // Create the status bar object.
  pstatbar =  new TStatbar(this);
}
```

Here, besides setting the frame window's size and position, the program also creates a `TStatbar` object and stores a pointer to the object in `pstatbar`. You can also find a change in the class' `WMSize()` function:

```
void TStatbarWnd::WMSize(RTMessage msg)
{
  // Process WM_SIZE message.
```

331

```
TMDIFrame::WMSize(msg);

// Set the size and position of the client window.
MoveWindow(ClientWnd->HWindow, 0, 0, msg.LP.Lo,
        msg.LP.Hi-22, TRUE);

// Set the size and position of the status bar.
pstatbar->MoveBar(msg.LP.Lo, msg.LP.Hi);
}
```

Here, the program resizes and repositions not only the client window but also the status window. The status window is resized with a call to the status window's `MoveBar()` function.

Not surprisingly, the status bar class is also similar to the previous one. Its constructor, however, has one important change:

```
TStatbar::TStatbar(PTWindowsObject AParent):
        TWindow(AParent, NULL)
{
  SetFlags(WB_MDICHILD, FALSE);
  Attr.Style = WS_CHILD ¦ WS_VISIBLE ¦ WS_BORDER;
}
```

Notice the call to the `SetFlags()` function. This function is a member of the ObjectWindows `TWindowsObject` class, from which all windows are derived. By calling this function with the parameters of `WM_MDICHILD` and `FALSE`, the program informs ObjectWindows that this object is not an MDI child window, which it's assumed to be in an MDI application.

If the program doesn't call `SetFlags()`, the status bar object will have as its parent the client window, not the frame window. In this case, when the program tries to draw the status bar at the bottom of the frame window, it is drawn in the client window instead.

At first, it looks as though the status bar wasn't drawn, because its coordinates are below the visible portion of the client window. However, the addition of scroll bars to the main window is a hint that if you scroll the window you see the status window, as shown in Figure 9.11. Notice that the status window is missing its display string and 3-D outline, but has gained a few controls. This is because it has inherited the type of controls an MDI child window must have. This bizarre new status bar can be sized, as shown in Figure 9.12, proving that it has indeed metamorphosed into a full-fledged MDI child window.

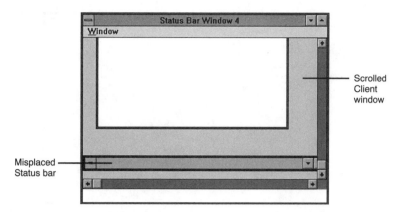

Figure 9.11. The status bar transformed into a regular child window.

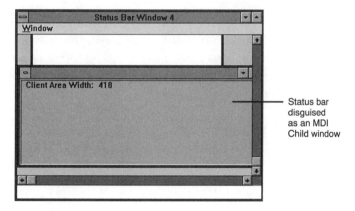

Figure 9.12. The child-window status bar can even be resized.

You're now ready to add a toolbar to the developing application. In the next section, you discover that a toolbar is little more than a status bar with controls.

Adding a Toolbar

It may have occurred to you that, if you can change the size of the client window to make room at the bottom of the frame window, you can make room also in other areas of the frame window. All you have to do is resize and reposition the client window as necessary. You can reserve space all the way around the client window, as shown in Figure 9.13.

333

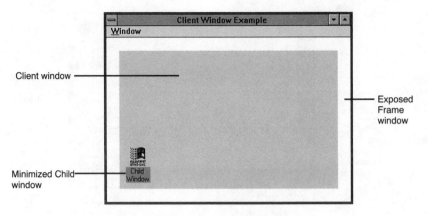

Client window ——

Minimized Child——
window

—— Exposed
Frame
window

Child
Window

Figure 9.13. The client window can be reduced to any size.

So, the first step in adding a toolbar to your application is to reserve room at the top of the frame window, while leaving room at the bottom for the status bar. Then you can create a toolbar using the same techniques you used to create the status bar. Compile and run Listings 9.20 through 9.24 to see the toolbar application.

Listing 9.20. TOOLAPP.CPP—the toolbar application.

```
// ToolAPP.CPP: Tool bar application.

#include <owl.h>
#include <mdi.h>
#include "childwnd.h"
#include "toolwnd.h"

class TToolbarApp : public TApplication
{
public:
  TToolbarApp(LPSTR AName, HINSTANCE hInstance,
      HINSTANCE hPrevInstance, LPSTR lpCmdLine,
      int nCmdShow): TApplication(AName, hInstance,
      hPrevInstance, lpCmdLine, nCmdShow) {};
  virtual void InitMainWindow();
};


////////////////////////////////////////////////////////
// TToolbarApp::InitMainWindow()
```

```
//
// This function creates the application's main window.
/////////////////////////////////////////////////////
void TToolbarApp::InitMainWindow()
{
  MainWindow = new TToolbarWnd(Name);
}


/////////////////////////////////////////////////////
// WinMain()
/////////////////////////////////////////////////////
int PASCAL WinMain(HINSTANCE hInstance,
                   HINSTANCE hPrevInstance,
            LPSTR lpCmdLine, int nCmdShow)
{
  TToolbarApp ToolbarApp("Tool Bar Window", hInstance,
            hPrevInstance, lpCmdLine, nCmdShow);
  ToolbarApp.Run();
  return ToolbarApp.Status;
}
```

Listing 9.21. TOOLWND.H—the frame window's header file.

```
// TOOLWND.H -- Header file for the frame window.

#ifndef _TOOLWND_H
#define _TOOLWND_H

#include <owl.h>
#include "toolbar.h"
#include "statbar4.h"

_CLASSDEF(TToolbarWnd)
class TToolbarWnd: public TMDIFrame
{
private:
  PTStatbar pstatbar;
  PTToolbar ptoolbar;

public:
```

continues

335

Listing 9.21. Continued

```cpp
    TToolbarWnd(LPSTR ATitle);
    virtual void SetupWindow();
    virtual PTWindowsObject InitChild();
    virtual void WMSize(RTMessage msg)
        = [WM_FIRST + WM_SIZE];
};


#endif
```

Listing 9.22. TOOLWND.CPP—the frame window's implementation.

```cpp
// TOOLWND.CPP -- Implementation for the frame window.

#include <stdio.h>
#include <owl.h>
#include <mdi.h>
#include "toolwnd.h"
#include "childwnd.h"
#include "statbar4.h"
#include "toolbar.h"


/////////////////////////////////////////////////////////
// TToolbarWnd::TToolbarWnd()
//
// This is the frame window's constructor.
/////////////////////////////////////////////////////////
TToolbarWnd::TToolbarWnd(LPSTR ATitle):
            TMDIFrame(ATitle, "STATMENU")
{
    // Set size and position of frame window.
    Attr.X = 40;
    Attr.Y = 40;
    Attr.H = GetSystemMetrics(SM_CYSCREEN) / 1.5;
    Attr.W = GetSystemMetrics(SM_CXSCREEN) / 1.5;

    // Create status bar and tool bar objects.
    pstatbar =  new TStatbar(this);
    ptoolbar = new TToolbar(this);
}
```

```
/////////////////////////////////////////////////////
// TToolbarWnd::SetupWindow()
//
// This function creates the starting child window for
// the application.
/////////////////////////////////////////////////////
void TToolbarWnd::SetupWindow()
{
  TMDIFrame::SetupWindow();
  CreateChild();
  HWND childh = GetWindow(ClientWnd->HWindow, GW_CHILD);
  SendMessage(ClientWnd->HWindow, WM_MDIMAXIMIZE, childh, 0);
}


/////////////////////////////////////////////////////
// TToolbarWnd::InitChild()
//
// This function creates a new child window.
/////////////////////////////////////////////////////
PTWindowsObject TToolbarWnd::InitChild()
{
  return(new TMyMDIChild(this));
}


/////////////////////////////////////////////////////
// TToolbarWnd::WMSize()
//
// This function sets the size and position of the
// client window, the status bar, and the tool bar
// whenever the frame window is moved.
/////////////////////////////////////////////////////
void TToolbarWnd::WMSize(RTMessage msg)
{
  // Process WM_SIZE message.
  TMDIFrame::WMSize(msg);

  // Set the size and position of the client window.
  MoveWindow(ClientWnd->HWindow, 0, 26, msg.LP.Lo,
             msg.LP.Hi-48, TRUE);

  // Set the size and position of the status bar.
  pstatbar->MoveBar(msg.LP.Lo, msg.LP.Hi);
  ptoolbar->MoveBar(msg.LP.Lo);
}
```

Listing 9.23. TOOLBAR.H—the toolbar class' header file.

```
// TOOLBAR.H: Header file for the tool bar class.

#ifndef _TOOLBAR_H
#define _TOOLBAR_H

_CLASSDEF(TToolbar)
class TToolbar: public TWindow {
public:
  TToolbar(PTWindowsObject AParent);
  virtual LPSTR GetClassName();
  virtual void GetWindowClass(WNDCLASS &AWndClass);
  virtual void Paint(HDC PaintDC, PAINTSTRUCT &);
  virtual void ButtonMsg()
      = [ID_FIRST + 100];
  void MoveBar(int w);
};

#endif
```

Listing 9.24. TOOLBAR.CPP—the toolbar class' implementation.

```
// TOOLBAR.CPP: Implementation for the tool bar class.

#include <owl.h>
#include <button.h>
#include "toolbar.h"

//////////////////////////////////////////////////////////
// TToolbar::TToolbar()
//
// Tool bar constructor.
//////////////////////////////////////////////////////////
TToolbar::TToolbar(PTWindowsObject AParent):
        TWindow(AParent, NULL)
{
  SetFlags(WB_MDICHILD, FALSE);
  Attr.Style = WS_CHILD ¦ WS_VISIBLE ¦ WS_BORDER;
  new TButton(this,100,"Create",100,2,200,20,FALSE);
```

```
}


/////////////////////////////////////////////////////
// TToolbar::GetWindowClass()
//
// Set up a window class for the tool bar.
/////////////////////////////////////////////////////
void TToolbar::GetWindowClass(WNDCLASS &AWndClass)
{
  // Allow normal processing.
  TWindow::GetWindowClass(AWndClass);

  // Set the window background color to light gray.
  AWndClass.hbrBackground = GetStockObject(LTGRAY_BRUSH);
}


/////////////////////////////////////////////////////
// TToolbar::GetClassName()
//
// Supply a class name for the tool bar.
/////////////////////////////////////////////////////
LPSTR TToolbar::GetClassName()
{
  return "ToolBar";
}


/////////////////////////////////////////////////////
// TToolbar::MoveBar()
//
// Respond to the message from main window to move the
// tool bar to a new location.
/////////////////////////////////////////////////////
void TToolbar::MoveBar(int w)
{
  MoveWindow(HWindow, 0, 0, w, 26, TRUE);
}


/////////////////////////////////////////////////////
// TToolbar::Paint()
//
```

continues

339

Listing 9.24. Continued

```
// Draw a 3-D outline and text into the tool bar.
/////////////////////////////////////////////////////////
void TToolbar::Paint(HDC DC, PAINTSTRUCT&)
{
  RECT r;

  // Get the size of the client area.
  GetClientRect(HWindow, &r);

  // Draw 3-D graphics.
  HPEN new_pen = GetStockObject(BLACK_PEN);
  HPEN prev_pen = SelectObject(DC, new_pen);
  MoveTo(DC, r.left+4, r.bottom-4);
  LineTo(DC, r.left+4, r.top+4);
  LineTo(DC, r.left+90, r.top+4);
  new_pen = GetStockObject(WHITE_PEN);
  SelectObject(DC, new_pen);
  MoveTo(DC, r.left+4, r.bottom-4);
  LineTo(DC, r.left+90, r.bottom-4);
  LineTo(DC, r.left+90, r.top+4);

  new_pen = GetStockObject(BLACK_PEN);
  SelectObject(DC, new_pen);
  MoveTo(DC, r.left+309, r.bottom-4);
  LineTo(DC, r.left+309, r.top+4);
  LineTo(DC, r.right-4, r.top+4);
  new_pen = GetStockObject(WHITE_PEN);
  SelectObject(DC, new_pen);
  MoveTo(DC, r.left+309, r.bottom-4);
  LineTo(DC, r.right-4, r.bottom-4);
  LineTo(DC, r.right-4, r.top+4);

  // Restore the old pen and mode.
  SelectObject(DC, prev_pen);
}


/////////////////////////////////////////////////////////
// TToolbar::ButtonMsg()
//
// When the user clicks the tool bar's button, this
// function responds by sending a CM_CREATECHILD message
```

```
// to the frame window.
////////////////////////////////////////////////////////
void TToolbar::ButtonMsg()
{
  SendMessage(Parent->HWindow,
          WM_COMMAND, CM_CREATECHILD, 0);
}
```

Besides the now-familiar status bar, this application has a toolbar containing a single button, as shown in Figure 9.14. When you click this button, a new child window appears. This button, then, is a shortcut for choosing the Create option of the Window menu.

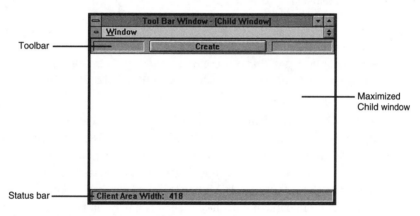

Figure 9.14. The toolbar application.

Because much of the application is similar to the previous versions, you look at only the functions that play an important role in adding the toolbar to the program. The first function on the list is the frame window's constructor:

```
TToolbarWnd::TToolbarWnd(LPSTR ATitle):
        TMDIFrame(ATitle, "STATMENU")
{
  // Set the size and position of the frame window.
  Attr.X = 40;
  Attr.Y = 40;
  Attr.H = GetSystemMetrics(SM_CYSCREEN) / 1.5;
  Attr.W = GetSystemMetrics(SM_CXSCREEN) / 1.5;

  // Create the status bar and tool bar objects.
```

```
  pstatbar =  new TStatbar(this);
  ptoolbar = new TToolbar(this);
}
```

Here, the program sets the size and position of the window, as usual. Then, after creating a new status bar object, it creates a new toolbar object, too. The `ptoolbar` pointer, like `pstatbar`, is a data member of the frame window class, `TToolbarWnd`.

When you ran this program, you may have been surprised to see that the first child window was not only already created, but also maximized. This little piece of prestidigitation is accomplished in the frame window's `SetupWindow()` function:

```
void TToolbarWnd::SetupWindow()
{
  TMDIFrame::SetupWindow();
  CreateChild();
  HWND childh = GetWindow(ClientWnd->HWindow, GW_CHILD);
  SendMessage(ClientWnd->HWindow, WM_MDIMAXIMIZE, childh, 0);
}
```

To maximize the child window, you get its handle by a call to the Windows API `GetWindow()` function. Then you call the Windows API `SendMessage()` function to send a `WM_MDIMAXIMIZE` message to the child window. (The message is actually sent to the client window, which then passes it to the window indicated by the `childh` handle.) When the child window receives the message, it responds by maximizing itself, just as if the user had clicked its maximize button.

The last important change in the frame window class is in its `WMSize()` function:

```
void TToolbarWnd::WMSize(RTMessage msg)
{
  // Process WM_SIZE message.
  TMDIFrame::WMSize(msg);

  // Set the size and position of the client window.
  MoveWindow(ClientWnd->HWindow, 0, 26, msg.LP.Lo,
          msg.LP.Hi-48, TRUE);

  // Set the size and position of the status bar.
  pstatbar->MoveBar(msg.LP.Lo, msg.LP.Hi);
  ptoolbar->MoveBar(msg.LP.Lo);
}
```

Just as the program sends a move message to the status bar to keep it in position when the frame window is moved, it must send a move message to the toolbar. The only difference is that your toolbar must know only the window's new width; the height is unnecessary because the toolbar is always drawn at the coordinates 0, 0.

Here is the toolbar's class definition:

```
_CLASSDEF(TToolbar)
class TToolbar: public TWindow {
public:
  TToolbar(PTWindowsObject AParent);
  virtual LPSTR GetClassName();
  virtual void GetWindowClass(WNDCLASS &AWndClass);
  virtual void Paint(HDC PaintDC, PAINTSTRUCT &);
  virtual void ButtonMsg()
      = [ID_FIRST + 100];
  void MoveBar(int w);
};
```

Everything looks similar to the status bar class definition, except for the addition of the `ButtonMsg()` message-response function. As you saw when you ran the program, the toolbar contains a button that, when clicked, creates a new child window. This function responds to those button clicks. The button is added to the toolbar in the toolbar's constructor:

```
TToolbar::TToolbar(PTWindowsObject AParent):
        TWindow(AParent, NULL)
{
  SetFlags(WB_MDICHILD, FALSE);
  Attr.Style = WS_CHILD | WS_VISIBLE | WS_BORDER;
  new TButton(this,100,"Create",100,2,200,20,FALSE);
}
```

Here, the program first informs Windows that the toolbar is not an MDI child window. Then it sets the window's style attributes and adds the button to the toolbar by using `new` to create a `TButton` object on the heap.

The `this` parameter is the button's parent window, which is the toolbar. The first integer parameter, 100, is the button's ID. The string parameter is the text that appears on the button. The remaining integer parameters are the button's `x` and `y` coordinates, with respect to its parent window, and its width and height.

Finally, the last parameter indicates whether the button is the default button, the one that is automatically selected when the user presses Enter. This applies mainly to windows that contain many buttons, such as dialog boxes.

 Note: Remember that every call to an object's functions includes the hidden `this` parameter, which is a pointer to the object that called the function.

When the user clicks the toolbar button, the class' `ButtonMsg()` message-response function, which is keyed to the button's ID number, takes over:

```
void TToolbar::ButtonMsg()
{
  SendMessage(Parent->HWindow,
          WM_COMMAND, CM_CREATECHILD, 0);
}
```

Here, the program simply sends a `CM_CREATECHILD` message to the frame window, which yields the same result as selecting the Create option of the Window menu.

You should be able to figure out the rest of the source code for the toolbar application with little difficulty. Much of it is similar to code you went over earlier in this chapter. In addition, the code is liberally commented.

Conclusion

Keep in mind that, although the example toolbar contains only a single button, you can add as many controls as you like to a toolbar—not only buttons, but also list boxes, check boxes, and any other controls that fit. As users of power applications know, there's nothing like having the tools you need right at your fingertips (or mouse tip, to be precise). As a power programmer, you can provide that consideration to your users.

10

Designing Custom Controls

I n the last chapter, you learned to create custom toolbars for your application's main window. By adding a toolbar to your applications, you provide convenient access to menu commands and frequently needed tools. Most professional applications with toolbars, however, use custom buttons rather than conventional window buttons. Other types of custom controls include graphical menu items and floating toolboxes. All these items are easy to create, after you learn a few techniques.

In this chapter, you add a custom button to the status bar application. In addition, you add a graphical menu item to the Window menu and create a toolbox window that, like the toolbar, provides quick and easy access to sets of related tools.

345

Customized Buttons

When Windows was designed, its programmers went to great lengths to provide a flexible and powerful graphical interface. To this end, they created many types of controls that you can use in your programs—controls that are easily modified to suit a specific application. For example, button controls can contain any text, can be almost any size, and can be placed virtually anywhere on-screen. List boxes (and most other controls), too, can be modified a number of basic ways.

Although you can change the size, placement, and text of controls, they all look basically the same from one program to the next. Because buttons are the most prevalent control in a Windows program, they can become boring. To avoid this problem, the Windows designers provided ways for application programmers to add their own buttons (and other custom controls). These custom buttons are used like regular Windows buttons, but can look any way you like.

As with any Windows programming option, there are several ways to create custom buttons. The most common way is through the use of owner-draw buttons.

Owner-Draw Buttons

Owner-draw buttons work like other Windows buttons, but they can take on any appearance because Windows turns the button-drawing tasks over to your program. You can draw any kind of button you like, from conventional Windows-like buttons to objects that look like controls from another universe.

Amazingly, even if your program draws no button image, the button still works; if you click the button's location, the function assigned to the button is selected, yet you see no button animation. This is because Windows gives you control of the appearance of the button only, not the way it functions. Figure 10.1 shows a window with an undrawn owner-draw button in the toolbar. Although the button's image hasn't been drawn on-screen, the button still functions. When the user clicks in the white rectangle, a new child window is created.

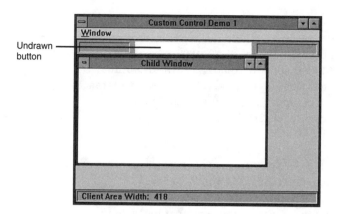

Figure 10.1. A window with an undrawn owner-draw button in the toolbar.

To create an owner-draw button, you must do only four things:

1. Create a new button class descended from the TButton class.

2. Make the button's style BS_OWNERDRAW.

3. Write the functions to draw the button in its various states.

4. In the button's parent window class, provide a message-response function for the WM_DRAWITEM message.

Listings 10.1 through 10.9 are the files needed to create an MDI application with an owner-draw button in its toolbar. (The files CHILDWND.H, STATBAR4.H, and STATBAR4.CPP are not shown because they are identical to the listings of the same names in Chapter 9.)

Listing 10.1. CUSCTL1.CPP—version 1 of the custom control application.

```
// CUSCTL1.CPP: Custom control application, version 1.

#include <owl.h>
#include <mdi.h>
#include "childwnd.h"
#include "cusctlw1.h"

// Class for the application.
class TCusCtlApp : public TApplication
{
public:
```

continues

Listing 10.1. Continued

```
  TCusCtlApp(LPSTR AName, HINSTANCE hInstance,
        HINSTANCE hPrevInstance, LPSTR lpCmdLine,
        int nCmdShow): TApplication(AName, hInstance,
        hPrevInstance, lpCmdLine, nCmdShow) {};
  virtual void InitMainWindow();
};


/////////////////////////////////////////////////////
// TCusCtlApp::InitMainWindow()
//
// This function creates the application's main window.
/////////////////////////////////////////////////////
void TCusCtlApp::InitMainWindow()
{
  MainWindow = new TCusCtlWnd(Name);
}


/////////////////////////////////////////////////////
// WinMain()
/////////////////////////////////////////////////////
int PASCAL WinMain(HINSTANCE hInstance,
                   HINSTANCE hPrevInstance,
                   LPSTR lpCmdLine, int nCmdShow)
{
  TCusCtlApp CusCtlApp("Custom Control Demo 1", hInstance,
                       hPrevInstance, lpCmdLine, nCmdShow);
  CusCtlApp.Run();
  return CusCtlApp.Status;
}
```

Listing 10.2. CUSCTLW1.H—the frame window's header file.

```
// CUSCTLW1.H: Header file for frame window.

#ifndef _CUSCTLW1_H
#define _CUSCTLW1_H

#include <owl.h>
#include "toolbar2.h"
```

```
#include "statbar4.h"

_CLASSDEF(TCusCtlWnd)
class TCusCtlWnd: public TMDIFrame
{
private:
  PTStatbar pstatbar;
  PTToolbar ptoolbar;

public:
  TCusCtlWnd(LPSTR ATitle);
  void SetupWindow();
  virtual PTWindowsObject CreateChild();
  virtual void WMSize(RTMessage msg)
      = [WM_FIRST + WM_SIZE];
};


#endif
```

Listing 10.3. CUSCTLW1.CPP—the frame window's implementation.

```
// CUSCTLW1.CPP: Implementation for frame window.

#include <owl.h>
#include <mdi.h>
#include "cusctlw1.h"
#include "childwnd.h"
#include "statbar4.h"
#include "toolbar2.h"


/////////////////////////////////////////////////////
// TCusCtlWnd::TCusCtlWnd()
//
// This is the frame window's constructor.
/////////////////////////////////////////////////////
TCusCtlWnd::TCusCtlWnd(LPSTR ATitle):
          TMDIFrame(ATitle, "CUSCTLMENU")
{
  // Set size and position of frame window.
  Attr.X = 40;
  Attr.Y = 40;
```

continues

Listing 10.3. Continued

```
  Attr.H = GetSystemMetrics(SM_CYSCREEN) / 1.5;
  Attr.W = GetSystemMetrics(SM_CXSCREEN) / 1.5;

  // Create status bar and tool bar objects.
  pstatbar =  new TStatbar(this);
  ptoolbar = new TToolbar(this);
}


//////////////////////////////////////////////////////////
// TCusCtlWnd::SetupWindow()
//
// This function creates the starting child window for
// the application.
//////////////////////////////////////////////////////////
void TCusCtlWnd::SetupWindow()
{
  TMDIFrame::SetupWindow();
  CreateChild();
}


//////////////////////////////////////////////////////////
// TCusCtlWnd::CreateChild()
//
// This function creates a new child window.
//////////////////////////////////////////////////////////
PTWindowsObject TCusCtlWnd::CreateChild()
{
  return GetApplication()->
    MakeWindow(new TMyMDIChild(this));
}


//////////////////////////////////////////////////////////
// TCusCtlWnd::WMSize()
//
// This function sets the size and position of the
// client window, the status bar, and the tool bar
// whenever the frame window is moved.
//////////////////////////////////////////////////////////
void TCusCtlWnd::WMSize(RTMessage msg)
```

```
{
  // Process WM_SIZE message.
  TMDIFrame::WMSize(msg);

  // Set the size and position of the client window.
  MoveWindow(ClientWnd->HWindow, 0, 26, msg.LP.Lo,
          msg.LP.Hi-48, TRUE);

  // Set the size and position of the status bar.
  pstatbar->MoveBar(msg.LP.Lo, msg.LP.Hi);
  ptoolbar->MoveBar(msg.LP.Lo);
}
```

Listing 10.4. TOOLBAR2.H—the toolbar class' header file.

```
// TOOLBAR2.H: Header file for tool bar class.

#ifndef _TOOLBAR2_H
#define _TOOLBAR2_H

#include "custmbut.h"

_CLASSDEF(TToolbar)
class TToolbar: public TWindow
{
  PTCustmBut pcustmbut;
public:
  TToolbar(PTWindowsObject AParent);
  virtual LPSTR GetClassName();
  virtual void GetWindowClass(WNDCLASS &AWndClass);
  virtual void Paint(HDC PaintDC, PAINTSTRUCT &);
  virtual void ButtonMsg(void)
      = [ID_FIRST + 100];
  void WMDrawItem(RTMessage msg)
      = [WM_FIRST + WM_DRAWITEM];
  void MoveBar(int w);
};

#endif
```

Listing 10.5. TOOLBAR2.CPP—the toolbar class' implementation.

```cpp
// TOOLBAR2.CPP -- Tool bar class implementation.

#include <owl.h>
#include <button.h>
#include "toolbar2.h"

//////////////////////////////////////////////////////////
// TToolbar::TToolbar()
//
// Tool bar constructor.
//////////////////////////////////////////////////////////
TToolbar::TToolbar(PTWindowsObject AParent):
         TWindow(AParent, NULL)
{
  SetFlags(WB_MDICHILD, FALSE);
  Attr.Style = WS_CHILD | WS_VISIBLE | WS_BORDER;
  pcustmbut = new TCustmBut(this,100,"Create",
                            100,2,200,20,FALSE);

}


//////////////////////////////////////////////////////////
// TToolbar::GetWindowClass()
//
// Set up a window class for the tool bar.
//////////////////////////////////////////////////////////
void TToolbar::GetWindowClass(WNDCLASS &AWndClass)
{
  // Allow normal processing.
  TWindow::GetWindowClass(AWndClass);

  // Set window background color to light gray.
  AWndClass.hbrBackground = GetStockObject(LTGRAY_BRUSH);
}


//////////////////////////////////////////////////////////
// TToolbar::GetClassName()
//
// Supply a class name for the tool bar.
//////////////////////////////////////////////////////////
LPSTR TToolbar::GetClassName()
```

```
{
  return "ToolBar2";
}


//////////////////////////////////////////////////////
// TToolbar::MoveBar()
//
// Respond to message from main window to move tool
// bar to new location.
//////////////////////////////////////////////////////
void TToolbar::MoveBar(int w)
{
  MoveWindow(HWindow, 0, 0, w, 26, TRUE);
}


//////////////////////////////////////////////////////
// TToolbar::Paint()
//
// Draw 3-D outline and text into tool bar.
//////////////////////////////////////////////////////
void TToolbar::Paint(HDC DC, PAINTSTRUCT&)
{
  RECT r;

  // Get size of client area.
  GetClientRect(HWindow, &r);

  // Draw 3-D graphics.
  HPEN new_pen = GetStockObject(BLACK_PEN);
  HPEN prev_pen = SelectObject(DC, new_pen);
  MoveTo(DC, r.left+4, r.bottom-4);
  LineTo(DC, r.left+4, r.top+4);
  LineTo(DC, r.left+90, r.top+4);
  new_pen = GetStockObject(WHITE_PEN);
  SelectObject(DC, new_pen);
  MoveTo(DC, r.left+4, r.bottom-4);
  LineTo(DC, r.left+90, r.bottom-4);
  LineTo(DC, r.left+90, r.top+4);

  new_pen = GetStockObject(BLACK_PEN);
  SelectObject(DC, new_pen);
  MoveTo(DC, r.left+309, r.bottom-4);
  LineTo(DC, r.left+309, r.top+4);
```

continues

Listing 10.5. Continued

```
LineTo(DC, r.right-4, r.top+4);
new_pen = GetStockObject(WHITE_PEN);
SelectObject(DC, new_pen);
MoveTo(DC, r.left+309, r.bottom-4);
LineTo(DC, r.right-4, r.bottom-4);
LineTo(DC, r.right-4, r.top+4);

  // Restore old pen and mode.
  SelectObject(DC, prev_pen);
}


/////////////////////////////////////////////////////
// TToolbar::ButtonMsg()
//
// This function responds when the user clicks the tool
// bar's button, by sending a CM_CREATECHILD message to
// the frame window.
/////////////////////////////////////////////////////
void TToolbar::ButtonMsg(void)
{
  SendMessage(Parent->HWindow,
          WM_COMMAND, CM_CREATECHILD, 0);
}


/////////////////////////////////////////////////////
// TToolbar::WMDrawItem()
//
// This function is called when the program receives a
// WM_DRAWITEM message. It determines which object needs
// to be drawn and calls the appropriate drawing
// function.
/////////////////////////////////////////////////////
void TToolbar::WMDrawItem(RTMessage msg)
{
  LPDRAWITEMSTRUCT p = (DRAWITEMSTRUCT FAR*) msg.LParam;
  if (p->CtlID == 100)
    pcustmbut->DrawButton(p);
}
```

Listing 10.6. CUSTMBUT.H—the button class' header file.

```
// CUSTMBUT.H: Header file for button class.

#ifndef _CUSTMBUT_H
#define _CUSTMBUT_H

#include <button.h>

_CLASSDEF(TCustmBut)
class TCustmBut: public TButton
{
public:
  TCustmBut(PTWindowsObject AParent, int AnID,
        LPSTR ATitle, int x, int y, int w,
        int h, BOOL IsDfault);
  void DrawButton(LPDRAWITEMSTRUCT p);
  void DrawSelected(LPDRAWITEMSTRUCT p);
  void DrawUnselected(LPDRAWITEMSTRUCT p);
  void DrawFocused(LPDRAWITEMSTRUCT p);
};

#endif
```

Listing 10.7. CUSTMBUT.CPP—the button class' implementation.

```
// CUSTMBUT.CPP: Button class implementation.

#include <button.h>
#include "custmbut.h"

/////////////////////////////////////////////////////////
// TCustmBut::TCustmBut()
//
// This is the custom button's constructor.
/////////////////////////////////////////////////////////
TCustmBut::TCustmBut(PTWindowsObject AParent, int AnID,
            LPSTR ATitle, int x, int y, int w,
            int h, BOOL IsDefault): TButton
```

continues

355

Listing 10.7. Continued

```
                (AParent, AnID, ATitle, x, y, w, h,
                IsDefault)
{
  Attr.Style = BS_OWNERDRAW ¦ WS_CHILD ¦ WS_VISIBLE;
}


/////////////////////////////////////////////////////
// TCustmBut::DrawUnselected()
//
// This function draws the unselected version of the
// button.
/////////////////////////////////////////////////////
void TCustmBut::DrawUnselected(LPDRAWITEMSTRUCT p)
{
  // Select new pen and brush into the display context.
  HPEN new_pen = GetStockObject(NULL_PEN);
  HPEN prev_pen = SelectObject(p->hDC, new_pen);
  HBRUSH new_brush = GetStockObject(LTGRAY_BRUSH);
  HBRUSH prev_brush = SelectObject(p->hDC, new_brush);

  // Fill button's background area with gray.
  Rectangle(p->hDC, 0, 0, Attr.W+1, Attr.H+1);

  // Change pen and brush.
  new_pen = GetStockObject(BLACK_PEN);
  SelectObject(p->hDC, new_pen);
  new_brush = GetStockObject(NULL_BRUSH);
  SelectObject(p->hDC, new_brush);

  // Draw button's 3-D outline.
  Ellipse(p->hDC, 1, 1, 198, 19);
  new_pen = GetStockObject(WHITE_PEN);
  SelectObject(p->hDC, new_pen);
  Ellipse(p->hDC, 0, 0, 197, 18);

  // Change drawing mode and print button label.
  HANDLE prev_mode = SetBkMode(p->hDC, TRANSPARENT);
  TextOut(p->hDC, 79, 2, "Create", 6);

  // Restore device context to defaults.
  SelectObject(p->hDC, prev_pen);
  SelectObject(p->hDC, prev_brush);
```

```
    SetBkMode(p->hDC, prev_mode);

  // Draw button's focused image, if necessary.
  if (p->itemState & ODS_FOCUS)
    DrawFocused(p);
}


/////////////////////////////////////////////////////////
// TCustmBut::DrawSelected()
//
// This function draws the button in its selected form.
/////////////////////////////////////////////////////////
void TCustmBut::DrawSelected(LPDRAWITEMSTRUCT p)
{
  // Select new pen and brush into the device context.
  HPEN new_pen = GetStockObject(NULL_PEN);
  HPEN prev_pen = SelectObject(p->hDC, new_pen);
  HBRUSH new_brush = CreateSolidBrush(RGB(255, 0, 0));
  HBRUSH prev_brush = SelectObject(p->hDC, new_brush);

  // Draw button filled with red.
  Ellipse(p->hDC, 1, 1, 198, 19);

  // Set drawing mode and draw button text.
  HANDLE prev_mode = SetBkMode(p->hDC, TRANSPARENT);
  TextOut(p->hDC, 79, 2, "Create", 6);

  // Restore device context to defaults.
  SelectObject(p->hDC, prev_pen);
  SelectObject(p->hDC, prev_brush);
  SetBkMode(p->hDC, prev_mode);

  // Delete custom brush object.
  DeleteObject(new_brush);

  // Draw button's focused image, if necessary.
  if (p->itemState & ODS_FOCUS)
    DrawFocused(p);
}


/////////////////////////////////////////////////////////
// TCustmBut::DrawFocused()
//
```

continues

Listing 10.7. Continued

```cpp
// This function draws the button in its focused form.
/////////////////////////////////////////////////////////
void TCustmBut::DrawFocused(LPDRAWITEMSTRUCT p)
{
  RECT r = {74, 3, 125, 17};
  DrawFocusRect(p->hDC, &r);
}


/////////////////////////////////////////////////////////
// TCustmBut::DrawButton()
//
// This function is called when the tool bar receives a
// WM_DRAWITEM message.
/////////////////////////////////////////////////////////
void TCustmBut::DrawButton(LPDRAWITEMSTRUCT p)
{
  // Respond to action.
  switch (p->itemAction)
  {
    // Draw full button.
    case ODA_DRAWENTIRE:
      DrawUnselected(p);
      break;

    // Check button state and draw appropriate image.
    case ODA_SELECT:
      if (p->itemState & ODS_SELECTED)
     DrawSelected(p);
      else
        DrawUnselected(p);
      break;

    // Draw button's focused image, if necessary.
    case ODA_FOCUS:
      if (p->itemState & ODS_FOCUS)
        DrawFocused(p);
      break;
  }
}
```

Listing 10.8. CUSCTL1.RC—the application's resource file.

```
#include <owlrc.h>

CUSCTLMENU MENU LOADONCALL MOVEABLE PURE DISCARDABLE
BEGIN
  POPUP "&Window"
  BEGIN
    MenuItem   "C&reate", CM_CREATECHILD
    MenuItem   "&Cascade", CM_CASCADECHILDREN
    MenuItem   "&Tile", CM_TILECHILDREN
    MenuItem   "C&lose All", CM_CLOSECHILDREN
  END
END
```

Listing 10.9. CUSTMCTL.DEF—the application's definition file.

```
EXETYPE WINDOWS
CODE PRELOAD MOVEABLE DISCARDABLE
DATA PRELOAD MOVEABLE MULTIPLE
HEAPSIZE 4096
STACKSIZE 5120
```

When you run the program, you see the window shown in Figure 10.2. The only difference between this window and the one in your toolbar application in Chapter 9 is that this toolbar now sports a custom button. If you click the button, it flashes red and a new child window appears.

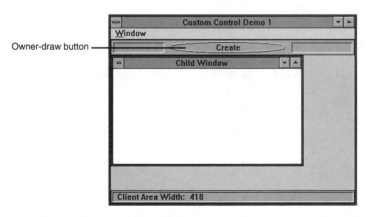

Figure 10.2. A window with an owner-draw button in the toolbar.

359

The listings for CUSCTL1.CPP, CUSCTLW1.H, and CUSCTLW1.CPP contain nothing new, so they aren't discussed here. Still, look them over to be sure you understand them.

The new toolbar class, too, is similar to the first version, which you saw in Chapter 9, but one function contains an important change:

```
TToolbar::TToolbar(PTWindowsObject AParent):
        TWindow(AParent, NULL)
{
  SetFlags(WB_MDICHILD, FALSE);
  Attr.Style = WS_CHILD ¦ WS_VISIBLE ¦ WS_BORDER;
  pcustmbut = new TCustmBut(this,100,"Create",
                            100,2,200,20,FALSE);
}
```

This is the toolbar's constructor. In the first version of the toolbar, the TButton object was created here. Notice that this time, something called TCustmBut is created. This is the custom button class, which is described shortly.

Besides this simple change in the TToolBar class, a new function has been added:

```
void TToolbar::WMDrawItem(RTMessage msg)
{
  LPDRAWITEMSTRUCT p = (DRAWITEMSTRUCT FAR*) msg.LParam;
  if (p->CtlID == 100)
    pcustmbut->DrawButton(p);
}
```

This function informs the custom button when it must be redrawn and what its current state is. The function does this by responding to the Windows WM_DRAWITEM message, which is sent whenever an object must be drawn. If you have more than one owner-draw object, many WM_DRAWITEM messages pass through your application. To draw an object properly, you must know for which object the message is intended. You can find this information by examining the message's DRAWITEMSTRUCT, a pointer to which is stored in the message's LParam field.

DRAWITEMSTRUCT contains nine fields, each of which holds information about the item to be drawn. Four of these fields—CtlId, itemAction, itemState, and hDC—are of interest in this program.(You can find the full description of the DRAWITEMSTRUCT structure in your Borland manuals, Borland's on-line help, or most Windows programming manuals.) The `CtlId` field holds the ID of the item to be drawn. The `itemAction` field indicates the action the object has to take. The `itemState` field holds the object's current state. And, finally, the `hDC` field contains a handle to the item's device context.

In the `WMDrawItem()` function, a pointer to `DRAWITEMSTRUCT` is first obtained. Then, the `CtlId` field is examined. If `CtlId` is the same as the button's ID (it always will be in this program because there's only one owner-draw item), the program calls the function to draw the button. This brings you to the custom button class:

```
_CLASSDEF(TCustmBut)
class TCustmBut: public TButton
{
public:
  TCustmBut(PTWindowsObject AParent, int AnID,
        LPSTR ATitle, int x, int y, int w,
        int h, BOOL IsDfault);
  void DrawButton(LPDRAWITEMSTRUCT p);
  void DrawSelected(LPDRAWITEMSTRUCT p);
  void DrawUnselected(LPDRAWITEMSTRUCT p);
  void DrawFocused(LPDRAWITEMSTRUCT p);
};
```

Here, a button class named `TCustmBut` is declared that is derived from OWL's `TButton` class. The `TCustmBut` class includes a constructor and four functions that handle button-drawing duties. Look at the constructor first:

```
TCustmBut::TCustmBut(PTWindowsObject AParent, int AnID,
            LPSTR ATitle, int x, int y, int w,
            int h, BOOL IsDefault): TButton(
            AParent, AnID, ATitle, x, y, w, h,
            IsDefault)
{
  Attr.Style = BS_OWNERDRAW ¦ WS_CHILD ¦ WS_VISIBLE;
}
```

The constructor first calls the `TButton` constructor to create a normal button object. Then, in the main body of the constructor, the button's style is set, including the `BS_OWNERDRAW` flag. This is all you must do to change the button from a conventional Windows button to one that you can draw on your own. After setting the button's style, it still operates like any other Windows button, except you are in charge of drawing the object. If you don't draw the object, the button appears as a blank rectangle (as shown in Figure 10.1).

Three Button States

When Windows sends a `WM_DRAWITEM` message, the button's parent window (the toolbar) checks the message to make sure it is intended for the button and then calls the button's `DrawButton()` function:

```
void TCustmBut::DrawButton(LPDRAWITEMSTRUCT p)
{
  // Respond to action.
  switch (p->itemAction)
  {
    // Draw full button.
    case ODA_DRAWENTIRE:
      DrawUnselected(p);
      break;

    // Check button state and draw appropriate image.
    case ODA_SELECT:
      if (p->itemState & ODS_SELECTED)
        DrawSelected(p);
      else
        DrawUnselected(p);
      break;

    // Draw button's focused image, if necessary.
    case ODA_FOCUS:
      if (p->itemState & ODS_FOCUS)
        DrawFocused(p);
      break;
  }
}
```

Here, the function first checks the `itemAction` field of `DRAWITEMSTRUCT`, which can have three states: `ODA_DRAWENTIRE`, `ODA_SELECT`, or `ODA_FOCUS`. If `itemAction` is set to `ODA_STATE`, the entire button must be drawn in its unselected state. If `itemAction` is set to `ODA_SELECT`, the button's selection state has changed. And, if `itemAction` is set to `ODA_FOCUS`, the button's focus has changed.

In the case of `ODA_DRAWENTIRE`, the program's task is easy: simply draw the complete button, in its unselected state, which must be done the first time the button is drawn. If `itemAction` equals `ODA_SELECT`, the program must change the button's selection state, drawing it as either selected or unselected. To know which image to draw, the program has to know the button's current state.

It finds this information by checking the `itemState` field. If `itemState` is set to `ODS_SELECTED`, the button should be drawn in its selected state. Otherwise, the button should be drawn in its unselected state.

The same is true when `itemAction` is set to `IDA_FOCUS`. This informs the program that the button's focus state has changed—but to draw the button properly, its current state must be known. This state is found by checking the `itemState` field as before. If it is set to `ODS_FOCUS`, the program draws the button's focus rectangle. Otherwise, it leaves the button as it is.

The `DrawButton()` function does no drawing. Instead, it routes program execution to the appropriate drawing function based on the `itemAction` and `itemState` fields of `DRAWITEMSTRUCT`. Because every button can be in one of three states—*unselected, selected,* and *focused*—there are three functions to draw the button. The first is `DrawUnselected()`:

```
void TCustmBut::DrawUnselected(LPDRAWITEMSTRUCT p)
{
  // Select new pen and brush into the display context.
  HPEN new_pen = GetStockObject(NULL_PEN);
  HPEN prev_pen = SelectObject(p->hDC, new_pen);
  HBRUSH new_brush = GetStockObject(LTGRAY_BRUSH);
  HBRUSH prev_brush = SelectObject(p->hDC, new_brush);

  // Fill button's background area with gray.
  Rectangle(p->hDC, 0, 0, Attr.W+1, Attr.H+1);

  // Change pen and brush.
  new_pen = GetStockObject(BLACK_PEN);
  SelectObject(p->hDC, new_pen);
  new_brush = GetStockObject(NULL_BRUSH);
  SelectObject(p->hDC, new_brush);

  // Draw button's 3-D outline.
  Ellipse(p->hDC, 1, 1, 198, 19);
  new_pen = GetStockObject(WHITE_PEN);
  SelectObject(p->hDC, new_pen);
  Ellipse(p->hDC, 0, 0, 197, 18);

  // Change drawing mode and print button label.
  HANDLE prev_mode = SetBkMode(p->hDC, TRANSPARENT);
  TextOut(p->hDC, 79, 2, "Create", 6);

  // Restore device context to defaults.
  SelectObject(p->hDC, prev_pen);
```

```
    SelectObject(p->hDC, prev_brush);
    SetBkMode(p->hDC, prev_mode);

    // Draw button's focused image, if necessary.
    if (p->itemState & ODS_FOCUS)
      DrawFocused(p);
}
```

This function draws the entire button image, using standard GDI calls to select pens and brushes and to draw various shapes. You've seen most of these graphics functions before. In `DrawUnselected()`, a gray rectangle is first drawn to fill the empty button area (the white area shown in Figure 10.1). Then a three-dimensional ellipse is drawn for the button's border. Finally, the button's text label is printed.

At the end of the function, the button's focus state is checked. A button can retain the focus regardless of its selection state, so the button's focus must be checked whenever it's redrawn.

The `DrawSelected()` function draws the button in its selected state:

```
void TCustmBut::DrawSelected(LPDRAWITEMSTRUCT p)
{
  // Select new pen and brush into the device context.
  HPEN new_pen = GetStockObject(NULL_PEN);
  HPEN prev_pen = SelectObject(p->hDC, new_pen);
  HBRUSH new_brush = CreateSolidBrush(RGB(255, 0, 0));
  HBRUSH prev_brush = SelectObject(p->hDC, new_brush);

  // Draw button filled with red.
  Ellipse(p->hDC, 1, 1, 198, 19);

  // Set drawing mode and draw button text.
  HANDLE prev_mode = SetBkMode(p->hDC, TRANSPARENT);
  TextOut(p->hDC, 79, 2, "Create", 6);

  // Restore device context to defaults.
  SelectObject(p->hDC, prev_pen);
  SelectObject(p->hDC, prev_brush);
  SetBkMode(p->hDC, prev_mode);

  // Delete custom brush object.
  DeleteObject(new_brush);
```

```
  // Draw button's focused image, if necessary.
  if (p->itemState & ODS_FOCUS)
    DrawFocused(p);
}
```

This function fills the button's interior with a red ellipse. Because the Windows GDI does not include a stock red brush, the function must create one. It does this with a call to `CreateSolidBrush()`, after which the ellipse is drawn. When creating your own pens, brushes, or other objects, you must be sure to delete them as soon as possible because they take up valuable Windows resources. In this example, this is done near the end of the function, with a call to `DeleteObject()`. Finally, the function again checks the button's focus and draws the focus rectangle, if necessary.

The button's focused state is drawn easily:

```
void TCustmBut::DrawFocused(LPDRAWITEMSTRUCT p)
{
  RECT r = {74, 3, 125, 17};
  DrawFocusRect(p->hDC, &r);
}
```

Here, the function simply calls the Windows `DrawFocusRect()` function, using a rectangle that is large enough to surround the button's text label. The function could have used the `rcItem` rectangle, which is included as one of the fields in `DRAWITEMSTRUCT`. However, the `rcItem` rectangle is set to the entire button area. If the program uses the `rcItem` rectangle coordinates, the focus rectangle is drawn around the perimeter of the button, rather than around the button's text, as is usually the case with buttons.

Note: It is customary on toolbars not to draw the button's focus state, because toolbars are not accessible with the keyboard, only with the mouse. In the sample program, the button's focussed state is included only to demonstrate the handling of that state. Normally, a toolbar button has only two states: *selected* and *unselected*.

Any Look You Want

That's all there is to incorporating user-draw buttons. As you can see, you can give buttons any look you want, virtually anything that you can draw on-screen. Drawing buttons with GDI calls, however, can generate a lot of source code.

Another way to draw custom buttons is simply to transfer a bitmap to the button's screen location. Using bitmaps, you can design all types of sophisticated looking buttons containing icons and other graphical elements. You learn how to do this later in the chapter, when you design a toolbox window. But, as an introduction to bitmaps, you'll now add a graphical menu entry to the application's Window menu.

Customized Menus

Although a menu item is not a control in the usual Windows sense, it can still be modified to look any way you like. The easiest way to do this is by adding to the menu a bitmap, rather than the usual text string. Using a bitmap, you can display not only text, but also all kinds and sizes of graphical images. This is particularly useful in programs in which the user has to choose graphics tools, fonts, or other types of objects that are more easily displayed as a bitmap than as text.

Listings 10.10 through 10.13 are the new files needed to add a bitmap menu item to the application. (Listings shown in Chapter 9 are not repeated here.)

Listing 10.10. CUSCTL2.CPP—version 2 of the custom control application.

```
// CUSCTL2.CPP: Custom control application, version 2.

#include <owl.h>
#include <mdi.h>
#include "childwnd.h"
#include "cusctlw2.h"

// Class for the application.
class TCusCtlApp : public TApplication
{
public:
  TCusCtlApp(LPSTR AName, HINSTANCE hInstance,
      HINSTANCE hPrevInstance, LPSTR lpCmdLine,
      int nCmdShow): TApplication(AName, hInstance,
      hPrevInstance, lpCmdLine, nCmdShow) {};
```

```
  virtual void InitMainWindow();
};


///////////////////////////////////////////////////
// TCusCtlApp::InitMainWindow()
//
// This function creates the application's main window.
///////////////////////////////////////////////////
void TCusCtlApp::InitMainWindow()
{
  MainWindow = new TCusCtlWnd(Name);
}


///////////////////////////////////////////////////
// WinMain()
///////////////////////////////////////////////////
int PASCAL WinMain(HINSTANCE hInstance,
                   HINSTANCE hPrevInstance,
                   LPSTR lpCmdLine, int nCmdShow)
{
  TCusCtlApp CusCtlApp("Custom Control Demo 2", hInstance,
                   hPrevInstance, lpCmdLine, nCmdShow);
  CusCtlApp.Run();
  return CusCtlApp.Status;
}
```

Listing 10.11. CUSCTLW2.H—the frame window's header file.

```
// CUSCTLW2.H: Header file for frame window.

#ifndef _CUSCTLW2_H
#define _CUSCTLW2_H

#include <owl.h>
#include "toolbar2.h"
#include "statbar4.h"

_CLASSDEF(TCusCtlWnd)
class TCusCtlWnd: public TMDIFrame
{
  PTStatbar pstatbar;
```

continues

Listing 10.11. Continued

```
  PTToolbar ptoolbar;
  HBITMAP hBitmap;

public:
  TCusCtlWnd(LPSTR ATitle);
  void SetupWindow();
  virtual PTWindowsObject CreateChild();
  virtual BOOL CanClose();
  virtual void WMSize(RTMessage msg)
      = [WM_FIRST + WM_SIZE];
  virtual void Save()
      = [CM_FIRST + 100];
};


#endif
```

Listing 10.12. CUSCTLW2.CPP—the frame window's implementation.

```
// CUSCTLW2.CPP: Implementation for frame window.

#include <owl.h>
#include <mdi.h>
#include "cusctlw2.h"
#include "childwnd.h"
#include "statbar4.h"
#include "toolbar2.h"


/////////////////////////////////////////////////////
// TCusCtlWnd::TCusCtlWnd()
//
// This is the frame window's constructor.
/////////////////////////////////////////////////////
TCusCtlWnd::TCusCtlWnd(LPSTR ATitle):
        TMDIFrame(ATitle, "CUSCTLMENU")
{
  // Set size and position of frame window.
  Attr.X = 40;
  Attr.Y = 40;
```

```
  Attr.H = GetSystemMetrics(SM_CYSCREEN) / 1.5;
  Attr.W = GetSystemMetrics(SM_CXSCREEN) / 1.5;

  // Create status bar and tool bar objects.
  pstatbar =  new TStatbar(this);
  ptoolbar = new TToolbar(this);
}


/////////////////////////////////////////////////////
// TCusCtlWnd::SetupWindow()
//
// This function creates the starting child window for
// the application. It also loads a bitmap and appends
// it to the application's Window menu.
/////////////////////////////////////////////////////
void TCusCtlWnd::SetupWindow()
{
  TMDIFrame::SetupWindow();
  hBitmap = LoadBitmap(
           GetApplication()->hInstance, "BITMAP_1");
  HMENU hMenu1 = GetMenu(HWindow);
  HMENU hMenu2 = GetSubMenu(hMenu1, 0);
  AppendMenu(hMenu2, MF_BITMAP | MF_ENABLED,
          100, LPCSTR(hBitmap));

  CreateChild();
}


/////////////////////////////////////////////////////
// TCusCtlWnd::CreateChild()
//
// This function creates a new child window.
/////////////////////////////////////////////////////
PTWindowsObject TCusCtlWnd::CreateChild()
{
  return GetApplication()->
    MakeWindow(new TMyMDIChild(this));
}


/////////////////////////////////////////////////////
// TCusCtlWnd::WMSize()
//
```

continues

369

Listing 10.12. Continued

```
// This function sets the size and position of the
// client window, the status bar, and the tool bar
// whenever the frame window is moved.
/////////////////////////////////////////////////////
void TCusCtlWnd::WMSize(RTMessage msg)
{
  // Process WM_SIZE message.
  TMDIFrame::WMSize(msg);

  // Set the size and position of the client window.
  MoveWindow(ClientWnd->HWindow, 0, 26, msg.LP.Lo,
          msg.LP.Hi-48, TRUE);

  // Set the size and position of the status bar.
  pstatbar->MoveBar(msg.LP.Lo, msg.LP.Hi);
  ptoolbar->MoveBar(msg.LP.Lo);
}


/////////////////////////////////////////////////////
// TCusCtlWnd::Save()
//
// This function responds to the menu's save command.
/////////////////////////////////////////////////////
void TCusCtlWnd::Save()
{
  MessageBox(HWindow, "Save Menu Selected",
          "Save", MB_OK);
}


/////////////////////////////////////////////////////
// TCusCtlWnd::CanClose()
//
// This function deletes the bitmap object from memory
// before the application closes.
/////////////////////////////////////////////////////
BOOL TCusCtlWnd::CanClose()
{
  DeleteObject(hBitmap);
  return TRUE;
}
```

Listing 10.13. CUSCTL2.RC—the application's resource file.

```
BITMAP_1 BITMAP "disk.bmp"
CUSCTLMENU MENU
BEGIN
    POPUP "&Window"
    BEGIN
        MENUITEM "C&reate", 24339
        MENUITEM "&Cascade", 24337
        MENUITEM "&Tile", 24336
        MENUITEM "C&lose All", 24338
    END
END
```

When you run the program, you see the same window as in Figure 10.2. When you pull down the Window menu, however, you see a disk bitmap, as shown in Figure 10.3. This bitmap represents a file-save function that might be used in a program for children. When you select this item, a message box pops up, verifying that you've selected the file-save function.

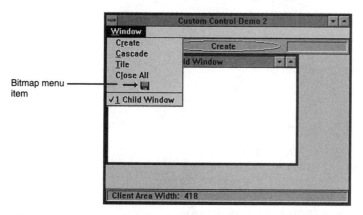

Figure 10.3. A disk bitmap used as a menu item.

Surprisingly little has been added to the original program. But before you get into the actual program, you should learn about bitmaps.

371

A Little About Bitmaps

Bitmaps are nothing more than screen images that can be loaded from disk and "pasted" anywhere on-screen. Because bitmaps can contain any image that can be displayed on-screen, they are the perfect objects for sprucing up a program. You've seen many bitmaps in other Windows programs. Most custom buttons, for example, are bitmaps.

How do you create a bitmap? You can use the bitmap editor supplied with Borland's Resource Workshop. This editor works much like a paint program, except it limits your drawing to the area you've defined as a bitmap (which can be any size). After creating the bitmap, you save it to disk as a .BMP file and then include the bitmap's filename in the application's resource file (see Listing 10.13).

Adding Images to a Menu

Now look at the declaration for the new frame-window class, which contains the menu to which you'll be adding the bitmap:

```
_CLASSDEF(TCusCtlWnd)
class TCusCtlWnd: public TMDIFrame
{
  PTStatbar pstatbar;
  PTToolbar ptoolbar;
  HBITMAP hBitmap;

public:
  TCusCtlWnd(LPSTR ATitle);
  void SetupWindow();
  virtual PTWindowsObject CreateChild();
  virtual BOOL CanClose();
  virtual void WMSize(RTMessage msg)
      = [WM_FIRST + WM_SIZE];
  virtual void Save()
      = [CM_FIRST + 100];
};
```

Besides pointers to the status bar and toolbar, the declaration contains hBitmap, which is a handle to a bitmap. The class also includes the Save()

message-response function, which is called whenever the user selects the bitmap menu item. Finally, a virtual function called `CanClose()` has been added. This function, which is a member of the OWL `TWindowsObject` class, is called whenever a window tries to close, and normally does nothing more than return true. By overriding this function, you can perform whatever functions you need before a window closes. In this case, the program uses `CanClose()` to delete the bitmap from memory when it's no longer needed.

The bitmap is loaded into memory by the window's `SetupWindow()` function:

```
void TCusCtlWnd::SetupWindow()
{
  TMDIFrame::SetupWindow();
  hBitmap = LoadBitmap(
          GetApplication()->hInstance, "BITMAP_1");
  HMENU hMenu1 = GetMenu(HWindow);
  HMENU hMenu2 = GetSubMenu(hMenu1, 0);
  AppendMenu(hMenu2, MF_BITMAP | MF_ENABLED,
            100, LPCSTR(hBitmap));

  CreateChild();
}
```

Here, the program calls the `SetupWindow()` ancestor function, after which it loads the bitmap into memory using the Windows `LoadBitmap()` function. `LoadBitmap()`'s parameters are the application's instance handle and the bitmap's name (or ID). After loading the bitmap, the program calls `GetMenu()` to retrieve the handle of the window's menu. Using that handle, `GetSubMenu()` is called to get the handle of the pop-up menu into which the bitmap should be placed. The second parameter to this function is the position of the pop-up menu in the menu bar. In usual C fashion, the first pop-up is 0.

After getting the pop-up menu's handle, the program calls `AppendMenu()` to add the bitmap to the end of the menu's entries. The first parameter to this function is the pop-up menu's handle. The second parameter comprises the menu-item flags. In this case, the program is informing Windows that the menu item is a bitmap and that the menu item should be enabled rather than grayed. The third parameter is the menu item's ID. The fourth parameter is the bitmap's handle stored in the low word of a long pointer to a character string. Normally, this parameter would be the text string you wanted to add to the menu, such as:

```
AppendMenu(hMenu2, MF_STRING | MF_ENABLED,
          100, "&Save");
```

That's all there is to inserting the bitmap into the menu. Now, when the user displays the menu, the bitmap is in position, and when the user selects the bitmap, it triggers a menu message as any other menu item does. The program grabs that message with the window's `Save()` message-response function:

```
void TCusCtlWnd::Save()
{
  MessageBox(HWindow, "Save Menu Selected",
             "Save", MB_OK);
}
```

This function doesn't do much, it simply brings up a message box so you know the menu worked. In a real program, you can do something wildly wonderful here...or maybe you can simply save a file.

The last function to examine is the window's `CanClose()` function:

```
BOOL TCusCtlWnd::CanClose()
{
  DeleteObject(hBitmap);
  return TRUE;
}
```

As mentioned, this function, which is a member of the OWL `TObjectWindows` class, is called immediately before a window is allowed to close. If this function returns true, the window closes. If this function returns false, the window is not allowed to close. In a full application, this is where you would check whether all new or changed files have been saved. The `CanClose()` function is also a good place to do clean-up. In this example, the program must delete the bitmap it previously loaded. It does this with a quick call to `DeleteObject()`.

 Caution: It's extremely important that you delete bitmaps you load. If you don't, they stay in memory after the program ends, stealing valuable Windows resource space from other programs that might need it. If enough resource space is used up, Windows comes to a screaming halt.

You're probably surprised to see how easy it is to add a bitmap to a menu. The hardest part is drawing the bitmap in the first place. Creating a toolbox, on the other hand, is trickier, as you see in the next section.

Creating a Toolbox

N ow that you know a bit about owner-draw buttons and using bitmaps, you can put together a toolbox object that users can call up like a dialog box. Unlike most dialog boxes, though, your toolbox does not force users to close it before they can return to the application's main window. Instead, the toolbox floats over the main window, enabling users to select tools and immediately return to work. Listings 10.14 through 10.23 are the files needed to create the toolbox program.

Listing 10.14. TOOLBAPP.H—the toolbox application's header file.

```
// TOOLBAPP.H: Header file for Tool box application.

#ifndef _TOOLBAPP_H
#define _TOOLBAPP_H

#include <owl.h>

// Custom button IDs.
#define ID_BUT1 101
#define ID_BUT2 102
#define ID_BUT3 103
#define ID_BUT4 104

// User-defined message.
#define PM_CHANGELINE WM_USER
#define PM_CLOSETOOLS WM_USER + 1

#endif
```

Listing 10.15. TOOLBAPP.CPP—the toolbox application.

```
// TOOLBAPP.CPP: Toolbox application.

#include <owl.h>
#include "toolbapp.h"
#include "toolbxw.h"
```

continues

Listing 10.15. Continued

```
// Class for the application.
class TToolBoxApp : public TApplication
{
public:
  TToolBoxApp(LPSTR AName, HINSTANCE hInstance,
       HINSTANCE hPrevInstance, LPSTR lpCmdLine,
       int nCmdShow): TApplication(AName, hInstance,
       hPrevInstance, lpCmdLine, nCmdShow) {};
  virtual void InitMainWindow();
};


////////////////////////////////////////////////////////
// TToolBoxApp::InitMainWindow()
//
// This function creates the application's main window.
////////////////////////////////////////////////////////
void TToolBoxApp::InitMainWindow()
{
  MainWindow = new TToolbxWnd(NULL, "Toolbox Demo");
}


////////////////////////////////////////////////////////
// WinMain()
////////////////////////////////////////////////////////
int PASCAL WinMain(HINSTANCE hInstance,
                   HINSTANCE hPrevInstance,
                   LPSTR lpCmdLine, int nCmdShow)
{
  TToolBoxApp ToolBoxApp("ToolBoxDemo", hInstance,
                   hPrevInstance, lpCmdLine, nCmdShow);
  ToolBoxApp.Run();
  return ToolBoxApp.Status;
}
```

Listing 10.16. TOOLBXW.H—the frame window's header file.

```
// TOOLBXW.H: Header file for frame window.

#ifndef _TOOLBXW_H
#define _TOOLBXW_H
```

```
#include <owl.h>
#include "toolapp.h"
#include "tooldlg.h"

_CLASSDEF(TToolbxWnd)
class TToolbxWnd: public TWindow
{
  int linewidth, // Currently selected line width.
      button,    // Mouse-button flag.
      new_pen,   // Handle for drawing pen.
      prev_pen;  // Handle for old pen.
  HDC lineDC;    // Window's device context handle.
  PTToolDlg pdialog; // Pointer to the tool box object.

public:
  TToolbxWnd(PTWindowsObject AParent, LPSTR ATitle);
  virtual void WMLButtonDown(RTMessage msg)
      = [WM_FIRST + WM_LBUTTONDOWN];
  virtual void WMLButtonUp()
      = [WM_FIRST + WM_LBUTTONUP];
  virtual void WMMouseMove(RTMessage msg)
      = [WM_FIRST + WM_MOUSEMOVE];
  virtual void Dialog()
      = [CM_FIRST + 101];
  virtual void PMChangeLine(RTMessage msg)
      = [WM_FIRST + PM_CHANGELINE];
  virtual void PMCloseTools()
      = [WM_FIRST + PM_CLOSETOOLS];
};

#endif
```

Listing 10.17. TOOLBXW.CPP—the frame window's implementation.

```
// TOOLBXW.CPP: Implementation for frame window.

#include <owl.h>
#include "toolbxw.h"
#include "tooldlg.h"
```

continues

377

Listing 10.17. Continued

```
///////////////////////////////////////////////////////
// TToolbxWnd::TToolbxWnd()
//
// This is the frame window's constructor.
///////////////////////////////////////////////////////
TToolbxWnd::TToolbxWnd(PTWindowsObject AParent,
            LPSTR ATitle): TWindow(AParent, ATitle)
{
  // Add menu to window.
  AssignMenu("TOOLMENU");

  // Set size and position of frame window.
  Attr.X = 40;
  Attr.Y = 40;
  Attr.H = GetSystemMetrics(SM_CYSCREEN) / 1.5;
  Attr.W = GetSystemMetrics(SM_CXSCREEN) / 1.5;

  // Initialize variables.
  linewidth = 1;
  button = FALSE;
  pdialog = NULL;
}


///////////////////////////////////////////////////////
// TToolbxWnd::Dialog()
//
// This function responds to the menu's Dialog command.
///////////////////////////////////////////////////////
void TToolbxWnd::Dialog()
{
  // If you don't already have a tool box...
  if (!pdialog)
  {
    // Create and display a new tool box.
    pdialog = new TToolDlg(this, "DIALOG_1", linewidth);
    GetApplication()->MakeWindow(pdialog);
  }
}
```

```
///////////////////////////////////////////////////////
// TToolbxWnd::WMLButtonDown()
//
// This function responds to a WM_LBUTTONDOWN message.
///////////////////////////////////////////////////////
void TToolbxWnd::WMLButtonDown(RTMessage msg)
{
  // If this is a new button press...
  if (!button)
  {
    // Get device context and pen.
    lineDC = GetDC(HWindow);
    HPEN new_pen = CreatePen(PS_SOLID, linewidth*2,
                   BLACK_PEN);
    prev_pen = SelectObject(lineDC, new_pen);

    // Direct all mouse input to the window.
    SetCapture(HWindow);

    // Set line start to the mouse coords.
    MoveTo(lineDC, msg.LP.Lo, msg.LP.Hi);

    // Set mouse-button flag.
    button = TRUE;
  }
}


///////////////////////////////////////////////////////
// TToolbxWnd::WMLButtonUp()
//
// This function responds to a WM_LBUTTONUP message.
///////////////////////////////////////////////////////
void TToolbxWnd::WMLButtonUp()
{
  // Restore and release device context.
  SelectObject(lineDC, prev_pen);
  ReleaseDC(HWindow, lineDC);

  // Delete custom pen object.
  DeleteObject(new_pen);

  // Turn off button flag.
  button = FALSE;
```

continues

Listing 10.17. Continued

```
  // Release mouse capture.
  ReleaseCapture();
}


///////////////////////////////////////////////////////
// TToolbxWnd::WMMouseMove()
//
// This function responds to a WM_MOUSEMOVE message.
///////////////////////////////////////////////////////
void TToolbxWnd::WMMouseMove(RTMessage msg)
{
  if (button)
    LineTo(lineDC, msg.LP.Lo, msg.LP.Hi);
}


///////////////////////////////////////////////////////
// TToolbxWnd::PMChangeLine()
//
// This function responds to the user-defined
// PM_CHANGELINE message, issued by the tool box when a
// new line width is selected.
///////////////////////////////////////////////////////
void TToolbxWnd::PMChangeLine(RTMessage msg)
{
  linewidth = msg.WParam;
}


///////////////////////////////////////////////////////
// TToolbxWnd::PMCloseTools()
//
// This function responds to the user-defined
// PM_CLOSETOOLS message, issued by the tool box when it
// is closed.
///////////////////////////////////////////////////////
void TToolbxWnd::PMCloseTools()
{
  pdialog = NULL;
}
```

380

Listing 10.18. TOOLDLG.H—the toolbox dialog's header file.

```
// TOOLDLG.H: Header file for the toolbox dialog.

#ifndef _TOOLDLG_H
#define _TOOLDLG_H

#include <owl.h>
#include "toolbutn.h"
#include "toolbapp.h"

_CLASSDEF(TToolDlg)
class TToolDlg: public TDialog
{
  HBITMAP hBitmap1, // Handles to button bitmaps.
          hBitmap2;
  PTToolButn ptoolbutn[4]; // Array of button pointers.
  int selected;        // Current button selected.

public:
  TToolDlg(PTWindowsObject AParent, LPSTR AName,
           int linewidth);
virtual void SetupWindow();
virtual void TToolDlg::WMDrawItem(RTMessage msg)
   = [WM_FIRST + WM_DRAWITEM];
virtual void IDBut1() = [ID_FIRST + ID_BUT1];
virtual void IDBut2() = [ID_FIRST + ID_BUT2];
virtual void IDBut3() = [ID_FIRST + ID_BUT3];
virtual void IDBut4() = [ID_FIRST + ID_BUT4];
virtual void WMDestroy(RTMessage msg)
   = [WM_FIRST + WM_DESTROY];
};

#endif
```

Listing 10.19. TOOLDLG.CPP—the toolbox's implementation.

```
// TOOLDLG.CPP: Tool box implementation.

#include "tooldlg.h"
#include "toolbutn.h"
```

continues

Listing 10.19. Continued

```c
#include "toolbapp.h"

////////////////////////////////////////////////////////
// TToolDlg::TToolDlg()
//
// This is the tool box's constructor.
////////////////////////////////////////////////////////
TToolDlg::TToolDlg(PTWindowsObject AParent, LPSTR AName,
                int linewidth): TDialog(AParent, AName)
{
  // Load button bitmaps.
  hBitmap1 = LoadBitmap(
      GetApplication()->hInstance, "BITMAP_1");
  hBitmap2 = LoadBitmap(
      GetApplication()->hInstance, "BITMAP_2");

  // Add custom buttons to dialog window.
  ptoolbutn[0] =
    new TToolButn(this,ID_BUT1,1,1,46,26,FALSE);
  ptoolbutn[1] =
    new TToolButn(this,ID_BUT2,48,1,46,26,FALSE);
  ptoolbutn[2] =
    new TToolButn(this,ID_BUT3,1,28,46,26,FALSE);
  ptoolbutn[3] =
    new TToolButn(this,ID_BUT4,48,28,46,26,FALSE);

  // Set selected button.
  selected = linewidth + 100;
}


////////////////////////////////////////////////////////
// TToolDlg::SetupWindow()
//
// This function is called after the tool-box object
// is created, but before it is drawn.
////////////////////////////////////////////////////////
void TToolDlg::SetupWindow()
{
  // Call ancestor function.
  TDialog::SetupWindow();
```

```
  // Post message to give focus to the
  // currently selected control.
  HWND hButton = GetDlgItem(HWindow, selected);
  PostMessage(HWindow, WM_NEXTDLGCTL, hButton, 0x1L);
}


///////////////////////////////////////////////////////
// TToolDlg::WMDrawItem
//
// This function responds to the WM_DRAWITEM message,
// by setting the selected-button flag if necessary and
// then drawing the button in its appropriate state.
///////////////////////////////////////////////////////
void TToolDlg::WMDrawItem(RTMessage msg)
{
  // Get a pointer to the DrawItemStruct.
  LPDRAWITEMSTRUCT p = (DRAWITEMSTRUCT FAR*) msg.LParam;

  // Check whether ID is one of the buttons.
  if ((p->CtlID >= ID_BUT1) && (p->CtlID <= ID_BUT4))
  {
    // If the button is being selected, set the
    // selected flag to the control's ID.
    if ((p->itemAction == ODA_SELECT) &&
        (p->itemState & ODS_SELECTED))
      selected = p->CtlID;

    // Draw button in appropriate state.
    ptoolbutn[p->CtlID-ID_BUT1]->
      DrawButton(p, selected, hBitmap1, hBitmap2);
  }
}


///////////////////////////////////////////////////////
// TToolDlg::IDBut1()
//
// This function responds to a mouse click on button
// #1, by sending a user-defined PM_CHANGELINE message
// to the main window.
///////////////////////////////////////////////////////
```

Listing 10.19. Continued

```
void TToolDlg::IDBut1()
{
  SendMessage(GetApplication()->MainWindow->HWindow,
              PM_CHANGELINE, 1, 0x0L);
}


///////////////////////////////////////////////////////
// TToolDlg::IDBut2()
//
// This function responds to a mouse click on button
// #2, by sending a user-defined PM_CHANGELINE message
// to the main window.
///////////////////////////////////////////////////////
void TToolDlg::IDBut2()
{
  SendMessage(GetApplication()->MainWindow->HWindow,
              PM_CHANGELINE, 2, 0x0L);
}


///////////////////////////////////////////////////////
// TToolDlg::IDBut3()
//
// This function responds to a mouse click on button
// #3, by sending a user-defined PM_CHANGELINE message
// to the main window.
///////////////////////////////////////////////////////
void TToolDlg::IDBut3()
{
  SendMessage(GetApplication()->MainWindow->HWindow,
              PM_CHANGELINE, 3, 0x0L);
}


///////////////////////////////////////////////////////
// TToolDlg::IDBut4()
//
// This function responds to a mouse click on button
// #4, by sending a user-defined PM_CHANGELINE message
// to the main window.
///////////////////////////////////////////////////////
void TToolDlg::IDBut4()
{
  SendMessage(GetApplication()->MainWindow->HWindow,
              PM_CHANGELINE, 4, 0x0L);
```

```
}
////////////////////////////////////////////////////
// TToolDlg::WMDestroy()
//
// This function is called immediately before the tool
// box window is destroyed. It deletes the bitmaps and
// notifies the parent window that the tool box is
// closing.
////////////////////////////////////////////////////
void TToolDlg::WMDestroy(RTMessage msg)
{
  // Delete bitmaps from memory.
  DeleteObject(hBitmap1);
  DeleteObject(hBitmap2);

  // Notify main window that tool box is gone.
  SendMessage(GetApplication()->MainWindow->HWindow,
          PM_CLOSETOOLS, 0, 0x0L);

  // Perform normal WM_DESTROY processing.
  TDialog::WMDestroy(msg);
}
```

Listing 10.20. TOOLBUTN.H—the button class' header file.

```
// TOOLBUTN.H: Header file for button class.

#ifndef _TOOLBUTN_H
#define _TOOLBUTN_H

#include <button.h>

_CLASSDEF(TToolButn)
class TToolButn: public TButton
{
public:
  TToolButn(PTWindowsObject AParent, int AnID,
          int x, int y, int w, int h, BOOL IsDfault);
  void DrawLine(LPDRAWITEMSTRUCT p, int offset);
  void DrawButton(LPDRAWITEMSTRUCT p, int selected,
                  HBITMAP hBitmap1, HBITMAP hBitmap2);
```

continues

385

Listing 10.20. Continued

```
  void DrawSelected(LPDRAWITEMSTRUCT p,
                    HBITMAP hBitmap2);
  void DrawUnselected(LPDRAWITEMSTRUCT p,
                      HBITMAP hBitmap1);
  void DrawFocused(LPDRAWITEMSTRUCT p);
};


#endif
```

Listing 10.21. TOOLBUTN.CPP—the button class' implementation.

```
// TOOLBUTN.CPP: Button class implementation.

#include <button.h>
#include "toolbutn.h"


//////////////////////////////////////////////////////
// TToolButn::TToolButn()
//
// This is the custom button's constructor.
//////////////////////////////////////////////////////
TToolButn::TToolButn(PTWindowsObject AParent, int AnID,
             int x, int y, int w, int h,
             BOOL IsDefault): TButton(
             AParent, AnID, "", x, y, w, h,
             IsDefault)
{
  Attr.Style =
    BS_OWNERDRAW ¦ WS_CHILD ¦ WS_VISIBLE;
}


//////////////////////////////////////////////////////
// TToolButn::DrawLine()
//
// This function draws the appropriate-sized line on the
// button's face. The offset is used to simulate
// movement when the button is selected, by drawing the
// line down and to the right one pixel.
//////////////////////////////////////////////////////
```

```
void TToolButn::DrawLine(LPDRAWITEMSTRUCT p, int offset)
{
  // Select new pen and brush.
  HPEN custom_pen = CreatePen(PS_SOLID, (p->CtlID-100)*2,
                              BLACK_PEN);
  HPEN prev_pen = SelectObject(p->hDC, custom_pen);
  HBRUSH new_brush = GetStockObject(LTGRAY_BRUSH);
  HBRUSH prev_brush = SelectObject(p->hDC, new_brush);

  // Draw line on button.
  MoveTo(p->hDC, 8+offset, 13+offset);
  LineTo(p->hDC, 39+offset, 13+offset);

  // Square the lines' rounded ends.
  HPEN new_pen = GetStockObject(NULL_PEN);
  SelectObject(p->hDC, new_pen);
  Rectangle(p->hDC, 4+offset, 6+offset,
            8+offset, 22+offset);
  Rectangle(p->hDC, 40+offset, 4+offset,
              44+offset, 22+offset);

  // Restore device context.
  SelectObject(p->hDC, prev_pen);
  SelectObject(p->hDC, prev_brush);
  DeleteObject(custom_pen);
}


///////////////////////////////////////////////////////
// TToolButn::DrawUnselected()
//
// This function draws the unselected version of the
// button.
///////////////////////////////////////////////////////
void TToolButn::DrawUnselected(LPDRAWITEMSTRUCT p,
                               HBITMAP hBitmap1)
{
  // Create memory device context.
  HDC hMemDC = CreateCompatibleDC(p->hDC);

  // Select bitmap into device context.
  HBITMAP hOldBitmap = SelectObject(hMemDC, hBitmap1);

  // Copy the bitmap to the screen.
```

continues

Listing 10.21. Continued

```
  BitBlt(p->hDC, 1, 1, 47, 27, hMemDC, 0, 0, SRCCOPY);

  // Restore old memory DC.
  SelectObject(hMemDC, hOldBitmap);
  DeleteDC(hMemDC);

  // Draw the appropriate line on the button.
  DrawLine(p, 0);

  // Draw focus rectangle, if necessary.
  if (p->itemState & ODS_FOCUS)
    DrawFocused(p);
}


/////////////////////////////////////////////////////
// TToolButn::DrawSelected()
//
// This function draws the button in its selected form.
/////////////////////////////////////////////////////
void TToolButn::DrawSelected(LPDRAWITEMSTRUCT p,
                             HBITMAP hBitmap2)
{
  // Create a memory device context.
  HDC hMemDC = CreateCompatibleDC(p->hDC);

  // Select the bitmap into the memory DC.
  HBITMAP hOldBitmap = SelectObject(hMemDC, hBitmap2);

  // Draw the bitmap.
  BitBlt(p->hDC, 1, 1, 47, 27, hMemDC, 0, 0, SRCCOPY);

  // Restore old memory DC.
  SelectObject(hMemDC, hOldBitmap);
  DeleteDC(hMemDC);

  // Draw the appropriate line on the button.
  DrawLine(p, 1);

  // Draw focus rectangle, if necessary.
  if (p->itemState & ODS_FOCUS)
```

```
      DrawFocused(p);
}


/////////////////////////////////////////////////////
// TToolButn::DrawFocused()
//
// This function draws the button in its focused form.
/////////////////////////////////////////////////////
void TToolButn::DrawFocused(LPDRAWITEMSTRUCT p)
{
  // Set a rectangle to just larger than the
  // button's line image.
  RECT r = {5, 7, 43, 20};

  // Draw the focus rectangle.
  DrawFocusRect(p->hDC, &r);
}


/////////////////////////////////////////////////////
// TToolButn::DrawButton()
//
// This function is called when the tool box receives a
// WM_DRAWITEM message.
/////////////////////////////////////////////////////
void TToolButn::DrawButton(LPDRAWITEMSTRUCT p,
      int selected, HBITMAP hBitmap1, HBITMAP hBitmap2)
{
  // Respond to action.
  switch (p->itemAction)
  {
    // Draw full button.
    case ODA_DRAWENTIRE:
      if (selected != p->CtlID)
    DrawUnselected(p, hBitmap1);
      else
    DrawSelected(p, hBitmap2);
      break;

    // Check button state and draw appropriate image.
    case ODA_SELECT:
      if (p->itemState & ODS_SELECTED)
    DrawSelected(p, hBitmap2);
      else if (p->CtlID != selected)
```

continues

Listing 10.21. Continued

```
    DrawUnselected(p, hBitmap1);
      break;

    // Draw button's focused image, if necessary.
    case ODA_FOCUS:
      if (p->itemState & ODS_FOCUS)
        DrawFocused(p);
      break;
  }
}
```

Listing 10.22. TOOLBAPP.RC—the application's resource file.

```
BITMAP_1 BITMAP "button1.bmp"
BITMAP_2 BITMAP "button2.bmp"
TOOLMENU MENU
BEGIN
    POPUP "&File"
    BEGIN
        MENUITEM "&Tool Box", 101
    END
END
DIALOG_1 DIALOG 11, 19, 48, 28
STYLE WS_POPUP ¦ WS_VISIBLE ¦ WS_CAPTION ¦ WS_SYSMENU
CAPTION "Tool Box"
BEGIN
END
```

Listing 10.23. TOOLBAPP.DEF—the application's definition file.

```
EXETYPE WINDOWS
CODE PRELOAD MOVEABLE DISCARDABLE
DATA PRELOAD MOVEABLE MULTIPLE
HEAPSIZE 4096
STACKSIZE 5120
```

When you run the program, the main window appears, as shown in Figure 10.4. You can draw in the window by holding the left mouse button down and moving the mouse pointer over the window's client area. To choose another line thickness, select the Tool Box entry of the File menu. The line-thickness toolbox appears. Select a new line thickness by clicking the appropriate button.

You can move the toolbox out of the way by dragging it outside the main window, where it stays accessible.

 Note: This program cannot redraw its main window, so if you change the size of the window or move the toolbox over your drawing, the screen image is partially or fully erased.

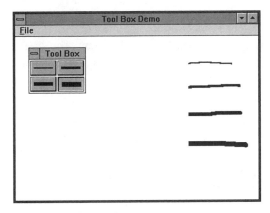

Figure 10.4. The toolbox application.

Now that you've had a chance to draw a few masterpieces (sorry, you can't save them), you can learn how the toolbox works. Start with the TToolbxWnd class, which is the application's main window:

```
_CLASSDEF(TToolbxWnd)
class TToolbxWnd: public TWindow
{
  int linewidth, // Currently selected line width.
      button,    // Mouse-button flag.
      new_pen,   // Handle for drawing pen.
      prev_pen;  // Handle for old pen.
  HDC lineDC;    // Window's device context handle.
```

```
    PTToolDlg pdialog; // Pointer to the tool box object.

public:
  TToolbxWnd(PTWindowsObject AParent, LPSTR ATitle);
  virtual void WMLButtonDown(RTMessage msg)
      = [WM_FIRST + WM_LBUTTONDOWN];
  virtual void WMLButtonUp()
      = [WM_FIRST + WM_LBUTTONUP];
  virtual void WMMouseMove(RTMessage msg)
      = [WM_FIRST + WM_MOUSEMOVE];
  virtual void Dialog()
      = [CM_FIRST + 101];
  virtual void PMChangeLine(RTMessage msg)
      = [WM_FIRST + PM_CHANGELINE];
  virtual void PMCloseTools()
      = [WM_FIRST + PM_CLOSETOOLS];
};
```

As you can see, this class contains a number of private data members, all of which you learn more about as you examine the listings. This class also contains six message-response functions besides the usual constructor. These functions control the drawing process, as well as activate the toolbox. The class' constructor gets things started:

```
TToolbxWnd::TToolbxWnd(PTWindowsObject AParent,
        LPSTR ATitle): TWindow(AParent, ATitle)
{
  // Add menu to window.
  AssignMenu("TOOLMENU");

  // Set size and position of frame window.
  Attr.X = 40;
  Attr.Y = 40;
  Attr.H = GetSystemMetrics(SM_CYSCREEN) / 1.5;
  Attr.W = GetSystemMetrics(SM_CXSCREEN) / 1.5;

  // Initialize variables.
  linewidth = 1;
  button = FALSE;
  pdialog = NULL;
}
```

Here, the program constructs the window, assigns the window's menu, sets the window's size and position, and initializes a few data members. The `linewidth` variable keeps track of the currently selected line width, `button` is a flag that indicates whether the left mouse button is down, and `pdialog` is a pointer to the toolbox dialog. Because the toolbox is not on-screen when the program begins, this pointer is set to NULL.

When the user selects the Tool Box entry of the File menu, the `Dialog()` function is called:

```
void TToolbxWnd::Dialog()
{
  // If you don't already have a toolbox...
  if (!pdialog)
  {
    // Create and display a new toolbox.
    pdialog = new TToolDlg(this, "DIALOG_1", linewidth);
    GetApplication()->MakeWindow(pdialog);
  }
}
```

If a toolbox is not present, this function creates and displays the toolbox dialog. If the user has already opened the toolbox, the `pdialog` pointer is not NULL, and this function does nothing. Notice that the program calls `MakeWindow()`, which creates a modeless dialog box, rather than `ExecDialog()`, which creates a modal dialog box.

What's the difference? A *modal* dialog box takes over the application until the dialog is closed. If you used this type of dialog for a toolbox, users would have to bring up the toolbox, select their tool, then close the toolbox every time they wanted to change line thicknesses. This is clearly a major inconvenience. A *modeless* dialog, on the other hand, doesn't take over the application, enabling users to freely switch from window to window while the toolbox remains visible. This type of dialog is perfect for a toolbox.

Drawing in a Window

In addition to creating a toolbox, the program enables the user to draw simple line shapes in the window. The drawing functions are called when the user presses the left mouse button while the pointer is over the window's client area, generating a `WM_LBUTTONDOWN` message. When the program receives this message, the `WMLButtonDown()` message-response function takes over:

```
void TToolbxWnd::WMLButtonDown(RTMessage msg)
{
  // If this is a new button press...
  if (!button)
  {
    // Get device context and pen.
    lineDC = GetDC(HWindow);
    HPEN new_pen = CreatePen(PS_SOLID, linewidth*2,
                  BLACK_PEN);
    prev_pen = SelectObject(lineDC, new_pen);

    // Direct all mouse input to your window.
    SetCapture(HWindow);

    // Set line start to the mouse coordinates.
    MoveTo(lineDC, msg.LP.Lo, msg.LP.Hi);

    // Set the mouse-button flag.
    button = TRUE;
  }
}
```

Here, the program starts the drawing process by creating a device context. Then, it uses `linewidth` in a call to the Windows `CreatePen()` function to set the pen to the right line thickness and color, after which it selects the pen into the device context. A call to the Windows `SetCapture()` function ensures that all mouse input is directed to the window, even if the mouse isn't over the window. If the program didn't do this, strange side effects would result.

For example, if the user dragged the mouse pointer out of the window and released the button, the program wouldn't know that the button was up and consequently wouldn't set the `button` flag to the button's new state. When the user brought the mouse pointer back over the window, the drawing would continue even though the button was no longer down. `SetCapture()` guards against this type of problem, because mouse releases that occur outside the window are still directed to the window.

Finally, after setting the mouse capture to the window, the program positions the line's starting point to the mouse's current coordinates and sets the mouse-button flag to true, which indicates that the button is down.

When the user moves the mouse pointer across the window, a long series of `WM_MOUSEMOVE` messages is generated. This activates the `WMMouseMove()` message-response function:

```
void TToolbxWnd::WMMouseMove(RTMessage msg)
{
  if (button)
    LineTo(lineDC, msg.LP.Lo, msg.LP.Hi);
}
```

Here, the program first checks whether the button is down. It must do this because the mouse generates WM_MOUSEMOVE messages whether a button is pressed or not. You don't want to draw lines when the button is up, so the program checks button first. If button is true, indicating that the mouse button is pressed, the program draws a line from the mouse's previous position (originally set by the MoveTo() call in WMLButtonDown(), but updated by every call to Line()) to the mouse's current position.

When the mouse button is released, it generates a WM_LBUTTONUP message, which is grabbed by the WMLButtonUp() message-response function:

```
void TToolbxWnd::WMLButtonUp()
{
  // Restore and release device context.
  SelectObject(lineDC, prev_pen);
  ReleaseDC(HWindow, lineDC);

  // Delete the custom pen object.
  DeleteObject(new_pen);

  // Turn off the button flag.
  button = FALSE;

  // Release mouse capture.
  ReleaseCapture();
}
```

This function restores and deletes the device context, deletes the custom pen, sets the button flag to false (indicating the button is now up), and allows mouse input to be sent to other windows.

The last two functions in the main window class handle messages sent from the toolbox. The first responds to the user-defined PM_CHANGELINE message, which is sent when the user clicks a button on the toolbox:

```
void TToolbxWnd::PMChangeLine(RTMessage msg)
{
  linewidth = msg.WParam;
}
```

All the program does here is set the line width to the value returned in the message's `WParam` field.

The second function responds to the user-defined `PM_CLOSETOOLS` message, which is sent by the toolbox when the user closes it:

```
void TToolbxWnd::PMCloseTools()
{
  pdialog = NULL;
}
```

Caution: Use the `PMCloseTools()` function to set the `pdialog` pointer to NULL when the toolbox shuts down. Failure to reset this pointer results in the inability to reopen the toolbox, because the pointer must be NULL before the toolbox can be opened.

If you've never used user-defined messages before, the `PM_CHANGELINE` and `PM_CLOSETOOLS` messages may be perplexing. You won't find them in your Windows or Borland manuals. Why? They are user-defined—in other words, they are made up. Although Windows defines hundreds of messages, it can't possibly anticipate the needs of every Windows program. Therefore, the developers of Windows set aside a range of messages that applications can define and use internally. These message identifiers range in value from `WM_USER` through `WM_USER + 0x7FFF`. The user-defined messages used in this program are defined in the application's header file, TOOLBAPP.H:

```
// Custom button IDs.
#define ID_BUT1 101
#define ID_BUT2 102
#define ID_BUT3 103
#define ID_BUT4 104

// User-defined message.
#define PM_CHANGELINE WM_USER
#define PM_CLOSETOOLS WM_USER + 1
```

You see how the toolbox uses these messages when you examine the toolbox's class. What's important to realize here is that you can create message-response functions for your own messages just as you can for regular Windows messages. And, because you can have over 32,000 different user-defined messages in your program, there's virtually no limit to the special messages your applications can send between their objects. (If you ever write a program in which you use all possible user-defined messages, you'll win the *Most Inefficient Programmer of the Year* award, hands down.)

The Toolbox Class

Now, look at the toolbox class. Here is its declaration:

```
_CLASSDEF(TToolDlg)
class TToolDlg: public TDialog
{
  HBITMAP hBitmap1, // Handles to button bitmaps.
          hBitmap2;
  PTToolButn ptoolbutn[4]; // Array of button pointers.
  int selected;      // Current button selected.

public:
  TToolDlg(PTWindowsObject AParent, LPSTR AName,
           int linewidth);
virtual void SetupWindow();
virtual void TToolDlg::WMDrawItem(RTMessage msg)
    = [WM_FIRST + WM_DRAWITEM];
virtual void IDBut1() = [ID_FIRST + ID_BUT1];
virtual void IDBut2() = [ID_FIRST + ID_BUT2];
virtual void IDBut3() = [ID_FIRST + ID_BUT3];
virtual void IDBut4() = [ID_FIRST + ID_BUT4];
virtual void WMDestroy(RTMessage msg)
    = [WM_FIRST + WM_DESTROY];
};
```

This class, like the TToolbxWnd class, also has several private data members. First are handles for the bitmaps that represent the custom buttons in selected and unselected form. Then, there's an array of pointers to these custom buttons. Having these pointers in an array simplifies sections of the code, eliminating some case or if statements. Finally, there's a variable that holds the ID number of the currently selected button. In the function declarations, notice that there are message-response functions for each button. The program also responds to the WM_DRAWITEM and WM_DESTROY messages.

Next is the class' implementation. The toolbox dialog, like all objects, is created in its constructor:

```
TToolDlg::TToolDlg(PTWindowsObject AParent, LPSTR AName,
            int linewidth): TDialog(AParent, AName)
```

```
{
  // Load button bitmaps.
  hBitmap1 = LoadBitmap(
    GetApplication()->hInstance, "BITMAP_1");
  hBitmap2 = LoadBitmap(
    GetApplication()->hInstance, "BITMAP_2");

  // Add custom buttons to the dialog window.
  ptoolbutn[0] =
    new TToolButn(this,ID_BUT1,1,1,46,26,FALSE);
  ptoolbutn[1] =
    new TToolButn(this,ID_BUT2,48,1,46,26,FALSE);
  ptoolbutn[2] =
    new TToolButn(this,ID_BUT3,1,28,46,26,FALSE);
  ptoolbutn[3] =
    new TToolButn(this,ID_BUT4,48,28,46,26,FALSE);

  // Set the selected button.
  selected = linewidth + 100;
}
```

Here, after calling the ancestor function, the program loads the two bitmaps for the buttons. The bitmaps were created using the Resource Workshop's bitmap editor. Figure 10.5 shows what these bitmaps look like.

Figure 10.5. Button bitmaps created with the Resource Workshop's bitmap editor.

Next, the program creates a button object for each button in the toolbox, saving the pointers in the array. Finally, it uses linewidth to initialize selected to the number of the last selected button. The program must do this so the toolbox always appears with the currently active tool selected. Suppose, for example, that the user closes the toolbox after selecting the thickest line. If the user brings the toolbox back up, the thickest line should still be selected.

After the constructor finishes its work, `SetupWindow()` gets a call:

```
void TToolDlg::SetupWindow()
{
  // Call ancestor function.
  TDialog::SetupWindow();

  // Post message to give focus to the
  // currently selected control.
  HWND hButton = GetDlgItem(HWindow, selected);
  PostMessage(HWindow, WM_NEXTDLGCTL, hButton, 0x1L);
}
```

This function ensures that the selected button has the focus. Because the program uses the `WM_DRAWITEM` message to update the buttons, the dialog must begin with the focus on the selected button. (You see why later.) The focus for the selected button is set by posting a `WM_NEXTDLGCTL` message to the dialog. The program has to do it this way, rather than use a call to `SetFocus()`, because a control's focus cannot be changed until it has been created and drawn. By posting a message, the program allows time for these actions to take place.

The buttons are drawn in their proper form by capturing the `WM_DRAWITEM` message, as was done for the first program in this chapter:

```
void TToolDlg::WMDrawItem(RTMessage msg)
{
  // Get a pointer to the DrawItemStruct.
  LPDRAWITEMSTRUCT p = (DRAWITEMSTRUCT FAR*) msg.LParam;

  // Check whether ID is one of the buttons.
  if ((p->CtlID >= ID_BUT1) && (p->CtlID <= ID_BUT4))
  {
    // If the button is being selected, set the
    // selected flag to the control's ID.
    if ((p->itemAction == ODA_SELECT) &&
        (p->itemState & ODS_SELECTED))
      selected = p->CtlID;

    // Draw the button in the appropriate state.
    ptoolbutn[p->CtlID-ID_BUT1]->
      DrawButton(p, selected, hBitmap1, hBitmap2);
  }
}
```

This function is not unlike the one you looked at in Listing 10.5. Here, however, the program also changes the value of `selected`, which holds the ID of the currently selected button. To do this, the program checks whether `itemAction` is set to `ODA_SELECT`. If it is, the program knows that a new button has been selected. By checking `itemState`, the program can determine whether it's the current button instance that has been selected, rather than one of the other three. If so, it sets `selected` to the button's ID.

Each of the buttons has its own message-response function in the dialog. All are similar, so you have to examine only the first one:

```
void TToolDlg::IDBut1()
{
  SendMessage(GetApplication()->MainWindow->HWindow,
           PM_CHANGELINE, 1, 0x0L);
}
```

Here, the program sends a message to the main window, informing it to switch to a new line thickness, the value for which is placed in the message's `WParam` field. The `PM_CHANGELINE` message is one of the user-defined messages. If you look back a few paragraphs, you see that when the main window receives this message, it sets `linewidth` to the value sent in the message's `WParam` field. The other button message-response functions vary only in the `WParam` value: the larger the value, the thicker the line.

The last function in this class is `WMDestroy()`:

```
void TToolDlg::WMDestroy(RTMessage msg)
{
  // Delete the bitmaps from memory.
  DeleteObject(hBitmap1);
  DeleteObject(hBitmap2);

  // Notify the main window that the toolbox is gone.
  SendMessage(GetApplication()->MainWindow->HWindow,
           PM_CLOSETOOLS, 0, 0x0L);

  // Perform normal WM_DESTROY processing.
  TDialog::WMDestroy(msg);
}
```

This message-response function takes control when the user closes the toolbox, either by clicking its close box or by closing the entire application.

 Note: You cannot use the WM_CLOSEWINDOW message to close the toolbox. Although the WM_CLOSEWINDOW message-response function is called when the user clicks the toolbox's Close box, it is not called when the application closes with the toolbox still open. In this class, using WMCloseWindow() rather than WMDestroy() can lead to undeleted bitmaps.

In WMDestroy(), the program first deletes the button bitmaps. Then it sends another user-defined message, PM_CLOSETOOLS, to the main window, notifying it that the toolbox is closing and the pdialog pointer has to be set to NULL. The program then calls the TDialog::WMDestroy() ancestor function to finish the toolbox's destruction.

The Custom Button Class

Your toolbox wouldn't be very useful without its buttons. The new custom button class is not unlike the one in this chapter's first program:

```
_CLASSDEF(TToolButn)
class TToolButn: public TButton
{
public:
  TToolButn(PTWindowsObject AParent, int AnID,
            int x, int y, int w, int h, BOOL IsDfault);
  void DrawLine(LPDRAWITEMSTRUCT p, int offset);
  void DrawButton(LPDRAWITEMSTRUCT p, int selected,
                  HBITMAP hBitmap1, HBITMAP hBitmap2);
  void DrawSelected(LPDRAWITEMSTRUCT p,
                    HBITMAP hBitmap2);
  void DrawUnselected(LPDRAWITEMSTRUCT p,
                      HBITMAP hBitmap1);
  void DrawFocused(LPDRAWITEMSTRUCT p);
};
```

In this class, there are many of the same functions used in the first user-draw button class. In addition, there's the `DrawLine()` function, which draws the appropriate line graphic on each button's face. The biggest difference in this class, though, is that it draws each button's main image with bitmaps, rather than with GDI calls. Also, it uses the `WM_DRAWITEM` message to ensure that only one button at a time is selected in the toolbox.

As in the first user-draw button program, the buttons in the toolbox are drawn by the `DrawButton()` function, which is called when the toolbox receives a `WM_DRAWITEM` message:

```
void TToolButn::DrawButton(LPDRAWITEMSTRUCT p,
      int selected, HBITMAP hBitmap1, HBITMAP hBitmap2)
{
  // Respond to the action.
  switch (p->itemAction)
  {
    // Draw the full button.
    case ODA_DRAWENTIRE:
      if (selected != p->CtlID)
        DrawUnselected(p, hBitmap1);
      else
        DrawSelected(p, hBitmap2);
      break;

    // Check button state and draw appropriate image.
    case ODA_SELECT:
      if (p->itemState & ODS_SELECTED)
        DrawSelected(p, hBitmap2);
      else if (p->CtlID != selected)
        DrawUnselected(p, hBitmap1);
      break;

    // Draw the button's focused image, if necessary.
    case ODA_FOCUS:
      if (p->itemState & ODS_FOCUS)
        DrawFocused(p);
      break;
  }
}
```

Recall how, in the `TToolDlg` class just before calling `DrawButton()`, the program set `selected` to the currently selected button's ID. The program passes `selected`, along with the bitmap handles, to `DrawButton()`, where it uses `selected` to redraw the buttons in a way that mimics radio buttons. (Radio buttons allow only one button to be selected at any given time.) First, the program checks for the `ODA_DRAWENTIRE` action. If it has one, it must check whether the button it's drawing is selected and draw the button in its appropriate state.

 Note: Although the `ODA_DRAWENTIRE` action occurs only when the buttons are first drawn, the program can't draw all the buttons in their unselected states. This is because, from the start, the toolbox has one button selected. In fact, the toolbox always has one—and only one—button selected.

If `itemAction` is set to `ODA_SELECT`, the selection state of the button has changed. As usual, the program checks the button's state and draws the appropriate button image. In the case of `ODA_FOCUS`, the program draws the button's focus rectangle. You may now wonder why the images of two buttons change when you click a button on the toolbox, with the button you clicked drawn selected and the old button changed to unselected.

When you click a new button, it not only is selected, but also gets the focus. Why is this important? Only one button can have the focus at one time. When a new button is selected, the old button loses its focus. This causes a `WM_DRAWITEM` message to be sent for both buttons.

Drawing Bitmapped Buttons

Drawing buttons in this program is both less and more complicated than it was in the first custom-button program. The drawing is less complicated because you don't have to painstakingly create a button's image with many GDI calls, but it's more complicated in that you have to manipulate bitmaps.

Look at the `DrawUnselected()` function:

```
void TToolButn::DrawUnselected(LPDRAWITEMSTRUCT p,
                               HBITMAP hBitmap1)
{
  // Create memory device context.
  HDC hMemDC = CreateCompatibleDC(p->hDC);
```

```
// Select bitmap into device context.
HBITMAP hOldBitmap = SelectObject(hMemDC, hBitmap1);

// Copy the bitmap to the screen.
BitBlt(p->hDC, 1, 1, 47, 27, hMemDC, 0, 0, SRCCOPY);

// Restore old memory DC.
SelectObject(hMemDC, hOldBitmap);
DeleteDC(hMemDC);

// Draw the appropriate line on the button.
DrawLine(p, 0);

// Draw the focus rectangle, if necessary.
if (p->itemState & ODS_FOCUS)
  DrawFocused(p);
}
```

This function first creates a device context (DC) in memory where it can manipulate the bitmap. This memory DC must be compatible with the button's DC, a pointer to which is included in `DRAWITEMSTRUCT`. Luckily, Windows provides a function called `CreateCompatibleDC()` that creates compatible device contexts. The program uses this function to create the memory DC, after which it selects the appropriate bitmap into the newly created DC.

The program can then display the bitmap by calling `BitBlt()`, which copies the bitmap in memory to the screen. The parameters for this function are the destination DC, the x,y coordinates of the upper-left corner of the destination rectangle, the width and height of the bitmap, the source DC, the x,y coordinates of the upper-left corner of the source bitmap, and the raster operation to be performed. The *raster operation* is the way in which the source and destination values are combined. For more information on this topic, consult your Borland C++ manuals.

Finally, after the program displays the bitmap, it restores and deletes the memory DC, draws the appropriate line image on the button's face, and checks whether it must draw a focus rectangle.

The selected form of the button is drawn by the `DrawSelected()` function. This function is identical to `DrawUnselected()`, except it draws a different bitmap.

The last function of interest in this class is `DrawLine()`:

```
void TToolButn::DrawLine(LPDRAWITEMSTRUCT p, int offset)
{
  // Select new pen and brush.
  HPEN custom_pen = CreatePen(PS_SOLID, (p->CtlID-100)*2,
                              BLACK_PEN);
  HPEN prev_pen = SelectObject(p->hDC, custom_pen);
  HBRUSH new_brush = GetStockObject(LTGRAY_BRUSH);
  HBRUSH prev_brush = SelectObject(p->hDC, new_brush);

  // Draw the line on the button.
  MoveTo(p->hDC, 8+offset, 13+offset);
  LineTo(p->hDC, 39+offset, 13+offset);

  // Square the lines' rounded ends.
  HPEN new_pen = GetStockObject(NULL_PEN);
  SelectObject(p->hDC, new_pen);
  Rectangle(p->hDC, 4+offset, 6+offset,
            8+offset, 22+offset);
  Rectangle(p->hDC, 40+offset, 4+offset,
            44+offset, 22+offset);

  // Restore device context.
  SelectObject(p->hDC, prev_pen);
  SelectObject(p->hDC, prev_brush);
  DeleteObject(custom_pen);
}
```

This function draws the appropriate line image on a button's face. First, it calls `CreatePen()` to get a pen of the right line thickness, using the button's ID to determine the thickness of the line needed. Then, it draws the line on the button. Because the thicker lines are drawn with rounded ends, the function next squares the ends of the lines by drawing two small gray rectangles over them. Finally, the function restores the DC and deletes the custom pen.

Notice the `offset` variable in all the drawing operations. If a button is being drawn unselected, `offset` is 0. If a button is being drawn selected, `offset` is 1. By adding 1 to the coordinates of all drawing operations for a selected button, the line on the face of the button is drawn one pixel down and to the right, which gives the button the illusion of movement.

405

Full-Size Toolboxes

Although your toolbox has only four buttons, it doesn't take a lot of extra programming to expand it. You only have to increase the size of the dialog box and the button-pointer array. Depending on your application, you may also have to create additional button bitmaps, especially if the images on the buttons' faces cannot be drawn easily with GDI calls. Still, you can use the techniques presented here to create the perfect toolbox for almost any application.

A final note about this type of toolbox: You must not allow the user to change button focus with the Tab key. In other words, the buttons' style must not include the WS_TABSTOP flag. This is because the toolbox assumes that the selected button is also the one with the focus. If this were not the case, the buttons would be drawn incorrectly.

As an experiment, add the WS_TABSTOP flag to the button class by adding ¦ WS_TABSTOP to the end of the line Attr.Style = BS_OWNERDRAW ¦ WS_CHILD ¦ WS_VISIBLE in the buttons' constructor. Now run the program, bring up the toolbox, change the button focus with the Tab key, and click an unselected button. Whoops! Now you have two pressed buttons, as shown in Figure 10.6. To allow users to select tools with the keyboard, you have to add a tool menu (which you should do, anyway).

Two buttons pressed ⸻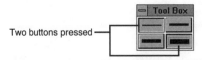

Figure 10.6. The results of allowing tabbing in the toolbox.

Conclusion

As you can see, custom controls give your programs any look you want. Moreover, they enable you to create new kinds of objects—such as the toolbox presented here—that make your programs more professional looking. In business, they say the customer is always right. In the programming business, it's the user who's always right, and users want programs that are easy and convenient to use.

11

Scaling Printer Output

ne of the greatest advantages of running applications in Windows is *device independence*. This means that Windows can handle most graphics cards, printers, or sound cards (as well as other devices) almost invisibly to the user. All the user has to do is install Windows with the correct drivers. From then on Windows takes care of itself. Unfortunately, this device independence means that programmers must work a little harder. They must write their programs such that they never access devices directly. This goes double for printers, especially considering that many DOS programmers are accustomed to accessing printers directly. This habit must be broken when programming in Windows.

In this chapter, you learn to not only send output to a printer—a complicated process in Windows—but also to scale the output so it looks similar from one printer device to the next. To demonstrate the printer techniques presented here, this chapter includes a small Windows application that prints audio-cassette labels.

Example Application: WinCassette

L istings 11.1 through 11.6 contain the files needed to create this chapter's sample program, WinCassette. As mentioned, this application is a label printer for audio cassettes.

Listing 11.1. WINCASS.H—the WinCassette application's header file.

```
// WINCASS.H: Header file for the WinCassette application.

#ifndef _WINCASS_H
#define _WINCASS_H

#define ID_SIDE        201
#define ID_PRINT       202
#define ID_ABOUT       203
#define ID_SIDETITLE   102
#define ID_TITLESTRING 300

#endif
```

Listing 11.2. WINCASS.CPP—the WinCassette application's implementation.

```
// WINCASS.CPP: Implementation for the
//              WinCassette application.

#include <owl.h>
#include "twnd.h"
#include "twcwnd.h"
#include "bwcc.h"

// WinCassette application class.
class TWCApp: public TApplication
{
public:
  TWCApp(LPSTR AName, HINSTANCE hInstance,
         HINSTANCE hPrevInstance, LPSTR lpCmdLine,
         int nCmdShow): TApplication(AName, hInstance,
         hPrevInstance, lpCmdLine, nCmdShow) {};
```

```
  virtual void InitMainWindow();
};


//////////////////////////////////////////////////////
// TWCApp::InitMainWindow()
//
// This function creates the application's main window.
//////////////////////////////////////////////////////
void TWCApp::InitMainWindow()
{
  MainWindow = new TWCWnd(NULL, "DIALOG1");
}


//////////////////////////////////////////////////////
// WinMain()
//////////////////////////////////////////////////////
int PASCAL WinMain(HINSTANCE hInstance,
                   HINSTANCE hPrevInstance,
             LPSTR lpCmdLine, int nCmdShow)
{
  BWCCGetVersion();
  TWCApp WCApp("WinCassette", hInstance,
               hPrevInstance, lpCmdLine, nCmdShow);
  WCApp.Run();
  return WCApp.Status;
}
```

Listing 11.3. TWCWND.H—the main window's header file.

```
// TWCWND.H: Header file for the WinCassette main window.

#ifndef _TWCWND_H
#define _TWCWND_H

#include "owl.h"
#include "wincass.h"


typedef struct
{
  char cassTitle[38], // Title for cassette.
       sideTitle[38]; // Title for side A or B.
```

continues

Listing 11.3. Continued

```
        // Song titles.
   char edit1[38], edit2[38], edit3[38],
        edit4[38], edit5[38], edit6[38],
        edit7[38], edit8[38], edit9[38],
        edit10[38], edit11[38], edit12[38],
        edit13[38], edit14[38], edit15[38],
        edit16[38];
} TRANSFERREC;


_CLASSDEF(TWCWnd)
class TWCWnd: public TDialog
{
   int sideA,               // Cassette side flag.
       result;              // Printer error flag.
   TRANSFERREC dlgStrgs,    // Transfer buffer for dialog.
            sideAStrgs,  // Storage for side A data.
            sideBStrgs;  // Storage for side B data.
   HDC pDC;                 // Printer device context.
   char *dlgEdits[18],      // Pointers to edit field strings.
        *sideAEdits[18],
        *sideBEdits[18];

public:
   TWCWnd(PTWindowsObject AParent, LPSTR AName);
   virtual void IDSide()
      = [ID_FIRST + ID_SIDE];
   virtual void IDPrint()
      = [ID_FIRST + ID_PRINT];
   virtual void IDAbout()
      = [ID_FIRST + ID_ABOUT];

private:
   void LoadStrings(char **s, char **d);
   int StartPrinting();
   void StopPrinting();
   void PrintLabel();
   void DrawLabel(int horDots, int verDots);
   void DrawBodyText(int horDots, int verDots);
```

```
  void DrawTitleText(int horDots, int verDots);
  HFONT CreateCassFont(int hSize, int vSize);
};


#endif
```

Listing 11.4. TWCWND.CPP—the main window's implementation.

```
// TWCWND.CPP: The main window implementation for
//             WinCassette.

#include "twcwnd.h"
#include "edit.h"
#include "string.h"


////////////////////////////////////////////////////////
// TWCWnd::TWCWnd()
//
// This is the main window's constructor.
////////////////////////////////////////////////////////
TWCWnd::TWCWnd(PTWindowsObject AParent, LPSTR AName):
              TDialog(AParent, AName)
{
  // Create OWL edit-control objects.
  for (int x=101; x<=119; ++x)
    new TEdit(this, x, 38);

  // Initialize the buffers to all NULLs.
  memset(&dlgStrgs, 0, sizeof dlgStrgs);
  memset(&sideAStrgs, 0, sizeof sideAStrgs);
  memset(&sideBStrgs, 0, sizeof sideBStrgs);

  // Set the address of the dialog's transfer buffer.
  TransferBuffer = &dlgStrgs;

  // Initialize string-pointer arrays by storing the
  // address of each of the 38-character strings that
  // make up each buffer.
  for (x=0; x<18; ++x)
  {
```

continues

411

Listing 11.4. Continued

```
      dlgEdits[x] = dlgStrgs.cassTitle + x*38;
      sideAEdits[x] = sideAStrgs.cassTitle + x*38;
      sideBEdits[x] = sideBStrgs.cassTitle + x*38;
  }

  // Start on side A.
  sideA = TRUE;
}


///////////////////////////////////////////////////////
// TWCWnd::LoadStrings()
//
// This function transfers the contents of one
// TRANSFERREC structure to another. To simplify the
// transfer, you don't address the structures directly,
// but instead find their strings by the pointer arrays
// you initialized for each buffer.
///////////////////////////////////////////////////////
void TWCWnd::LoadStrings(char **s, char **d)
{
  for (int x=0; x<18; ++x)
    strcpy(d[x], s[x]);
}


///////////////////////////////////////////////////////
// TWCWnd::IDSide()
//
// This function responds when the user clicks the
// Side button.
///////////////////////////////////////////////////////
void TWCWnd::IDSide()
{
  HWND hControl1, hControl2;

  // Transfer data from the dialog's edit controls
  // to the transfer buffer.
  TransferData(TF_GETDATA);

  // Get handles to the Side button and the
  // dialog's static string for the side label.
  hControl1 = GetDlgItem(HWindow,ID_SIDE);
```

```
hControl2 = GetDlgItem(HWindow, ID_TITLESTRING);

// If the user was on side A...
if (sideA)
{
  // Copy the dialog's data to the side A buffer.
  LoadStrings(dlgEdits, sideAEdits);

  // Change the Side button's text and the
  // side static string's text.
  SetWindowText(hControl1, "&Side A");
  SetWindowText(hControl2, "Side B:");

  // Copy the cassette's title because it is the
  // same for side B.
  strcpy(sideBStrgs.cassTitle, sideAStrgs.cassTitle);

  // Copy the side B buffer to the transfer buffer.
  LoadStrings(sideBEdits, dlgEdits);

  sideA = FALSE;
}
// Else if on side B...
else
{
  // Copy the dialog's data to the side B buffer.
  LoadStrings(dlgEdits, sideBEdits);

  // Change the text in the Side button and the
  // side static string.
  SetWindowText(hControl1, "&Side B");
  SetWindowText(hControl2, "Side A:");

  // Copy the cassette's title, in case it has changed.
  strcpy(sideAStrgs.cassTitle, sideBStrgs.cassTitle);

  // Copy the side A buffer to the transfer buffer.
  LoadStrings(sideAEdits, dlgEdits);

  sideA = TRUE;
}
```

continues

Listing 11.4. Continued

```
  // Set focus to the side-title edit field.
  hControl1 = GetDlgItem(HWindow, ID_SIDETITLE);
  SetFocus(hControl1);

  // Copy the data in the transfer buffer to
  // the dialog's controls.
  TransferData(TF_SETDATA);
}


/////////////////////////////////////////////////////////
// TWCWnd::IDPrint()
//
// This function responds when the user clicks the
// Print button.
/////////////////////////////////////////////////////////
void TWCWnd::IDPrint()
{
  // Copy data from the dialog's edit controls
  // into the transfer buffer.
  TransferData(TF_GETDATA);

  // Copy the transfer buffer into the appropriate
  // buffer, depending on the current side.
  if (sideA)
    LoadStrings(dlgEdits, sideAEdits);
  else
    LoadStrings(dlgEdits, sideBEdits);

  // Initialize the printer.
  result = StartPrinting();

  // Print the label.
  if (result > 0)
    PrintLabel();

  // Shut down printing.
  StopPrinting();
}
```

```
//////////////////////////////////////////////////////
// TWCWnd::PrintLabel()
//
// This function sends the cassette label to the
// printer.
//////////////////////////////////////////////////////
void TWCWnd::PrintLabel()
{
  // Get horizontal and vertical resolution for printer.
  int horDots = GetDeviceCaps(pDC, LOGPIXELSX);
  int verDots = GetDeviceCaps(pDC, LOGPIXELSY);

  // Draw the cassette label's outline.
  DrawLabel(horDots, verDots);

  // Print the side titles and song titles.
  DrawBodyText(horDots, verDots);

  // Print the main cassette titles.
  DrawTitleText(horDots, verDots);
}


//////////////////////////////////////////////////////
// TWCWnd::DrawLabel()
//
// This function draws the cassette label's outline.
//////////////////////////////////////////////////////
void TWCWnd::DrawLabel(int horDots, int verDots)
{
  MoveTo(pDC, horDots/2, verDots/2);
  LineTo(pDC, horDots*4.5, verDots/2);
  LineTo(pDC, horDots*4.5, verDots*4.3);
  LineTo(pDC, horDots/2, verDots*4.3);
  LineTo(pDC, horDots/2, verDots/2);
  MoveTo(pDC, horDots/2, verDots*0.75);
  LineTo(pDC, horDots*4.5, verDots*0.75);
  MoveTo(pDC, horDots/2, verDots*0.93);
  LineTo(pDC, horDots*4.5, verDots*0.93);
  MoveTo(pDC, horDots/2, verDots*3.1);
  LineTo(pDC, horDots*4.5, verDots*3.1);
  MoveTo(pDC, horDots/2, verDots*3.62);
  LineTo(pDC, horDots*4.5, verDots*3.62);
```

continues

415

Listing 11.4. Continued

```
  MoveTo(pDC, horDots*2.5, verDots*0.75);
  LineTo(pDC, horDots*2.5, verDots*3.1);
}


/////////////////////////////////////////////////////////
// TWCWnd::DrawBodyText()
//
// This function prints the cassette's side and song
// titles.
/////////////////////////////////////////////////////////
void TWCWnd::DrawBodyText(int horDots, int verDots)
{
  TEXTMETRIC metrics;   // Physical font description.
  char s[80];           // Output text line.

  // Create and select the font for the cassette text.
  HFONT newFont = CreateCassFont(horDots/30, verDots/8);
  HFONT oldFont = SelectObject(pDC, newFont);

  // Get the size of the physical font.
  GetTextMetrics(pDC, &metrics);

  // Construct and print side A and side B titles.
  strcpy(s, "Side A: ");
  strcpy(&s[strlen(s)], sideAStrgs.sideTitle);
  TextOut(pDC, horDots*0.6, verDots*0.77, s, strlen(s));
  strcpy(s, "Side B: ");
  strcpy(&s[strlen(s)], sideBStrgs.sideTitle);
  TextOut(pDC, horDots*2.6, verDots*0.77, s, strlen(s));

  // Print song titles for sides A and B.
  for (int x=2; x<18; ++x)
  {
    TextOut(pDC, horDots*0.6, (verDots*0.87)+((x-1)
        *metrics.tmHeight), sideAEdits[x],
        strlen(sideAEdits[x]));
    TextOut(pDC, horDots*2.6, (verDots*0.87)+((x-1)
        *metrics.tmHeight), sideBEdits[x],
        strlen(sideBEdits[x]));
  }
```

```
  // Restore the device context.
  SelectObject(pDC, oldFont);
  DeleteObject(newFont);
}


/////////////////////////////////////////////////////////
// TWCWnd::DrawTitleText()
//
// This function prints the cassette's main titles.
/////////////////////////////////////////////////////////
void TWCWnd::DrawTitleText(int horDots, int verDots)
{
  int strWidth;        // Width of text line.
  long textExtent;     // Width and height of text line.

  // Create the new title font.
  HFONT newFont = CreateCassFont(horDots/20, verDots/5);
  HFONT oldFont = SelectObject(pDC, newFont);

  // Get the width and height of the title string.
  textExtent = GetTextExtent(pDC, sideAStrgs.cassTitle,
                  strlen(sideAStrgs.cassTitle));

  // Extract the width of the title string.
  strWidth = LOWORD(textExtent);

  // Print the main cassette titles.
  TextOut(pDC, (horDots*2.5)-(strWidth/2), verDots*0.52,
      sideAStrgs.cassTitle, strlen(sideAStrgs.cassTitle));
  TextOut(pDC, (horDots*2.5)-(strWidth/2), verDots*3.25,
      sideAStrgs.cassTitle, strlen(sideAStrgs.cassTitle));

  // Restore the device context.
  SelectObject(pDC, oldFont);
  DeleteObject(newFont);
}


/////////////////////////////////////////////////////////
// TWCWnd::CreateCassFont()
//
// This function creates fonts for the cassette label.
// Fonts vary only in their horizontal and vertical
// size.
/////////////////////////////////////////////////////////
```

continues

417

Listing 11.4. Continued

```
HFONT TWCWnd::CreateCassFont(int hSize, int vSize)
{
  LOGFONT cassLogFont; // Logical font description.

  // Fill in LOGFONT structure.
  cassLogFont.lfHeight = vSize;
  cassLogFont.lfWidth = hSize;
  cassLogFont.lfEscapement = 0;
  cassLogFont.lfOrientation = 0;
  cassLogFont.lfWeight = FW_NORMAL;
  cassLogFont.lfItalic = 0;
  cassLogFont.lfUnderline = 0;
  cassLogFont.lfStrikeOut = 0;
  cassLogFont.lfCharSet = ANSI_CHARSET;
  cassLogFont.lfOutPrecision = OUT_DEFAULT_PRECIS;
  cassLogFont.lfClipPrecision = CLIP_DEFAULT_PRECIS;
  cassLogFont.lfQuality = PROOF_QUALITY;
  cassLogFont.lfPitchAndFamily = VARIABLE_PITCH ¦ FF_ROMAN;
  strcpy(cassLogFont.lfFaceName, "Times New Roman");

  // Create new font.
  return CreateFontIndirect(&cassLogFont);
}


//////////////////////////////////////////////////////
// TWCWnd::IDAbout()
//
// This function responds when the user clicks the
// About button.
//////////////////////////////////////////////////////
void TWCWnd::IDAbout()
{
  char s[100];

  // Construct the string to display.
  strcpy(s, "  WinCassette 1.0");
  s[17] = 13;
  strcpy(&s[18], "by Clayton Walnum");
  s[35] = 13;
  s[36] = 13;
  strcpy(&s[37], "   Copyright 1992");
  s[55] = 13;
```

```
    strcpy(&s[56], "    by Prentice Hall");
    s[76] = 13;
    strcpy(&s[77], "Computer Publishing");

    // Use messageBox to display "About" info.
    MessageBox(HWindow, s, "About", MB_OK);
}


/////////////////////////////////////////////////////////////
// TWCWnd::StartPrinting()
//
// This function creates a device context for the
// user's printer and initializes the printer.
/////////////////////////////////////////////////////////////
int TWCWnd::StartPrinting()
{
    char buffer[80], // Storage for profile string.
         *cp,        // Character pointer.
         *driver,    // Pointer to driver string.
         *device,    // Pointer to device string.
         *output;    // Pointer to output port string.

    // Change the cursor to an hourglass shape.
    SetCursor(LoadCursor(0, IDC_WAIT));

    // Get the printer device string from WIN.INI.
    GetProfileString("windows", "device", ",,",
             buffer, sizeof buffer);

    // Parse the printer device string to get the
    // device, driver, and output port strings.
    device = buffer;            // Set device to start of string.
    cp = strchr(buffer, ',');   // Get address of first comma.
    *cp = 0;                    // Change comma to null.
    driver = &cp[1];            // Get adr of char after device.
    cp = strchr(driver, ',');   // Get address of next comma.
    *cp = 0;                    // Change comma to null.
    output = &cp[1];            // Set pointer to port string.

    // Create a printer device context.
    pDC = CreateDC(driver, device, output, NULL);

    // Begin printing the document.
```

continues

419

Listing 11.4. Continued

```
if (pDC != 0)
{
  DOCINFO tdi;
  tdi.cbSize = 5;
  tdi.lpszDocName = "Label";
  tdi.lpszOutput = output;
  result = StartDoc(pDC, &tdi);
    // Escape(pDC, STARTDOC, 5, "LABEL", NULL);
  if (result > 0)
    result = StartPage(pDC);
}
if ((result <= 0) ¦¦ (pDC == NULL))
  MessageBox(0, "Printer initialization failed",
             "Error", MB_ICONEXCLAMATION ¦ MB_OK);
return result;
}


/////////////////////////////////////////////////////
// TWCWnd::StopPrinting()
//
// This function shuts down the printing job.
/////////////////////////////////////////////////////
void TWCWnd::StopPrinting()
{
  EndPage(pDC); // Escape(pDC, NEWFRAME, 0, NULL, NULL);
  EndDoc(pDC);   // Escape(pDC, ENDDOC, 0, NULL, NULL);
  SetCursor(LoadCursor(0, IDC_ARROW));
  DeleteDC(pDC);
}
```

Listing 11.5. WINCASS.RC—the application's resource file.

```
DIALOG1 DIALOG 12, 13, 276, 202
STYLE DS_MODALFRAME ¦ WS_POPUP ¦ WS_VISIBLE ¦
     WS_CAPTION ¦ WS_SYSMENU
CLASS "BorDlg"
CAPTION "WinCassette"
BEGIN
    CONTROL "", 101, "EDIT", ES_LEFT ¦ ES_AUTOHSCROLL ¦
      WS_CHILD ¦ WS_VISIBLE ¦ WS_BORDER ¦ WS_TABSTOP,
      24, 6, 98, 12
```

```
CONTROL "", 102, "EDIT", ES_LEFT ¦ ES_AUTOHSCROLL ¦
  WS_CHILD ¦ WS_VISIBLE ¦ WS_BORDER ¦ WS_TABSTOP,
  158, 6, 97, 12
CONTROL "", 103, "EDIT", ES_LEFT ¦ ES_AUTOHSCROLL ¦
  WS_CHILD ¦ WS_VISIBLE ¦ WS_BORDER ¦ WS_TABSTOP,
  23, 28, 100, 12
CONTROL "", 104, "EDIT", ES_LEFT ¦ ES_AUTOHSCROLL ¦
  WS_CHILD ¦ WS_VISIBLE ¦ WS_BORDER ¦ WS_TABSTOP,
  23, 45, 100, 12
CONTROL "", 105, "EDIT", ES_LEFT ¦ ES_AUTOHSCROLL ¦
  WS_CHILD ¦ WS_VISIBLE ¦ WS_BORDER ¦ WS_TABSTOP,
  23, 63, 100, 12
CONTROL "", 106, "EDIT", ES_LEFT ¦ ES_AUTOHSCROLL ¦
  WS_CHILD ¦ WS_VISIBLE ¦ WS_BORDER ¦ WS_TABSTOP,
  23, 81, 100, 12
CONTROL "", 107, "EDIT", ES_LEFT ¦ ES_AUTOHSCROLL ¦
  WS_CHILD ¦ WS_VISIBLE ¦ WS_BORDER ¦ WS_TABSTOP,
  23, 99, 100, 12
CONTROL "", 108, "EDIT", ES_LEFT ¦ ES_AUTOHSCROLL ¦
  WS_CHILD ¦ WS_VISIBLE ¦ WS_BORDER ¦ WS_TABSTOP,
  23, 117, 100, 12
CONTROL "", 109, "EDIT", ES_LEFT ¦ ES_AUTOHSCROLL ¦
  WS_CHILD ¦ WS_VISIBLE ¦ WS_BORDER ¦ WS_TABSTOP,
  23, 135, 100, 12
CONTROL "", 110, "EDIT", ES_LEFT ¦ ES_AUTOHSCROLL ¦
  WS_CHILD ¦ WS_VISIBLE ¦ WS_BORDER ¦ WS_TABSTOP,
  23, 153, 100, 12
CONTROL "", 111, "EDIT", ES_LEFT ¦ ES_AUTOHSCROLL ¦
  WS_CHILD ¦ WS_VISIBLE ¦ WS_BORDER ¦ WS_TABSTOP,
  155, 28, 100, 12
CONTROL "", 112, "EDIT", ES_LEFT ¦ ES_AUTOHSCROLL ¦
  WS_CHILD ¦ WS_VISIBLE ¦ WS_BORDER ¦ WS_TABSTOP,
  155, 45, 100, 12
CONTROL "", 113, "EDIT", ES_LEFT ¦ ES_AUTOHSCROLL ¦
  WS_CHILD ¦ WS_VISIBLE ¦ WS_BORDER ¦ WS_TABSTOP,
  155, 63, 100, 12
CONTROL "", 114, "EDIT", ES_LEFT ¦ ES_AUTOHSCROLL ¦
  WS_CHILD ¦ WS_VISIBLE ¦ WS_BORDER ¦ WS_TABSTOP,
  155, 81, 100, 12
CONTROL "", 115, "EDIT", ES_LEFT ¦ ES_AUTOHSCROLL ¦
  WS_CHILD ¦ WS_VISIBLE ¦ WS_BORDER ¦ WS_TABSTOP,
  155, 99, 100, 12
```

continues

Listing 11.5. Continued

```
CONTROL "", 116, "EDIT", ES_LEFT | ES_AUTOHSCROLL |
  WS_CHILD | WS_VISIBLE | WS_BORDER | WS_TABSTOP,
  155, 117, 100, 12
CONTROL "", 117, "EDIT", ES_LEFT | ES_AUTOHSCROLL |
  WS_CHILD | WS_VISIBLE | WS_BORDER | WS_TABSTOP,
  155, 135, 100, 12
CONTROL "", 118, "EDIT", ES_LEFT | ES_AUTOHSCROLL |
  WS_CHILD | WS_VISIBLE | WS_BORDER | WS_TABSTOP,
  155, 153, 100, 12
CONTROL "&Side B", 201, "BorBtn", BS_PUSHBUTTON |
  WS_CHILD | WS_VISIBLE | WS_TABSTOP,
  14, 176, 32, 20
CONTROL "&Print", 202, "BorBtn", BS_PUSHBUTTON |
  WS_CHILD | WS_VISIBLE | WS_TABSTOP,
  57, 176, 32, 20
CONTROL "&About", 203, "BorBtn", BS_PUSHBUTTON |
  WS_CHILD | WS_VISIBLE | WS_TABSTOP,
  100, 176, 32, 20
CONTROL "Quit", 2, "BorBtn", 0 | WS_CHILD |
  WS_VISIBLE | WS_TABSTOP, 230, 176, 34, 20
LTEXT "Side A:", 300, 133, 8, 24, 8
LTEXT "1", -1, 15, 30, 5, 8
LTEXT "2", -1, 15, 47, 5, 8
LTEXT "3", -1, 15, 65, 5, 8
LTEXT "4", -1, 15, 83, 5, 8
LTEXT "5", -1, 15, 101, 5, 8
LTEXT "6", -1, 15, 119, 5, 8
LTEXT "7", -1, 15, 137, 5, 8
LTEXT "8", -1, 15, 155, 5, 8
LTEXT "9", -1, 147, 30, 5, 8
LTEXT "10", -1, 144, 47, 8, 8
LTEXT "11", -1, 144, 65, 8, 8
LTEXT "12", -1, 144, 83, 8, 8
LTEXT "13", -1, 144, 101, 8, 8
LTEXT "14", -1, 144, 119, 8, 8
LTEXT "15", -1, 144, 137, 8, 8
LTEXT "16", -1, 144, 155, 8, 8
LTEXT "Title:", -1, 6, 8, 16, 8
CONTROL "", 119, "BorShade", 2 | WS_CHILD |
  WS_VISIBLE, 4, 22, 269, 2
CONTROL "", 120, "BorShade", 2 | WS_CHILD |
  WS_VISIBLE, 4, 170, 269, 1
END
```

Listing 11.6. WINCASS.DEF—the application's definition file.

```
EXETYPE WINDOWS
CODE PRELOAD MOVEABLE DISCARDABLE
DATA PRELOAD MOVEABLE MULTIPLE
HEAPSIZE 4096
STACKSIZE 5120
```

When you run the program, you see the window shown in Figure 11.1. In the first edit box (the one in the upper-left corner), type the main title of the cassette. Then press Tab and type the title for side A. Next, type up to 16 song titles for side A of the cassette, then click the Side B button to enter song titles for side B. Finally, click the Print button to print the cassette label.

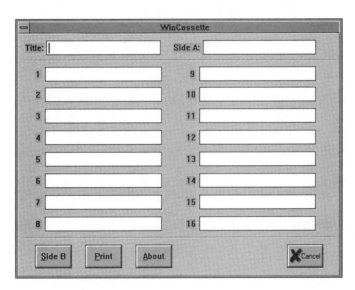

Figure 11.1. The WinCassette main window.

Thanks to the power of a Windows dialog box, this program does little more than format and print data. But as you can see from the size of the listing, it takes many lines of code to print even something as simple as a cassette label. You must select fonts, create printer device contexts, and scale output for the printer. Because you want the application to work with more than one type of printer, you must handle all this processing in a general way, assuming nothing about the output device.

WinCassette accomplishes this goal to produce similar labels on any printer. Read on to see how the program works.

A Dialog Main Window

W inCassette's main window requires many controls: four buttons and 18 edit fields. To create these controls in the program would be a major chore. You would have to experiment with different control sizes and coordinates by typing values into the program, compiling the program, seeing how the controls look, then readjusting them. A way around this meticulous process is to create a dialog box using the Resource Workshop, and then use the dialog as your main window.

Although it may seem at first that this is a tricky task, using a dialog box for a main window is no more complex than using a regular window. This fact can be seen in the application's `InitMainWindow()` function:

```
void TWCApp::InitMainWindow()
{
  MainWindow = new TWCWnd(NULL, "DIALOG1");
}
```

Here, the program substitutes the dialog box's constructor for the usual `TWindow` constructor (or a window derived from `TWindow`). When the program runs now, the screen displays the dialog box instead of a conventional main window. This dialog window, however, has some limitations. For example, a dialog box doesn't have a menu (except for the system menu) and normally can't specify an icon or a cursor, as a window derived from `TWindow` can.

Except for having a dialog box as a main window, this application class is almost identical to the other application classes you've used. This is typical of an ObjectWindows program. With only minimal changes, the application class you've been using all along can be the basis for practically any program.

The Dialog Window Class

Virtually all of WinCassette's functionality is in the `TWCWnd` class:

```
_CLASSDEF(TWCWnd)
class TWCWnd: public TDialog
{
  int sideA,              // Cassette side flag.
      result;             // Printer error flag.
  TRANSFERREC dlgStrgs,   // Transfer buffer for dialog.
          sideAStrgs,     // Storage for side A data.
          sideBStrgs;     // Storage for side B data.
```

424

```
    HDC pDC;                    // Printer device context.
    char *dlgEdits[18],    // Pointers to edit field strings.
         *sideAEdits[18],
         *sideBEdits[18];

public:
    TWCWnd(PTWindowsObject AParent, LPSTR AName);
    virtual void IDSide()
        = [ID_FIRST + ID_SIDE];
    virtual void IDPrint()
        = [ID_FIRST + ID_PRINT];
    virtual void IDAbout()
        = [ID_FIRST + ID_ABOUT];

private:
    void LoadStrings(char **s, char **d);
    int StartPrinting();
    void StopPrinting();
    void PrintLabel();
    void DrawLabel(int horDots, int verDots);
    void DrawBodyText(int horDots, int verDots);
    void DrawTitleText(int horDots, int verDots);
    HFONT CreateCassFont(int hSize, int vSize);
};
```

This class contains a number of private data members. The sideA flag indicates whether the user is working on side A or B of the cassette. The result integer contains the results of certain printer operations.

Next are three copies of the dialog's *transfer buffer*. (The transfer buffers are described in more detail in the next section.) The first, dlgStrgs, is the transfer buffer OWL uses to transfer data from your dialog box. The other two, sideAStrgs and sideBStrgs, provide storage for data copied from the main transfer buffer. The pDC handle holds the handle to a printer device context.

Finally, the dlgEdits[], sideAEdits[], and sideBEdits[] character pointer arrays hold pointers to each of the fields in the three TRANSFERREC structures. By having these pointer arrays, the program can access the strings in the buffers more easily.

The public member functions in this class include only the class' constructor and three message-response functions, one each for the Side, Print, and About buttons. The class doesn't need to declare a message-response method for the Cancel button because it has inherited that function from the OWL TDialog class.

Finally, the private member functions handle all the printing operations. They also allow the transfer of data between the TRANSFERREC structures and the selection of new fonts.

Handling Dialog Data

The WinCassette dialog box contains 18 edit fields, any or all of which may hold the information you need to print a cassette label. Before you can print the label, you must be able to access this data. In a traditional Windows program, handling dialog data requires checking each control before the dialog closes; the data in the controls must be saved in a buffer or processed before the dialog closes. When the dialog closes, the data is gone.

Borland C++ programmers, however, don't care about the details of accessing dialog data, because ObjectWindows supplies a transfer mechanism that automatically copies this data into a buffer when the dialog closes. You can then process the data any way you like, in your own good time.

To enable this transfer mechanism, you must first define a transfer buffer. This *transfer buffer* is a structure that contains a field for each control that you want involved in the transfer. The types of fields in the structure vary depending on the type of control. For example, an edit control requires a character array, whereas an option button requires only a single integer in which to store its state (checked or unchecked).

The transfer buffer for WinCassette is defined in the TWCWND.H file and looks like this:

```
typedef struct
{
  char cassTitle[38], // Title for cassette.
       sideTitle[38]; // Title for side A or B.

       // Song titles.
  char edit1[38], edit2[38], edit3[38],
       edit4[38], edit5[38], edit6[38],
       edit7[38], edit8[38], edit9[38],
       edit10[38], edit11[38], edit12[38],
       edit13[38], edit14[38], edit15[38],
       edit16[38];
} TRANSFERREC;
```

The dialog box has two title fields and 16 song title fields. As you can see, each edit field has a 38-element character array. You don't have to provide fields in this structure for the dialog's buttons because the buttons do not contain information you need after the dialog closes.

Supplying the transfer buffer is only the first step in setting up the transfer mechanism. Next, you have to associate the controls of your dialog box with OWL controls, because only OWL controls can participate in the transfer. Moreover, you must create these OWL controls in the same order in which they are represented in your transfer buffer. Finally, you must supply OWL with the address of the transfer buffer.

All this happens in the dialog's constructor:

```
TWCWnd::TWCWnd(PTWindowsObject AParent, LPSTR AName):
                TDialog(AParent, AName)
{
  // Create OWL edit-control objects.
  for (int x=101; x<=119; ++x)
    new TEdit(this, x, 38);

  // Initialize the buffers to all NULLs.
  memset(&dlgStrgs, 0, sizeof dlgStrgs);
  memset(&sideAStrgs, 0, sizeof sideAStrgs);
  memset(&sideBStrgs, 0, sizeof sideBStrgs);

  // Set the address of the dialog's transfer buffer.
  TransferBuffer = &dlgStrgs;

  // Initialize string-pointer arrays by storing the
  // address of each of the 38-character strings that
  // make up each buffer.
  for (x=0; x<18; ++x)
  {
    dlgEdits[x] = dlgStrgs.cassTitle + x*38;
    sideAEdits[x] = sideAStrgs.cassTitle + x*38;
    sideBEdits[x] = sideBStrgs.cassTitle + x*38;
  }

  // Start on side A.
  sideA = TRUE;
}
```

Here, the program first creates 18 OWL edit controls. The first control stores its data in the first field of the transfer buffer, the second stores its data in the second field, and so on. After creating the controls, the program calls `memset()` to initialize all the buffers to NULLs. In the case of `dlgStrgs`, which is the transfer buffer, this call ensures that all fields in the dialog box are blank when the box first appears.

After clearing the buffers, the program gives OWL the address of the transfer buffer by setting the dialog's `TransferBuffer` data member. At this point, the transfer mechanism is fully initialized and ready to go. Next, the pointer arrays are initialized, using pointer math in a `for` loop. Because each edit control is 38 characters long, calculating the address of a control is only a matter of multiplying the loop variable `x` by 38 and adding the result to the address of the first field in the structure. Finally, the `sideA` flag is set to true, which indicates that the dialog is currently on side A.

When the user first runs the program, the dialog box basically takes care of itself. The user can type and edit data in any of the displayed edit fields with no help from the program. WinCassette kicks into action when the user selects one of its buttons (unless this button happens to be Cancel, which does nothing more than close the dialog).

A Two-Faced Dialog

Because all the edit fields needed for both sides of the cassette cannot fit into one dialog box, the dialog box displays only one side's worth of data at a time. In a way, this window is really two dialogs in one. Because of this design, when users finish entering data for side A of the cassette, they must press the Side B button to switch the dialog to side B.

When the user selects the Side button, the faces must switch, as it were, to display the edit fields for the other side. This bit of magic is performed by the `IDSide()` message-response function:

```
void TWCWnd::IDSide()
{
  HWND hControl1, hControl2;

  // Transfer data from the dialog's edit controls
  // to the transfer buffer.
  TransferData(TF_GETDATA);
```

```
// Get handles to the Side button and the
// dialog's static string for the side label.
hControl1 = GetDlgItem(HWindow,ID_SIDE);
hControl2 = GetDlgItem(HWindow, ID_TITLESTRING);

// If the user was on side A...
if (sideA)
{
  // Copy the dialog's data to the side A buffer.
  LoadStrings(dlgEdits, sideAEdits);

  // Change the Side button's text and the
  // side static string's text.
  SetWindowText(hControl1, "&Side A");
  SetWindowText(hControl2, "Side B:");

  // Copy the cassette's title because it's the same
  // for side B.
  strcpy(sideBStrgs.cassTitle, sideAStrgs.cassTitle);

  // Copy the side B buffer to the transfer buffer.
  LoadStrings(sideBEdits, dlgEdits);

  sideA = FALSE;
}
// Else if on side B...
else
{
  // Copy the dialog's data to the side B buffer.
  LoadStrings(dlgEdits, sideBEdits);

  // Change the text in the Side button and the
  // side static string.
  SetWindowText(hControl1, "&Side B");
  SetWindowText(hControl2, "Side A:");

  // Copy the cassette's title, in case it's changed.
  strcpy(sideAStrgs.cassTitle, sideBStrgs.cassTitle);

  // Copy the side A buffer to the transfer buffer.
  LoadStrings(sideAEdits, dlgEdits);

  sideA = TRUE;
}
```

429

```
// Set the focus to the side-title edit field.
hControl1 = GetDlgItem(HWindow, ID_SIDETITLE);
SetFocus(hControl1);

// Copy the data in the transfer buffer to
// the dialog's controls.
TransferData(TF_SETDATA);
}
```

In this function, a call to TransferData() first copies the data from the dialog to the transfer buffer. (The automatic data transfer takes place only when the user closes the dialog box. Thus, here, the program must inform the transfer mechanism when it needs data and when it needs the dialog updated with new data.) After this call, the text the user typed into the dialog's edit fields is in the dlgStrgs structure.

After transferring the data, the program must modify a few of the dialog's controls so it appears as if it has switched sides. First, the program gets handles to the ID_SIDE button and the ID_TITLESTRING static text controls. After getting the handles, the program determines which side is being processed. If the user is on side A, LoadStrings() is called to copy the transfer buffer into the side A buffer. This short function looks like this:

```
void TWCWnd::LoadStrings(char **s, char **d)
{
  for (int x=0; x<18; ++x)
    strcpy(d[x], s[x]);
}
```

This function takes as parameters the arrays of pointers the program initialized previously. Using a for loop, it iterates through the arrays, copying the source strings (pointed to by the pointers in s[ ]) into the destination strings (pointed to by the pointers in d[ ]).

Getting back to IDSide(), after saving the data in the transfer buffer, the program calls SetWindowText() to change the text strings displayed in the two controls for which it got handles. It changes the button's text to *Side A* (because the button now will be used to switch to side A) and the static text string to *Side B* (because this is the side the user is now on). Then, because the cassette's main title is the same for either side, the title is copied to side B's buffer. Next, side B's strings are copied to the transfer buffer so OWL can display them. Before the function ends, SetFocus() is called to place the text cursor in the side B text field, where the user will most likely want to begin typing. Finally, the program copies the new data to the dialog's edit fields by calling TransferData().

430

The process is almost identical when switching from side B back to side A, so the `else` statement is not discussed here.

When the users have entered all the data for the cassette label, they'll want to print it. They do this by selecting the Print button, which calls the `IDPrint()` message-response function:

```
void TWCWnd::IDPrint()
{
  // Copy data from the dialog's edit controls
  // into the transfer buffer.
  TransferData(TF_GETDATA);

  // Copy the transfer buffer into the appropriate
  // buffer, depending on the current side.
  if (sideA)
    LoadStrings(dlgEdits, sideAEdits);
  else
    LoadStrings(dlgEdits, sideBEdits);

  // Initialize the printer.
  result = StartPrinting();

  // Print the label.
  if (result > 0)
    PrintLabel();

  // Shut down printing.
  StopPrinting();
}
```

Here, the program copies the data from the dialog box to the transfer buffer and then copies the transfer buffer to the appropriate storage buffer, depending on the current side. Then `StartPrinting()` is called to start the printing job. If the job starts okay, `PrintLabel()` is called to print the label and then `StopPrinting()` is called to end the print job. These three functions contain the details of the printing process.

The Printer Device Context

When outputting graphics to a window, you don't write directly to the screen. Instead, you get a device context for the currently active window and use GDI calls to draw the output. In this way, you are sure that the output is translated by the active graphics driver, so it's displayed properly on the monitor. The device context acts as a middle layer between your program and the physical devices.

Sending output to the printer works similarly. In your Windows programs, you should never write directly to the printer. Rather, you should create a device context for the printer and use GDI calls to send data to the device context. This is accomplished with the StartPrinting() function:

```
int TWCWnd::StartPrinting()
{
  char buffer[80], // Storage for profile string.
       *cp,        // Character pointer.
       *driver,    // Pointer to driver string.
       *device,    // Pointer to device string.
       *output;    // Pointer to output port string.

  // Change the cursor to an hourglass shape.
  SetCursor(LoadCursor(0, IDC_WAIT));

  // Get the printer device string from WIN.INI.
  GetProfileString("windows", "device", ",,",
          buffer, sizeof buffer);

  // Parse the printer device string to get the
  // device, driver, and output port strings.
  device = buffer;            // Set device to start of string.
  cp = strchr(buffer, ',');   // Get address of first comma.
  *cp = 0;                    // Change comma to null.
  driver = &cp[1];            // Get adr of char after device.
  cp = strchr(driver, ',');   // Get address of next comma.
  *cp = 0;                    // Change comma to null.
  output = &cp[1];            // Set pointer to port string.

  // Create a printer device context.
  pDC = CreateDC(driver, device, output, NULL);

  // Begin printing the document.
  if (pDC != 0)
  {
    DOCINFO tdi;
    tdi.cbSize = 5;
```

```
      tdi.lpszDocName = "Label";
      tdi.lpszOutput = output;
      result = StartDoc(pDC, &tdi);
        // Escape(pDC, STARTDOC, 5, "LABEL", NULL);
      if (result > 0)
        result = StartPage(pDC);
    }
  if ((result <= 0) ¦¦ (pDC == NULL))
    MessageBox(0, "Printer initialization failed",
              "Error", MB_ICONEXCLAMATION ¦ MB_OK);
  return result;
}
```

First, `SetCursor()` is called to change the mouse cursor to the hourglass, informing the user that the system is busy sending data to the printer. Next, the program has to get a device context for the active printer. To do this, it first must know which printer driver to use, which printer is active, and to which port the printer is connected. This information is in the user's WIN.INI file. A call to `GetProfileString()` with the parameters shown results in the profile string for the current printer, for example:

`HP DeskJet Plus,HPDSKJET,LPT1:`

The first part of the string is the type of printer, the second part is the printer driver's name, and the third part is the port to which the printer is connected. In `StartPrinting()`, the program does some tricky pointer handling to parse the string and separate it into the `driver`, `device`, and `output` strings. Finally, it creates the printer DC by calling `CreateDC()`.

After the program has a handle to the DC, it can start the print job. To do this with older versions of Windows, devices had to be accessed by the clumsy `Escape()` function. Functions have been added to Windows 3.1 to simplify the printing process. To start the job, the program calls the Windows `StartDoc()` function, with parameters that are the printer DC and a pointer to the `DOCINFO` structure. The `DOCINFO` structure contains three fields. The first, `cbSize`, is the length of the document's name. The second, `lpszDocName`, is the document's name (used to identify the document in the print queue). And the third, `lpszOutput`, is the string containing the output-port identifier.

If the print job starts without error, a call to `StartPage()` sets up the printer device and begins printing the document. This function also notifies Windows that a page is about to be printed, which prohibits changes to the device mode (including such things as paper size and orientation) until the page is fully printed.

Printer Output

Although sending output to a printer is much more complicated than sending it to a window, both processes have much in common. To generate printer output, you simply call the appropriate GDI functions, directing them to your device context, just as you do with a window. Windows can translate GDI function calls into appropriate graphics commands for a specific printer, but it can't scale the output so it looks similar on different printers. It's up to your program to translate the output's logical coordinates into physical coordinates that take into consideration the resolution of the device.

For example, consider a dot-matrix printer with a horizontal resolution of 120 DPI and a laser printer with a horizontal resolution of 300 DPI. If you were to send the `Rectangle(10,10,310,10)` command to each printer, you'd get different results. With the dot-matrix printer, the rectangle would be almost three inches wide. The laser printer, however, would produce a rectangle only one inch wide. When dealing with printers, the coordinates in the GDI `Rectangle()` function (and other GDI drawing functions) are dot coordinates, just as they are pixel coordinates for a window. In other words, on both the 120-DPI and 300-DPI printer, the rectangle is 300 dots wide, but because the dot-matrix printer has larger dots, the rectangle comes out larger.

 Note: Windows uses various mapping modes to translate logical coordinates to physical coordinates. The default mapping mode, which is used in WinCassette, is MM_TEXT, a mode in which logical and physical coordinates are the same. The MM_TEXT mapping mode also specifies that values of x increase as you move to the right and values of y increase as you move down. This is probably the type of coordinate system you're used to working with. For a more in-depth look at mapping modes, consult your Borland C++ manuals or Windows programming guide.

So, to produce drawings of the same physical dimensions on different printers, you must scale the coordinates to the printer. In the `PrintLabel()` function, the program gets the printer's resolution and uses the resolution to scale the output:

```
void TWCWnd::PrintLabel()
{
```

```
    // Get horizontal and vertical resolution for printer.
    int horDots = GetDeviceCaps(pDC, LOGPIXELSX);
    int verDots = GetDeviceCaps(pDC, LOGPIXELSY);

    // Draw the cassette label's outline.
    DrawLabel(horDots, verDots);

    // Print the side titles and song titles.
    DrawBodyText(horDots, verDots);

    // Print the main cassette titles.
    DrawTitleText(horDots, verDots);
}
```

First, the Windows `GetDeviceCaps()` function is called to get the printer's horizontal and vertical resolutions, which are given as dots per inch. Then, the program calls the functions that draw the label's various elements, passing the printer's horizontal and vertical resolution as parameters.

The first drawing function, `DrawLabel()`, draws the label's outline with a series of calls to `MoveTo()` and `LineTo()`:

```
void TWCWnd::DrawLabel(int horDots, int verDots)
{
  MoveTo(pDC, horDots/2, verDots/2);
  LineTo(pDC, horDots*4.5, verDots/2);
  LineTo(pDC, horDots*4.5, verDots*4.3);
  LineTo(pDC, horDots/2, verDots*4.3);
  LineTo(pDC, horDots/2, verDots/2);
  MoveTo(pDC, horDots/2, verDots*0.75);
  LineTo(pDC, horDots*4.5, verDots*0.75);
  MoveTo(pDC, horDots/2, verDots*0.93);
  LineTo(pDC, horDots*4.5, verDots*0.93);
  MoveTo(pDC, horDots/2, verDots*3.1);
  LineTo(pDC, horDots*4.5, verDots*3.1);
  MoveTo(pDC, horDots/2, verDots*3.62);
  LineTo(pDC, horDots*4.5, verDots*3.62);
  MoveTo(pDC, horDots*2.5, verDots*0.75);
  LineTo(pDC, horDots*2.5, verDots*3.1);
}
```

Because the `horDots` and `verDots` variables represent the number of dots per inch both horizontally and vertically, you can easily think of your printer output in terms of inches. For example, you want to start drawing your cassette label a half an inch from the top and left of the page, so you simply move to the coordinates given by `horDots/2` and `verDots/2`. On a 120-DPI printer, this is 60 dots from the top and left. On a 300-DPI printer, this is 150 dots from the top and left. In both cases, it is half an inch, resulting in an identical location on the page for either printer. Using similar calculations, the program can draw the entire cassette label's outline with no further fuss.

Creating and Using Fonts

After drawing the cassette's outline, the program must print text for the side titles and the song titles. Because these titles use a smaller font than the font for the cassette's main title, the program can't rely on default fonts. It must create fonts that are not only the proper size for both types of titles, but also scaled for the current printer. The `CreateCassFont()` function handles these font-creation duties:

```
HFONT TWCWnd::CreateCassFont(int hSize, int vSize)
{
  LOGFONT cassLogFont; // Logical font description.

  // Fill in LOGFONT structure.
  cassLogFont.lfHeight = vSize;
  cassLogFont.lfWidth = hSize;
  cassLogFont.lfEscapement = 0;
  cassLogFont.lfOrientation = 0;
  cassLogFont.lfWeight = FW_NORMAL;
  cassLogFont.lfItalic = 0;
  cassLogFont.lfUnderline = 0;
  cassLogFont.lfStrikeOut = 0;
  cassLogFont.lfCharSet = ANSI_CHARSET;
  cassLogFont.lfOutPrecision = OUT_DEFAULT_PRECIS;
  cassLogFont.lfClipPrecision = CLIP_DEFAULT_PRECIS;
  cassLogFont.lfQuality = PROOF_QUALITY;
  cassLogFont.lfPitchAndFamily = VARIABLE_PITCH | FF_ROMAN;
  strcpy(cassLogFont.lfFaceName, "Times New Roman");

  // Create new font.
  return CreateFontIndirect(&cassLogFont);
}
```

The parameters passed to this function are the horizontal and vertical size of the font. To create a font, the program first must initialize a LOGFONT (logical font) structure, which holds a complete description of the font. This structure contains 14 fields, although many of the fields can be set to 0 or their default values, depending on the program's needs. Each field of LOGFONT is briefly described in Table 11.1.

Table 11.1. *LOGFONT* fields and their descriptions.

Field	Description
lfHeight	Height of font in logical units
lfWidth	Width of font in logical units
lfEscapement	Angle at which to draw the text
lfOrientation	Character tilt in tenths of a degree
lfWeight	Used to select normal (400) or boldface (700) text
lfItalic	A nonzero value indicates italics
lfUnderline	A nonzero value indicates an underlined font
lfStrikeOut	A nonzero value indicates a strikethrough font
lfCharSet	Font character set
lfOutPrecision	How to match requested font to actual font
lfClipPrecision	How to clip characters that run over clip area
lfQuality	Print quality of the font
lfPitchAndFamily	Pitch and font family
lfFaceName	Typeface name

The LOGFONT description in Table 11.1 gives only an overview of the structure. Before experimenting with custom fonts, you may want to look up this structure in your Borland manual or on-line help, where you'll find a more

437

complete description of each of its fields, including the many constants that are already defined for use with the structure. In any case, you can use `CreateCassFont()` to create fonts of different sizes quickly.

In `CreateCassFont()`, the program sets the `lfHeight` and `lfWidth` fields to the height and width of the requested font. These values are the parameters passed to the function. Note that, in most cases, you should set the width to 0, which allows Windows to select a width that better matches the height. With your cassette labels, however, you have to conserve space. The font width selected in the function yields a compressed font that enables the program to print longer song titles.

Finally, in `CreateCassFont()`, the program sets many of the other `LOGFONT` fields to zero or to their default values and selects the variable-pitch Roman font family and the Times New Roman face.

After filling in the `LOGFONT` structure, the font is created by calling `CreateFontIndirect()`, which returns a handle to the new font. `CreateCassFont()` returns this handle, to be used by the calling function.

There's still more to know about using a custom font, though, as you can see in the `DrawBodyText()` function:

```
void TWCWnd::DrawBodyText(int horDots, int verDots)
{
  TEXTMETRIC metrics;   // Physical font description.
  char s[80];           // Output text line.

  // Create and select the font for the cassette text.
  HFONT newFont = CreateCassFont(horDots/30, verDots/8);
  HFONT oldFont = SelectObject(pDC, newFont);

  // Get the size of the physical font.
  GetTextMetrics(pDC, &metrics);

  // Construct and print side A and side B titles.
  strcpy(s, "Side A: ");
  strcpy(&s[strlen(s)], sideAStrgs.sideTitle);
  TextOut(pDC, horDots*0.6, verDots*0.77, s, strlen(s));
  strcpy(s, "Side B: ");
  strcpy(&s[strlen(s)], sideBStrgs.sideTitle);
  TextOut(pDC, horDots*2.6, verDots*0.77, s, strlen(s));

  // Print song titles for sides A and B.
```

```
for (int x=2; x<18; ++x)
{
  TextOut(pDC, horDots*0.6, (verDots*0.87)+((x-1)
      *metrics.tmHeight), sideAEdits[x],
      strlen(sideAEdits[x]));
  TextOut(pDC, horDots*2.6, (verDots*0.87)+((x-1)
      *metrics.tmHeight), sideBEdits[x],
      strlen(sideBEdits[x]));
}

// Restore the device context.
SelectObject(pDC, oldFont);
DeleteObject(newFont);
}
```

This function draws the text for the side and song titles. It first calls `CreateCassFont()` to create an appropriately sized font, scaling `horDots` and `verDots` as needed for the application. It then selects the new font into the printer DC. Because Windows cannot always guarantee that you will get exactly the font requested, the program must check the selected font's *metrics* (characteristics). It does this with a call to `GetTextMetrics()`, which fills in a `TEXTMETRIC` structure, a pointer to which is one of the function's parameters. The `TEXTMETRIC` structure contains 20 fields that describe the selected font. See Table 11.2.

Table 11.2. *TEXTMETRIC* fields and their descriptions.

Field	Description
tmHeight	Height of a character in logical units
tmAscent	Height of a character above the baseline in logical units
tmDescent	Height of a character below the baseline in logical units
tmInternalLeading	The difference between the point size and the physical size of the font
tmExternalLeading	Spacing between rows of text
tmAveCharWidth	Average width of characters in logical units

continues

439

Table 11.2. *TEXTMETRIC* fields and their descriptions *(continued)*.

Field	Description
tmMaxCharWidth	The maximum width of a character in logical units
tmWeight	Indicates normal or boldface font
tmItalic	A nonzero value indicates an italic font
tmUnderlined	A nonzero value indicates an underlined font
tmStruckOut	A nonzero value indicates a strikethrough font
tmFirstChar	The code for the first character in the font
tmLastChar	The code for the last character in the font
tmDefaultChar	Character displayed by Windows for characters not included in the selected font
tmBreakChar	Character used for breaks between words
tmPitchAndFamily	Pitch and font family
tmCharSet	Character set of font
tmOverhang	Extra space needed for italic or bold characters
tmDigitizedAspectX tmDigitizedAspectY	Aspect ratio of the device for which the font was selected

In this program, you are concerned only with the height of the font, so you can determine the proper line spacing.

After the program calls `GetTextMetrics()`, it builds the side A and B title strings and prints them on the label. Each line is printed by calling the GDI `TextOut()` function, scaling `horDots` and `verDots` to position the titles. After printing the side titles, the program then prints the song titles, using a `for` loop to iterate through the edit-field pointer arrays. Notice how the `tmHeight` field of the `metrics` `TEXTMETRIC` structure is used to space the text vertically. Finally, the function exits, the program restores the old DC by selecting the old font and deleting the new one.

Now that the cassette's outline has been drawn and the side and song titles have been printed, the only thing left to do is to print the cassette's main title, which is accomplished in the DrawTitleText() function:

```
void TWCWnd::DrawTitleText(int horDots, int verDots)
{
  int strWidth;         // Width of text line.
  long textExtent;      // Width and height of text line.

  // Create the new title font.
  HFONT newFont = CreateCassFont(horDots/20, verDots/5);
  HFONT oldFont = SelectObject(pDC, newFont);

  // Get the width and height of the title string.
  textExtent = GetTextExtent(pDC, sideAStrgs.cassTitle,
                  strlen(sideAStrgs.cassTitle));

  // Extract the width of the title string.
  strWidth = LOWORD(textExtent);

  // Print the main cassette titles.
  TextOut(pDC, (horDots*2.5)-(strWidth/2), verDots*0.52,
      sideAStrgs.cassTitle, strlen(sideAStrgs.cassTitle));
  TextOut(pDC, (horDots*2.5)-(strWidth/2), verDots*3.25,
      sideAStrgs.cassTitle, strlen(sideAStrgs.cassTitle));

  // Restore the device context.
  SelectObject(pDC, oldFont);
  DeleteObject(newFont);
}
```

Here, a new, larger font is created for the main title and selected into the DC. Then GetTextExtent() is called to determine the size of the title string. This function returns a long integer with the height of the string in the high word and the width of the string in the low word. Because the title string should be centered on the label, the program must extract the value of the low word; this is done by invoking the LOWORD macro. Then, using strWidth, horDots, and verDots (all scaled appropriately), the program calls TextOut() to print the title centered on the label. Finally, the old font is selected into the DC, and the new font is deleted.

Ending a Print Job

N ow that the label is printed, the program has to close the print job. The StopPrinting() function takes care of this:

```
void TWCWnd::StopPrinting()
{
  EndPage(pDC); // Escape(pDC, NEWFRAME, 0, NULL, NULL);
  EndDoc(pDC);  // Escape(pDC, ENDDOC, 0, NULL, NULL);
  SetCursor(LoadCursor(0, IDC_ARROW));
  DeleteDC(pDC);
}
```

First, EndPage() is called, which ejects the finished page from the printer. Then a call to EndDoc() ends the print job. (These are two of the new Windows 3.1 functions that replace an Escape() call.) Finally, the program sets the cursor back to the arrow and deletes the printer DC.

That's it. The user's cassette label is now printed, and the user can exit the program by clicking the Cancel button or selecting the Close entry in the System menu. You do not have to provide a message-response function for the Cancel button, because OWL handles it for you.

Conclusion

A lthough handling printer output in Windows is a meticulous process, you should have little difficulty producing device-independent programs if you follow the rules and assume nothing about the active printer.

This chapter presented the basics of handling and scaling printer output. However, dealing with printers in Windows is a complex topic, one that can fill a book of its own. If you plan to write applications that use printers extensively, you should research this topic further. Besides the Borland C++ manuals, you should pick up a copy of *Programming in Windows 3.1*, Second Edition, published by Que Corporation, and Charles Petzold's book, *Programming Windows 3.1*, published by Microsoft Press.

12

The Windows Clipboard

haring data is more than a convenience in Windows—it's a way of life. Because it's so important, Windows provides several ways of sharing data between applications, each of varying complexity. These methods of sharing data include the following:

- the Windows Clipboard
- Dynamic Data Exchange (DDE)
- Object Linking and Embedding (OLE)
- Dynamic Link Libraries (DLLs)

DDE and *OLE* require that applications process messages not only from Windows, but also messages that originate from other applications. The message-passing and response can become fairly complex. In fact, entire books have been written on these topics.

The Clipboard, on the other hand, provides a simple mechanism for transferring data between applications. Although it is limited in some respects, it still offers a great deal of flexibility, allowing applications to exchange not only text, but even bitmaps, metafiles, spreadsheet data, .TIFF files, color palettes, and user-defined (or *private*) data formats.

Anything placed on the Clipboard is instantly available to any application that supports the Clipboard. And virtually any application that provides standard editing features such as cut and paste supports the Clipboard.

In this chapter, you learn how to copy data to the Clipboard, as well as how to extract data that other applications have placed there. Along the way, you learn to keep menu items current, based on the format of data in the Clipboard. Chapter 13 discusses *Dynamic Link Libraries* in detail.

Introducing the Clipboard

The Windows Clipboard is not some magical software wonder that only a computer scientist can understand. It's really nothing more than a buffer manager. You've worked with buffers before, right? In order to use a buffer, a program needs a way to place information into the buffer, to extract information from the buffer, and to determine the type of information stored in the buffer. In traditional applications, the actual program creates the buffer and decides how to handle it.

One big difference between the Clipboard and other buffers is that the Clipboard doesn't go away when a program ends. Moreover, Windows, rather than an application program, determines, by a set of predefined rules, how the buffer must be handled. The fine folks who designed Windows developed these rules, which are represented by a group of functions and messages. To access the Clipboard, a program must call Windows functions.

Because the Clipboard is a resource that's shared by all Windows applications, programs must have permission to use it. When a program is finished with the Clipboard, the program must then make the Clipboard available to other applications. This is not unlike the way a program gets and releases device contexts, which are also a shared resource (although, unlike the Clipboard, you can have more than one device context). Using the Clipboard in an application requires following the rules. In the sections that follow, you learn not only how to use the Clipboard, but also how to ensure that other applications have their fair share of Clipboard access.

Clipboard Formats

The Clipboard can hold many types of data. Because of this flexibility, programs can easily transfer text, graphics, spreadsheet data, and more, all the while retaining the data's original formatting information. All told, the Clipboard supports nine data formats, with other private, user-defined formats available. The supported Clipboard formats are listed in Table 12.1.

Table 12.1. Clipboard data formats.

Format	Description
CF_TEXT	NULL-terminated ANSI text, including carriage returns and linefeeds.
CF_BITMAP	Device-dependent bitmaps.
CF_METAFILEPICT	Metafile pictures.
CF_SYLK	Microsoft Symbolic Link data, used by Multiplan, Chart, and Excel.
CF_DIF	Data Interchange Format data used by VisiCalc.
CF_TIFF	Tag Image File Format data for bitmaps.
CF_OEMTEXT	Text using the OEM (standard IBM) character set.
CF_DIB	Device-independent bitmaps.
CF_PALETTE	A color palette handle.

As you can see, the Clipboard is a versatile beast. But because most programs need only the CF_TEXT and CF_BITMAP formats, it is these formats that you learn to handle in this chapter.

Handling Text with the Clipboard

The simplest Clipboard data is CF_TEXT, which is plain vanilla ANSI text. The only special characters recognized by this format are carriage returns, linefeeds, and NULLs. Carriage returns and linefeeds mark the end of lines, of course, whereas a NULL marks the end of the text. This type of data is usually transferred to the Clipboard when a user cuts or copies text from a text editor of some type. The Borland IDE editor, for example, transfers text in this format.

When an application transfers text to the Clipboard, the text no longer belongs to the application. For this reason, the application must create in global memory a copy of the item being transferred, then hand this copy over to the Clipboard. If the application needs the data again, it must extract the data from the Clipboard in the same way any application does.

Listings 12.1 through 12.5 are the files needed to create CLIPBRD1, a simple text-editing program that provides Clipboard support. When you run the program, the window shown in Figure 12.1 appears. You can type text in the window, as well as copy and paste text. To copy text to the Clipboard, highlight the text by dragging the mouse pointer over it, then select the Copy entry of the Edit menu. To paste the text back to the Window, select the Edit menu's Paste entry.

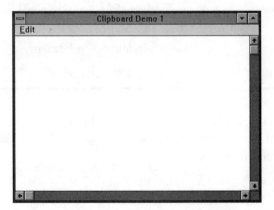

Figure 12.1. An example Clipboard application—version 1.

The program's Edit menu is smart enough to know when the Clipboard contains the correct type of data—that is, if the data in the Clipboard is not of format CF_TEXT, the Paste entry is disabled. To check this out, run Windows Paintbrush and copy a bitmap to the Clipboard (simply use the scissors tool to copy part of the Paintbrush window). Then switch back to the text editor and look at the Edit menu. The Paste option should be disabled, as shown in Figure 12.2. Now, switch to another text-editing program and copy some text to the Clipboard. Return to CLIPBRD1 and note that the Paste entry is again enabled.

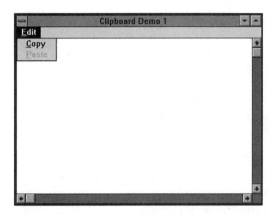

Figure 12.2. The Paste option is disabled when copied data is not of format *CF_TEXT*.

Look now at the main window's declaration, found in CLIPWND1.H:

```
_CLASSDEF(TClipWnd)
class TClipWnd: public TEditWindow
{
public:
  TClipWnd(PTWindowsObject AParent, LPSTR ATitle);
  virtual void WMSetFocus(RTMessage msg)
      = [WM_FIRST + WM_SETFOCUS];
  virtual void CMCopy()
      = [CM_FIRST + CM_COPY];
  virtual void CMPaste()
      = [CM_FIRST + CM_PASTE];
};
```

As you can see, the main window is an *OWL edit window,* which is a special window that offers full text-editing functions. By using a window of this class, you can type text, select text with the mouse, and copy and paste text (and more) without providing code for these functions in the program. In addition,

447

the `TClipWnd` window class provides message-response functions for the Copy and Paste menu items, as well as for the Windows message `WM_SETFOCUS`.

The edit window, like any object, is created by its constructor:

```
TClipWnd::TClipWnd(PTWindowsObject AParent, LPSTR ATitle):
        TEditWindow(AParent, ATitle)
{
  // Add menu to window.
  AssignMenu("CLIP1MENU");

  // Set the size and position of the window.
  Attr.X = 40;
  Attr.Y = 40;
  Attr.H = GetSystemMetrics(SM_CYSCREEN) / 1.5;
  Attr.W = GetSystemMetrics(SM_CXSCREEN) / 1.5;
}
```

Here, after calling the ancestor class' constructor, `TEditWindow()`, the program assigns a menu to the window and sets the window's position and size. You've seen similar constructors in this book before, but there's something special about this program's edit menu, as you see in the next section.

Enabling and Disabling Paste

In this text-editing demonstration, the program enables Paste when the Clipboard contains `CF_TEXT` data and disables Paste when the Clipboard contains another type of data. Strangely, you can't fool the menu, even by switching to another program and changing the contents of the Clipboard. By some miracle of Windows magic, when you switch back to the editor, the Paste menu is changed to reflect the new contents of the Clipboard. This so-called miracle is possible due to the `WM_SETFOCUS` message.

Windows sends the `WM_SETFOCUS` message to a window whenever the window is activated, either by switching to the window from another application or by running the program that creates the window. By responding to this message, a program can immediately check the contents of the Clipboard and update the Paste menu appropriately. This is all done before the user has a chance to reach for her keyboard, let alone select the Edit menu.

The edit window responds to a `WM_SETFOCUS` message with the function `WMSetFocus()`:

```
void TClipWnd::WMSetFocus(RTMessage msg)
{
  // Perform normal WM_SETFOCUS processing.
  TEditWindow::WMSetFocus(msg);

  // Get handle to the menu.
  HMENU hMenu = GetMenu(HWindow);

  // Check for text in Clipboard.
  if (!IsClipboardFormatAvailable(CF_TEXT))
  {
    // If there's no text in the Clipboard,
    // turn off the Paste menu item.
    EnableMenuItem(hMenu, CM_PASTE, MF_GRAYED);
  }
  else
    // If text is available, turn on Paste.
    EnableMenuItem(hMenu, CM_PASTE, MF_ENABLED);
}
```

In this function, the program first calls `TEditWindow::WMSetFocus()`, because the `TEditWindow` base class must also process the `WM_SETFOCUS` message. A call to the function `IsClipboardFormatAvailable()` with a parameter of `CF_TEXT` then checks whether the Clipboard contains text. (To check for other types of data, you need only replace `CF_TEXT` with a format from Table 12.1.) If this function returns a true, the Clipboard contains text, so the program enables the Paste menu item by calling the Windows function `EnableMenuItem()`. Otherwise, the program disables the Paste menu item.

Surprisingly easy, no?

Copying Text to the Clipboard

If the program receives a `CM_COPY` message (defined in CLIPWND1.H), the user has selected the Edit menu's Copy item and wants to copy data from the main window to the Clipboard. This message is handled by the message-response function `CMCopy()`:

```
void TClipWnd::CMCopy()
{
  int startPos, endPos;
```

```
// Get starting and ending positions of the
// selected text.
Editor->GetSelection(startPos, endPos);

// Get a handle to a block of memory big enough
// to hold the selected text.
HANDLE hMem = GlobalAlloc(GHND, endPos-startPos+1);

// Get a pointer to the block and lock the
// block in memory.
LPSTR s = GlobalLock(hMem);

// Copy the selected text and unlock the memory block.
Editor->GetSubText(s, startPos, endPos);
GlobalUnlock(hMem);

// Open and clear the Clipboard.
OpenClipboard(HWindow);
EmptyClipboard();

// Give the selected text to the Clipboard.
SetClipboardData(CF_TEXT, hMem);

// Close the Clipboard.
CloseClipboard();

// Turn on Paste menu item.
HMENU hMenu = GetMenu(HWindow);
EnableMenuItem(hMenu, CM_PASTE, MF_ENABLED);
}
```

Normally, a `TEditWindow` handles all the cut, copy, and paste functions automatically, transferring data to and from the Clipboard as needed. However, to demonstrate how the Clipboard works, CLIPBRD1 takes over some of these functions. First, it retrieves the starting and ending character positions of the selected text by calling the edit control's `GetSelection()` function. The text indicated by `startPos` and `endPos` is the text that must be copied to the Clipboard.

The program next calls `GlobalAlloc()`, requesting enough memory to hold the text. (This function's `GHND` parameter requests a moveable memory block that's initialized to zeros. The function's second parameter is the size of the block.) When the block is allocated, the program receives a handle to the memory block, rather than an address. A NULL handle means memory cannot be allocated. Although CLIPBRD1 doesn't check for a NULL handle, you should do so in your own programs.

In order to use RAM as efficiently as possible, Windows does a lot of memory shuffling. This means that a program must never assume that an object will stay at one address. Therefore, before copying the selected text into the allocated memory block, CLIPBRD1 must inform Windows not to move the block until it's through with it.

CLIPBRD1 does this by calling the function `GlobalLock()` with the block's handle. `GlobalLock()` nails the object in memory and returns a pointer to it. After this call, the program can safely call the edit control's `GetSubText()` function to copy the selected text into the memory block. Then, a call to `GlobalUnlock()` informs Windows that the program is finished with the block. After unlocking the block, the pointer s is no longer valid. CLIPBRD1 must now refer to the memory block only by its handle.

Now that the selected text has been copied into memory, the program can give the text to the Clipboard. First, the program calls `OpenClipboard()` with its window's handle. This action prevents other applications from accessing the Clipboard while CLIPBRD1 is using it. When the program has the Clipboard, its first task is to empty the Clipboard by calling the Windows function `EmptyClipboard()`.

This function actually does more than empty the Clipboard. It also makes the calling program the Clipboard's *owner* and releases from memory whatever data the Clipboard contained. The Clipboard's owner is the last application to place data into the Clipboard. Being the Clipboard's owner doesn't actually mean a program owns the Clipboard, but rather that it was the source of the data presently in the Clipboard.

After emptying the Clipboard, CLIPBRD1 calls the Windows function `SetClipboardData()`, which gives the text to the Clipboard. This function's first parameter is the type of data being placed into the Clipboard (from Table 12.1). The second parameter is an unlocked handle to the data. After copying the text into the Clipboard, the program calls `CloseClipboard()` to release the Clipboard so other applications can access it.

 Note: When a program empties the Clipboard, it becomes the Clipboard's owner and remains the owner even after the program closes the Clipboard. A program loses ownership when another application empties the Clipboard.

The last thing CMCopy() does is enable the Paste entry of the Edit menu, so the user can paste the text she just copied. In this case, the program has no need to check the data format of the Clipboard, because it placed the data there itself.

Extracting Text from the Clipboard

Copying data into the Clipboard is only half the battle. An application that supports the Clipboard also has to retrieve data. In a text-editing program, the signal to perform this operation is sent when the user selects the Edit menu's Paste item. In CLIPBRD1, this generates a CM_PASTE message (defined in CLIPWND1.H), which is handled by the function CMPaste():

```
void TClipWnd::CMPaste()
{
  // Check that there is text in the Clipboard.
  if (IsClipboardFormatAvailable(CF_TEXT))
  {
    // Open Clipboard and get a handle to its text.
    OpenClipboard(HWindow);
    HANDLE hMem = GetClipboardData(CF_TEXT);

    // Check for valid handle.
    if (hMem)
    {
      // Get a pointer to the text.
      LPSTR s = GlobalLock(hMem);

      // Add text to edit window.
      Editor->Insert(s);

      // Unlock the memory block holding the text.
      GlobalUnlock(hMem);
    }

    // Close the Clipboard.
    CloseClipboard();
  }
}
```

Before copying the contents of the Clipboard to its window, the program must ensure that the data is in the correct format. This is done, as before, with a call to `IsClipboardFormatAvailable()`. If this function returns a false, `CMPaste()` does nothing. Of course, in CLIPBRD1, this call should never fail, because each time the window gets the focus, the program checks the Clipboard's data format. Thus, the Paste menu is never accessible when the Clipboard contains something other than `CF_TEXT`.

After validating the data format, the program opens the Clipboard and obtains a handle to the Clipboard's data by calling `GetClipboardData()`. This function's parameter is the data format the program needs. If this type of data is not in the Clipboard, the function returns a NULL handle.

Once CLIPBRD1 has a handle to the Clipboard's contents, it has to determine the data's address. It does this by calling `GlobalLock()`, which not only returns a pointer to the data, but also locks the data in memory so Windows can't move it. Next, the program displays the Clipboard's text by calling the edit control's `Insert()` function. Finally, it unlocks the memory block and closes the Clipboard.

Listings 12.1 through 12.5, which follow, are the complete code listings for this program. Study them carefully until you're sure you understand what's going on. In the next section, you learn to use the Clipboard with bitmapped graphics.

Listing 12.1. CLIPBRD1.CPP—version 1 of the Clipboard demo application.

```
// CLIPBRD1.CPP -- Implementation for Clipboard Demo 1.

#include <owl.h>
#include "clipwnd1.h"

// Application Class.
class TClip1App: public TApplication
{
public:
  TClip1App(LPSTR AName, HINSTANCE hInstance,
        HINSTANCE hPrevInstance, LPSTR lpCmdLine,
        int nCmdShow): TApplication(AName, hInstance,
        hPrevInstance, lpCmdLine, nCmdShow) {};
  virtual void InitMainWindow();
};
```

continues

453

Listing 12.1. Continued

```
///////////////////////////////////////////////////////
// TWCApp::InitMainWindow()
//
// This function creates the application's main window.
///////////////////////////////////////////////////////
void TClip1App::InitMainWindow()
{
  MainWindow = new TClipWnd(NULL, "Clipboard Demo 1");
}


///////////////////////////////////////////////////////
// WinMain()
///////////////////////////////////////////////////////
int PASCAL WinMain(HINSTANCE hInstance,
                   HINSTANCE hPrevInstance,
              LPSTR lpCmdLine, int nCmdShow)
{
  TClip1App Clip1App("Clipbrd1", hInstance,
               hPrevInstance, lpCmdLine, nCmdShow);
  Clip1App.Run();
  return Clip1App.Status;
}
```

Listing 12.2. CLIPWND1.H—Clipboard demo 1 main window header file.

```
// CLIPWND1.H -- Main Window Declaration.

#ifndef _CLIPWND1_H
#define _CLIPWND1_H

#include <editwnd.h>

#define CM_COPY  101
#define CM_PASTE 102

_CLASSDEF(TClipWnd)
class TClipWnd: public TEditWindow
```

```
{
public:
  TClipWnd(PTWindowsObject AParent, LPSTR ATitle);
  virtual void WMSetFocus(RTMessage msg)
      = [WM_FIRST + WM_SETFOCUS];
  virtual void CMCopy()
      = [CM_FIRST + CM_COPY];
  virtual void CMPaste()
      = [CM_FIRST + CM_PASTE];
};


#endif
```

Listing 12.3. CLIPWND1.CPP—Clipboard demo 1 main window implementation.

```
// CLIPWND1.CPP -- Main Window Implementation.

#include "clipwnd1.h"

///////////////////////////////////////////////////////
// TClipWnd::TClipWnd()
//
// This is the main window's constructor.
///////////////////////////////////////////////////////
TClipWnd::TClipWnd(PTWindowsObject AParent, LPSTR ATitle):
        TEditWindow(AParent, ATitle)
{
  // Add menu to window.
  AssignMenu("CLIP1MENU");

  // Set the size and position of the window.
  Attr.X = 40;
  Attr.Y = 40;
  Attr.H = GetSystemMetrics(SM_CYSCREEN) / 1.5;
  Attr.W = GetSystemMetrics(SM_CXSCREEN) / 1.5;
}


///////////////////////////////////////////////////////
// TClipWnd::WMSetFocus()
//
```

continues

Listing 12.3. Continued

```
// This function is called when the program's main
// window receives the focus.
/////////////////////////////////////////////////////
void TClipWnd::WMSetFocus(RTMessage msg)
{
  // Perform normal WM_SETFOCUS processing.
  TEditWindow::WMSetFocus(msg);

  // Get handle to the menu.
  HMENU hMenu = GetMenu(HWindow);

  // Check for bitmap in Clipboard.
  if (!IsClipboardFormatAvailable(CF_TEXT))
  {
    // If there's no text in the Clipboard,
    // turn off the Paste menu item.
    EnableMenuItem(hMenu, CM_PASTE, MF_GRAYED);
  }
  else
    // If text is available, turn on Paste.
    EnableMenuItem(hMenu, CM_PASTE, MF_ENABLED);
}


/////////////////////////////////////////////////////
// TClipWnd::CMCopy()
//
// This function is called when the user clicks the Copy
// entry of the Edit menu.
/////////////////////////////////////////////////////
void TClipWnd::CMCopy()
{
  int startPos, endPos;

  // Get starting and ending positions of the
  // selected text.
  Editor->GetSelection(startPos, endPos);
```

```
  // Get a handle to a block of memory big enough
  // to hold the selected text.
  HANDLE hMem = GlobalAlloc(GHND, endPos-startPos+1);

  // Get a pointer to the block and lock the
  // block in memory.
  LPSTR s = GlobalLock(hMem);

  // Copy the selected text and unlock the memory block.
  Editor->GetSubText(s, startPos, endPos);
  GlobalUnlock(hMem);

  // Open and clear the Clipboard.
  OpenClipboard(HWindow);
  EmptyClipboard();

  // Give the selected text to the Clipboard.
  SetClipboardData(CF_TEXT, hMem);

  // Close the Clipboard.
  CloseClipboard();

  // Turn on Paste menu item.
  HMENU hMenu = GetMenu(HWindow);
  EnableMenuItem(hMenu, CM_PASTE, MF_ENABLED);
}


//////////////////////////////////////////////////////
// TClipWnd::CMPaste()
//
// This function is called when the user clicks the
// Paste entry of the Edit menu.
//////////////////////////////////////////////////////
void TClipWnd::CMPaste()
{
  // Check that there is text in the Clipboard.
  if (IsClipboardFormatAvailable(CF_TEXT))
  {
    // Open Clipboard and get a handle to its text.
    OpenClipboard(HWindow);
```

continues

457

Listing 12.3. Continued

```
    HANDLE hMem = GetClipboardData(CF_TEXT);

    // Check for valid handle.
    if (hMem)
    {
      // Get a pointer to the text.
      LPSTR s = GlobalLock(hMem);

      // Add text to edit window.
      Editor->Insert(s);

      // Unlock the memory block holding the text.
      GlobalUnlock(hMem);
    }

    // Close the Clipboard.
    CloseClipboard();
  }
}
```

Listing 12.4. CLIPBRD1.RC—Clipboard demo 1 resource file.

```
CLIP1MENU MENU
BEGIN
    POPUP "&Edit"
    BEGIN
        MENUITEM "&Copy", 101
        MENUITEM "&Paste", 102
    END

END
```

Listing 12.5. CLIPBRD.DEF—Clipboard demo 1 definition file.

```
EXETYPE WINDOWS
CODE PRELOAD MOVEABLE DISCARDABLE
DATA PRELOAD MOVEABLE MULTIPLE
HEAPSIZE 4096
STACKSIZE 5120
```

Handling Bitmaps with the Clipboard

A lthough most data transferred to and from the Clipboard is in CF_TEXT format, bitmaps, which are data format CF_BITMAP, are also handy objects to cut and paste. And, believe it or not, handling bitmaps with the Clipboard is not much more difficult than handling text. The basics are the same. You simply have to understand how to manipulate bitmaps in memory.

Listings 12.6 through 12.10 are the files needed to create CLIPBRD2, a version of the editor program that handles bitmaps. This program, which is based on the drawing program developed in Chapter 10, enables you to draw shapes on-screen, then cut parts of the screen to the Clipboard.

Listing 12.6. CLIPBRD2.CPP—version 2 of the Clipboard demo application.

```
// CLIPBRD2.CPP -- Implementation for Clipboard Demo 2.

#include <owl.h>
#include "clipwnd2.h"

// Application Class.
class TClip2App: public TApplication
{
public:
  TClip2App(LPSTR AName, HINSTANCE hInstance,
          HINSTANCE hPrevInstance, LPSTR lpCmdLine,
          int nCmdShow): TApplication(AName, hInstance,
          hPrevInstance, lpCmdLine, nCmdShow) {};
  virtual void InitMainWindow();
};


//////////////////////////////////////////////////////
// TWCApp::InitMainWindow()
//
// This function creates the application's main window.
//////////////////////////////////////////////////////
void TClip2App::InitMainWindow()
{
  MainWindow = new TClipWnd(NULL, "Clipboard Demo 2");
}
```

continues

459

Listing 12.6. Continued

```
///////////////////////////////////////////////////////
// WinMain()
///////////////////////////////////////////////////////
int PASCAL WinMain(HINSTANCE hInstance,
                   HINSTANCE hPrevInstance,
             LPSTR lpCmdLine, int nCmdShow)
{
  TClip2App Clip2App("Clipbrd2", hInstance,
                hPrevInstance, lpCmdLine, nCmdShow);
  Clip2App.Run();
  return Clip2App.Status;
}
```

Listing 12.7. CLIPWND2.H—Clipboard demo 2 main window header file.

```
// CLIPWND2.H -- Header file for main window.

#ifndef _CLIPWND2_H
#define _CLIPWND2_H

#include <owl.h>

#define CM_PASTE 101

_CLASSDEF(TClipWnd)
class TClipWnd: public TWindow
{
  int lButton,   // Mouse-button flags.
      rButton,
      paste,     // Paste mode flag.
      newPen,    // Handle for drawing pen.
      oldPen;    // Handle for old pen.
  HDC lineDC,    // Device context handles.
      rectDC;
  RECT rect;     // Rectangle for defining block.

public:
  TClipWnd(PTWindowsObject AParent, LPSTR ATitle);
  virtual void WMSetFocus(RTMessage msg)
      = [WM_FIRST + WM_SETFOCUS];
```

```
    virtual void WMLButtonDown(RTMessage msg)
        = [WM_FIRST + WM_LBUTTONDOWN];
    virtual void WMLButtonUp()
        = [WM_FIRST + WM_LBUTTONUP];
    virtual void WMMouseMove(RTMessage msg)
        = [WM_FIRST + WM_MOUSEMOVE];
    virtual void WMRButtonDown(RTMessage msg)
        = [WM_FIRST + WM_RBUTTONDOWN];
    virtual void WMRButtonUp()
        = [WM_FIRST + WM_RBUTTONUP];
    virtual void CMPaste()
        = [CM_FIRST + CM_PASTE];

private:
  void PasteBitmap(RTMessage msg);
};


#endif
```

Listing 12.8. CLIPWND2.CPP—Clipboard demo 2 main window implementation.

```
// CLIPWND2.CPP -- Implementation for main window.

#include "clipwnd2.h"

//////////////////////////////////////////////////////////
// TClipWnd::TClipWnd()
//
// This is the main window's constructor.
//////////////////////////////////////////////////////////
TClipWnd::TClipWnd(PTWindowsObject AParent,
          LPSTR ATitle): TWindow(AParent, ATitle)
{
  // Add a menu to the window.
  AssignMenu("CLIP2MENU");

  // Set the size and position of the window.
  Attr.X = 40;
  Attr.Y = 40;
  Attr.H = GetSystemMetrics(SM_CYSCREEN) / 1.5;
  Attr.W = GetSystemMetrics(SM_CXSCREEN) / 1.5;
```

continues

461

Listing 12.8. Continued

```
  // Initialize variables.
  lButton = FALSE;
  rButton = FALSE;
  paste = FALSE;
  SetRectEmpty(&rect);
}


/////////////////////////////////////////////////////////
// TClipWnd::WMSetFocus()
//
// This function is called when the program's main
// window receives the focus.
/////////////////////////////////////////////////////////
void TClipWnd::WMSetFocus(RTMessage msg)
{
  // Perform normal WM_SETFOCUS processing.
  TWindow::DefWndProc(msg);

  // Get a handle to the menu.
  HMENU hMenu = GetMenu(HWindow);

  // Check for a bitmap in the Clipboard.
  if (!IsClipboardFormatAvailable(CF_BITMAP))
  {
    // If there's not a bitmap in the Clipboard,
    // turn off the Paste menu item.
    EnableMenuItem(hMenu, CM_PASTE, MF_GRAYED);
  }
  else
    // If there is a bitmap available, turn on
    // the Paste menu item.
    EnableMenuItem(hMenu, CM_PASTE, MF_ENABLED);
}


/////////////////////////////////////////////////////////
// TClipWnd::WMLButtonDown()
//
// This function responds to a WM_LBUTTONDOWN message.
/////////////////////////////////////////////////////////
```

```
void TClipWnd::WMLButtonDown(RTMessage msg)
{
  // If the program is in paste mode...
  if (paste)
    PasteBitmap(msg);

  // If this is a new left button press...
  else if (!lButton)
  {
    // Get device context and pen.
    lineDC = GetDC(HWindow);
    newPen = CreatePen(PS_SOLID, 2, BLACK_PEN);
    oldPen = SelectObject(lineDC, newPen);

    // Direct all mouse input to this window.
    SetCapture(HWindow);

    // Set line start to the mouse coords.
    MoveTo(lineDC, msg.LP.Lo, msg.LP.Hi);

    // Set mouse-button flag.
    lButton = TRUE;
  }
}


////////////////////////////////////////////////////
// TClipWnd::WMLButtonUp()
//
// This function responds to a WM_LBUTTONUP message.
////////////////////////////////////////////////////
void TClipWnd::WMLButtonUp()
{
  if (lButton)
  {
    // Restore and release device context.
    SelectObject(lineDC, oldPen);
    ReleaseDC(HWindow, lineDC);

    // Delete custom pen object.
    DeleteObject(newPen);

    // Turn off button flag.
    lButton = FALSE;
```

continues

463

Listing 12.8. Continued

```
    // Release mouse capture.
    ReleaseCapture();
  }
}


//////////////////////////////////////////////////////
// TClipWnd::WMMouseMove()
//
// This function responds to a WM_MOUSEMOVE message.
//////////////////////////////////////////////////////
void TClipWnd::WMMouseMove(RTMessage msg)
{
  // If the left button is down, draw a line.
  if (lButton)
    LineTo(lineDC, msg.LP.Lo, msg.LP.Hi);

  // If the right button is down...
  else if (rButton)
  {
    // Set the drawing mode to XOR.
    SetROP2(rectDC, R2_XORPEN);

    // Erase the old rectangle.
    DrawFocusRect(rectDC, &rect);

    // Set new rectangle to new coords.
    SetRect(&rect, rect.left, rect.top,
        msg.LP.Lo, msg.LP.Hi);

    // Draw the new rectangle.
    DrawFocusRect(rectDC, &rect);
  }
}


//////////////////////////////////////////////////////
// TClipWnd::WMRButtonDown()
//
// This function responds to a WM_RBUTTONDOWN message.
//////////////////////////////////////////////////////
void TClipWnd::WMRButtonDown(RTMessage msg)
```

```
{
  if (!rButton)
  {
    rButton = TRUE;

    // Get device context and set starting rectangle
    // to the mouse's coordinates.
    rectDC = GetDC(HWindow);
    SetRect(&rect, msg.LP.Lo, msg.LP.Hi,
            msg.LP.Lo, msg.LP.Hi);

    // Direct all mouse input to this window.
    SetCapture(HWindow);
  }
}


/////////////////////////////////////////////////////////
// TClipWnd::WMRButtonUp()
//
// This function responds to a WM_RBUTTONUP message.
/////////////////////////////////////////////////////////
void TClipWnd::WMRButtonUp()
{
  rButton = FALSE;

  // Erase the outline rectangle.
  SetROP2(rectDC, R2_XORPEN);
  DrawFocusRect(rectDC, &rect);

  // Release DC and mouse capture.
  ReleaseDC(HWindow, rectDC);
  ReleaseCapture();

  // Calculate the width and height of block.
  int width = rect.right - rect.left;
  int height = rect.bottom - rect.top;

  // If the bitmap is not empty...
  if ((width > 0) && (height > 0))
  {
    // Get a window and memory DC.
    HDC hDC = GetDC(HWindow);
```

continues

465

Listing 12.8. Continued

```
HDC hMemDC = CreateCompatibleDC(hDC);

// Create the bitmap.
HBITMAP hBitmap = CreateCompatibleBitmap(hDC,
 width, height);

// If the bitmap was created okay...
if (hBitmap)
{
  // Select the bitmap into the memory DC.
  SelectObject(hMemDC, hBitmap);

  // Copy the bitmap into the memory DC.
  BitBlt(hMemDC, 0, 0, width, height,
   hDC, rect.left, rect.top, SRCCOPY);

  // Give the bitmap to the Clipboard.
  OpenClipboard(HWindow);
  EmptyClipboard();
  SetClipboardData(CF_BITMAP, hBitmap);
  CloseClipboard();

  // Notify user all went well.
  MessageBox(HWindow,"Bitmap captured", "Copy", MB_OK);

  // Turn on the Paste menu item.
  HMENU hMenu = GetMenu(HWindow);
  EnableMenuItem(hMenu, CM_PASTE, MF_ENABLED);
}

// Release the window and memory DCs.
ReleaseDC(HWindow, hDC);
DeleteDC(hMemDC);
  }
}


//////////////////////////////////////////////////////
// TClipWnd::CMPaste()
//
// This function is called when the user clicks the
// Paste entry of the Edit menu.
//////////////////////////////////////////////////////
```

```
void TClipWnd::CMPaste()
{
  // Set paste mode and change cursor.
  paste = TRUE;
  SetClassWord(HWindow, GCW_HCURSOR,
            LoadCursor(NULL, IDC_CROSS));
}


/////////////////////////////////////////////////////////
// TClipWnd::PasteBitmap()
//
// This function pastes a bitmap from the Clipboard to
// the screen.
/////////////////////////////////////////////////////////
void TClipWnd::PasteBitmap(RTMessage msg)
{
  BITMAP bitmap;

  // Get window DC.
  HDC hDC = GetDC(HWindow);

  // Open the Clipboard and get a handle to the data.
  OpenClipboard(HWindow);
  HBITMAP hBitmap = GetClipboardData(CF_BITMAP);

  // If the Clipboard contains a bitmap...
  if (hBitmap)
  {
    // Create memory DC and select bitmap into it.
    HDC hMemDC = CreateCompatibleDC(hDC);
    SelectObject(hMemDC, hBitmap);

    // Fill in bitmap structure.
    GetObject(hBitmap, sizeof(BITMAP), (LPSTR) &bitmap);

    // Copy the bitmap to the screen.
    BitBlt(hDC, msg.LP.Lo, msg.LP.Hi, bitmap.bmWidth,
      bitmap.bmHeight, hMemDC, 0, 0, SRCCOPY);

    // Delete the memory DC.
    DeleteDC(hMemDC);
  }
```

continues

467

Listing 12.8. Continued

```
// Release the window DC.
ReleaseDC(HWindow, hDC);

// Close the Clipboard and turn off paste mode.
CloseClipboard();
paste = FALSE;

// Restore cursor to Arrow.
SetClassWord(HWindow, GCW_HCURSOR,
        LoadCursor(NULL, IDC_ARROW));
}
```

Listing 12.9. CLIPBRD2.RC—Clipboard demo 2 resource file.

```
CLIP2MENU MENU
BEGIN
    POPUP "&Edit"
    BEGIN
        MENUITEM "&Paste", 101
    END

END
```

Listing 12.10. CLIPBRD.DEF—Clipboard demo 2 definition file.

```
EXETYPE WINDOWS
CODE PRELOAD MOVEABLE DISCARDABLE
DATA PRELOAD MOVEABLE MULTIPLE
HEAPSIZE 4096
STACKSIZE 5120
```

When you run the program, you see the window shown in Figure 12.3.

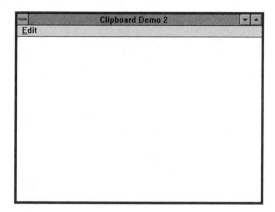

Figure 12.3. Version 2 of the Clipboard application—handling bitmaps.

To use the program, first place your mouse pointer in the window's client area, hold down the left button, and draw a shape. Then, place the mouse cursor on the upper-left corner of the shape you want to capture, hold down the right mouse button, and drag the mouse pointer to the lower-right corner of the shape. A dotted rectangle follows the mouse pointer, outlining the shape you're selecting, as shown in Figure 12.4. To copy the contents of the rectangle, release the right mouse button. A message box appears, informing you that the shape has been captured.

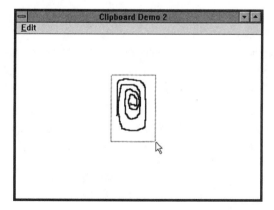

Figure 12.4. Copying a bitmap object to the Clipboard.

To paste the captured image, select the Paste entry of the Edit menu. The mouse cursor changes to a cross. Place the cross where you want to paste the

469

shape and press the left mouse button. Finally, to prove that the Clipboard is functioning properly, run Windows Paintbrush and select its Paste menu item. The shape you selected appears on Paintbrush's client area. (You can also view the bitmap using Windows Clipboard Viewer.)

Copying a Bitmap to the Clipboard

As mentioned previously, copying a bitmap to the Clipboard is not much more complicated than copying text. The main difference is in the way the data is prepared—that is, whereas text needs only to be copied into memory, a bitmap requires obtaining device contexts, creating device compatible bitmaps in memory, and *blitting* a bitmap from one device context to another. (Blitting is the process of quickly transferring data between sections of memory, usually from RAM to screen memory.)

Look at the main window's declaration, which is found in the file CLIPWND2.CPP:

```
_CLASSDEF(TClipWnd)
class TClipWnd: public TWindow
{
  int lButton,   // Mouse-button flags.
      rButton,
      paste,     // Paste mode flag.
      newPen,    // Handle for drawing pen.
      oldPen;    // Handle for old pen.
  HDC lineDC,    // Device context handles.
      rectDC;
  RECT rect;     // Rectangle for defining block.

public:
  TClipWnd(PTWindowsObject AParent, LPSTR ATitle);
  virtual void WMSetFocus(RTMessage msg)
      = [WM_FIRST + WM_SETFOCUS];
  virtual void WMLButtonDown(RTMessage msg)
      = [WM_FIRST + WM_LBUTTONDOWN];
  virtual void WMLButtonUp()
      = [WM_FIRST + WM_LBUTTONUP];
  virtual void WMMouseMove(RTMessage msg)
      = [WM_FIRST + WM_MOUSEMOVE];
```

```
    virtual void WMRButtonDown(RTMessage msg)
        = [WM_FIRST + WM_RBUTTONDOWN];
    virtual void WMRButtonUp()
        = [WM_FIRST + WM_RBUTTONUP];
    virtual void CMPaste()
        = [CM_FIRST + CM_PASTE];

private:
    void PasteBitmap(RTMessage msg);
};
```

This class is obviously much more complicated than CLIPBRD1's edit-window class. This is because OWL has no graphics-editing window class, so the program must provide its own graphics-editing services. This new TClipWnd class includes a number of private data members, all of which are commented. (You see how the program uses these variables later in this section.) The functions WMLButtonDown(), WMLButtonUp(), WMMouseMove(), WMRButtonDown(), and WMRButtonUp() provide CLIPBRD2 with its graphics-editing features. (Some code in these functions is borrowed from Chapter 10's toolbox demo program.) The function WMSetFocus() provides the same service it did in CLIPBRD1, except that it now checks the Clipboard for CF_BITMAP data rather than for CF_TEXT data. Finally, the private member function PasteBitmap() copies a bitmap from the Clipboard to the screen.

Look now at the class' constructor:

```
TClipWnd::TClipWnd(PTWindowsObject AParent,
        LPSTR ATitle): TWindow(AParent, ATitle)
{
    // Add a menu to the window.
    AssignMenu("CLIP2MENU");

    // Set the size and position of the window.
    Attr.X = 40;
    Attr.Y = 40;
    Attr.H = GetSystemMetrics(SM_CYSCREEN) / 1.5;
    Attr.W = GetSystemMetrics(SM_CXSCREEN) / 1.5;

    // Initialize variables.
    lButton = FALS;
    rButton = FALSE;
    paste = FALSE;
    SetRectEmpty(&rect);
}
```

Here, as in CLIPBRD1, the program assigns a menu to its window and then sets the window's position and size. Next, it initializes a few important variables. The Boolean `lButton` indicates whether the left mouse button is pressed. The Boolean `rButton` does the same for the right mouse button. The Boolean `paste` indicates whether the program is currently in paste mode. The `RECT rect` contains the coordinates of the rectangle the user outlines on-screen. Finally, the function `SetRectEmpty()` sets the rectangle's coordinates to zero.

CLIPBRD2 kicks into action when the user presses her left mouse button in the window's client area, generating a `WM_LBUTTONDOWN` message. The program handles this message with the function `WMLButtonDown()`:

```
void TClipWnd::WMLButtonDown(RTMessage msg)
{
  // If the program is in paste mode...
  if (paste)
    PasteBitmap(msg);

  // If this is a new left button press...
  else if (!lButton)
  {
    // Get device context and pen.
    lineDC = GetDC(HWindow);
    newPen = CreatePen(PS_SOLID, 2, BLACK_PEN);
    oldPen = SelectObject(lineDC, newPen);

    // Direct all mouse input to this window.
    SetCapture(HWindow);

    // Set line start to the mouse coords.
    MoveTo(lineDC, msg.LP.Lo, msg.LP.Hi);

    // Set mouse-button flag.
    lButton = TRUE;
  }
}
```

This function is almost identical to its counterpart in Chapter 10's toolbox program. The biggest difference is where the program checks the Boolean variable `paste`. If `paste` is true, the program is in paste mode, which means the user is not trying to draw a line. Rather, she is trying to paste the contents of the Clipboard to the screen. If `paste` is false, the program starts the drawing operation.

472

The drawing concludes when the user releases the left mouse button, generating a `WM_LBUTTONUP` message. This message is handled by `WMLButtonUp()` just as before, so there's no need to discuss it here.

When the user presses the right mouse button, he's informing the program that he wants to select a new bitmap. The message-response function `WMRButtonDown()` starts this process:

```
void TClipWnd::WMRButtonDown(RTMessage msg)
{
  if (!rButton)
  {
    rButton = TRUE;

    // Get device context and set starting rectangle
    // to the mouse's coordinates.
    rectDC = GetDC(HWindow);
    SetRect(&rect, msg.LP.Lo, msg.LP.Hi,
            msg.LP.Lo, msg.LP.Hi);

    // Direct all mouse input to this window.
    SetCapture(HWindow);
  }
}
```

Here, the program checks that the right button is not already down, after which it sets `rButton` to true. Then, as when starting a drawing operation, the program obtains a DC for the window. Because a right-button click marks the upper-left corner of the rectangle the user wants to capture, the program uses the mouse's current coordinates in a call to `SetRect()`, which sets `rect` to these coordinates.

By setting the left and right rectangle coordinates to the same value and the top and bottom rectangle coordinates to the same value, the program creates a rectangle with a width and height of zero. Finally, after initializing the rectangle, the program calls `SetCapture()` to direct all mouse input to its window, regardless of where the mouse is located.

When the user moves the mouse, he generates a series of `WM_MOUSEMOVE` messages, which are handled by the function `WMMouseMove()`:

```
void TClipWnd::WMMouseMove(RTMessage msg)
{
  // If the left button is down, draw a line.
```

473

```
    if (lButton)
      LineTo(lineDC, msg.LP.Lo, msg.LP.Hi);

    // If the right button is down...
    else if (rButton)
    {
      // Set the drawing mode to XOR.
      SetROP2(rectDC, R2_XORPEN);

      // Erase the old rectangle.
      DrawFocusRect(rectDC, &rect);

      // Set new rectangle to new coords.
      SetRect(&rect, rect.left, rect.top,
          msg.LP.Lo, msg.LP.Hi);

      // Draw the new rectangle.
      DrawFocusRect(rectDC, &rect);
    }
}
```

If the user doesn't have the left or right mouse buttons pressed, this function does nothing. If the user has the left button pressed, this function draws a new line, as it did in the toolbox program. However, if the right button is pressed, the user is outlining a rectangle on-screen, which means CLIPBRD2 has a bit of work to do.

First, the program calls SetROP2() to change the drawing mode to XOR (exclusive OR). This drawing mode is perfect for outlining a rectangle, because it allows the program to draw a rectangle on-screen without disturbing the screen's display. This is accomplished by drawing exactly the same shape twice, at exactly the same coordinates. The first time the program draws the shape, it highlights the pixels over which it is drawn. The second time it draws the shape, the pixels are unhighlighted, leaving the screen as it was before the rectangle was drawn.

After setting the drawing mode, CLIPBRD2 erases the old rectangle by redrawing it in XOR mode. (The first time through this function, rect has a width and height of zero, so nothing is drawn.) The Windows function DrawFocusRect() provides the perfect shape and line style for drawing an outlining rectangle, without the program's having to create and select custom pens into the device context. After erasing the old rectangle, CLIPBRD2 calls SetRect() to copy the new rectangle's coordinates into rect. The coordinates of the upper-left part of the rectangle are always the same coordinates that are originally stored in the `left` and `top` members of `rect`. The right and bottom coordinates, however, are the new position of the mouse. Finally, the program draws the new rectangle with another call to `DrawFocusRect()`. Because the program is still in `XOR` drawing mode, the rectangle highlights the pixels over which it is drawn.

As long as the user holds down the right mouse button while she moves the mouse, she continues to generate `WM_MOUSEMOVE` messages that result in the erasing and drawing of rectangles. This gives the illusion of an expanding and contracting outline. When the user finally releases the button, the program must create the selected bitmap. It does this in the function `WMRButtonUp()`:

```
void TClipWnd::WMRButtonUp()
{
  rButton = FALSE;

  // Erase the outline rectangle.
  SetROP2(rectDC, R2_XORPEN);
  DrawFocusRect(rectDC, &rect);

  // Release DC and mouse capture.
  ReleaseDC(HWindow, rectDC);
  ReleaseCapture();

  // Calculate the width and height of block.
  int width = rect.right - rect.left;
  int height = rect.bottom - rect.top;

  // If the bitmap is not empty...
  if ((width > 0) && (height > 0))
  {
    // Get a window and memory DC.
    HDC hDC = GetDC(HWindow);
    HDC hMemDC = CreateCompatibleDC(hDC);

    // Create the bitmap.
    HBITMAP hBitmap = CreateCompatibleBitmap(hDC,
     width, height);

    // If the bitmap was created okay...
    if (hBitmap)
    {
```

```
// Select the bitmap into the memory DC.
SelectObject(hMemDC, hBitmap);

// Copy the bitmap into the memory DC.
BitBlt(hMemDC, 0, 0, width, height,
 hDC, rect.left, rect.top, SRCCOPY);

// Give the bitmap to the Clipboard.
OpenClipboard(HWindow);
EmptyClipboard();
SetClipboardData(CF_BITMAP, hBitmap);
CloseClipboard();

// Notify user all went well.
MessageBox(HWindow,"Bitmap captured", "Copy", MB_OK);

// Turn on the Paste menu item.
HMENU hMenu = GetMenu(HWindow);
EnableMenuItem(hMenu, CM_PASTE, MF_ENABLED);
}

// Release the window and memory DCs.
ReleaseDC(HWindow, hDC);
DeleteDC(hMemDC);
}
}
```

Here, the program sets rButton to false, indicating that the button is no longer down. Then, it erases the rectangle and releases the device context and the mouse capture. To calculate the size of the selected bitmap, the program subtracts the rectangle's left coordinate from its right coordinate to determine its width, and subtracts the top from the bottom to determine its height.

If the width and height are greater than zero, the user selected a valid rectangle, so the program receives a new DC for the window and creates a memory DC that's compatible with it. A call to CreateCompatibleBitmap() creates an empty bitmap that's compatible with the window DC (and thus, the memory DC). If this function returns a valid bitmap handle, the program selects that bitmap into the memory DC by calling SelectObject(). It then calls BitBlt() to copy the outlined screen area into the bitmap.

At this point, there is a copy of the selected bitmap in memory. Because the program has a handle to this bitmap, it can now pass the bitmap to the

Clipboard by first opening and emptying the Clipboard, and then calling `SetClipboardData()` with the parameters `CF_BITMAP` and `hBitmap`. Finally, the program closes the Clipboard and displays a message box to inform the user that the bitmap was copied. The program's last tasks are to update the Paste menu item and release the device contexts.

Pasting a Bitmap from the Clipboard

Now, the bitmap belongs to the Clipboard, where it can be accessed by any program that supports the `CF_BITMAP` format. CLIPBRD2, of course, can access it as well, which it must do when the user wants to paste the image. The user selects the Paste entry of the Edit menu, which generates a `CM_PASTE` message. This message is handled by the message-response function `CMPaste()`:

```
void TClipWnd::CMPaste()
{
  // Set paste mode and change cursor.
  paste = TRUE;
  SetClassWord(HWindow, GCW_HCURSOR,
          LoadCursor(NULL, IDC_CROSS));
}
```

Here, the program sets the variable `paste` to true, indicating that it is now in paste mode. Then, it calls the Windows function `SetClassWord()` to change the window's cursor style to the crosshair. Why not call `SetCursor()`? When Windows returns from processing the menu and the user brings the mouse pointer over the window's client area, Windows changes the cursor to the one defined in the window class. If the program changes the cursor in `CMPaste()` with a `SetCursor()` call, Windows sets the cursor back to the arrow. To get around this stubborn bit of behavior on Windows' part, the program simply changes the default cursor for the window class.

Now that the user is in the paste mode, he moves the crosshair cursor where he wants to paste the bitmap and presses the left mouse button. This generates a `WM_LBUTTONDOWN` message, which calls `WMLButtonDown()`. As seen before, when in the paste mode, `WMLButtonDown()` calls `PasteBitmap()` to fulfill the user's request:

```
void TClipWnd::PasteBitmap(RTMessage msg)
{
  BITMAP bitmap;
```

477

```
// Get window DC.
HDC hDC = GetDC(HWindow);

// Open the Clipboard and get a handle to the data.
OpenClipboard(HWindow);
HBITMAP hBitmap = GetClipboardData(CF_BITMAP);

// If the Clipboard contains a bitmap...
if (hBitmap)
{
  // Create memory DC and select bitmap into it.
  HDC hMemDC = CreateCompatibleDC(hDC);
  SelectObject(hMemDC, hBitmap);

  // Fill in bitmap structure.
  GetObject(hBitmap, sizeof(BITMAP), (LPSTR) &bitmap);

  // Copy the bitmap to the screen.
  BitBlt(hDC, msg.LP.Lo, msg.LP.Hi, bitmap.bmWidth,
     bitmap.bmHeight, hMemDC, 0, 0, SRCCOPY);

  // Delete the memory DC.
  DeleteDC(hMemDC);
}

// Release the window DC.
ReleaseDC(HWindow, hDC);

// Close the Clipboard and turn off paste mode.
CloseClipboard();
paste = FALSE;

// Restore cursor to Arrow.
SetClassWord(HWindow, GCW_HCURSOR,
        LoadCursor(NULL, IDC_ARROW));
}
```

This function first declares a `BITMAP` structure to hold the information needed to define a bitmap. Then, it obtains a device context for the window, opens the Clipboard, and retrieves a handle to the bitmap in the Clipboard. If the Clipboard doesn't contain a bitmap, the handle returned is NULL.

Next, the program creates a memory device context and selects the bitmap into it. Then, it calls `GetObject()`, which fills in the `BITMAP` structure `bitmap`, after which `bitmap.bmWidth` and `bitmap.bmHeight` contain the bitmap's width and height, respectively. A call to `BitBlt()` displays the bitmap in the window, and a call to `DeleteDC()` deletes the memory device context. Finally, the program releases the window's device context, closes the Clipboard, sets the paste mode to false, and restores the mouse cursor to the arrow form.

Clipboard Etiquette

Because the Clipboard is a resource that is shared by every application in a Windows session, it is imperative that you abide by the rules set forth for its use. Failure to do so could cause every other application in the current Windows session to misbehave. For example, if you forget to close the Clipboard, Windows assumes that you are still using it. This prevents other applications from opening it for as long as your application is active. (Luckily, Windows takes back the Clipboard when an application closes.)

 Note: Close the Clipboard as soon as possible after opening it. Don't retain control of it any longer than absolutely necessary. Other applications cannot access the Clipboard as long as you have control over it.

Conclusion

In this chapter, you learned the basics of handling the Windows' Clipboard. What you learned here will serve you well in just about any programming project. However, the Clipboard is capable of much more than is described in this intermediate text.

For example, it is possible to use data formats of your own design with the Clipboard. These data formats (called *private* data formats) are specified by the `CF_OWNERDISPLAY` constant. When using private data formats with the Clipboard, it is up to your application to display the data whenever its requested to do so. This means handling several extra Windows messages, including `WM_ASKCBFORMATNAME`, `WM_SIZECLIPBOARD`, and `WM_PAINTCLIPBOARD`.

In addition, the three Windows functions `SetClipboardViewer()`, `ChangeClipboardChain()`, and `GetClipboardViewer()` allow your application to become a *Clipboard viewer,* which is an application that receives messages about the Clipboard from Windows. For example, whenever the contents of the Clipboard change, Windows sends a `WM_DRAWCLIPBOARD` message to all applications registered as Clipboard viewers, so they can update their displays.

The details of using private data formats and creating Clipboard viewers, while not difficult to learn, are beyond the scope of this book. If you're interested in these topics, you should refer to your Windows programming references for further information. In Chapter 13, you learn yet another way Windows can share resources between programs—*Dynamic Link Libraries.*

13

Writing Dynamic Link Libraries

I n Chapter 12, you learned ways that Windows applications can share data. The methods mentioned were the Clipboard, Dynamic Data Exchange, and Object Linking and Embedding. *Dynamic Link Libraries* (DLLs) are another way to share data among applications. By placing data into a DLL, that data is available to every application that uses the DLL.

Windows fonts, for example, are stored in DLLs (although they don't have the file extension .DLL), which means all programs can use them. However, DLLs provide an even more important service. They enable the programmer to create libraries of functions which, like data in a DLL, can be shared between applications.

In this chapter, you learn to create DLLs and use them in your applications. The simple DLL you will develop enables your programs to draw different types of shapes on-screen—shapes that are not included in the Windows GDI. This shape library can be the starting point for a children's drawing program, or you can extend the idea to provide shapes for electronics programs, flow-charting programs, or any other type of application that requires unique shapes.

Sharing Functions Among Applications

S haring code among applications using DLLs is extremely important to Windows. In fact, without DLLs, Windows would be a crippled system, indeed. Windows comprises many DLLs. By placing most of the Windows API into DLLs, for example, an application doesn't have to have the Windows API functions linked into its executable file. Instead, the necessary libraries are loaded into memory as they're requested. If all the functions required by a Windows application had to be linked into the application, .EXE files would be huge. Moreover, each application would require its own copy of the functions.

The functions or data in a DLL can be shared by as many applications as can run at once. Yet, only one copy of the DLL is necessary in memory. The first time an application needs a DLL, Windows loads the DLL providing the DLL's file has the .DLL extension. (A DLL with a different extension must be loaded explicitly by your program). Subsequent applications also can call functions in the DLL without loading another copy. When the last application that uses the DLL closes, Windows unloads the DLL from memory, freeing the memory for other uses.

Because the functions and data in a DLL can be shared by every application running in the system, in a way, you can think of DLLs as an extension to the Windows API—they add functions that the original Windows designers omitted. Just like the regular Windows DLLs, your DLL can be distributed to many users—users who can then write programs with the functions or data contained in the DLL.

> **Note:** When Windows loads a DLL, it uses *dynamic linking* to link function calls in your program to the appropriate functions in the DLL (thus, the words "dynamic link" in the term "dynamic link library"). Unlike *static linking,* which occurs when you link a program with Borland C++'s linker, dynamic linking occurs at runtime.

DLLs Versus Programs

A lthough DLLs may contain functions your programs can call, a DLL alone is not an executable file. Not even changing the file's extension to .EXE fools Windows into running a DLL. (In fact, many of Windows' DLLs do have the .EXE extension, including USER.EXE and GDI.EXE. A DLL can have any file extension. However, Windows automatically loads *only* DLLs with the .DLL extension.) If you want to use the functions contained in a DLL, the DLL must be loaded by Windows or by your program with the LoadLibrary() call.

Because a DLL is not an executable program, you are right to assume that there are some major differences in the ways you create a DLL and an executable file. One difference is the type of definition file used for a DLL. Here's an example DLL definition file:

```
LIBRARY       SHAPELIB
DESCRIPTION   'Shape DLL for Windows'
EXETYPE       WINDOWS
CODE          PRELOAD MOVEABLE DISCARDABLE
DATA          PRELOAD MOVEABLE SINGLE
HEAPSIZE      1024
```

A definition file for an executable program includes a NAME field, but a DLL's definition file requires a LIBRARY field instead. The LIBRARY line identifies the module as a library, as well as supplies the library's name. The EXETYPE and CODE lines are used the same way for executable programs or DLLs. However, there's an important difference in the DATA line. The word SINGLE means that the DLL has only one data segment. Because a DLL can never have more than one instance loaded into Windows, it never needs more than one data segment. Executable files can have multiple data segments because each instance of the program requires its own segment. You can have a DLL with no data segment by using the line DATA NONE.

The final line in the previous definition file indicates the starting size of the DLL's heap. If this value proves to be too small, Windows can increase its size when needed. Notice that the definition file has no STACKSIZE line. This is because a DLL always shares the stack of the program that called it, so it doesn't need one of its own. This difference between DLLs and programs, however, leads to a sticky situation known in the industry as DS != SS. Luckily, the Borland IDE knows how to handle these problems and doesn't, if properly set up, assume that DS == SS for a DLL. If you're interested in knowing more about this situation, please refer to the accompanying note box.

483

Note: In C, all global and static variables are stored in static memory (on the heap) and all parameters to functions and local variables are stored on the stack. Static memory is addressed as an offset from the DS (*data segment*) register. Similarly, the stack is addressed as an offset from the SS (*stack segment*) register. Unfortunately, for reasons beyond the scope of this discussion, a C compiler has no way of knowing whether a `near` pointer represents an offset from DS or SS. To solve this problem, C (and C++) programs set the data segment and the stack segment to the same address. In other words, DS == SS. In regular Windows programs, which have their own data and stack segments, this represents no problem.

A DLL, however, has its own data segment, yet uses the stack of the calling program, which means DS != SS. In this case, functions in the DLL that use `near` pointers to address the stack segment are not able to find their data. When using the Borland C++ IDE to develop your DLL, however, you don't have to worry too much about this problem, because you can set the compiler so it knows, in a DLL, that DS never equals SS.

A Simple DLL: SHAPELIB.DLL

O ther differences between a DLL and an executable program show up in the DLL's source code. But before looking at that code, run the sample test program with the sample DLL, which are both shown in Listings 13.1 through 13.7. You don't have to compile the DLL, because it's already on this book's disk. However, you should load the DLL's project file (SHAPELIB.PRJ) and examine the compiler options that are set for the DLL.

Notice in particular the settings in the Application Options dialog box (Figure 13.1), the Code Generation dialog box (Figure 13.2), the Entry/Exit Code Generation dialog box (Figure 13.3), and the Linker Settings dialog box (Figure 13.4). The important settings in these dialog boxes are discussed next.

The Applications Options dialog box is where you choose whether you're compiling a Windows application or a DLL. By choosing one of these compilation options, you set many of the compiler's default settings appropriately for the type of module you are producing. For example, you can see in Figure 13.1 that when you select a DLL, the compiler automatically assumes that DS never equals SS.

484

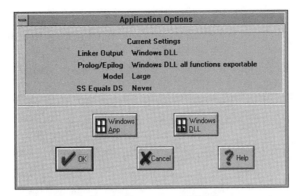

Figure 13.1. The Applications Options dialog box for a DLL.

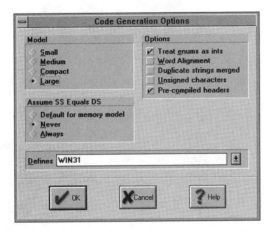

Figure 13.2. The Code Generation Options dialog box for a DLL.

In the Code Generation Options dialog box (Figure 13.2), checking the Large Model option ensures that all addresses are treated as FAR. (You can use the Small Model, if you like. However, if you do, you have to construct the library module for that model [TCLASSC.LIB], because, to save space, Borland doesn't include that library on your Borland C++ disks. You also must be sure that all the .DLL's functions use the FAR keyword in their declarations.) Notice also that "Assume SS Equals DS" is set to Never.

In the Entry/Exit Code Generation dialog box (Figure 13.3), setting "Windows DLL all functions exportable" informs the compiler that you want all functions in your DLL to be accessible to other modules (specifically, other applications using the DLL). If you use the "Windows DLL explicit functions exported," it's up to you to inform the compiler which functions to export by using the export

485

keyword when declaring a function. The calling convention can be set to C or Pascal. For a DLL, it doesn't matter much which you use, although the Pascal calling convention is more efficient. You can also specify the Pascal calling convention by using the PASCAL keyword when declaring a function.

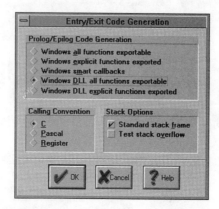

Figure 13.3. The Entry/Exit Code Generation dialog box for a DLL.

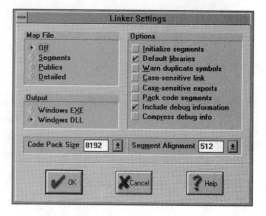

Figure 13.4. The Linker Settings dialog box for a DLL.

In the Linker Settings dialog box (Figure 13.4), the linker's output is set to Windows DLL. This setting, like many of the other compiler options, is automatically selected when you choose Windows DLL from the Applications Options dialog box.

Getting back to the example DLL, when you run the test program, place your mouse pointer over the window and click any button. If you click the left button, a face shape appears at the location of your click (that's Fred). If you click the right button, you get a triangle. And, finally, if you click the middle button, you get the squiggle shape. The program's main window is shown in Figure 13.5.

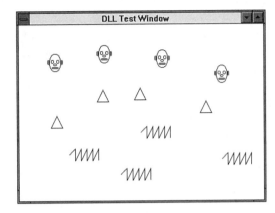

Figure 13.5. The DLL test application's main window.

Now that you know what the program does, look at the function declarations in the header file for the shapes DLL, SHAPELIB.H:

```
extern "C"
{
  void _export FAR PASCAL
    Triangle(HDC hDC, int x, int y);
  void _export FAR PASCAL
    Squiggle(HDC hDC, int x, int y);
  void _export FAR PASCAL
    Fred(HDC hDC, int x, int y);
}
```

All the functions in the DLL are declared as extern "C". This declaration protects against an infamous C++ compiler convention called *name-mangling*. What's name-mangling? When you compile a C++ program, the compiler changes function names by adding information about the function's parameters and return value. Unfortunately, it is this changed name that your program must use when calling functions.

You wouldn't have noticed this name change until now because the compiler takes care of all the name matching for you. However, keep in mind that DLLs can be called from many other programs, programs that may or may not have been written in the same language or with the same compiler as the DLL—that's where the trouble appears.

487

If you allow name-mangling to occur, the DLL can be called only by programs that were compiled on the same compiler as the DLL. It doesn't even matter if the programs were written with the same language, because, although all C++ compilers incorporate name-mangling, no two do it the same way. So, if you compile your DLL on Borland's C++ compiler, you can't call the DLL's functions with programs written with the Microsoft C++ compiler. The way around this problem is to use the `extern "C"` declaration and not allow name-mangling.

 Caution: Don't forget—if you want any application written with any programming language to be able to call your DLLs—you must not allow C++'s infamous name-mangling to occur. Use the `extern "C"` declaration to avoid name-mangling in a DLL.

The listing in the header file SHAPELIB.H declares the functions that draw the shapes. The _extern keyword informs the linker to export these functions for use in other modules. If you fail to export these functions and try to compile the program that calls them, you receive a linker error.

Now look at the implementation code for the DLL, starting with the `LibMain()` function:

```
int FAR PASCAL LibMain(HINSTANCE hInstance,
                WORD wDataSeg, WORD cbHeapSize,
                LPSTR lpstrCmdLine)
{
  // Unlock data segment.
  if (cbHeapSize)
    UnlockData(0);

  return TRUE;
}
```

Just as every executable Windows program must have a `WinMain()` function, every DLL must have a `LibMain()` function, which is where execution of the DLL begins. It is in `LibMain()` that you perform whatever initialization your DLL requires. The `LibMain()` function takes four parameters, as listed:

- the DLL's instance handle
- the DLL's data segment address

- the size of the DLL's heap

- a command line

In the previous code example, `LibMain()` unlocks its data segment, which is always locked by the DLL's start-up code. `LibMain()` then returns true, which indicates that the DLL initialized properly. If `LibMain()` returns false, Windows unloads the DLL.

DLLs also must have a deinitialization function called `WEP()` (*Windows Exit Procedure*), which Windows automatically calls when it unloads the DLL:

```
int FAR PASCAL WEP(int nParam)
{
  return TRUE;
}
```

This is where you can do any necessary cleanup. The parameter `nParam` is passed to the procedure by Windows and can be one of two values. A value of `WEP_FREE_DLL` is sent to `WEP()` when Windows is unloading the DLL, and `WEP_SYSTEMEXIT` is sent when Windows shuts down completely. Like `LibMain()`, `WEP()` must return true if all went well. In the previous example, there is no cleanup to be done, so the function simply returns true.

 Note: All functions in a DLL that will be called from other modules must be exported and declared as FAR. By exporting a function, you make it visible to other modules, rather than visible only to the module in which it's declared. The functions must be declared as FAR because they will be called from a different code segment.

Except that every exported function must be declared as FAR, there's nothing unusual about the functions that make up the body of a DLL. You write these functions the same way as any other functions, as you can see with `Fred()`, which draws the face shape:

```
void FAR PASCAL _export Fred(HDC hDC, int x, int y)
{
  Ellipse(hDC, x, y, x+20, y+30);
  Ellipse(hDC, x+3, y+10, x+8, y+16);
  Ellipse(hDC, x+12, y+10, x+17, y+16);
  Ellipse(hDC, x+7, y+16, x+13, y+20);
```

```
  Ellipse(hDC, x+4, y+22, x+16, y+25);
  Ellipse(hDC, x-3, y+10, x, y+18);
  Ellipse(hDC, x+20, y+10, x+23, y+18);
}
```

In the previous code, the function calls the Windows GDI function `Ellipse()`
to draw the component's of Fred's face. `Fred()`'s parameters are the handle to
the window's DC and Fred's x- and y-coordinates. The other shape functions,
`Triangle()` and `Squiggle()`, work similarly, so there's no point in discussing
them here. You can see them in Listings 13.1 through 13.3, which include the
header file, implementation, and definition file for the shape DLL.

Listing 13.1. SHAPELIB.H—header file for the shape DLL.

```
// SHAPELIB.H -- Header file for the shape DLL.

#ifndef _SHAPELIB_H
#define _SHAPELIB_H

// Use extern "C" to prevent C++ name mangling.

extern "C"
{
  void FAR PASCAL _export
    Triangle(HDC hDC, int x, int y);
  void FAR PASCAL _export
    Squiggle(HDC hDC, int x, int y);
  void FAR PASCAL _export
    Fred(HDC hDC, int x, int y);
}

#endif
```

Listing 13.2. SHAPELIB.CPP—implementation for the shape DLL.

```
// SHAPELIB.CPP -- Implementation for the shape DLL.

#include <windows.h>
#include "shapelib.h"
```

```
// Prevent name mangling.
extern "C"
{
  int FAR PASCAL WEP(int nParam);
}

#pragma argsused

//////////////////////////////////////////////////////
// LibMain()
//
// This function is the DLL's entry point.
//////////////////////////////////////////////////////
int FAR PASCAL LibMain(HINSTANCE hInstance,
                WORD wDataSeg, WORD cbHeapSize,
                LPSTR lpstrCmdLine)
{
  // Unlock data segment.
  if (cbHeapSize)
    UnlockData(0);

  return TRUE;
}

#pragma argsused

//////////////////////////////////////////////////////
// WEP()
//
// The DLL exits here. WEP = Windows Exit Procedure.
//////////////////////////////////////////////////////
int FAR PASCAL WEP(int nParam)
{
  return TRUE;
}

//////////////////////////////////////////////////////
// Fred()
//
// This function draws Fred.
//////////////////////////////////////////////////////
```

continues

491

Listing 13.2. Continued

```
void FAR PASCAL _export Fred(HDC hDC, int x, int y)
{
  Ellipse(hDC, x, y, x+20, y+30);
  Ellipse(hDC, x+3, y+10, x+8, y+16);
  Ellipse(hDC, x+12, y+10, x+17, y+16);
  Ellipse(hDC, x+7, y+16, x+13, y+20);
  Ellipse(hDC, x+4, y+22, x+16, y+25);
  Ellipse(hDC, x-3, y+10, x, y+18);
  Ellipse(hDC, x+20, y+10, x+23, y+18);
}


///////////////////////////////////////////////////////
// Triangle()
//
// This function draws a triangle.
///////////////////////////////////////////////////////
void FAR PASCAL _export Triangle(HDC hDC, int x, int y)
{
  MoveTo(hDC, x, y);
  LineTo(hDC, x-10, y+20);
  LineTo(hDC, x+10, y+20);
  LineTo(hDC, x, y);
}


///////////////////////////////////////////////////////
// Squiggle()
//
// This function draws a squiggle.
///////////////////////////////////////////////////////
void FAR PASCAL _export Squiggle(HDC hDC, int x, int y)
{
  MoveTo(hDC, x, y);
  for (int i=1; i<6; ++i)
  {
    LineTo(hDC, x+(i*10), y-10);
    LineTo(hDC, x+(i*10), y+10);
  }
}
```

Listing 13.3. SHAPELIB.DEF—definition file for shape DLL.

```
LIBRARY        SHAPELIB
DESCRIPTION    'Shape DLL for Windows'
EXETYPE        WINDOWS
CODE           PRELOAD MOVEABLE DISCARDABLE
DATA           PRELOAD MOVEABLE SINGLE
HEAPSIZE       1024
```

Calling Functions in a DLL

N ow that you know how to write a DLL, you might wonder how you can call that DLL from another program. First, before compiling the program, you must supply the linker with the names of the functions your program is importing from the DLL. If you fail to do this, the linker generates undefined symbol errors for each imported function. There are three ways of informing the linker about imported functions:

- Add an IMPORTS section to the program's definition file, listing the names of the functions to be imported.

- Add an EXPORTS section to the DLL's definition file that assigns ordinal values to each exported function. Then, add an IMPORTS section to your application's definition file that equates the function names with the ordinal values.

- Create an import library.

 Caution: You must supply the linker with the names of the functions your program is importing from the DLL. If you fail to do this, the linker generates undefined symbol errors for each imported function.

You add an IMPORTS section to the program's definition file like this:

```
EXETYPE WINDOWS
CODE PRELOAD MOVEABLE DISCARDABLE
DATA PRELOAD MOVEABLE MULTIPLE
HEAPSIZE 4096
STACKSIZE 5120
```

```
IMPORTS SHAPELIB.Fred
        SHAPELIB.Triangle
        SHAPELIB.Squiggle
```

This method is adequate for programs that import only a few functions. However, listing all the functions imported from a large DLL can be a long and tedious process.

A twist on the previous technique is to assign ordinal values to each of the functions that your DLL exports. This is done by adding an EXPORTS section to the DLL's definition file, as shown here:

```
EXPORTS Fred       @1
        Triangle @2
        Squiggle @3
```

These ordinal values, preceded by the @ symbol, can be any unique positive integers.

Now, in the IMPORT section of your application's definition file, you can assign appropriate function names to the ordinal values, like this:

```
IMPORTS Fred       = SHAPELIB.1
        Triangle = SHAPELIB.2
        Squiggle = SHAPELIB.3
```

By storing ordinal values rather than function names, your program's executable file will be a bit smaller. But listing all the functions included in a large DLL can be a tedious chore.

Creating an import library is an easier way to inform the linker about imported DLL functions. After creating your DLL, run Borland's IMPLIBW.EXE program (called Import Lib in the Borland C++ 3.1 group window). Then, give IMPLIBW the name of the DLL that it should convert to an import library.

When the import library is created, it has the extension .LIB. Add this new library file to your application's project file list, and then compile the application. That's all there is to it. You don't have to list all the functions manually; the import library does this for you.

When writing your program, you can now call the DLL's functions as if they were part of your program, as you see as you examine the program's main window class, starting with the class' definition:

```
_CLASSDEF(TDLLWnd)
class TDLLWnd: public TWindow
{
public:
```

```
    TDLLWnd(PTWindowsObject AParent, LPSTR ATitle);
    virtual void WMLButtonDown(RTMessage msg)
        = [WM_FIRST + WM_LBUTTONDOWN];
    virtual void WMRButtonDown(RTMessage msg)
        = [WM_FIRST + WM_RBUTTONDOWN];
    virtual void WMMButtonDown(RTMessage msg)
        = [WM_FIRST + WM_MBUTTONDOWN];
};
```

In this example, the main window is derived from the TWindow class. The main window's only functions, besides the constructor, are message-response functions for all three mouse buttons. When the user presses a mouse button, the appropriate function is called to draw the required shape in the window. For example, the function WMLButtonDown() draws Fred:

```
void TDLLWnd::WMLButtonDown(RTMessage msg)
{
  HDC hDC = GetDC(HWindow);
  Fred(hDC, msg.LP.Lo, msg.LP.Hi);
  ReleaseDC(HWindow, hDC);
}
```

In this example, the function obtains a device context for the window and calls the function Fred() to draw the shape. Although Fred() is in the DLL, WMLButtonDown() calls it exactly as it does any other function in the program. Then, after the shape is drawn, WMLButtonDown() releases the DC and exits. The WMRButtonDown() and WMMButtonDown() functions work similarly.

Listings 13.4 through 13.7 include the header file, the implementation, and the definition file for the DLL test application.

Listing 13.4. DLLAPP.CPP—DLL test application.

```
// DLLAPP.CPP -- Application that uses shape DLL.

#include <owl.h>
#include "dllwnd.h"

// Application class declaration.
class TDLLApp: public TApplication {
public:
  TDLLApp(LPSTR AName, HINSTANCE AnInstance,
          HINSTANCE APrevInstance, LPSTR ACmdLine,
```

continues

495

Listing 13.4. Continued

```
            int ACmdShow): TApplication(AName,
            AnInstance, APrevInstance, ACmdLine,
            ACmdShow) {};
  virtual void InitMainWindow();
};


///////////////////////////////////////////////////////
// TDLLApp::InitMainWindow()
//
// This function creates the application's main window.
///////////////////////////////////////////////////////
void TDLLApp::InitMainWindow()
{
  MainWindow = new TDLLWnd(NULL, "DLL Test Window");
}


///////////////////////////////////////////////////////
// WinMain()
///////////////////////////////////////////////////////
int PASCAL WinMain(HINSTANCE hInstance,
                   HINSTANCE hPrevInstance,
             LPSTR lpszCmdLine, int nCmdShow)
{
  TDLLApp DLLApp("DLLApp", hInstance,
                   hPrevInstance, lpszCmdLine, nCmdShow);
  DLLApp.Run();
  return DLLApp.Status;
}
```

Listing 13.5. DLLWND.H—header file for main window.

```
#ifndef _DLLWND_H
#define _DLLWND_H

_CLASSDEF(TDLLWnd)
class TDLLWnd: public TWindow
{
public:
```

```
    TDLLWnd(PTWindowsObject AParent, LPSTR ATitle);
    virtual void WMLButtonDown(RTMessage msg)
        = [WM_FIRST + WM_LBUTTONDOWN];
    virtual void WMRButtonDown(RTMessage msg)
        = [WM_FIRST + WM_RBUTTONDOWN];
    virtual void WMMButtonDown(RTMessage msg)
        = [WM_FIRST + WM_MBUTTONDOWN];
};


#endif
```

Listing 13.6. DLLWND.CPP—implementation for main window.

```
// DLLWND.CPP -- Implementation for main window.

#include <owl.h>
#include "dllwnd.h"
#include "shapelib.h"

//////////////////////////////////////////////////////
// TDLLWnd::TDLLWnd()
//
// This is the main window's constructor.
//////////////////////////////////////////////////////
TDLLWnd::TDLLWnd(PTWindowsObject AParent,
                LPSTR ATitle): TWindow(AParent, ATitle)
{
  // Set the window's size.
  Attr.X = 40;
  Attr.Y = 40;
  Attr.H = GetSystemMetrics(SM_CYSCREEN) / 1.5;
  Attr.W = GetSystemMetrics(SM_CXSCREEN) / 1.5;
}


//////////////////////////////////////////////////////
// TDLLWnd::WMLButtonDown()
//
// This function responds to a WM_LBUTTONDOWN message.
//////////////////////////////////////////////////////
void TDLLWnd::WMLButtonDown(RTMessage msg)
```

continues

497

Listing 13.6. Continued

```
{
  HDC hDC = GetDC(HWindow);
  Fred(hDC, msg.LP.Lo, msg.LP.Hi);
  ReleaseDC(HWindow, hDC);
}


////////////////////////////////////////////////////////
// TDLLWnd::WMMButtonDown()
//
// This function responds to a WM_MBUTTONDOWN message.
////////////////////////////////////////////////////////
void TDLLWnd::WMMButtonDown(RTMessage msg)
{
  HDC hDC = GetDC(HWindow);
  Squiggle(hDC, msg.LP.Lo, msg.LP.Hi);
  ReleaseDC(HWindow, hDC);
}


////////////////////////////////////////////////////////
// TDLLWnd::WMRButtonDown()
//
// This function responds to a WM_RBUTTONDOWN message.
////////////////////////////////////////////////////////
void TDLLWnd::WMRButtonDown(RTMessage msg)
{
  HDC hDC = GetDC(HWindow);
  Triangle(hDC, msg.LP.Lo, msg.LP.Hi);
  ReleaseDC(HWindow, hDC);
}
```

Listing 13.7. DLLAPP.DEF—the DLL test application's definition file.

```
EXETYPE WINDOWS
CODE PRELOAD MOVEABLE DISCARDABLE
DATA PRELOAD MOVEABLE MULTIPLE
HEAPSIZE 4096
STACKSIZE 5120
```

498

DLL Caveats and Points of Interest

A s you can see, writing a simple DLL is easy. However, there are several things that you should keep in mind as you write your own DLLs, as follow:

- Unlike a program, which has its own code, data, and stack segments, a DLL can have only a code and a data segment. It uses the stack of the calling program, which leads to the DS != SS condition.

- All functions in a DLL must be declared as FAR and all pointer parameters passed to or from a DLL must also be FAR.

- DLL's do not have a message loop and, therefore, do not receive window messages. A DLL can, however, call GetMessage() or PeekMessage() to examine messages targeted for the program that called the DLL.

- Static data in a DLL is accessible by any program that calls the DLL.

- You can use modal dialog boxes in a DLL. When creating the dialog, use the DLL's instance handle and set the dialog's parent to NULL.

- You can register and create windows within a DLL. However, messages for these windows are sent to the calling program instance, not to the DLL.

- The normal start-up code that's added to a Windows program during linking is not added to a DLL. This means you can't use the getenv() or putenv() functions in a DLL.

- A DLL can allocate global memory for the program instance that called it. The allocated memory is released when the program instance terminates.

- A DLL can load resources either from its own file or from the file of the calling program instance. The file from which the resources are loaded depends on the instance handle used with the resource-loading function.

Conclusion

As you now know, DLLs allow many concurrently running programs to call a library of functions while having only a single instance of the library loaded in memory. This promotes efficient memory use and smaller executable files.

DLLs can be used in other ways, too. You might, for example, consider using DLLs for program modules that your application needs only infrequently. Using DLLs this way, you can keep the size of your main program small, loading the additional data or functions only when they are needed. In this case, use the `LoadLibrary()` and `FreeLibrary()` functions in your program to explicitly load and unload DLLs, rather than having Windows handle them for you.

Now that all the serious business is out of the way, it's time to have some fun. In Chapter 14, you learn to add multimedia sound to your programs. In Chapter 15, the concluding chapter, you create a Windows screen saver.

14

Using Multimedia Sound with Windows

N othing, outside of graphics, adds as much pizzazz to a program as the judicial use of sound. Not only can sound add pleasing effects to your software, but it can also alert the user to situations that warrant immediate attention.

In previous versions of Windows, there was only limited support for sound; but in Windows 3.1, you can handle many types of sound devices, including CD players, sound cards, and MIDI-compatible synthesizers.

Perhaps the most popular source of sound for Windows programs is a *waveform file,* which stores sampled sounds that can be played back by Windows. These sound files, which are identified by their .WAV filename extension, are responsible for most of the sounds you hear when running a Windows session with a multimedia-capable sound card installed.

In this chapter, you learn not only to play waveform sounds, but also to add such sound functions as pause and resume to your programs. Along the way, you are introduced to Windows 3.1's *Media Control Interface* (MCI), which provides a wealth of functions for controlling multimedia devices.

 Note: To receive the best results from the sound programs included in this chapter, you should have a multimedia-capable sound board, such as Sound Blaster, installed in your system. However, if you don't have a sound card, you might be able to use the programs by installing the PC speaker driver included on this book's disk. (Microsoft does not guarantee that this driver works on all systems.)

The Media Control Interface

The Media Control Interface is part of the Multimedia Extensions to Windows, which controls multimedia devices. This high-level interface gives you control over such devices as CD players, VCRs, videodisc players, MIDI synthesizers, and more.

Unfortunately, if you scan through the printed Windows documentation that came with your Borland C++ compiler, you'll find nary a mention of the MCI. In fact, if you check most Windows programming books, you'll find this important information missing there, too. You're not out of luck, though. In your Borland C++ main window, you will find on-disk documentation for the MCI. This documentation can be tough to figure out, though, so this chapter is designed to give you a head start.

You can control the MCI in two ways, as explained:

- By using the *command-message interface.* This method enables you to program the MCI using Windows messages and commands, much as you do with any part of the Windows API.

- By using the *command-string interface.* This method provides a scripting language for the MCI, enabling you to provide commands in string form that Windows then translates into the commands necessary to control the multimedia devices.

In this chapter, you learn about the command-message interface. Once you see how this works, you should be able to use the on-disk documentation (in the MCI reference) to figure out the command-string interface.

Playing a Waveform File

I f you've set up your PC for multimedia audio, you've undoubtedly seen waveform files, which are stored on your disk with various names, but all with the .WAV file extension. These files represent digitally sampled sounds that Windows can easily reproduce through the MCI. Sounds such as the famous Windows "ta-da" (heard on some systems when Windows boots) and the pleasant "ding!" used for the system bell are stored in .WAV files. You might think that playing digitized sounds in Windows is a headache and a half. If so, you are wrong.

By simply calling the MCI `sndPlaySound()` function, you can play any waveform file that fits in memory. Give the function the name of the file you want to play, add the sound-play options, and presto, you have digitized sound!

Is it really that easy? You bet! Listings 14.1 through 14.4 compose a simple sound application that plays a wave file named BOING.WAV. (This wave file is on this book's disk, along with the listings.) When you compile and run the program, you see the window in Figure 14.1. Click the Press Me button to hear the "boing" sound.

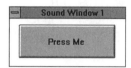

Figure 14.1. Sound application, version 1.

Now, look at the program, starting with the main window's declaration found in SNDWND1.H:

```
_CLASSDEF(TSndWnd)
class TSndWnd: public TWindow
{
public:
  TSndWnd(PTWindowsObject AParent, LPSTR ATitle);
  virtual void IDPressMe(RTMessage msg)
      = [ID_FIRST + ID_PRESSME];
};
```

The main window class is derived from `TWindow` and has only two member functions, the constructor and a message-response function for the window's single button. The constructor, found in the class' implementation file, SNDWND1.CPP, sets the main window so it can't be resized:

```
TSndWnd::TSndWnd(PTWindowsObject AParent,
                 LPSTR ATitle): TWindow(AParent, ATitle)
{
  // Set the window's style.
  Attr.Style = WS_POPUP | WS_SYSMENU |
          WS_BORDER | WS_CAPTION;

  // Set the window's size.
  Attr.X = 100;
  Attr.Y = 100;
  Attr.H = 100;
  Attr.W = 200;

  // Add a button to the window.
  new TButton(this, ID_PRESSME, "Press Me",
          16, 10, 165, 55, FALSE);
}
```

Besides changing the window's style so it has no thick frame for sizing the window (in other words, no WS_THICKFRAME) and setting its position and size, this function creates a single button for the window, giving it the ID that is defined in SNDWND1.H. This button is handled by the message-response function IDPressMe():

```
void TSndWnd::IDPressMe(RTMessage)
{
  if (!sndPlaySound("BOING.WAV",
                   SND_SYNC | SND_NODEFAULT))
    MessageBox(HWindow, "Couldn't find WAV file.",
              "SOUND", MB_OK | MB_ICONEXCLAMATION);
}
```

IDPressMe() does little more than call sndPlaySound() to generate the "boing" contained in the file BOING.WAV. The sndPlaySound() function returns a false if there's an error and a true if the sound played accurately. The if statement, therefore, checks the return value and, if it detects an error, a message box is displayed.

The sndPlaySound() function requires two parameters. The first is the name of the file you want to play. The function first searches the [sounds] section of the WIN.INI file for the sound. The sound names found there are not the names of waveform files, but rather names assigned to specific Windows events. A typical WIN.INI [sounds] section looks like this:

```
[sounds]
SystemAsterisk=chord.wav,Asterisk
SystemHand=chord.wav,Critical Stop
SystemDefault=C:\WINDOWS\DING.WAV,Default Beep
SystemExclamation=chord.wav,Exclamation
SystemQuestion=chord.wav,Question
SystemExit=chimes.wav,Windows Exit
SystemStart=tada.wav,Windows Start
```

To play the SystemAsterisk sound, you provide sndPlaySound() with the string "SystemAsterisk" as its first parameter. If sndPlaySound() can't find the sound represented by the string in WIN.INI, the function assumes that the sound string is the name of a waveform file. sndPlaySound() then searches for the file in the current directory, the main Windows directory, the Windows system directory, or directories included in the user's PATH environment variable. If the function can't find the file, it tries to play the SystemDefault sound, as defined in WIN.INI. Finally, if it can't find this sound, it returns an error.

The second parameter for sndPlaySound() is the *sound-play* option, which can be one or more of the following:

- SND_SYNC—The sound is played synchronously and the function returns only when the sound ends.

- SND_ASYNC—The sound is played asynchronously and the function returns immediately after the sound begins. You must call sndPlaySound() with a first parameter of NULL to end the sound.

- SND_NODEFAULT—If the sound specified in the first parameter can't be found, the function returns without playing the default sound.

- SND_MEMORY—Indicates that the first parameter in the sndPlaySound() call points to a waveform sound in memory.

- SND_LOOP—The sound plays repeatedly. To stop the loop, you must call sndPlaySound() with a first parameter of NULL. (You must also include the SND_ASYNC flag along with SND_LOOP.)

- SND_NOSTOP—The function does not play the requested sound if a sound is already playing. In this case, sndPlaySound() returns false.

505

Note: The constants used with the multimedia functions are defined in MMSYSTEM.H. Therefore, you must include MMSYSTEM.H in files that use these constants.

Listings 14.1 through 14.4 include the complete code for this simple sound application. You might want to enhance the program to a full waveform player by adding the functions necessary to choose any sound file on the disk. As written, this application plays only the BOING.WAV file.

Listing 14.1. SNDAPP1.CPP—sound application, version 1.

```
// SNDAPP1.CPP -- Sound Application, version 1.

#include <owl.h>
#include "sndwnd1.h"

// Application class declaration.
class TSndApp: public TApplication
{
public:
  TSndApp(LPSTR AName, HINSTANCE AnInstance,
          HINSTANCE APrevInstance, LPSTR ACmdLine,
          int ACmdShow): TApplication(AName,
          AnInstance, APrevInstance, ACmdLine,
          ACmdShow) {};
  virtual void InitMainWindow();
};


/////////////////////////////////////////////////////////
// TSndApp::InitMainWindow()
//
// This function creates the application's main window.
/////////////////////////////////////////////////////////
void TSndApp::InitMainWindow()
{
  MainWindow = new TSndWnd(NULL, "Sound Window 1");
}
```

```
//////////////////////////////////////////////////////
// WinMain()
//////////////////////////////////////////////////////
int PASCAL WinMain(HINSTANCE hInstance, HINSTANCE hPrevInstance,
                LPSTR lpszCmdLine, int nCmdShow)
{
  TSndApp SndApp("SndApp1", hInstance,
                hPrevInstance, lpszCmdLine, nCmdShow);
  SndApp.Run();
  return SndApp.Status;
}
```

Listing 14.2. SNDWND1.H—main window header file.

```
// SNDWND1.H -- Header file for main window.

#ifndef _SNDWND1_H
#define _SNDWND1_H

#define ID_PRESSME 100

_CLASSDEF(TSndWnd)
class TSndWnd: public TWindow
{
public:
  TSndWnd(PTWindowsObject AParent, LPSTR ATitle);
  virtual void IDPressMe(RTMessage msg)
      = [ID_FIRST + ID_PRESSME];
};

#endif
```

Listing 14.3. SNDWND1.CPP—main window implementation.

```
// SNDWND1.CPP -- Implementation for main window.

#include <owl.h>
#include <mmsystem.h>
```

continues

Listing 14.3. Continued

```cpp
#include <button.h>
#include "sndwnd1.h"

//////////////////////////////////////////////////////////
// TSndWnd::TSndWnd()
//
// This is the main window's constructor.
//////////////////////////////////////////////////////////
TSndWnd::TSndWnd(PTWindowsObject AParent,
                LPSTR ATitle): TWindow(AParent, ATitle)
{
  // Set the window's style.
  Attr.Style = WS_POPUP | WS_SYSMENU |
          WS_BORDER | WS_CAPTION;

  // Set the window's size.
  Attr.X = 100;
  Attr.Y = 100;
  Attr.H = 100;
  Attr.W = 200;

  // Add a button to the window.
  new TButton(this, ID_PRESSME, "Press Me",
          16, 10, 165, 55, FALSE);
}


//////////////////////////////////////////////////////////
// TSndWnd::IDPressMe()
//
// This function responds when the Press Me button is
// clicked.
//////////////////////////////////////////////////////////
void TSndWnd::IDPressMe(RTMessage)
{
  if (!sndPlaySound("BOING.WAV",
                  SND_SYNC | SND_NODEFAULT))
    MessageBox(HWindow, "Couldn't find WAV file.",
              "SOUND", MB_OK | MB_ICONEXCLAMATION);
}
```

Listing 14.4. SNDAPP.DEF—sound application's definition file.

```
EXETYPE WINDOWS
CODE PRELOAD MOVEABLE DISCARDABLE
DATA PRELOAD MOVEABLE MULTIPLE
HEAPSIZE 4096
STACKSIZE 5120
```

Having More Control Over Sound

The function `sndPlaySound()` is the highest level function available for playing waveform files in Windows 3.1. As such, it allows only a few options and always plays a sound from beginning to end. What if you want more control over the sounds in your programs? Then, you must step down one level and use the `mciSendCommand()` function to send specific commands to your sound device.

Although using `mciSendCommand()` requires learning a new list of Windows messages specially designed for multimedia applications, it is still a straight-forward process. In this process, devices are treated much like tape recorders with features like play, stop, pause, and resume. By using these different functions, you can stop a waveform file from playing at any point or pause the waveform file and resume playing exactly where it paused. You can, as you see in the next program, even hand control of the sounds over to the user.

Listings 14.5 through 14.8 compose a sound application that plays a sound-effect waveform and enables the user to manipulate the sound with the program's buttons.

When you compile and run the program, you see the window in Figure 14.2. To begin playing the sound, click the Play button. To stop the sound, click the Stop button. You can pause and resume the sound effect by clicking the Pause and Resume buttons, respectively.

Figure 14.2. Sound application, version 2.

509

Now that you've had a little fun with the program (recognize the sound effect?), look at the program code, starting with the main window's class definition, found in SNDWND2.H:

```
_CLASSDEF(TSndWnd)
class TSndWnd: public TWindow
{
  int deviceID;

public:
  TSndWnd(PTWindowsObject AParent, LPSTR ATitle);
  virtual void SetupWindow();
  virtual void IDPlay()
      = [ID_FIRST + ID_PLAY];
  virtual void IDStop()
      = [ID_FIRST + ID_STOP];
  virtual void IDPause()
      = [ID_FIRST + ID_PAUSE];
  virtual void IDResume()
      = [ID_FIRST + ID_RESUME];
  virtual void MMMCINotify(RTMessage msg)
      = [WM_FIRST + MM_MCINOTIFY];

private:
  void SetButtons(BOOL b1, BOOL b2, BOOL b3, BOOL b4);
  void StopSound();
};
```

This main window class is a bit more complicated than the previous one. First, the data member deviceID holds the ID for the currently open sound device. Because the ID is needed by most MCI functions, it is accessible to all member functions in the class. Following this single data member are the member functions for the class, including the constructor and four message-response functions, one for each of the window's four buttons. Finally, two private member functions, SetButtons() and StopSound(), provide services needed by more than one message-response function.

The fun begins in the main window's constructor, found in SNDWND1.CPP:

```
TSndWnd::TSndWnd(PTWindowsObject AParent,
              LPSTR ATitle): TWindow(AParent, ATitle)
{
  // Set the window's style.
```

510

```
Attr.Style = WS_POPUP | WS_SYSMENU |
          WS_BORDER | WS_CAPTION;

// Set the window's size.
Attr.X = 100;
Attr.Y = 100;
Attr.H = 90;
Attr.W = 372;

// Add buttons to the window.
new TButton(this, ID_PLAY, "Play",
        10, 10, 80, 50, FALSE);
new TButton(this, ID_STOP, "Stop",
        100, 10, 80, 50, FALSE);
new TButton(this, ID_PAUSE, "Pause",
        190, 10, 80, 50, FALSE);
new TButton(this, ID_RESUME, "Resume",
        280, 10, 80, 50, FALSE);
}
```

This constructor is similar to the one for the first sound application, except four buttons are added to the window rather than only one. Also, the window is sized differently so it has room for all four buttons.

Before the main window is displayed, its buttons must be set so only the Play button is enabled. A good place to handle this task is in the window's SetupWindow() function:

```
void TSndWnd::SetupWindow()
{
  // Perform regular setup.
  TWindow::SetupWindow();

  // Enable and disable buttons.
  SetButtons(TRUE, FALSE, FALSE, FALSE);
}
```

In this function, TWindow::SetupWindow() is called first because it provides required services for the class. Then, the function SetButtons() is called:

```
void TSndWnd::SetButtons(BOOL b1, BOOL b2, BOOL b3, BOOL b4)
{
  HWND h = GetDlgItem(HWindow, ID_PLAY);
```

```
  EnableWindow(h, b1);
  h = GetDlgItem(HWindow, ID_STOP);
  EnableWindow(h, b2);
  h = GetDlgItem(HWindow, ID_PAUSE);
  EnableWindow(h, b3);
  h = GetDlgItem(HWindow, ID_RESUME);
  EnableWindow(h, b4);
}
```

This function enables or disables the window's buttons based on the Boolean values supplied as its parameters. To enable or disable a button, the function has simply to obtain each button's handle with a call to `GetDlgItem()` and then to call `EnableWindow()`, passing the requested button state as the second parameter.

Once the main window is constructed and displayed, the program waits for the user to click the Play button. When she does, the message-response function `IDPlay()` takes over:

```
void TSndWnd::IDPlay()
{
  char str[161];
  char elementName[81] = "BEAMUP.WAV";

  MCI_OPEN_PARMS mciOpen;
  MCI_PLAY_PARMS mciPlay;

  // Set up the MCI open parameters.
  mciOpen.dwCallback = 0L;
  mciOpen.wDeviceID = 0;
  mciOpen.wReserved0 = 0;
  mciOpen.lpstrDeviceType = NULL;
  mciOpen.lpstrElementName = elementName;
  mciOpen.lpstrAlias = NULL;

  // Open the waveform audio device.
  DWORD error = mciSendCommand(0, MCI_OPEN,
                  MCI_WAIT | MCI_OPEN_ELEMENT,
              (DWORD) (LPMCI_OPEN_PARMS) &mciOpen);

  // Report an error, if one occurred.
  if (error != 0L)
  {
    // Get the error string.
```

```
      mciGetErrorString(error, str, sizeof(str));

      // Use the error string in a message box.
      MessageBox(HWindow, str, "SOUND",
              MB_OK | MB_ICONEXCLAMATION);
  }
  else
  {

      // Save the audio device's ID.
      deviceID = mciOpen.wDeviceID;

      // Update the buttons.
      SetButtons(FALSE, TRUE, TRUE, FALSE);

      // Set up the MCI play parameters.
      mciPlay.dwCallback = HWindow;
      mciPlay.dwFrom = 0;
      mciPlay.dwTo = 0;

      // Play the sound.
      mciSendCommand(deviceID, MCI_PLAY, MCI_NOTIFY,
          (DWORD) (LPMCI_PLAY_PARMS) &mciPlay);
  }
}
```

As you can see, producing sounds without `sndPlaySound()` is a bit more complicated. Most of the work, though, is accomplished by a single function, `mciSendCommand()`. It is this function's parameters that determine the command being sent to the device.

At the top of the function, the `MCI_OPEN_PARMS` and `MCI_PLAY_PARMS` structures are defined. These structures hold many of the parameters necessary to open and play a sound device. Remember when you defined a `LOGFONT` structure for creating fonts in Chapter 11? These structures work similarly, providing a handy container for the many parameters needed by the MCI functions.

To play a sound from the beginning using the default sound device, simply fill in the `MCI_OPEN_PARMS` structure `mciOpen` as shown in the program. The `lpstrElementName` is a complete path string to the sound you want to play. In this program, `elementName` is always `BEAMUP.WAV`. However, you can make this program more flexible by allowing the user to select any waveform file.

Note: Be sure the file BEAMUP.WAV is in the directory from which you run SNDAPP2. Otherwise, the program is unable to find the file and gives you an error message. If you want your .WAV files in a different directory, you must change `elementName` in `IDPlay()` to that directory.

After setting up the `MCI_OPEN_PARMS` structure, the function calls `mciSendCommand()` to open the sound device. The first parameter is the ID of the device to open. By using a zero, the first available device is chosen. The second parameter is the command message to be sent, in this case, `MCI_OPEN`. The third parameter includes the command flags for the options to be set. There are many, many of these flags, depending on the device being opened. (Refer to Borland's on-disk MCI documentation for a list of all the flags.)

In the function `IDPlay()`, two flags are used: `MCI_WAIT` and `MCI_OPEN_ELEMENT`. The first instructs the MCI to complete the open function before returning control to the program. The second instructs the MCI that `elementName` is a filename for the sound to open. Because this file has a .WAV extension, the MCI opens a waveform device. Finally, the fourth parameter is the address of the `MCI_OPEN_PARMS` structure. After calling `mciSendCommand()` with these parameters, the device ID—if the device was successfully opened—is in the `wDeviceID` field of the structure.

If `mciSendCommand()` manages to do its job, it returns a value of zero. If, however, there's an error, `mciSendCommand()` returns an error code. To display an error message, `IDPlay()` first calls `mciGetErrorString()`, which fills `str` with an appropriate error message. (A terrifically handy function, no? If only all error messages could be so easily constructed.)

The parameters for this function call are the error code received from `mciSendMessage()`, the address of the character array into which the error message should be stored, and the length of the character array. To display the message, the program simply uses `str` in a message box.

To play the sound once the device is opened, `IDPlay()` first fills the `MCI_PLAY_PARMS` structure, `mciPlay`, with appropriate values. The `dwFrom` and `dwTo` fields of this structure indicate where in the file to start the playing and where to end. To play the entire sound, these values are set at zero. The `dwCallback` field must contain the handle of the window to which `MM_MCINOTIFY` messages should be sent, which is, of course, the main window. The `MM_MCINOTIFY` message, as you soon see, informs the program when the sound is finished playing, among other things.

When the MCI_PLAY_PARMS structure is initialized, the program calls mciSendCommand() with a command value of MCI_PLAY to play the sound. This time the call's parameters include the device ID; the MCI_NOTIFY flag, which instructs the MCI to send MM_MCINOTIFY messages to the window with a handle stored in the dwCallback field of the MCI_PLAY_PARMS structure; and the address of the MCI_PLAY_PARMS structure.

If the user allows the entire sound to play, a MM_MCINOTIFY message is sent to the main window. This message is handled by the message-response function MMMCINotify():

```
void TSndWnd::MMMCINotify(RTMessage msg)
{
  // If the sound is done playing, close the device.
  if (msg.WParam == MCI_NOTIFY_SUCCESSFUL)
  {
    StopSound();
  }
}
```

When the MM_MCINOTIFY message's WParam is set to MCI_NOTIFY_SUCCESSFUL, the sound has played to the end. In this case, the sound must be stopped and the device closed, tasks handled by the function StopSound():

```
void TSndWnd::StopSound()
{
  MCI_GENERIC_PARMS mciGeneric;

  // Set up the MCI stop and close parameters.
  mciGeneric.dwCallback = 0L;

  // Stop the device from playing.
  mciSendCommand(deviceID, MCI_STOP, MCI_WAIT,
        (DWORD) (LPMCI_GENERIC_PARMS) &mciGeneric);

  // Close the device.
  mciSendCommand(deviceID, MCI_CLOSE, MCI_WAIT,
        (DWORD) (LPMCI_GENERIC_PARMS) &mciGeneric);

  // Update the buttons.
  SetButtons(TRUE, FALSE, FALSE, FALSE);
}
```

Here, the function first initializes an `MCI_GENERIC_PARMS` structure by setting the `dwCallback` field to zero, which is the only field in the structure. (The program no longer has to intercept `MM_MCINOTIFY` messages.) It then calls `mciSendMessage()` to close the device. Finally, the buttons are set appropriately with a call to `SetButtons()`.

All this work is basically equivalent to the single `sndPlaySound()` function used in the first program. Seems like a lot of work? Sure, but keep in mind that, by using `mciSendMessage()`, the program has greater control over sound. For example, the user can pause the sound by clicking the Pause button, which calls the message-response function `IDPause()`:

```
void TSndWnd::IDPause()
{
  MCI_GENERIC_PARMS mciGeneric;

  // Set up the MCI pause parameters.
  mciGeneric.dwCallback = 0L;

  // Pause the sound.
  mciSendCommand (deviceID, MCI_PAUSE, MCI_WAIT,
          (DWORD)(LPMCI_GENERIC_PARMS) &mciGeneric);

  // Update the buttons.
  SetButtons(FALSE, TRUE, FALSE, TRUE);
}
```

This function isn't much different from `StopSound()`, which you already looked at, except that here the function calls `mciSendMessage()` with a command value of `MCI_PAUSE`. This causes the current sound to stop playing, yet retain its current position. The function to resume play, called when the user clicks the Resume button, also follows the same form as `IDPause()`, except it sends the `MCI_RESUME` command:

```
void TSndWnd::IDResume()
{
  MCI_GENERIC_PARMS mciGeneric;

  // Set up the MCI resume parameters.
    mciGeneric.dwCallback = 0L;

  // Resume the sound.
```

```
mciSendCommand (deviceID, MCI_RESUME, MCI_WAIT,
        (DWORD)(LPMCI_GENERIC_PARMS) &mciGeneric);

  // Update the buttons.
  SetButtons(FALSE, TRUE, TRUE, FALSE);
}
```

This second version of the sound application is much like a CD or tape player because the user can do more than simply play a sound. He can stop the sound at any time, as well as pause the sound and continue play where it left off. Of course, these functions are more valuable for a device such as a CD player. Waveform files are usually too short to warrant anything more than a play command. Using what you've learned here, you should be able to extend your programs to handle other audio devices.

The full listings for the second sound application appear in Listings 14.5 through 14.8.

Listing 14.5. SNDAPP2.CPP—sound application, version 2.

```
// SNDAPP2.CPP -- Sound Application, version 2.

#include <owl.h>
#include "sndwnd2.h"

// Application class declaration.
class TSndApp: public TApplication
{
public:
  TSndApp(LPSTR AName, HINSTANCE AnInstance,
          HINSTANCE APrevInstance, LPSTR ACmdLine,
          int ACmdShow): TApplication(AName,
          AnInstance, APrevInstance, ACmdLine,
          ACmdShow) {};
  virtual void InitMainWindow();
};

///////////////////////////////////////////////////////
// TSndApp::InitMainWindow()
//
// This function creates the application's main window.
///////////////////////////////////////////////////////
```

continues

Listing 14.5. Continued

```
void TSndApp::InitMainWindow()
{
  MainWindow = new TSndWnd(NULL, "Sound Window 2");
}


//////////////////////////////////////////////////////////
// WinMain()
//////////////////////////////////////////////////////////
int PASCAL WinMain(HINSTANCE hInstance, HINSTANCE hPrevInstance,
                   LPSTR lpszCmdLine, int nCmdShow)
{
  TSndApp SndApp("SndApp2", hInstance,
                 hPrevInstance, lpszCmdLine, nCmdShow);
  SndApp.Run();
  return SndApp.Status;
}
```

Listing 14.6. SNDWND2.H—the main window's header file.

```
// SNDWND2.H -- Header file for main window.

#ifndef _SNDWND2_H
#define _SNDWND2_H

#include <mmsystem.h>

#define ID_PLAY    100
#define ID_STOP    101
#define ID_PAUSE   102
#define ID_RESUME  103


_CLASSDEF(TSndWnd)
class TSndWnd: public TWindow
{
  int deviceID;

public:
  TSndWnd(PTWindowsObject AParent, LPSTR ATitle);
  virtual void SetupWindow();
  virtual void IDPlay()
      = [ID_FIRST + ID_PLAY];
```

```
    virtual void IDStop()
        = [ID_FIRST + ID_STOP];
    virtual void IDPause()
        = [ID_FIRST + ID_PAUSE];
    virtual void IDResume()
        = [ID_FIRST + ID_RESUME];
    virtual void MMMCINotify(RTMessage msg)
        = [WM_FIRST + MM_MCINOTIFY];

private:
    void SetButtons(BOOL b1, BOOL b2, BOOL b3, BOOL b4);
    void StopSound();
};


#endif
```

Listing 14.7. SNDWND2.CPP—the main window's implementation.

```
// SNDWND2.CPP -- Implementation for main window.

#include <owl.h>
#include <mmsystem.h>
#include <button.h>
#include "sndwnd2.h"


///////////////////////////////////////////////////////
// TSndWnd::TSndWnd()
//
// This is the main window's constructor.
///////////////////////////////////////////////////////
TSndWnd::TSndWnd(PTWindowsObject AParent,
                LPSTR ATitle): TWindow(AParent, ATitle)
{
    // Set the window's style.
    Attr.Style = WS_POPUP | WS_SYSMENU |
            WS_BORDER | WS_CAPTION;

    // Set the window's size.
    Attr.X = 100;
    Attr.Y = 100;
```

continues

Listing 14.7. Continued

```
  Attr.H = 90;
  Attr.W = 372;

  // Add buttons to the window.
  new TButton(this, ID_PLAY, "Play",
          10, 10, 80, 50, FALSE);
  new TButton(this, ID_STOP, "Stop",
          100, 10, 80, 50, FALSE);
  new TButton(this, ID_PAUSE, "Pause",
          190, 10, 80, 50, FALSE);
  new TButton(this, ID_RESUME, "Resume",
          280, 10, 80, 50, FALSE);
}


/////////////////////////////////////////////////////
// TSndWnd::SetupWindow()
//
// This function disables the buttons that should not
// be functional at the start of the program.
/////////////////////////////////////////////////////
void TSndWnd::SetupWindow()
{
  // Perform regular setup.
  TWindow::SetupWindow();

  // Enable and disable buttons.
  SetButtons(TRUE, FALSE, FALSE, FALSE);
}


/////////////////////////////////////////////////////
// TSndWnd::IDPlay()
//
// This function responds when the Play button is
// clicked.
/////////////////////////////////////////////////////
void TSndWnd::IDPlay()
{
  char str[161];
  char elementName[81] = "C:\\BORLANDC\\BEAMUP.WAV";

  MCI_OPEN_PARMS mciOpen;
  MCI_PLAY_PARMS mciPlay;
```

```
    // Set up the MCI open parameters.
    mciOpen.dwCallback = 0L;
    mciOpen.wDeviceID = 0;
    mciOpen.wReserved0 = 0;
    mciOpen.lpstrDeviceType = NULL;
    mciOpen.lpstrElementName = elementName;
    mciOpen.lpstrAlias = NULL;

    // Open the waveform audio device.
    DWORD error = mciSendCommand(0, MCI_OPEN,
                  MCI_WAIT | MCI_OPEN_ELEMENT,
               (DWORD) (LPMCI_OPEN_PARMS) &mciOpen);

    // Report an error, if one occurred.
    if (error != 0L)
    {
      // Get the error string.
      mciGetErrorString(error, str, sizeof(str));

      // Use the error string in a message box.
      MessageBox(HWindow, str, "SOUND",
                  MB_OK | MB_ICONEXCLAMATION);
    }
    else
    {

      // Save the audio device's ID.
      deviceID = mciOpen.wDeviceID;

      // Update the buttons.
      SetButtons(FALSE, TRUE, TRUE, FALSE);

      // Set up the MCI play parameters.
      mciPlay.dwCallback = HWindow;
      mciPlay.dwFrom = 0;
      mciPlay.dwTo = 0;

      // Play the sound.
      mciSendCommand(deviceID, MCI_PLAY, MCI_NOTIFY,
          (DWORD) (LPMCI_PLAY_PARMS) &mciPlay);
    }
}
```

continues

Listing 14.7. Continued

```
////////////////////////////////////////////////////
// TSndWnd::IDStop()
//
// This function responds when the Stop button is
// clicked.
////////////////////////////////////////////////////
void TSndWnd::IDStop()
{
  StopSound();
}


////////////////////////////////////////////////////
// TSndWnd::IDPause()
//
// This function responds when the Pause button is
// clicked.
////////////////////////////////////////////////////
void TSndWnd::IDPause()
{
  MCI_GENERIC_PARMS mciGeneric;

  // Set up the MCI pause parameters.
  mciGeneric.dwCallback = 0L;

  // Pause the sound.
  mciSendCommand (deviceID, MCI_PAUSE, MCI_WAIT,
          (DWORD)(LPMCI_GENERIC_PARMS) &mciGeneric);

  // Update the buttons.
  SetButtons(FALSE, TRUE, FALSE, TRUE);
}


////////////////////////////////////////////////////
// TSndWnd::IDResume()
//
// This function responds when the Resume button is
// clicked.
////////////////////////////////////////////////////
void TSndWnd::IDResume()
{
  MCI_GENERIC_PARMS mciGeneric;
```

```
    // Set up the MCI resume parameters.
    mciGeneric.dwCallback = 0L;

    // Resume the sound.
    mciSendCommand (deviceID, MCI_RESUME, MCI_WAIT,
            (DWORD)(LPMCI_GENERIC_PARMS) &mciGeneric);

    // Update the buttons.
    SetButtons(FALSE, TRUE, TRUE, FALSE);
}


/////////////////////////////////////////////////////////
// TSndWnd::MMMCINotify()
//
// This function responds to the MM_MCINOTIFY message.
/////////////////////////////////////////////////////////
void TSndWnd::MMMCINotify(RTMessage msg)
{
    // If the sound is done playing, close the device.
    if (msg.WParam == MCI_NOTIFY_SUCCESSFUL)
    {
        StopSound();
    }
}


/////////////////////////////////////////////////////////
// TSndWnd::SetButtons()
//
// This function enables or disables the buttons per the
// Boolean parameters b1, b2, b3, and b4.
/////////////////////////////////////////////////////////
void TSndWnd::SetButtons(BOOL b1, BOOL b2, BOOL b3, BOOL b4)
{
    HWND h = GetDlgItem(HWindow, ID_PLAY);
    EnableWindow(h, b1);
    h = GetDlgItem(HWindow, ID_STOP);
    EnableWindow(h, b2);
    h = GetDlgItem(HWindow, ID_PAUSE);
    EnableWindow(h, b3);
    h = GetDlgItem(HWindow, ID_RESUME);
    EnableWindow(h, b4);
}
```

continues

Listing 14.7. Continued

```
/////////////////////////////////////////////////////
// TSndWnd::StopSound()
//
// This function stops the sound and closes the device.
/////////////////////////////////////////////////////
void TSndWnd::StopSound()
{
  MCI_GENERIC_PARMS mciGeneric;

  // Set up the MCI stop and close parameters.
  mciGeneric.dwCallback = 0L;

  // Stop the device from playing.
  mciSendCommand(deviceID, MCI_STOP, MCI_WAIT,
        (DWORD) (LPMCI_GENERIC_PARMS) &mciGeneric);

  // Close the device.
  mciSendCommand(deviceID, MCI_CLOSE, MCI_WAIT,
        (DWORD) (LPMCI_GENERIC_PARMS) &mciGeneric);

  // Update the buttons.
  SetButtons(TRUE, FALSE, FALSE, FALSE);
}
```

Listing 14.8. SNDAPP.DEF—sound application's definition file.

```
EXETYPE WINDOWS
CODE PRELOAD MOVEABLE DISCARDABLE
DATA PRELOAD MOVEABLE MULTIPLE
HEAPSIZE 4096
STACKSIZE 5120
```

 Caution: Although adding sound to your programs can make them more interesting, you should use sound sparingly. Too many beeps, boops, and zings are bound to annoy your users.

Conclusion

A lthough using the Media Control Interface is complicated at times, it adds a great deal of sound control to your programs. In this chapter, you studied the basics of dealing with sound in Windows. Using the `mciSendMessage()` function, you can also:

- Determine the capabilities of a device (command message `MCI_GETDEVCAPS`).

- Determine the status of a device (`MCI_STATUS`).

- Set a device's parameters (`MCI_SET`).

- Record sound (`MCI_RECORD`).

All these MCI functions (and many others not listed) work similarly to the ones you looked at here, so you should have little trouble incorporating them into your programs.

If you'd like to pursue multimedia sound, you should read the two Borland on-line documentation files, *Multimedia Reference* and *MCI Reference.* In fact, because this documentation is not included in Borland's printed manuals, it's a good idea to print the Help files and organize them into a binder for quick and easy reference. When you examine this documentation, you'll see the kind of power that Windows 3.1's Multimedia Extensions provide for applications programmers. Don't be afraid to tap into that power.

15

Writing Screen Savers for Windows 3.1

lthough computer monitors are no longer prone to screen burn-in (caused by displaying the same image for an extended time), screen savers are more popular than ever—so popular, in fact, that these once shareware-type or public-domain-type programs have graduated into full commercial packages such as Berkeley's *After Dark*. Why are people willing to spend big bucks for silly programs that are little more than glorified graphics demos? Who knows? But, one thing's for sure: If you want to catch a computer user's eye, write a clever screen saver.

In this chapter, you learn to write screen savers for Windows 3.1, a task that is much easier than you might believe because Windows 3.1 handles much of the work for you. The sample screen saver included here shows you how to perform these tricks:

- Blanking out a screen.

- Turning a screen saver off when the user touches a key or moves the mouse.

- Writing the code that is compatible with the Windows 3.1 screen-saver routines.

Where Is SCRNSAVE.LIB?

If you've ever tried to write a screen saver for Windows 3.1, you probably discovered that Microsoft's Software Development Kit (SDK) includes a library of screen-saver routines named SCRNSAVE.LIB—a library not included in Borland C++. Books and magazine articles that show how to write screen savers usually base their programs on this library, which leaves Borland C++ users out in the cold.

Does that mean you can't write a screen saver in Borland C++? Of course not. (You are reading a chapter on screen savers, after all.) The fact is, writing a screen saver with Borland C++ might actually be easier than writing one using SCRNSAVE.LIB, because you don't have to deal with the clumsy code conventions needed to take advantage of Microsoft's screen saver library.

So, chuck out all those old screen-saver tutorials written for Microsoft SDK users. Here, you learn to write Borland C++ screen savers—and you won't even miss SCRNSAVE.LIB.

The Bubbles Screen Saver

Listings 15.1 through 15.7 are the files needed to create Bubbles, a screen saver for Windows 3.1. To create the screen saver, follow these steps:

1. Compile the program, creating a file named BUBBLES.EXE.

2. Transfer BUBBLES.EXE to your Windows directory and rename it BUBBLES.SCR.

3. Bring up the Windows Control Panel and double-click the Desktop icon. The dialog box shown in Figure 15.1 appears on-screen.

4. In the Screen saver box in Figure 15.1, select the Bubbles screen saver, installing it in Windows.

Figure 15.1. The Desktop dialog box.

To see the screen saver in action, you can either wait the amount of time shown in the Desktop dialog's Delay edit field, or you can simply click the Test button. If you want to configure Bubbles, click the Setup button, which displays the dialog box shown in Figure 15.2. Use the listbox to set the number of bubbles that the screen saver must draw before changing colors. A value of 1,000 or 2,000 seems to work best, but experiment and come up with something you like.

Figure 15.2. The Bubbles configuration dialog box.

529

Once you have selected Bubbles and closed the Control Panel, Bubbles automatically kicks into action after your system has been idle for the time you set. After the screen saver has been running, you must only move your mouse, click one of the mouse buttons, or touch a key on your keyboard to turn the screen saver off.

The Screen Saver's Application Class

A screen saver is nothing more mysterious than a Windows application. As such, like the other programs you've developed in this book's Windows section, Bubbles has an *application class*. It is the implementation of this class that makes Bubbles compatible with Windows 3.1 screen savers.

Specifically, to take advantage of Windows' built-in screen saver support, a screen saver has to respond to the command-line switches /c (or -c) and /s (or -s). The /c command-line switch informs a screen saver that the user wants to see the configuration dialog box. The /s switch instructs the screen saver to run.

The user doesn't actually type these command lines (although he could if he wanted to). Windows automatically runs the screen saver with the /s or /c command-line switch when the user clicks the Test or Setup buttons, respectively, in the Desktop dialog. Windows also runs the screen saver with the /s switch when the system has been idle for the selected delay time. Because Bubbles must create its main window based on the /c and /s switches, the command line must be checked in the application class' InitMainWindow() function:

```
void TBubbleApp::InitMainWindow()
{
  // No screen saver window yet.
  pBubWnd = NULL;

  // If the user wants to configure the screen saver,
  // make the configuration dialog the main window.
  if ((((lpCmdLine[0] == '/') || (lpCmdLine[0] == '-')) &&
      ((lpCmdLine[1] == 'c') || (lpCmdLine[1] == 'C')))
    MainWindow = new TBubDlg(NULL, "DIALOG_1");

  // If the user isn't requesting the configuration
  // dialog, it must be time to start the screen saver.
```

```
  else
  {
    pBubWnd = new TBubWnd(NULL, "BUBBLES");
    MainWindow = pBubWnd;
  }
}
```

Here, the function first sets the pointer pBubWnd to null, indicating that there is not yet a screen saver window. Then it checks the command line (which is found in the TModule data member lpCmdLine) to see whether it is /c. If it is, the program creates a TBubDlg dialog box and makes it the application's main window. If the command line is not /c, the program creates a screen saver window of the class TBubWnd and makes it the application's main window. The program saves a pointer to this window in pBubWnd, so the application can call the window's DoSaver() function (described in the section entitled "The Case of the Invisible Window").

Windows automatically runs a screen saver when the user is inactive for the time set in the Desktop dialog box's Delay edit field (assuming, of course, that screen savers are not disabled).

Because a user is idle, though, doesn't mean that all applications are also idle. Suppose, for example, that you're downloading a large file from a BBS. Although you may not have touched the mouse or keyboard during the download, the system is anything but idle. Your telecommunications program is gathering data as fast as it can and storing it on your disk. This activity must not be interrupted. When a screen saver runs, then, it must allow any applications also running to continue unhampered in the background.

In short, a screen saver should draw on-screen only when the system is idle. And, in Windows, idle means that there are currently no messages for any applications in the message queue.

Thanks to ObjectWindows, detecting this idle time is simply a matter of overriding the function IdleAction() in the application:

```
void TBubbleApp::IdleAction()
{
  // If the screen saver window has been created,
  // draw the next shape on the screen.
  if (pBubWnd)
    pBubWnd->DoSaver();
}
```

The function IdleAction(), a member of the TApplication class, is called whenever there are no messages for any application. Here, the function first

531

checks that `pBubWnd` is not NULL, which indicates that the application's main window is indeed the screen-saver window and not the configuration dialog. (`IdleAction()` is called when the screen saver's configuration dialog is on-screen, too. In this case, the program doesn't want to call `DoSaver()`.) If `pBubWnd` is a valid pointer, the window's `DoSaver()` function is called, drawing a single bubble on-screen.

You learn about `DoSaver()` in a later section. But first, you have to know how to handle a screen saver's configuration dialog box.

The Configuration Dialog

Every Windows 3.1 screen saver must provide a configuration dialog box that can be displayed when the user clicks the Setup button. The options offered in this dialog are up to you, as the creator. It is also up to you to see that the configuration selected by the user is properly saved to the CONTROL.INI file, so when the screen saver is activated, it can find this data.

As you have seen, Bubbles' configuration dialog contains a listbox for selecting a bubble count, as well as two buttons—OK and Cancel. This dialog box is defined in the resource file BUBBLES.RC and is implemented in the `TBubDlg` class:

```
_CLASSDEF(TBubDlg)
class TBubDlg: public TDialog
{
  char LBStrg[10];

public:
  TBubDlg(PTWindowsObject AParent, LPSTR AName):
         TDialog( AParent, AName) {}
  virtual void SetupWindow();
  virtual void Ok(RTMessage msg)
    = [ID_FIRST + IDOK];
  virtual void IDListBox(RTMessage msg)
    = [ID_FIRST + ID_LISTBOX];
};
```

This class' private data member `LBStrg` is a character array that holds the string the user selects from the dialog's listbox. In addition, this class has a constructor and three member functions that set up the dialog window and respond to its controls. The first of these, `TBubDlg::SetupWindow()`, initializes the listbox control:

```
void TBubDlg::SetupWindow()
{
  // Do the basic window setup.
  TDialog::SetupWindow();

  // Add strings to the list box.
  SendDlgItemMsg(ID_LISTBOX, LB_ADDSTRING,
                 NULL, (DWORD) "1");
  SendDlgItemMsg(ID_LISTBOX, LB_ADDSTRING,
                 NULL, (DWORD) "10");
  SendDlgItemMsg(ID_LISTBOX, LB_ADDSTRING,
                 NULL, (DWORD) "100");
  SendDlgItemMsg(ID_LISTBOX, LB_ADDSTRING,
                 NULL, (DWORD) "200");
  SendDlgItemMsg(ID_LISTBOX, LB_ADDSTRING,
                 NULL, (DWORD) "400");
  SendDlgItemMsg(ID_LISTBOX, LB_ADDSTRING,
                 NULL, (DWORD) "1000");
  SendDlgItemMsg(ID_LISTBOX, LB_ADDSTRING,
                 NULL, (DWORD) "2000");
  SendDlgItemMsg(ID_LISTBOX, LB_ADDSTRING,
                 NULL, (DWORD) "4000");

  // Set the string to the default value.
  strcpy(LBStrg, "1000");
}
```

This function first calls `TWindow::SetupWindow()` to perform the setup for the basic window. It then calls `SendDlgItemMsg()`, a member function of the ObjectWindows `TDialog` class, for each string that has to be displayed in the dialog's listbox. Finally, the data member `LBStrg` is initialized to its default value.

After `TBubDlg::SetupWindow()` exits, Windows displays the configuration dialog box, and the user can manipulate its controls. If the user clicks the Cancel button, the `TDialog` class' `Cancel()` function closes the dialog. If the user manipulates the listbox (other than scrolling it, which is handled by Windows), the dialog box receives a message with the same ID as the listbox—in this case, `ID_LISTBOX`, which is defined in the dialog's header file BUBDLG.H. This message is handled by the function `IDListBox()`:

```
void TBubDlg::IDListBox(RTMessage msg)
{
  // Did the user change the selection?
```

```
if (msg.LP.Hi == LBN_SELCHANGE)
{
  // Get the index of the selected item.
  DWORD index =
    SendDlgItemMsg(ID_LISTBOX, LB_GETCURSEL, 0, 0L);

  // If the index is valid, get the string the user
  // selected in the list box.
  if (index != LB_ERR)
    SendDlgItemMsg(ID_LISTBOX, LB_GETTEXT,
                   index, (DWORD) LBStrg);
}
}
```

If the user clicks one of the listbox's items, the high word of the message's LParam contains the value LBN_SELCHANGE. (Other possible values include LBN_DBLCLK, LBN_ERRSPACE, LBN_KILLFOCUS, and LBN_SETFOCUS. You can find the descriptions of these messages in the Borland *Windows API Reference Guide,* Volume I, which is included with Borland C++.)

In this case, the program retrieves the selection's index by sending a LB_GETCURSEL message to the listbox. A call to SendDlgItemMsg(), a member function of the TDialog class, sends this message. The value returned is LB_ERR if no item is currently selected. Otherwise, this value is the zero-based index of the selected item. That is, a value of 0 means that the first item was selected, 1 means the second item was selected, and so on.

If index is not equal to LB_ERR, the function can send an LB_GETTEXT message to the listbox to retrieve the selected string. For this message, the WParam (SendDlgItemMsg()'s third parameter) is the index of the item to retrieve, and the LParam (SendDlgItemMsg()'s fourth parameter) is the address of a character array in which to store the selected string.

If the user clicks the OK button to exit, the dialog must save the user's chosen configuration to the Windows Control Panel's CONTROL.INI file. This is accomplished by the class' Ok() message-response function:

```
void TBubDlg::Ok(RTMessage msg)
{
  WritePrivateProfileString("Screen Saver.Bubbles", "Count",
                            LBStrg, "CONTROL.INI");
  TDialog::Ok(msg);
}
```

Saving information to an .INI file is much easier than you might think, because Windows handles most of the file details for you. You need only call the Windows function, `WritePrivateProfileString()` for each value you want to save.

This function's first parameter is the section of the .INI file to which you want the value saved. In the previous example, this section is `"Screen Saver.Bubbles."`. If the section doesn't yet exist in the file, Windows creates it. The second parameter is the label you want used for this value, which, in this function, is `"Count"`. The third parameter is the string that contains the value to be saved (`LBStrg`). Finally, the fourth parameter is the name of the .INI file to which you want the value saved. As stated before, in the case of a screen saver, this is usually the Control Panel's CONTROL.INI file.

After the previous function exits, the user's CONTROL.INI file includes a section that looks something like this:

```
[Screen Saver.Bubbles]
Count=1000
```

If you look at your CONTROL.INI file, you can find similar sections for each screen saver you have configured. For example, a section for the Flying Windows screen saver might look like this:

```
[Screen Saver.Flying Windows]
Density=25
WarpSpeed=5
PWProtected=0
```

The Case of the Invisible Window

N ow that you know how to configure a screen saver, it's time to learn how to run one. This job is handled by the screen saver's main window class, TBubWnd:

```
_CLASSDEF(TBubWnd)
class TBubWnd: public TWindow
{
  POINT mouseXY;
  int count;

public:
  TBubWnd(PTWindowsObject AParent, LPSTR ATitle);
```

535

```
    virtual void GetWindowClass(WNDCLASS &AWndClass);
    virtual LPSTR GetClassName();
    virtual void DefWndProc(RTMessage msg);
    virtual void WMSysCommand(RTMessage msg)
        = [WM_FIRST + WM_SYSCOMMAND];
    virtual void WMDestroy(RTMessage msg)
        = [WM_FIRST + WM_DESTROY];
    virtual void DoSaver();
};
```

This class includes two private data members. The first, `mouseXY`, holds the location of the mouse pointer when the screen saver is activated. The second, `count`, is the variable that holds the configuration value stored in the screen saver's CONTROL.INI section. Besides the usual constructor, this class includes functions to set up the window's class, to handle all the messages to which a screen saver must respond, and a function that produces the screen saver's display. The fun starts in the class' constructor:

```
TBubWnd::TBubWnd(PTWindowsObject AParent,
                 LPSTR ATitle): TWindow(AParent, ATitle)
{
  // Save the mouse pointer's position, and
  // turn the mouse off.
  GetCursorPos(&mouseXY);
  ShowCursor(FALSE);

  // Set the window's style, position, and size.
  Attr.Style = WS_POPUP;
  Attr.X = 0;
  Attr.Y = 0;
  Attr.W = GetSystemMetrics(SM_CXFULLSCREEN);
  Attr.H = GetSystemMetrics(SM_CYFULLSCREEN) +
           GetSystemMetrics(SM_CYCAPTION);

  // Read in the user's count setting.
  count = GetPrivateProfileInt("Screen Saver.Bubbles",
                    "Count", 1000, "CONTROL.INI");

  // Seed random-number generator.
  randomize();
}
```

Here, the program first calls the Windows function GetCursorPos() to get the current position of the mouse pointer, which is saved in mouseXY. Then, the mouse cursor is turned off by another Windows function, ShowCursor(). (When calling this function, a parameter of false turns off the mouse pointer and a value of true turns on the mouse pointer.)

After handling the mouse pointer, the function sets the window's style to WS_POPUP. A window with only this style bit set is no more than a large blank rectangle. In other words, it has no controls or any other graphical element; it's an invisible window.

After the function sets the window's style, it sets the window's size to the full screen. You can determine the width of a window by calling GetSystemMetrics() with a parameter of SM_CXFULLSCREEN, which returns the maximum width of a window's client area. To calculate the height of the window, you must call GetSystemMetrics() twice, once with a parameter of SM_CYFULLSCREEN, which returns the maximum height of a window's client area, and once with a value of SM_CYCAPTION, which returns the height of a window's caption bar. You must sum these two values to get the full height of the screen.

After sizing the window, the constructor reads the user's configuration settings from CONTROL.INI. This is accomplished with a call to the Windows function GetPrivateProfileInt(), which reads an integer value from an .INI file.

The function's first parameter is the section of the file that contains the value. The second parameter is the value's label. The third parameter is the default value to use if the requested value can't be found. Finally, the fourth parameter is the name of the .INI file. After this call, count contains the value the user saved when she configured the screen saver (or the default value of 1,000).

The last action this class' constructor takes is to seed the random-number generator by calling randomize().

 Note: Be sure to call randomize() in any program that uses random numbers. If you fail to do so, the sequence of numbers you receive from random-number functions is always the same.

When you run the Bubbles screen saver, you see that the screen turns black before the saver starts drawing bubbles. This happens because the window's background color is set to black, rather than the usual white, in the class' GetWindowClass() function:

```
void TBubWnd::GetWindowClass(WNDCLASS & AWndClass)
{
  TWindow::GetWindowClass(AWndClass);
  AWndClass.hbrBackground = GetStockObject(BLACK_BRUSH);
}
```

A window can have any background color you like. In this function, the background is set to black, which means the screen saver window isn't invisible, after all. Although it has no controls, this window's background color fills the screen.

 Note: If you like, you can make the screen saver window truly invisible by changing its background color to NULL_BRUSH. When you do this, the screen saver's window does not hide whatever was on-screen when it started. It seems, instead, to draw its graphics directly on top of your Windows desktop. This, of course, is only an illusion, because the screen saver still has its own client area, even though that client area has no background color. When the screen saver window closes, the old desktop is restored whether or not the screen saver window happened to have a background color.

As you saw when looking at the application class, whenever the system is idle, the screen saver's DoSaver() function is called:

```
void TBubWnd::DoSaver(   )
{
  static int cnt = 0;
  static COLORREF color = RND_RGB;
  LOGBRUSH lb;

  // Increment the draw count, and change
  // colors if it's time to change.
  ++cnt;
  if (cnt == count)
  {
    color = RND_RGB;
    cnt = 0;
  }

  // Create and select a new brush for drawing shapes.
```

```
        lb.lbColor = color;
        lb.lbStyle = BS_SOLID;
        lb.lbHatch = 0;
        HDC hDC = GetDC(HWindow);
        HBRUSH newBrush = CreateBrushIndirect(&lb);
        HBRUSH oldBrush = SelectObject(hDC, newBrush);

        // Get a random location for the next circle,
        // and draw the circle.
        int x = random(GetSystemMetrics(SM_CXFULLSCREEN));
        int y = random(GetSystemMetrics(SM_CYFULLSCREEN) +
                    GetSystemMetrics(SM_CYCAPTION));
        Ellipse(hDC, x-5, y-5, x+15, y+15);

        // Restore the DC and delete the custom brush.
        SelectObject(hDC, oldBrush);
        DeleteObject(newBrush);
        ReleaseDC(HWindow, hDC);
}
```

There's nothing too fancy here. This function simply draws circles of random colors on-screen. First, the static variable cnt is incremented and checked to determine whether it is equal to count, which, if you remember, is the value read from the user's configuration. If the values are equal, it's time to change the bubbles' color. This is accomplished by invoking the RND_RGB macro, which is defined at the top of the file as:

```
#define RND_RGB RGB(random(256),random(256),random(256))
```

This macro calls the Windows function RGB() to get a new color. The function's three parameters are the intensity of the red, green, and blue color elements, respectively. In this case, these three values are calculated by calling random() to get a random value.

Following the new color's calculation, cnt is set back to zero.

After checking cnt, the program creates a new solid brush of the current color, gets a DC for the window, selects the brush into the DC, and draws a circle at a random screen coordinate. Finally, the old brush is selected back into the DC, the custom brush is deleted, and the DC is released.

As you can see, this is a relatively simple screen saver. But you can add bells and whistles to it by adding code to the DoSaver() function, which is the heart of the screen saver's graphical display. In fact, you'll probably want to completely rewrite DoSaver() when you create your own screen savers. Let your imagination run wild. The crazier your screen saver is, the more people will like it.

 Note: The Bubbles screen saver draws one bubble on-screen each time the DoSaver() function is called by the application object. DoSaver() is called only when the system is idle. Still, even when there are applications running in the background, bubbles appear on-screen at an amazing rate. This shows how much free time Windows actually has, even when it's supposedly busy.

Avoiding Multiple Screen Savers

A screen saver is little more to Windows than another application. This means that, even when a screen saver is running, Windows keeps counting down its screen-saver delay clock. When the time expires, Windows tries to run the selected screen saver.

To avoid multiple instances of a screen saver, the program's main window must watch for WM_SYSCOMMAND messages, which signal several system activities, including the starting of screen savers. In Bubbles, this message is captured by the function WMSysCommand():

```
void TBubWnd::WMSysCommand(RTMessage msg)
{
  // If Windows is trying to start the screen saver
  // again, don't let it.
  if ((msg.WParam & 0xFFF0) == SC_SCREENSAVE)
  {
    msg.Result = 0;
  }
  else
    DefWndProc(msg);
}
```

Here, the function checks the message's WParam field to see whether it's set to SC_SCREENSAVE—the message that Windows sends when it wants to start a screen saver. (According to the Windows documentation, the WParam of the WM_SYSCOMMAND message must be ANDed with the mask 0xFFF0 before it's checked, because Windows sometimes uses the lowest four bits of WParam to store additional information.) If this function detects a `SC_SCREENSAVE` message, it returns a value of zero in the message's `Result` field, informing Windows that the program has handled this message and Windows can ignore it. Any other `WM_SYSCOMMAND` messages must be passed back to Windows by the `TWindowsObject` class' `DefWndProc()` function.

If you want to see what happens when a screen saver doesn't capture the `SC_SCREENSAVE` message, comment out all the lines in the previous function except the call to `DefWndProc()` and recompile the program. Install the new version of the screen saver, setting the screen saver's delay (in the Desktop dialog box, accessed by the Control Panel) to one minute. Watch the screen. After a minute, Windows starts the screen saver. Each following minute, Windows starts the screen saver again. Ouch!

Caution: In order to prevent Windows from running multiple instances of your screen saver, you must process `WM_SYSCOMMAND` messages in your program. When a `WM_SYSCOMMAND` message with a `WParam` of `SC_SCREENSAVE` is sent to your program, you should return a false to Windows, instead of passing the message back to Windows for processing.

Closing a Screen Saver

As you probably already know, every screen saver should automatically close when the user moves her mouse, types with her keyboard, or when another application tries to open a window. In a Windows screen saver, closing the screen saver is accomplished easily by watching messages. To watch for the appropriate types of messages, the screen saver's main window class must override `TWindowsObject`'s `DefWndProc()` function:

```
void TBubWnd::DefWndProc(RTMessage msg)
{
  switch(msg.Message)
  {
    // Check whether mouse has actually moved.
    // If not, do nothing.
    case WM_MOUSEMOVE:
      if (msg.LP.Lo == mouseXY.x &&
          msg.LP.Hi == mouseXY.y)
        break;
```

```
      // If another window wants to be activated,
      // shut down the screen saver.
      case WM_ACTIVATE:
      case WM_ACTIVATEAPP:
        if (msg.WParam != 0)
          break;

      // If any user input is received,
      // close the screen saver window.
      case WM_KEYDOWN:
      case WM_SYSKEYDOWN:
      case WM_LBUTTONDOWN:
      case WM_MBUTTONDOWN:
      case WM_RBUTTONDOWN:
        PostMessage(HWindow, WM_CLOSE, 0, 0L);

      default:
        break;
  }

  // Send messages for default processing.
  TWindow::DefWndProc(msg);
}
```

If the user moves her mouse, this function receives a WM_MOUSEMOVE message. Before acting on this message, however, the function first checks whether the current mouse location is the same as the mouse's location when the screen saver started. If it is, the mouse wasn't really moved. Rather, the screen saver window simply had a WM_MOUSEMOVE message in its message queue when the screen saver started. In this case, TBubWnd::DefWndProc() does nothing.

On the other hand, if the two sets of coordinates are not the same, the mouse has been moved and program execution falls through the other case statements to the call to PostMessage(), which closes the screen saver window by sending a WM_CLOSE message to Windows. If you fail to process the WM_MOUSEMOVE message this way in a screen saver application, the screen saver closes immediately after starting, just as if the user had moved the mouse.

This function must also check for WM_ACTIVATE and WM_ACTIVATEAPP messages, because these messages indicate that another application is trying to open a window. When another window is opening, the screen saver must yield the right of way, as it were, closing its window and letting the other application have the screen. If the WParam for these messages is non-zero, a window is trying to open.

The `case` statement reaches the `break` and program execution drops down to the call to `DefWndProc()`, which processes the message. If the message's `WParam` field is zero, Windows is informing the program that it wants to close the screen saver window. In this case, the program drops through the `case` statements and reaches the call to `PostMessage()`, which closes the window. Closing the window prevents the screen saver window from running behind another application's window.

Similarly, if this function receives a `WM_KEYDOWN`, `WM_SYSKEYDOWN`, `WM_LBUTTONDOWN`, `WM_MBUTTONDOWN`, or `WM_RBUTTONDOWN` message, this means the user has pressed either a keyboard key or a mouse button, in either case the screen saver must also be closed by calling `PostMessage()`. In any case, all messages are eventually passed back to Windows by `TWindow::DefWndProc()` for default handling.

The last action the screen saver must take before closing is to restore the mouse pointer. In Bubbles, this is accomplished by responding to the `WM_DESTROY` message, which Windows sends immediately before a window is destroyed:

```
void TBubWnd::WMDestroy(RTMessage msg)
{
  // Make the mouse pointer visible again.
  ShowCursor(TRUE);

  // Continue with normal WM_DESTROY processing.
  TWindow::WMDestroy(msg);
}
```

This function simply restores the mouse pointer, then passes the `WM_DESTROY` message to `TWindow::WMDestroy()` so the window can close.

Registering a Screen Saver with the Desktop

W hen the user opens the Desktop dialog box, Windows searches for screen savers and reads their names into the Name listbox of the Screen Saver's dialog box. (To be recognized as a screen saver by Windows, a program must have an .SCR file extension.)

Where does Windows find the screen savers' names? They are part of each executable file, placed there by the linker. You pass this name to the linker by placing it in the application's definition file, as so:

```
NAME          BUBBLES
DESCRIPTION 'SCRNSAVE :Bubbles'
EXETYPE WINDOWS
CODE PRELOAD MOVEABLE DISCARDABLE
DATA PRELOAD MOVEABLE MULTIPLE
HEAPSIZE 4096
STACKSIZE 5120
```

In this definition file, the DESCRIPTION line provides the name. You must include the string 'SCRNSAVE :' followed by the name you want to appear in the Desktop dialog. In this case, the name that appears is "Bubbles".

Listing 15.1. BUBBLES.CPP—the screen saver application.

```cpp
// BUBBLES.CPP -- Screen Saver Application.

#include <owl.h>
#include "bubwnd.h"
#include "bubdlg.h"

// Application class declaration.
class TBubbleApp: public TApplication
{
  PTBubWnd pBubWnd;

public:
  TBubbleApp(LPSTR AName, HINSTANCE AnInstance,
             HINSTANCE APrevInstance, LPSTR ACmdLine,
             int ACmdShow): TApplication(AName,
             AnInstance, APrevInstance, ACmdLine,
             ACmdShow) {}
  virtual void InitMainWindow();
  virtual void IdleAction();
};

/////////////////////////////////////////////////////////
// TBubbleApp::InitMainWindow()
//
// This function creates the application's main window.
/////////////////////////////////////////////////////////
void TBubbleApp::InitMainWindow()
{
  // No screen saver window yet.
  pBubWnd = NULL;
```

```
    // If the user wants to configure the screen saver,
    // make the configuration dialog the main window.
    if ((((lpCmdLine[0] == '/') || (lpCmdLine[0] == '-')) &&
        ((lpCmdLine[1] == 'c') || (lpCmdLine[1] == 'C')))
      MainWindow = new TBubDlg(NULL, "DIALOG_1");

    // If the user isn't requesting the configuration
    // dialog, it must be time to start the screen saver.
    else
    {
      pBubWnd = new TBubWnd(NULL, "BUBBLES");
      MainWindow = pBubWnd;
    }
}


/////////////////////////////////////////////////////////
// TBubbleApp::IdleAction()
//
// This function is called whenever there are no
// messages in the message queue for any application.
/////////////////////////////////////////////////////////
void TBubbleApp::IdleAction()
{
  // If the screen saver window has been created,
  // draw the next shape on the screen.
  if (pBubWnd)
    pBubWnd->DoSaver();
}


/////////////////////////////////////////////////////////
// WinMain()
/////////////////////////////////////////////////////////
int PASCAL WinMain(HINSTANCE hInstance,
                   HINSTANCE hPrevInstance,
                   LPSTR lpszCmdLine, int nCmdShow)
{
  TBubbleApp BubbleApp("Screen Saver.Bubbles", hInstance,
                  hPrevInstance, lpszCmdLine, nCmdShow);
  BubbleApp.Run();
  return BubbleApp.Status;
}
```

Listing 15.2. BUBWND.H—the main window header file.

```
// BUBWND.H -- Main window header file.

#ifndef _BUBWND_H
#define _BUBWND_H

#include <owl.h>

_CLASSDEF(TBubWnd)
class TBubWnd: public TWindow
{
  POINT mouseXY;
  int count;

public:
  TBubWnd(PTWindowsObject AParent, LPSTR ATitle);
  virtual void GetWindowClass(WNDCLASS &AWndClass);
  virtual LPSTR GetClassName();
  virtual void DefWndProc(RTMessage msg);
  virtual void WMSysCommand(RTMessage msg)
      = [WM_FIRST + WM_SYSCOMMAND];
  virtual void WMDestroy(RTMessage msg)
      = [WM_FIRST + WM_DESTROY];
  virtual void DoSaver();
};

#endif
```

Listing 15.3. BUBWND.CPP—the main window implementation.

```
// BUBWND.CPP -- Main window implementation.

#include <stdlib.h>
#include <time.h>
#include "bubwnd.h"

#define RND_RGB RGB(random(256),random(256),random(256))


//////////////////////////////////////////////////////
// TBubWnd::TBubWnd()
//
```

546

```
// This is the main window's constructor.
//////////////////////////////////////////////////////////
TBubWnd::TBubWnd(PTWindowsObject AParent,
                LPSTR ATitle): TWindow(AParent, ATitle)
{
  // Save the mouse pointer's position, and
  // turn the mouse off.
  GetCursorPos(&mouseXY);
  ShowCursor(FALSE);

  // Set the window's style, position, and size.
  Attr.Style = WS_POPUP;
  Attr.X = 0;
  Attr.Y = 0;
  Attr.W = GetSystemMetrics(SM_CXFULLSCREEN);
  Attr.H = GetSystemMetrics(SM_CYFULLSCREEN) +
           GetSystemMetrics(SM_CYCAPTION);

  // Read in the user's count setting.
  count = GetPrivateProfileInt("Screen Saver.Bubbles",
                     "Count", 1000, "CONTROL.INI");

  // Seed random-number generator.
  randomize();
}


//////////////////////////////////////////////////////////
// TBubWnd::GetWindowClass()
//
// This function sets up the new window class.
//////////////////////////////////////////////////////////
void TBubWnd::GetWindowClass(WNDCLASS & AWndClass)
{
  TWindow::GetWindowClass(AWndClass);
  AWndClass.hbrBackground = GetStockObject(BLACK_BRUSH);
}


//////////////////////////////////////////////////////////
// TBubWnd::GetClassName()
//
// This function returns the new class' name.
//////////////////////////////////////////////////////////
```

continues

547

Listing 15.3. Continued

```
LPSTR TBubWnd::GetClassName()
{
  return "BubblesWnd";
}


//////////////////////////////////////////////////////
// TBubWnd::DefWndProc()
//
// This function receives all the messages for this
// window. Messages that are not needed by the window
// are passed on for default processing.
//////////////////////////////////////////////////////
void TBubWnd::DefWndProc(RTMessage msg)
{
  switch(msg.Message)
  {
    // Check whether mouse has actually moved.
    // If not, do nothing.
    case WM_MOUSEMOVE:
      if (msg.LP.Lo == mouseXY.x &&
          msg.LP.Hi == mouseXY.y)
        break;

    // If another window wants to be activated,
    // shut down the screen saver.
    case WM_ACTIVATE:
    case WM_ACTIVATEAPP:
      if (msg.WParam != 0)
        break;

    // If any user input is received,
    // close the screen saver window.
    case WM_KEYDOWN:
    case WM_SYSKEYDOWN:
    case WM_LBUTTONDOWN:
    case WM_MBUTTONDOWN:
    case WM_RBUTTONDOWN:
      PostMessage(HWindow, WM_CLOSE, 0, 0L);

    default:
      break;
  }
```

```
  // Send messages for default processing.
  TWindow::DefWndProc(msg);
}


////////////////////////////////////////////////////
// TBubWnd::WMSysCommand()
//
// This function responds to the WM_SYSCOMMAND message,
// checking whether the screen saver is trying to
// start up while it's already active.
////////////////////////////////////////////////////
void TBubWnd::WMSysCommand(RTMessage msg)
{
  // If Windows is trying to start the screen saver
  // again, don't let it.
  if ((msg.WParam & 0xFFF0) == SC_SCREENSAVE)
  {
    msg.Result = 0;
  }
  else
    DefWndProc(msg);
}


////////////////////////////////////////////////////
// TBubWnd::WMDestroy()
//
// This function is called just before the window is
// destroyed.
////////////////////////////////////////////////////
void TBubWnd::WMDestroy(RTMessage msg)
{
  // Make the mouse pointer visible again.
  ShowCursor(TRUE);

  // Continue with normal WM_DESTROY processing.
  TWindow::WMDestroy(msg);
}


////////////////////////////////////////////////////
// TBubWnd::DoSaver()
//
```

continues

Listing 15.3. Continued

```
// This function draws the screen saver graphics. It is
// called by the screen saver's application object
// whenever the message queue is idle.
/////////////////////////////////////////////////////////
void TBubWnd::DoSaver()
{
  static int cnt = 0;
  static COLORREF color = RND_RGB;
  LOGBRUSH lb;

  // Increment the draw count, and change
  // colors if it's time to change.
  ++cnt;
  if (cnt == count)
  {
    color = RND_RGB;
    cnt = 0;
  }

  // Create and select a new brush for drawing shapes.
  lb.lbColor = color;
  lb.lbStyle = BS_SOLID;
  lb.lbHatch = 0;
  HDC hDC = GetDC(HWindow);
  HBRUSH newBrush = CreateBrushIndirect(&lb);
  HBRUSH oldBrush = SelectObject(hDC, newBrush);

  // Get a random location for the next circle,
  // and draw the circle.
  int x = random(GetSystemMetrics(SM_CXFULLSCREEN));
  int y = random(GetSystemMetrics(SM_CYFULLSCREEN) +
                 GetSystemMetrics(SM_CYCAPTION));
  Ellipse(hDC, x-5, y-5, x+15, y+15);

  // Restore the DC and delete the custom brush.
  SelectObject(hDC, oldBrush);
  DeleteObject(newBrush);
  ReleaseDC(HWindow, hDC);
}
```

Listing 15.4. BUBDLG.H—the configuration dialog header file.

```
// BUBDLG.H -- Dialog header file.

#ifndef _BUBDLG_H
#define _BUBDLG_H

#include <owl.h>

#define ID_LISTBOX 101

_CLASSDEF(TBubDlg)
class TBubDlg: public TDialog
{
  char LBStrg[10];

public:
  TBubDlg(PTWindowsObject AParent, LPSTR AName):
          TDialog( AParent, AName) {}
  virtual void SetupWindow();
  virtual void Ok(RTMessage msg)
     = [ID_FIRST + IDOK];
  virtual void IDListBox(RTMessage msg)
     = [ID_FIRST + ID_LISTBOX];
};

#endif
```

Listing 15.5. BUBDLG.CPP—the configuration dialog implementation.

```
// BUBDLG.CPP -- Settings dialog implementation.

#include <string.h>
#include "bubdlg.h"

/////////////////////////////////////////////////////////
// TBubDlg::SetupWindow()
//
// This function does last-minute window setup,
// including adding strings to the dialog's list box
// and initializing the string that will contain the
```

continues

551

Listing 15.5. Continued

```
// user's selection from the list box.
//////////////////////////////////////////////////////
void TBubDlg::SetupWindow()
{
  // Do the basic window setup.
  TDialog::SetupWindow();

  // Add strings to the list box.
  SendDlgItemMsg(ID_LISTBOX, LB_ADDSTRING,
                 NULL, (DWORD) "1");
  SendDlgItemMsg(ID_LISTBOX, LB_ADDSTRING,
                 NULL, (DWORD) "10");
  SendDlgItemMsg(ID_LISTBOX, LB_ADDSTRING,
                 NULL, (DWORD) "100");
  SendDlgItemMsg(ID_LISTBOX, LB_ADDSTRING,
                 NULL, (DWORD) "200");
  SendDlgItemMsg(ID_LISTBOX, LB_ADDSTRING,
                 NULL, (DWORD) "400");
  SendDlgItemMsg(ID_LISTBOX, LB_ADDSTRING,
                 NULL, (DWORD) "1000");
  SendDlgItemMsg(ID_LISTBOX, LB_ADDSTRING,
                 NULL, (DWORD) "2000");
  SendDlgItemMsg(ID_LISTBOX, LB_ADDSTRING,
                 NULL, (DWORD) "4000");

  // Set the string to the default value.
  strcpy(LBStrg, "1000");
}


//////////////////////////////////////////////////////
// TBubDlg::IDListBox()
//
// This function responds to the ID_LISTBOX message,
// which is generated whenever the user does something
// with the list box.
//////////////////////////////////////////////////////
void TBubDlg::IDListBox(RTMessage msg)
{
  // Did the user change the selection?
  if (msg.LP.Hi == LBN_SELCHANGE)
  {
    // Get the index of the selected item.
```

```
   DWORD index =
     SendDlgItemMsg(ID_LISTBOX, LB_GETCURSEL, 0, 0L);

   // If the index is valid, get the string the user
   // selected in the list box.
   if (index != LB_ERR)
     SendDlgItemMsg(ID_LISTBOX, LB_GETTEXT,
                    index, (DWORD) LBStrg);
 }
}


//////////////////////////////////////////////////////////
// TBubDlg::Ok()
//
// This function responds when the user selects the
// dialog's OK button. It writes the new count setting
// out to the CONTROL.INI file.
//////////////////////////////////////////////////////////
void TBubDlg::Ok(RTMessage msg)
{
  WritePrivateProfileString("Screen Saver.Bubbles", "Count",
                            LBStrg, "CONTROL.INI");

  TDialog::Ok(msg);
}
```

Listing 15.6. BUBBLES.RC—the application's resource file.

```
DIALOG_1 DIALOG 100, 80, 92, 86
STYLE DS_MODALFRAME ¦ WS_POPUP ¦ WS_CAPTION ¦ WS_SYSMENU
CAPTION "Bubbles Setup"
BEGIN
        PUSHBUTTON "OK", 1, 4, 68, 40, 14,
          WS_CHILD ¦ WS_VISIBLE ¦ WS_TABSTOP
        PUSHBUTTON "Cancel", 2, 49, 68, 39, 14,
          WS_CHILD ¦ WS_VISIBLE ¦ WS_TABSTOP
        CONTROL "", 101, "LISTBOX",
          LBS_NOTIFY ¦ WS_CHILD ¦ WS_VISIBLE ¦
          WS_BORDER ¦ WS_VSCROLL, 31, 28, 31, 33
        LTEXT "Set number of bubbles before color change:",
          -1, 9, 4, 77, 18,
          WS_CHILD ¦ WS_VISIBLE ¦ WS_GROUP
END
```

Listing 15.7. BUBBLES.DEF—the application's definition file.

```
NAME        BUBBLES
DESCRIPTION 'SCRNSAVE :Bubbles'
EXETYPE WINDOWS
CODE PRELOAD MOVEABLE DISCARDABLE
DATA PRELOAD MOVEABLE MULTIPLE
HEAPSIZE 4096
STACKSIZE 5120
```

Conclusion

That's all there is to writing Windows 3.1 screen savers. They may be trivial when compared with applications like Microsoft Word for Windows and the Borland C++ compiler, but, hey, they're fun to write and even more fun to watch. Who ever said you couldn't have fun with Windows?

Over the course of the last 15 chapters, you've learned a great deal about programming in DOS and Windows. This book has only hinted, however, at the power you have to create attractive, useful, and easy-to-use applications. To take advantage of that power, spend as much time programming as you can, and never be afraid to experiment. Practice and experimentation are the keys to becoming a masterful programmer.

III

References

DOS Window Library Quick Reference

Class *Windw*

This is a blank window with or without a border or screen-image buffering.

Data Members

`int *buffer`   Private

This is the pointer to the buffer containing the screen image to be restored when the window is erased. This buffer is active only when the window is created with `buf = 1`.

`int border`   Protected

A value of 1 means the window has a border. A value of 0 means the window has no border.

`int buffered`   Protected

A value of 1 means that the screen image behind the window has been buffered and should be redrawn when the window is erased. A value of 0 means there is no image buffering.

```
int wx, wy, ww, wh                                          Protected
```

These are the window's x,y position, width, and height.

```
Evntmsg evntmsg                                             Protected
```

The event-message structure for interactive windows.

Member Functions

```
Windw(int x, int y, int w, int h,
      int brd, int buf)                                     Public
```

This is the basic window's constructor. When constructing a `Windw`, you must supply the x,y coordinate of its upper-left corner, the width and height in pixels, and Boolean values indicating whether the window should have a border and whether the screen image behind the window should be buffered for redrawing.

```
~Windw(void)                                                Public
```

This is the basic window's destructor. If a window has image buffering turned on, the destructor restores the image to the screen and deletes the buffer. Otherwise, the destructor does nothing.

```
virtual void DrawWindow(void)                               Public
```

Call this function to draw a window on-screen. In addition to drawing the window's image, this function saves the screen image behind the window (if buffering is on, which is indicated by the value of `buffered`). Each derived window class should include its own virtual `DrawWindow()` function.

```
virtual void RunWindow(void)                                Public
```

Call this function to turn control over to an interactive window. Control returns to your program only after the user exits the window. In the case of the basic `Windw`, the user can exit the window by clicking the mouse or pressing any key. Each window class has its own virtual `RunWindow()` function.

```
void WindwError(char *s)                                    Private
```

This function reports the error message pointed to by `s`, then aborts the program. It is used for fatal errors, such as the incapability to create a new window.

Inherited Data Members

None.

Inherited Member Functions

None.

Class *CapWindw* <- *Windw*

This is a window with a caption bar at the top.

Data Members

```
char label[61]                                    Protected
```

This character array holds the caption to be displayed at the top of the window.

Member Functions

```
CapWindw(int x, int y, int w, int h,
      int brd, int buf, char *s)                   Public
```

This is the captioned window's constructor. When constructing `CapWindw`, you must supply the x,y coordinate of its upper-left corner, its width and height in pixels, and Boolean values indicating whether the window should have a border and whether the screen image behind the window should be buffered for redrawing. You should also supply the text for the label to be displayed.

```
virtual void DrawWindow(void)                      Public
```

Call this function to draw a captioned window on-screen. This function first calls `Windw::DrawWindow()` to draw the basic window.

```
void SetCaption(char *s)                           Public
```

This function changes the label displayed at the top of the window. The new label is in the character array pointed to by `s`.

```
void DrawCapBar(void)                             Private
```

This function draws the caption bar on the window.

Inherited Data Members

```
Windw ->  int wx, wy, ww, wh
      int border, buffered
      EvntMsg evntmsg
```

Inherited Member Functions

```
Windw -> RunWindow(void)
```

Class *CapTWindw <- CapWindw <- Windw*

This is a captioned window that can display two lines of text in the window's work area. The width of a captioned text window is determined by the width of the longest text line it must display. The height is set to 150 pixels. This type of window is automatically displayed in the center of the screen.

Data Members

```
char *line1, *line2
```
                                                                    Protected

These are pointers to the two text lines to be displayed in the labeled text window.

```
int button
```
                                                                    Protected

This is the value of the last pressed button. This field is not used in this class, but rather in classes derived from this class.

Member Functions

```
CapTWindw(char *s1, char *s2, char *s3)
```
                                                                      Public

This is the captioned text window's constructor. It first calls the `CapWindw` constructor. When constructing a captioned text window, you should supply the text for the label (`*s1`) and the text for the work area of the window (`*s2` and `*s3`).

```
virtual void DrawWindow(void)
```
                                                                      Public

Call this function to draw a labeled text window on-screen. This function first calls `CapWindw::DrawWindow()` to draw the labeled window. It then draws its text in the window's work area.

```
int GetButton(void)
```
                                                                      Public

Call this function to retrieve the value of the `button` data member, which holds the value of the last button pressed. This function is not used in this class, but rather in classes derived from this class.

Inherited Data Members

```
Windw ->  int wx, wy, ww, wh
     int border, buffered
     EvntMsg evntmsg
CapWindw ->    char label[61]
```

Inherited Member Functions

```
CapWindw ->    SetCaption(char *s)
Windw ->  RunWindow(void);
```

Class *OKWindw* <- *CapTWindw* <- *CapWindw* <- *Windw*

This is a message box that can display two lines of text in the window's work area, along with an OK button at the bottom of the window. The width of an OK window is determined by the width of the longest text line it must display. The height is set to 150 pixels. This type of window is automatically displayed in the center of the screen.

Data Members

```
Button *butn                                          Private
```

This is a pointer to the OK window's button.

Member Functions

```
OKWindw(char *s1, char *s2, char *s3)                 Public
```

This is the OK window's constructor. It first calls the `CapTWindw` constructor. When constructing an OK window, you should supply the text for the label (`*s1`) and the text message for the work area of the window (`*s2` and `*s3`).

```
~OKWindw(void)                                        Public
```

This is the OK window's destructor. It deletes the window's button object from memory before the OK window is deleted.

561

```
virtual void DrawWindow(void)                               Public
```

Call this function to draw an OK window on-screen. This function first calls `CapTWindw::DrawWindow()` to draw the captioned text window. It then draws the window's OK button.

```
virtual void RunWindow(void)                                Public
```

This function turns control of the program over to the OK window and returns only when the user closes the OK window, either by selecting its OK button or pressing the Esc key to cancel the dialog.

Inherited Data Members

```
Windw ->  int wx, wy, ww, wh
     int border, buffered
     EvntMsg evntmsg
CapWindw ->    char label[61]
CapTWindw ->   int button
     char *line1, *line2
```

Inherited Member Functions

```
CapWindw ->    SetCaption(char *s)
CapTWindw ->   GetButton(void)
```

Class *YesNoWindw* <- *CapTWindw* <- *CapWindw* <- *Windw*

This is a message box that can display two lines of text in the window's work area, along with Yes and No buttons at the bottom of the window. The width of a Yes/No window is determined by the width of the longest text line it must display. The height is set to 150 pixels. This type of window is automatically displayed in the center of the screen.

Data Members

```
Button *butn1, *butn2                                       Private
```

These are pointers to the Yes/No window's buttons.

Member Functions

```
YesNoWindw(char *s1, char *s2, char *s3)                    Public
```

This is the Yes/No window's constructor, which first calls the `CapTWindw` constructor. When constructing a Yes/No window, you should supply the text for the label (`*s1`) and the text message for the work area of the window (`*s2` and `*s3`).

`~YesNoWindw(void)`   Public

This is the Yes/No window's destructor. It deletes the window's button objects from memory before the window is deleted.

`virtual void DrawWindow(void)`   Public

Call this function to draw a Yes/No window on-screen. This function first calls `CapTWindw::DrawWindow()` to draw the captioned text window. It then draws the window's Yes and No buttons.

`virtual void RunWindow(void)`   Public

This function turns control of the program over to the Yes/No Window and returns only when the user closes the Window, either by selecting one of its buttons or by pressing the Esc key to cancel the dialog.

Inherited Data Members

```
Windw ->  int wx, wy, ww, wh
     int border, buffered
     EvntMsg evntmsg
CapWindw ->    char label[61]
CapTWindw ->   int button
     char *line1, *line2
```

Inherited Member Functions

```
CapWindw ->    SetCaption(char *s)
CapTWindw ->   GetButton(void)
```

Class *YesNoCanWindw* <- *CapTWindw* <- *CapWindw* <- *Windw*

This is a message box that can display two lines of text in the window's work area, along with Yes, No, and Cancel buttons at the bottom of the window. The width of the Yes/No/Cancel window is determined by the width of the longest text line it must display. The height is set to 150 pixels. This type of window is automatically displayed in the center of the screen.

Data Members

```
Button *butn1, *butn2, *butn3                          Private
```

These are pointers to the Yes/No/Cancel window's buttons.

Member Functions

```
YesNoCanWindw(char *s1, char *s2, char *s3             Public
```

This is the Yes/No/Cancel window's constructor, which first calls the `CapTWindw` constructor. When constructing a Yes/No/Cancel window, you should supply the text for the label (`*s1`) and the text message for the work area of the window (`*s2` and `*s3`).

```
~YesNoCanWindw(void)                                   Public
```

This is the Yes/No/Cancel window's destructor. It deletes the window's button objects from memory before the window is deleted.

```
virtual void DrawWindow(void)                          Public
```

Call this function to draw a Yes/No/Cancel window on-screen. This function first calls `CapTWindw::DrawWindow()` to draw the captioned text window. It then draws the window's Yes, No, and Cancel buttons.

```
virtual void RunWindow(void)                           Public
```

This function turns control of the program over to the Yes/No/Cancel window and returns only when the user closes the window, either by selecting one of its buttons or by pressing Esc to cancel the dialog.

Inherited Data Members

```
Windw ->  int wx, wy, ww, wh
     int border, buffered
     EvntMsg evntmsg
CapWindw ->   char label[61]
CapTWindw ->  int button
     char *line1, *line2
```

Inherited Member Functions

```
CapWindw ->    SetCaption(char *s)
CapTWindw ->   GetButton(void)
```

Class *InputWindw* <- *CapTWindw* <- *CapWindw* <- *Windw*

This is an input dialog that can display two lines of text in the window's work area, along with OK and Cancel buttons at the bottom of the window. The width of an input window is determined by the width of the longest text line it must display. The height is set to 150 pixels. This type of window is automatically displayed in the center of the screen. Use this window to accept single-line text strings from the user. Up to 80 characters can be entered into the window's scrolling text-entry field.

Data Members

```
Button *butn1, *butn2                              Private
```

These are pointers to the input window's buttons.

```
char input[81]                                     Private
```

This character array holds the user's input line.

Member Functions

```
InputWindw(char *s1, char *s2, char *s3)            Public
```

This is the input window's constructor, which first calls the `CapTWindw` constructor. When constructing an input window, you should supply the text for the label (`*s1`) and the text message for the work area of the window (`*s2` and `*s3`).

```
~InputWindw(void)                                   Public
```

This is the input window's destructor. It deletes the window's button objects from memory before the window is deleted.

```
virtual void DrawWindow(void)                       Public
```

Call this function to draw an input window on-screen. This function first calls `CapTWindw::DrawWindow()` to draw the captioned text window. It then draws the window's OK and Cancel buttons, as well as the text-entry field.

```
virtual void RunWindow(void)                          Public
```

This function turns control of the program over to the input window and returns only when the user closes the window, either by selecting one of its buttons or by pressing Esc to cancel the dialog.

```
void GetInput(char *s)                                Public
```

Call this function to retrieve the string input by the user. Its single parameter is a pointer to an 81-element character array.

Inherited Data Members

```
Windw ->  int wx, wy, ww, wh
     int border, buffered
     EvntMsg evntmsg
CapWindw ->    char label[61]
CapTWindw ->   int button
     char *line1, *line2
```

Inherited Member Functions

```
CapWindw ->    SetCaption(char *s)
CapTWindw ->   GetButton(void)
```

Class *Button* <- *Windw*

This is an animated button control that contains a single-word label. The button's size is preset by the class.

Data Members

```
char label[20]                                        Private
```

This character array holds the button's label. The character in the label that represents the button's hot key must be preceded by a caret (^), for example, ^Quit.

```
unsigned hotkey                                       Private
```

This is the Ctrl-key that selects the button from the keyboard.

```
int altkey                                                   Private
```

This is the button's alternate hot key. This field is valid only with an OK button or a Cancel button, in which case it contains the raw key value of the Enter or Esc key, respectively.

Member Functions

```
Button(int x, int y, char *s)                                Public
```

This is the button control's constructor, which first calls the `Windw` constructor. When constructing `Button`, you must supply the button's x,y coordinates and the button's label text.

```
virtual void DrawWindow(void)                                Public
```

Call this function to draw a button on-screen. This function first calls `Windw::DrawWindow()` to draw the basic window shape. It then draws the button's label, with the hot key underlined.

```
void SetButtonText(char *s)                                  Public
```

Call this function to change the label displayed in a button control.

```
int Clicked(EvntMsg evntmsg)                                 Public
```

This function returns true if the button has been selected or false if it hasn't been selected. If the button has been selected, this function also animates the button image.

```
int ClickButton(void)                                        Public
```

This function animates the button control and is normally called by `Clicked()`.

Inherited Data Members

```
Windw ->  int wx, wy, ww, wh
     int border, buffered
     EvntMsg evntmsg
```

Inherited Member Functions

```
Windw ->  RunWindow(void)
```

567

Detecting Whether a TSR Is Loaded

One thing you might have noticed about the clock TSR discussed in Chapter 8 is that it has no way of knowing whether it's already loaded. Because of this, you can accidentally load the TSR repeatedly, which eats up memory that can be used for other programs. To avoid this problem, the clock TSR needs some way of checking its status. But how? You can't use a flag in the main program, because each time you run the TSR, a new instance of the TSR is created, and each instance has it own data. The answer to this dilemma, as you may have guessed, is an *interrupt handler.*

The interrupt 0x2F is traditionally used for communicating between TSR programs. In fact, an entire standard for the use of this interrupt with TSR programs has been developed (the *TesSeRact* standard, information about which is provided at the end of this Appendix). There are many commands implemented in the standard, one of which, CHECK_INSTALL, is demonstrated in the third version of the clock TSR program from Chapter 8, shown here in

Listing B.1. This version of the program does not enable you to load the TSR if it's already in memory. If you try, you get the message "The clock TSR is already installed.".

Listing B.1. CLOCK3.CPP—on-screen clock TSR program, version 3.

```cpp
///////////////////////////////////////////////////////
// ON-SCREEN CLOCK TSR, VERSION 3
// by Clayton Walnum
// Written with Borland C++ 3.1
///////////////////////////////////////////////////////

#include <dos.h>
#include <iostream.h>

#define CLOCK 0x1c
#define ATTR 0x7900
#define FALSE 0
#define TRUE 1
#define CLOCK_ID 0xEB
#define CHECK_INSTALL 0x00

// Declare pointers to hold old vectors.
void interrupt (*old2f)(...);
void interrupt (*oldclock)(...);

// Declare a pointer to screen memory.
unsigned int (far *screen);

// Declare some global data.
struct time t;        // Struct for gettime().
int     tick,         // Interrupt counter.
        colon;        // Flag for colon visibility.
char clockstr[] = {"00:00"}; // Clock display string.

// Declare pointers to InDOS and CritErr flags.
char far *indos;
char far *criterr;

// Function prototypes.
void FormatClockStr();
void HandleColon();
```

```
void interrupt ClockIntr(...);
void interrupt New2f(unsigned, unsigned, unsigned, unsigned,
                unsigned, unsigned, unsigned, unsigned,
                unsigned, unsigned, unsigned, unsigned);


#pragma argsused
///////////////////////////////////////////////////////
// New2f()
//
// This is the interrupt handler used for communicating
// between TSRs. In this case, the handler notifies the
// caller that the CLOCK_ID TSR is loaded.
///////////////////////////////////////////////////////
void interrupt New2f(unsigned bp, unsigned di, unsigned si,
                unsigned ds, unsigned es, unsigned dx,
                unsigned cx, unsigned bx, unsigned ax,
                unsigned ip, unsigned cs, unsigned flags)
{
  // Check for the TSR's ID. If this request is not
  // for this clock TSR, chain to the old 2f.
  if (_AH != CLOCK_ID)
    _chain_intr(old2f);

  // If the caller is requesting whether the
  // clock TSR is loaded, tell it yes.
  if (_AL == CHECK_INSTALL)
  {
    ax = 0xFFFF;
    bx = _psp;
  }
}


///////////////////////////////////////////////////////
// FormatClockStr()
//
// This function uses the hour and minute counters to
// construct the clock's display.
///////////////////////////////////////////////////////
void FormatClockStr()
{
  // Format hour portion of string.
  if (t.ti_hour < 10)
```

continues

571

Listing B.1. Continued

```
    {
      clockstr[0] = '0';
      clockstr[1] = t.ti_hour + '0';
    }
    else
    {
      clockstr[0] = t.ti_hour / 10 + '0';
      clockstr[1] = t.ti_hour % 10 + '0';
    }

    // Format minute portion of string.
    if (t.ti_min < 10)
    {
      clockstr[3] = '0';
      clockstr[4] = t.ti_min + '0';
    }
    else
    {
      clockstr[3] = t.ti_min / 10 + '0';
      clockstr[4] = t.ti_min % 10 + '0';
    }
}


////////////////////////////////////////////////////////
// HandleColon()
//
// This function is responsible for the blinking colon
// in the clock display. Every 9 ticks (1/2 second),
// the colon is added or deleted from the string, which
// causes the colon to blink in one second intervals.
////////////////////////////////////////////////////////
void HandleColon()
{
  // Increment counter.
  ++tick;

  // If a half second has passed, set counter back
  // to zero, and then add or remove the colon.
  if (tick == 9)
  {
    tick = 0;

    // If colon is in string, remove it.
```

```
      if (colon)
      {
        clockstr[2] = ' ';
        colon = FALSE;
      }

      // If colon is not in string, add it.
      else
      {
        clockstr[2] = ':';
        colon = TRUE;
      }
  }
}


//////////////////////////////////////////////////////////
// ClockIntr()
//
// This is the interrupt handler. It displays the
// current clock string, checks the counters, and
// finally chains to the old interrupt.
//////////////////////////////////////////////////////////
void interrupt ClockIntr(...)
{
  // Handle the blinking colon.
  HandleColon();

  // Is it safe to call MS-DOS?
  if (!*indos && !*criterr)
  {
    // Use MS-DOS to get current time.
    gettime(&t);

    // Build clock display string.
    FormatClockStr();

    // Get the screen address.
    screen = (unsigned int far *) MK_FP(0xb800,0);

    // Get address of clock position on first screen line.
    screen += 75;

    // Write clock display string directly to screen memory.
    for (int x= 0; x<5; ++x)
```

continues

573

Listing B.1. Continued

```
      *screen++ = clockstr[x] + ATTR;
  }

  // Chain to old handler.
  _chain_intr(oldclock);
}


////////////////////////////////////////////////////////
// Main program.
////////////////////////////////////////////////////////
void main(void)
{
  _AH = CLOCK_ID;
  _AL = CHECK_INSTALL;
  geninterrupt(0x2f);
  if (_AL == 0xff)
    cout << "The clock TSR is already installed.\n";
  else
  {
    // Get address of inDOS flag.
    _AH = 0x34;
    geninterrupt(0x21);

    // Initialize InDOS and CritErr pointers.
    unsigned int seg = _ES;
    unsigned int off = _BX;
    indos = (char far *) MK_FP(seg, off);
    criterr = indos - 1;

    // Get old vectors and set new vectors.
    oldclock = getvect(CLOCK);
    setvect(CLOCK, ClockIntr);
    old2f = getvect(0x2f);
    setvect(0x2f, (void interrupt(*)(...)) New2f);

    // Initialize time counters and colon flag.
    tick = 0;
    colon = FALSE;

    // Go TSR.
    keep(0, (_SS + (_SP/16) - _psp));
  }
}
```

Look at main() first, because it's in main() that the program generates the request to check whether the TSR is already loaded:

```
void main(void)
{
  _AH = CLOCK_ID;
  _AL = CHECK_INSTALL;
  geninterrupt(0x2f);
  if (_AL == 0xff)
    cout << "The clock TSR is already installed.\n";
  else
  {
    // Get address of inDOS flag.
    _AH = 0x34;
    geninterrupt(0x21);

    // Initialize InDOS and CritErr pointers.
    unsigned int seg = _ES;
    unsigned int off = _BX;
    indos = (char far *) MK_FP(seg, off);
    criterr = indos - 1;

    // Get old vectors and set new vectors.
    oldclock = getvect(CLOCK);
    setvect(CLOCK, ClockIntr);
    old2f = getvect(0x2f);
    setvect(0x2f, (void interrupt(*)(...)) New2f);

    // Initialize time counters and colon flag.
    tick = 0;
    colon = FALSE;

    // Go TSR.
    keep(0, (_SS + (_SP/16) - _psp));
  }
}
```

Here, the program first sends a CHECK_INSTALL request to the 0x2f interrupt. This is accomplished by placing the TSR program's ID in AH, placing the command value (0x00 for CHECK_INSTALL) in AL, and then generating a 0x2f interrupt. The results of the request are returned in AL. If the clock TSR is already loaded, the value in AL is –1. In this case, the program must do nothing more than report that the TSR is already loaded, then exit. Otherwise, the program can install the TSR.

In order for the CHECK_INSTALL request to work properly, the TSR must install its own 0x2f interrupt handler:

```
void interrupt New2f(unsigned bp, unsigned di, unsigned si,
                unsigned ds, unsigned es, unsigned dx,
                unsigned cx, unsigned bx, unsigned ax,
                unsigned ip, unsigned cs, unsigned flags)
{
  // Check for the TSR's ID. If this request is not
  // for this clock TSR, chain to the old 2f.
  if (_AH != CLOCK_ID)
    _chain_intr(old2f);

  // If the caller is requesting whether the
  // clock TSR is loaded, tell it yes.
  if (_AL == CHECK_INSTALL)
  {
    ax = 0xFFFF;
    bx = _psp;
  }
}
```

When the clock TSR is not loaded, this interrupt handler is not active. The 0x2f interrupt generated in main(), then, is handled by whatever handler is installed at that time. It can be the system's default handler, or it might be a handler installed by another TSR. In any case, that handler doesn't recognize (hopefully) the clock TSR's ID and so does not respond with a −1 to the CHECK_INSTALL request.

 Caution: Because it's possible for two TSR programs to use the same ID, it's also possible for the CHECK_INSTALL request (and other commands) to return erroneous information. For example, if you try to load a TSR with the same ID as your clock TSR, the clock TSR might capture that TSR's CHECK_INSTALL request and not allow it to load. To help you avoid this type of problem, Microsoft Corporation keeps a list of registered TSR programs to which you can refer when choosing your TSR's ID number. When your TSR is complete, you can then register it with Microsoft so other developers are aware of your TSR's ID.

When the clock TSR is installed, however, its 0x2f interrupt handler can respond to main()'s CHECK_INSTALL request. First, this function checks the ID in AH. If AH doesn't contain the clock TSR's ID, the handler passes the buck, as it were, by chaining to the old 0x2f handler. If AH does contain the TSR's ID, the handler checks AL for the CHECK_INSTALL command value. If it finds this value, the program loads AX with –1 and loads BX with the TSR's *PSP*, which is found in the global variable _psp. (To comply with the TesSeRact standard, you must return the PSP in BX.)

Note: PSP stands for *program segment prefix*. The PSP is built by DOS when you run an executable file, and it contains the 256 bytes of data necessary for DOS to run your program. A complete discussion of the PSP is beyond the scope of this book, but it's helpful to know that the beginning of the PSP marks the beginning of your program in memory.

As you've already seen, the return values from the handler are easily checked by the program that generated the request, allowing any TSR to determine whether the clock TSR is loaded. In this way, you can make sure your TSR programs aren't loaded more than once, as well as communicate with other TSR programs with known IDs.

Note: Notice that, in some instructions, the 0x2f handler uses the register pseudovariables (_AH and _AL), and in others (where values are changed), it uses the register variables passed to the handler. It does this because, when the handler exits, the values in the register parameters are the ones used to restore the registers. If you try to make a change to a register using the pseudovariables, your change is overwritten by the values in the register parameters.

Caution: It's imperative that your 0x2f interrupt handlers chain to the old handler if the ID passed in AH does not belong to your TSR. This is the way you pass requests targeted for other TSR programs. If you fail to do this, other TSR programs loaded into the system might not function properly.

Index

Symbols

( ) parentheses, 230
* (multiplication) operator, 231
+ (addition) operator, 231
- (subtraction) operator, 231
-> (indirect component selector), 101
/ (division) operator, 231
@ symbol (ordinal values), 494
^ (caret character), 109-110
3-D
    graphics, 300
    outline (status bar), 301

A

ABS built-in function, 231
addition (+) operator, 231
AddNodes( ) function, 223
AddOp( ) function, 250-251
addresses
    CritErr flag, 284
    InDos flag, 284
    interrupt handlers, 263
    interrupt vector tables, 260
    saving in buffers, 97
    stack, 266, 484
    static memory, 484
allocation
    dynamic
        string classes, 42
        windows, 100

    global memory, DLLs, 499
    nodes, 152
ancestor classes, 23
animation (buttons), 218
ANSI text, 446
API (Application Program
    Interface), 293
AppendMenu( ) function, 373
application class screen savers,
    530-532
Application Options dialog box,
    484-485
applications, MDI (Multiple Docu-
    ment Interface), *see* MDI applica-
    tions
arguments
    default vs. overloading, 36-37
    maximum, 254
arrays
    character, 42, 50
    converting to String object, 52
    copying, 48
    passing, 199
    pointers, 425
    strings, inserting, 52
ASCII code, 70
assigning
    menus, 393, 448
    strings, assignment operator, 48
assignment operators, string
    constants, 48

K-L

program segment prefix (PSP), 577
programming
    basic windows, 98-101
    black-box routines, 12
    object-oriented, *see* object-oriented programming
    structures, 12
    switches, manual, 12
prototypes, functions, 163-164
pseudo-variables, 266
PSP (program segment prefix), 577

Q–R

quitting Life simulation, 162

`random( )` function, 539
random-numbers, 16
`randomize( )` function, 16

recalculation speed (Life simulation), 146
recording button press, 219
rectangles
    buttons, focus, 403
    drawing, 3-D graphics, 300
    windows, 92
`Rectngle` class, 32
recursion, 191-194
    backing out, 256
    breaking out, 197
    directory management, 197
    ending, 198
    mathematical expressions, 197
    parsing, 197
    routines, 197, 221
    stack, 197-199
recursive functions, 195-196
    arrays, passing, 199
    conditional statements, 193, 198
    parameters, 199
    stack frames, 197
recursive routines, 234
`Recursive( )` function, 192
recursive-descent parser, 237
redrawing
    buttons, 403
    windows, 294
`registerbgidriver( )` function, 165
registering
    graphics driver, 165
    screen savers, 543-554
    windows in DLLs, 499
registers
    DS (data segment), 484
    interrupts, 264
    loading, function numbers, 76
    SS (stack segment), 484
    stack-pointer, 266
    stack-segment, 266
repositioning
    client windows, 323
    status bar, parent window, 312
    status window, 332
resolution, printers, 435
Resource Workshop, 372, 398

605

U–V

W

.WAV file extension, 501
waveform files, 501-509
`WEP( )` function, 489
`while` loop, 16, 149
WIN.INI file
   settings, printers, 433
   `[sounds]` section, 505
`WinCassette`, 408-423
   definition file (Listing 11.6),
     423-442
   dialog, 426-431
   header files, 408-411
   implementation files, 408-409,
     411-420
   main window, 424-431
   printing labels, 431
   resource file (Listing 11.5),
     420-422
   transfer buffer, defining, 426
window classes, 299
window library
   `Button` class, 566-567
   `CapTWindw` class, 560-561
   `CapWindw` class, 559-560
   `InputWindw` class, 565-566
   `OKWindw` class, 561-562
   `Wndw` class, 557-559
   `YesNoCanWindw` class, 563-564
   `YesNoWindw`, 562-563
   see also individual listings
Windows
   Multimedia Extensions, 502
   ObjectWindows, 292-294
windows
   basic, 93-101
   bitmaps, displaying, 479
   blank, 92
   buffers, 97
   captioned, 101-106
   child
     maximizing, 342
     MDI applications, 314

classes
   buttons, 115-118
   header file (WINDW.H, Listing
     4.4), 125-128
   WINDW.CPP implementation
     file, 129-141
client, MDI applications, 314-315
color, background, 537-538
coordinates
   graphics elements, 97
   setting, 100
creating, 99
   dynamic allocation, 100
   heap, 299
   in DLLs, 499
   in memory, 100
deleting, dynamic allocation, 101
designing, 92-93
displaying, 100-101, 104
document, *see* document windows
drawing in, 393-397
dynamic allocation, 100
erasing destructors, 100
frame, *see* frame window
height/width, 299, 537
hierarchies, base classes, 93
input, 101, 120-125
labels, *see* captioned windows
libraries, 125-141
   designing, 92
   `YesNoCanWindw`, 119
main, creating, 298
menus, assigning, 393, 448
messages
   routing, 294
   `WM_DESTROY`, 397
   `WM_DRAWITEM`, 360, 397
   `WM_HSCROLL`, 301
   `WM_LBUTTONDOWN`, 393
   `WM_LBUTTONUP`, 395
   `WM_MDIMAXIMIZE`, 343
   `WM_MOUSEMOVE`, 473
   `WM_PAINT`, 294
   `WM_SIZE`, 309
   `WM_VSCROLL`, 301

X-Y-Z

If your computer uses
5 1/4-inch disks...

If your computer uses 5 1/4-inch disks, you can return this form to Que to obtain a
5 1/4-inch disk to use with this book. Complete the remainder of this form and mail to:

Borland C++ Power Programming
Disk Exchange
Que
11711 N. College Ave., Suite 140
Carmel, IN 46032

We will then send you, free of charge, the 5 1/4-inch version of the book's
software.

Name _____   Phone _____

Company _____   Title _____

Address _____

City _____   State ____   ZIP _____